Theory and Classification of Material Text Cultures

Materiale Textkulturen

Schriftenreihe des Sonderforschungsbereichs 933

Herausgegeben von
Ludger Lieb

Wissenschaftlicher Beirat:
Jan Christian Gertz, Markus Hilgert, Hanna Liss,
Bernd Schneidmüller, Melanie Trede
und Christian Witschel

Band 46.2

Theory and Classification of Material Text Cultures

Concluding Volume of the CRC 933

Edited by
Nikolaus Dietrich, Ludger Lieb and Nele Schneidereit

DE GRUYTER

This publication originated in the Collaborative Research Centre 933 'Material Text Cultures. Materiality and Presence of Writing in Non-Typographic Societies'. The CRC 933 is funded by the German Research Foundation (DFG).

This volume is also published in a German version (volume 46.1).

ISBN 978-3-11-132549-1
e-ISBN (PDF) 978-3-11-132551-4
e-ISBN (EPUB) 978-3-11-132613-9
ISSN 2198-6932
DOI https://doi.org/10.1515/9783111325514

This work is licensed under the Creative Commons Attribution-NonCommercial-NoDerivatives 4.0 International License. For details go to https://creativecommons.org/licenses/by-nc-nd/4.0/. Creative Commons license terms for re-use do not apply to any content (such as graphs, figures, photos, excerpts, etc.) not original to the Open Access publication and further permission may be required from the rights holder. The obligation to research and clear permission lies solely with the party re-using the material.

Library of Congress Control Number: 2024941942

Bibliographic information published by the Deutsche Nationalbibliothek
The Deutsche Nationalbibliothek lists this publication in the Deutsche Nationalbibliografie; detailed bibliographic data are available on the internet at http://dnb.dnb.de.

© 2024 with the author(s), editing © 2024 Nikolaus Dietrich, Ludger Lieb und Nele Schneidereit, publiziert von Walter de Gruyter GmbH, Berlin/Boston.
Dieses Buch ist als Open-Access-Publikation verfügbar über www.degruyter.com.

Editorial and typesetting: Nicolai Dollt (Sonderforschungsbereich 933, Heidelberg)
Cover image: Stained glass in Ebstorf Abbey from the 16th century. (Credo). Foto by Sabine Wehking, cropping and editing by Nicolai Dollt. © Kloster Ebstorf. See also: Deutsche Inschriften, Bd. 76, Lüneburger Klöster, Nr. 169 (Sabine Wehking), www.inschriften.net, urn:nbn:de:0238-di076g013k0016906.
Printing and binding: CPI books GmbH, Leck

www.degruyter.com

Acknowledgments

The success of a Collaborative Research Centre (in German 'Sonderforschungsbereich', one of the largest formats for collaborative university projects funded by the German Research Foundation) is due to the efforts, care, and openness of many individuals. Researchers from different academic disciplines engage with one other, develop joint questions and ideas, and have to formulate these in a commonly understood language that is compatible with their respective subject areas and thus able to have an impact in these fields afterwards. This volume is the result of many years of this work in the Collaborative Research Centre 933 'Material Text Cultures' at the University of Heidelberg.

As editors, we wish to express our sincere thanks to the 55 authors for the tireless labours invested in the joint writing of this volume. Special thanks go to the authors first named in each chapter, who were responsible for the individual chapters as a whole. We would also like to thank the student assistants Hannah Oberholz and Katharina von Recum for their work on Index I and Oliver Huber for work on the bibliographies.

We are indebted to Christoph Forster (CRC Information Infrastructure Service Project) for the idea of presenting the results of the CRC 933 as theses. This form, which initially seemed resistant to our work, forced us to state as precisely as possible which statements we could agree upon after more than twelve years of interdisciplinary research.

The publication series *Materiale Textkulturen* (MTK) has been published by de Gruyter since 2014. The present volume (no. 46.2) and the German version thereof (no. 46.1, published in 2023) bring this series to an end. On behalf of the members of the CRC 933 and all the authors in the MTK series, we would like to thank Mirko Vonderstein as the main editor and Anne Hiller for the excellent supervision of the many beautiful volumes at de Gruyter. We would also like to thank Gabriela Rus from Konvertus for her conscientious print data control and express our gratitude to the many reviewers involved in the peer review process, especially the academic advisory board of the series, for their time and effort.

Our colleague Nicolai Dollt has supervised, coordinated, edited, and typeset the series from volume 22 onwards, for which we are especially grateful. Thanks to his care, expertise, and commitment, numerous volumes have been published in the MTK series in the recent years, and his unremitting work on this volume has once again shown how important he has been for the quality of the volumes.

Christopher Sprecher has made the present volume possible through his conscientious and informed translation, and some of the authors of the volume have also contributed significantly with their meticulous and time-consuming examination. We would like to expressly thank both him and the many authors who contributed to the translation project for their labours.

Not only the *Materiale Textkulturen* series, but also the entire research of the CRC 933 would have been impossible without the generous and continued funding of the German Research Foundation. We would especially like to thank Heike Bock, Nora Böttcher, and Hans-Dieter Bienert for their trustworthy support and manifold assistance.

Heidelberg, January 2024
Nikolaus Dietrich, Ludger Lieb, Nele Schneidereit

Contents

Introduction —— 1

Nikolaus Dietrich, Ludger Lieb, Nele Schneidereit

    Preliminary Remarks —— 1
    Foundations of a Theory of Material Text Cultures —— 5
    Concepts and Elements of a Theory of Material Text Cultures —— 14
    Overview of Thematic Fields and Theses —— 20

Chapter 1:
Reflecting on Writing and Writtenness —— 29

Stephanie Béreiziat-Lang, Nele Schneidereit, Dennis Disselhoff, Robert Folger, Marina Aurora Garzón Fernández, Jonas Grethlein, Ludger Lieb, Christina Schulz, Sarina Tschachtli, Laura Velte

    Thesis 1 —— 33
    Thesis 2 —— 40
    Thesis 3 —— 44
    Thesis 4 —— 48
    Thesis 5 —— 52
    Thesis 6 —— 56

Chapter 2:
Layout, Design, Text-Image —— 65

Nikolaus Dietrich, Lisa Horstmann, Andrea Bernini, Susanne Börner, Sarah Braun, Johannes Fouquet, Tobias Frese, Adrian Heinrich, Rebecca Hirt, Carina Kühne-Wespi, Giuditta Mirizio, Rebecca Müller, Gustavo Fernández Riva, Anett Rózsa, Anna Sitz, Friederike Stahlke, Chun Fung Tong, Sebastian Watta

    Thesis 7 —— 69
    Thesis 8 —— 74
    Thesis 9 —— 83
    Thesis 10 —— 92
    Thesis 11 —— 96

Chapter 3:
Memory and Archive —— 111

Nikolas Jaspert, Kirsten Wallenwein, Barbara Frenk, Matthias Kuhn, Solvejg Langer, Tino Licht, Joachim Friedrich Quack, Loreleï Vanderheyden, Franziska Wenig, Wolf Zöller

    Thesis 12 —— **120**
    Thesis 13 —— **125**
    Thesis 14 —— **127**
    Thesis 15 —— **132**
    Thesis 16 —— **136**
    Thesis 17 —— **140**
    Thesis 18 —— **142**

Chapter 4:
Material Change —— 155

Sylvia Brockstieger, Paul Schweitzer-Martin, Johanna Baumgärtel, Federico Dal Bo, Friederike Elias, Rebecca Hirt, Radu Leca, Hanna Liss, Bernd Schneidmüller, Melanie Trede

    Thesis 19 —— **161**
    Thesis 20 —— **165**
    Thesis 21 —— **173**
    Thesis 22 —— **180**
    Thesis 23 —— **184**

Chapter 5:
Sacralisation —— 201

Tobias Frese, Wolf Zöller, Stefan Ardeleanu, Nikolaus Dietrich, Dennis Disselhoff, Annette Hornbacher, Lisa Horstmann, Jiří Jákl, Tino Licht, Hanna Liss, Giuditta Mirizio, Anett Rózsa, Anna Sitz, Mandy Telle, Sebastian Watta, Franziska Wenig

    Thesis 24 —— **205**
    Thesis 25 —— **214**
    Thesis 26 —— **224**
    Thesis 27 —— **231**

Chapter 6:
Political Rule and Administration —— 251

Abigail S. Armstrong, Rodney Ast, Enno Giele, Julia Lougovaya, Hannah Mieger, Jörg Peltzer, Joachim Friedrich Quack, Chun Fung Tong, Sarina Tschachtli, Banban Wang

    Thesis 28 —— **258**
    Thesis 29 —— **267**
    Thesis 30 —— **271**
    Thesis 31 —— **278**
    Thesis 32 —— **280**
    Thesis 33 —— **283**
    Thesis 34 —— **286**
    Thesis 35 —— **288**

Indexes —— 303

    Index I: Names (places, persons, figures) and works/artefacts —— **305**
    Index II: Terms, Concepts, and Materials —— **309**

Introduction

Nikolaus Dietrich, Ludger Lieb, Nele Schneidereit

Introduction

Nikolaus Dietrich, Ludger Lieb, Nele Schneidereit

Preliminary Remarks

This volume presents a clearly structured and focused synthesis of the research undertaken over the past twelve years by the Heidelberg Collaborative Research Centre 'Material Text Cultures' (CRC 933) and aims to collate the CRC's most important findings in a way that is at once concise, transparent, and accessible to a broad scholarly audience. With the CRC having come to an end in 2023, it is our goal and hope that as many scholars as possible will continue to work on its topics beyond this date and outside of Heidelberg. Furthermore, we hope that many will be inspired to take the foundations we have laid as a launchpad for making new contributions to the broad field of the materiality of inscriptions and manuscripts. The present volume has several aims: (1) to provide readers with an orientation in this field of research; (2) to be an easy-to-use guidebook and methodological aid for research on specific objects at the intersection of materiality, textuality, and practices; and (3) to serve as a reference work both for a theory of material text cultures and for studies on pre-modern cultures from the perspective of comparative cultural studies.

With this in mind, the volume has been divided into six thematic fields (Chapters 1–6) covering essential areas of the CRC's research on material text cultures (see the overview below), with each chapter being written collaboratively by an interdisciplinary group of CRC members. Each chapter first defines the given subject area and provides an outline of the content, which is then followed by four to eight theses succinctly summarising the CRC's most important insights and results in the respective area of research. Each thesis is then fleshed out, justified, or problematised. The theses' discussions present individual examples and refer to further research completed by the CRC 933 in the years of 2011–2023 and by others. The volume thus offers a good introduction to the research landscape and to the extensive publications of the CRC as a whole. All 35 theses of this volume are additionally listed at the end of this introduction (each with its respective page number) for quick reference and an easy survey of all topics at a glance; the appendix with two indexes has also been prepared to this end.

This volume has been published in both German and English, with both versions appearing in print and being available online via open access. By their very nature, the two versions—the original and its translation—are not entirely congruent. Moreover, the concise formulation of the complex phenomena of material text cultures in the theses presented here has required in some places that different terminological decisions be made in both languages so as to ensure as much convergence of content as possible.

∂ Open Access. © 2024 the authors, published by De Gruyter. [CC BY-NC-ND] This work is licensed under the Creative Commons Attribution-NonCommercial-NoDerivatives 4.0 International License.
https://doi.org/10.1515/9783111325514-001

The CRC 933 'Material Text Cultures' has focused on texts written on things: columns, portals, gravestones, clay tablets, pottery shards, amulets, bamboo splices, scrolls, manuscripts, and books made of papyrus, parchment, or paper, etc. Our interest lay in the materiality of these things as well as in their *presence,* i. e. the situations and spaces in which their effects unfolded. The practices, or 'routinised' actions of human actors, into which these things were once integrated, are closely interrelated to their material and presentic properties; some of these practices have been handed down to us from other sources, and some have to be inferred from the things themselves. We call such a connection of the material and practical dimensions in spaces and situations of things on which something is written ('inscribed artefacts') a 'text culture'. Given our primary focus on materiality, we have studied 'material' text cultures, and have done so primarily in societies in which writing had not yet become available en masse through technical procedures of reproduction (what we term 'non-typographic societies'). This strategic research decision assumed that the relationship between text, materiality, space, and related practices fundamentally changed as a result of the invention of printing, which in many cases led to a relative loss of meaning for the materiality of the individual inscribed artefact. An analysis of situations of material change within text cultures—notable examples being the inventions of paper and the printing press—serves to confirm this assumption as well as substantiate and differentiate it: how people dealt with texts and written materials did indeed change, even if the 'inertia' of established text cultures is often surprising, with the phenomena of selective persistence leaving a more lasting impression.

With non-typographic cultures at the core of the research presented here, we are thus dealing with text cultures situated in pre-modernity. The spectrum of fields ranges from Ancient Studies (Assyriology, Egyptology, Archaeology, Ancient History, Papyrology, Numismatics, Classical Philology, and Byzantine Art History), which also research the earliest preserved inscribed artefacts, to Medieval Studies (Medieval History, Art History, Medieval Latin, German Studies, Romance Studies, Jewish Studies, Islamic Studies) as well as to specific fields analysing the early modern transition to the typographic age. With Chinese Studies, East Asian Art History, and Ethnology, we also take a look at past and present text cultures in China, Japan, Bali, and Java. Even if some disciplines are still missing, a large number of research fields have been brought together here and open up access to very different cultural areas. This makes it possible to develop a theory of material text cultures drawing from numerous individual case studies while also standing on the broad foundation of a comprehensive data set[1] and remaining aware of the inherently different dynamics of individual material text cultures.

---

1 Cf. the databases published online: https://www.materiale-textkulturen.de/daten.php (accessed 13/3/2023).

In its analysis of inscribed artefacts (historical, archaeological, and philological) over the past twelve years, the CRC has systematically developed and utilised an array of methods that is interdisciplinary in nature. The present volume is an attempt to bundle the findings and insights of this interdisciplinary work with regard to the contribution they make towards a theory of material text cultures, thereby also formulating such findings in a systematic way and offering them up for wider discussion and debate. This kind of result does not have the uniformity and systematic organisation that one might expect from theoretical texts which are usually presented by individual authors rather than by collaborative teams of writers. In the pages to follow, then, we understand by the concept of a theory of material text cultures a systematic compilation of well-founded and coherent statements ('theses') about material text cultures, as well as an exposition of the premises that essentially underlie these statements insofar as they guide methodological procedures and set forth epistemic goals. As explained in greater detail below, we have drawn primarily on theoretical models presented in the course of the material turn in the humanities. Whatever our theoretical outline presented here might lack in terms of uniformity is to be compensated for by the richness of the scientific approaches it incorporates and by the depth of the general statements based on concrete, close-up research. Nevertheless, this diversity is held together by the premises set out in the following two sections: namely, common theoretical foundations and a number of concepts and elements which have been identified as being important.

Foundations of a Theory of Material Text Cultures

The goal of the research programme developed in the CRC has been to produce textual scholarship that investigates and reconstructs text cultures through the material, spatial (topological), and praxeologically oriented analysis of inscribed artefacts. This programme is based on the hermeneutic premise that the textual meaning and cultural significance of an inscribed artefact are not something bestowed once and for all, but rather are constantly refashioned in the artefact's reception, and that these practices of reception are inseparably linked to the materiality and presence of the artefacts. Reception practices, however, encompass more than just reading: the memorising, singing, reciting, and copying of such inscriptions also fall under this umbrella, as do the practices of looking at, marvelling at, highlighting, concealing, and destroying such artefacts—not to mention all forms of (inter)acting *with* inscribed artefacts, such as spell-casting, warding off, protecting, damaging, worshipping, presenting, boasting, and so forth. Through this change of perspective, the inscribed artefact comes to be seen as having a great influence in shaping all the contexts of action in which it participates. At the outset, the praxeologically oriented reconstruction of a material text culture and its phenomena of presence methodologically requires restraint with regard to textual hermeneutics. First, the relevant materiality and topology are described, and based on this, the probable practices and effects of presence that constitute the material text culture under study are reconstructed. Such a praxeologically oriented analysis of artefacts in the process of reconstructing material text cultures is a special 'hermeneutic strategy' for understanding texts and their cultural meaning—a meaning that can sometimes deviate from, contradict, or be completely independent of the text's possible semantic meaning.[2] Note that we understand hermeneutics explicitly *not* as an attempt to reconstruct an author's original intent, but rather as a methodological effort to secure an understanding of a text in conjunction with the text culture(s) that can be culturally and historically determined as enveloping this text.

This strategic approach to research thus courses along two distinct, albeit inextricably linked, paths:

1. The hermeneutic dimension: The texts' potential for sense and signification is not determined solely by the conventional philological methods of textual interpretation. First, the materiality of the text support and its spatial situation are recorded, and then the plausibility of likely reception practices is determined based on these, on the traces of use or other writings as well as the specific presence of the artefact. This praxeologically oriented analysis of the artefact is included in the interpretation of the texts, by means of which we go beyond the long-established hermeneutic practice of understanding texts from their historical contexts. 'Context' is more narrowly understood through the analysis of materiality, spatiality, traces of use, and the effects of presence, and is more controllable in terms of methodology than the inclusion of a broad and often arbitrary historical context in textual interpretation. Since efforts to gain understanding in this approach extend beyond the text to materiality, spatial surroundings, and practices, it can be understood as a methodologically 'extended hermeneutics', which can always have the result that the meaning of the text, initially thought as being obvious, becomes diffuse or is even negated.

2. The cultural-historical dimension: The praxeologically oriented analysis of inscribed artefacts renders plausible the presence of such artefacts in a specific cultural-historical situation, with such an analysis enabling us to sketch out a culture of texts that both surrounds and is constituted by the artefacts in question. Going beyond the level of textual content, it becomes clear that the meaning of inscribed artefacts themselves can be completely or partially independent of their textual content. The value and effect of an inscribed artefact, for example, are connected to its materiality (the material and effort behind its production) or can be inferred from where it was found or how it was received. Not infrequently, a tense or even contradictory relation-

---

[2] Hilgert 2010.

ship emerges between the textual meaning, the reconstructed effects of presence, and other aspects of a given artefact. The cultural-historical meaning of a text and/or of an inscribed artefact for a given social space—building on the technique of a methodologically extended hermeneutics—can thus also be determined independently of the textual content. The converse is also true: the cultural-historical elucidation of the textual culture surrounding an artefact can expand our understanding of the text's meaning. Based on these results, cultural-historical research can incorporate textual testimonies into its work in a methodologically sound new way.

The methodological and theoretical premises on which the two preceding dimensions are based built on the theories of the material turn and developed them further. Discussion of this turn was taken up by our research programme on material text cultures, first developed in 2010,[3] when talk of these theories was still in its infancy in the German-speaking world. The focus then was on the status of 'thingness' and 'materiality' in cultural studies analyses, which had become increasingly important since the mid-1980s under the moniker of 'material culture studies'.[4] By relating the typical focus of the material turn—on what is material, namely, things and thingness—to the special class of inscribed things, a deliberate advance was made towards the boundary between textual and material approaches to cultural-historical research. On the one hand, this pushes the ideas of material culture studies consistently further for text-related scholarship. On the other hand, more material-focused disciplines now place front and centre artefacts that have thus far often been 'consigned' to other disciplines due to their textual nature.

In order to situate the theory of material text cultures within the material turn of cultural studies, the main aspects of the more archaeologically/ethnologically oriented field of material culture studies should be noted here, as exemplified by (among others) Daniel Miller, Arjun Appadurai, Ian Hodder, and Henry Glassie,[5] and as received by the broader material turn of cultural studies.[6]

---

[3] Cf. Hilgert 2010 and 2016.
[4] Cf. Woodward 2007; Miller 1987; Hahn 2005, 2015a, and 2015b; Hicks/Beaudry 2010; Samida/Eggert/Hahn 2014. See also Daston 2004; Hilgert/Simon/Hofmann 2018; as well as Lake 2020.
[5] Cf. Miller 1987; Appadurai 1988; Hodder 1986; Glassie 1999.
[6] On the material turn, cf. Reckwitz 2006 and 2008; Goll/Keil/Telios 2013; Samida/Eggert/Hahn 2014; Keupp/Schmitz-Esser 2015; Kalthoff/Cress/Röhl 2016; Samida 2016; and critically: Keupp 2017. The establishment of the material turn in the humanities can be seen, among other things, in its inclusion in very different subject areas and thematic fields. For example, most recently in Schreiber et al. 2016 on prehistory and early history; in Aronin/Hornsby/Kiliańska-Przybyło 2018 on multilingualism; in Caroll/Walford/Walton 2021 on anthropology; in Kotrosits 2020 on the history of early Christianity; in Hedreen 2021 on the literature of antiquity and its reception in the Renaissance; and in Tacke/Münche/Augustyn 2018 on the role of things in the didactics of history.

1. The turn towards things: Things are included in the study of cultures in a new way. The assumption is that the material presence of things is not incidental to, but constitutive of, our relationship with them. This presence influences both us and our actions. Cultural theories of the material turn are interested in how human action and cognition, and the material preconditions for both, mutually influence one another. This new consideration of things and their materiality is to be understood as a counter-movement to the linguistic turn,[7] which had criticised and refuted the view that language was a neutral medium. According to its basic thesis, the way we speak to each other about the things of the world is what constitutes both us and things in the first place. This rather comprehensive claim on the part of the linguistic turn in cultural studies (as well as the constructivism of the cultural turn that builds on it) is restricted by material culture theory through paying new attention to things (as a non-linguistic field of phenomena).

2. 'Textual analogy': In some respects, however, the dawning of the material turn in the 1980s can also be seen as a continuation of the linguistic and cultural turns, which conceive of world and culture as a whole as being 'text', because of its premise that things can be read like texts.[8] More recent material turn theories have criticised this premise, since what this entails is merely the appropriation of things with the aim of getting at their effectively dematerialised semantic meaning. Instead, such newer approaches call for a turn to things with respect to their almost individual independence and resistance.[9]

3. The de-essentialisation of meaning: The meaning of culturally formed things does not lie in the things themselves. Bjørnar Olsen describes the 'textual analogy' of the early theories of the material turn as the adoption of structuralist and poststructuralist theories into the study of material culture within the disciplines of Archaeology and Ethnology.[10] The structuralist impetus lies in seeking the meaning of things not in themselves, but in the typified relations they have with each other and with whoever interacts with them. The poststructuralist impetus, in turn, radicalises the attitude towards the concept of meaning, with meaning always seen to be the result of a reception-centred process of negotiation. The meaning of a cultural thing arises individually and historically in each case. By de-essentialising meaning, the reception situation is accorded a radical increase in value vis-à-vis the production situation. Since meaning is now determined neither by the authority of an author nor by the relations of things, one must assume an openness of things to meaning and a

---

[7] Cf. Bennett/Joyce 2010.
[8] Cf. Hodder 1986; Tilley 1990 and 1991; on this, see also Olsen 2010.
[9] Cf. Hahn 2015a and 2015b; Olsen 2010, 59–62.
[10] Cf. Olsen 2010, chapter 2 (esp. 40–59).

'semiotic surplus'[11] on their part. A multitude of other things, texts, and actors is connected to each thing, overlapping with and contradicting each other and thus entering into the meaning that is constructed in each case. Poststructuralist material culture studies emphasise how things have the meanings they do, in which situations and for whom, all while recognising that there is a plethora of possible meanings.

4. Praxeology: The design of this theory requires on the part of material culture studies a precise analysis of the reception situation or—more comprehensively—of the situation in which a thing was handled or acted upon. On the one hand, the methodological design of this analysis must be directed towards the surrounding culture as an ensemble of practices qua socially shared patterns of action. On the other hand, such design must also take into account the re-evaluation of the relation between things and people, which is conditioned by the shift in the generation of cultural meaning from producer to recipient and user.[12]

5. Actor-network theory: The relationship between things and people is understood as an interaction in which things are not passive, but rather have an effect on their recipients through their materiality and their spatial reality, thereby influencing the actions of these recipients and prescribing certain modes of action. To describe this character of the reception situation, theories of the material turn have drawn on the sociological theory of technology (Latour, Schulz-Schaeffer) or on the Theory of Science (Serres, Rheinberger, Knorr Cetina), both of which conceive of the interaction of people and things as being fundamentally symmetrical positions in human-thing networks. Especially Bruno Latour's actor-network theory (ANT) has been taken up by material turn theories. ANT assumes a symmetrical relationship between things and people in systematically organised networks that enable joint actions. In this theory, based methodologically on the extremely precise and detailed empirical description of specific human-thing networks, objects are not treated as passive functions, but rather as independent actors (or 'actants', in Latour's words).[13]

In summary, we can note the following. First, the material turn in cultural studies can be understood as a theoretically informed turn towards things and their materiality, which holds that this materiality must be included in the determination of cultural meaning. Further aspects of this change of perspective include, second, the assumption that the material world of cultural things can be read like a text; third, the poststructuralist de-essentialisation of the meaning of cultural things by stating that it is only generated through how things are received an actively handled; fourth, a con-

---

11 Cf. Olsen 2010.
12 On the practice turn, cf. Knorr Cetina/Schatzki 2001; Schatzki 1996 and 2003; Schüttpelz et al. 2021; on 'praxeology', cf. Reckwitz 2006 and 2012; Elias et al. 2014; Haasis/Rieske 2015.
13 Cf. Latour 1996 and 2005; Schulz-Schaeffer 2000.

sequence of this being the turn towards practice and practices. Fifth, the interaction between things and people is understood as being one of independent actors/actants acting together in networks.

In forming its theories, the CRC 933 has adopted these elements of the material turn and developed them further in such a way as to enable the methodologically controlled analysis of inscribed artefacts and the formulation of an independent theory of material text cultures. We take a stand against the "privileging of [...] textual content",[14] focusing first on the material and topological reality of the text support and then trying—even if only partially—to reconstruct from this its specific presence and the practices that were probably related to it. The hermeneutic effort undertaken in order to understand the meaning of the text is not abandoned, but rather methodologically expanded and supplemented; admittedly, such a procedure could be understood as a semanticisation of the text support and its (cultural) environment and thus corresponding to the 'textual analogy' of the world of things as found in material culture studies.[15] In this sense, the theory of material text cultures can be understood as a methodologically 'expanded hermeneutics' that encompasses the materiality, the spatiality, and the presence of what is written. Consequently, the material form, spatial situation, and practices surrounding what is written must also be 'read', as it were.

As mentioned above, the approach of material culture studies—namely, to read the world of things like a text—has long been subject to critique. Some critics have said that the 'textual analogy' approach has appropriated the world of things and loosened the tongue of this mute world, only to misunderstand it in the process by not taking a serious look at things with respect to their individuality, unwieldiness, and incomprehensibility, but rather by reading them like signs in a unifying way.[16] Such criticism of material culture studies stands in the broader tradition of the critique of hermeneutics, which has always viewed the enterprise of determining meaning as an inadmissible simplification down to some original, authorised textual meaning. Now, this criticism would also apply—*ceteris paribus*—to the 'extended hermeneutics' we propose here, but we deal with this methodologically as follows. First, we stop only *reading* texts and instead also endeavour to describe their material and spatial conditions as precisely as possible. On the basis of this description—together with the inclusion of traces of use, as well as contemporary texts that speak of the handling of texts (so-called 'metatexts')—we seek to determine what practices could have been plausibly carried out on or in conjunction with the inscribed artefacts in question. This descriptive reconstruction methodologically expands the conventional forms of hermeneutics that focus on one meaning of the text, while also aiming to assess the cultural presence of inscribed artefacts. Materiality, spatiality, and practices are thus not 'read' in the literal sense, but are rather described as precisely as possible.

---

[14] Hilgert 2016, 255, our translation, German text: "Privilegierung des [...] Textinhalts".
[15] Cf. Olsen 2010, 42.
[16] Cf. Hahn 2015a and 2015b; Olsen 2010.

Second, this approach can disrupt the hermeneutic concern of understanding texts in the classical sense: materiality, presence, and practices can stand in a tense relationship with the meaning of the text and even contradict it. One therefore cannot speak of an appropriation of inscribed artefacts through conventional forms of hermeneutics.

With this poststructuralist view of inscribed artefacts as being signs that bear meaning, material text culture theory adopts the premise of the material turn's de-essentialised meaning of things in a more consistent way. The presence of texts, their materiality, topology, and use (i. e., practices) are all taken into account; yet the focus is no longer on the illusion of some authorial intent claiming sole validity, but rather on the analysis of scenarios of reception and handling, in which the meaning of a materially and spatially present inscribed artefact arises or is created by means of various practices. Authorship and text production still do play a role: they are to be understood as the initial attribution of meaning. However, since they do not hold any privileged status for the methodologically expanded hermeneutic approach vis-à-vis subsequent or competing attributions of meaning, such an approach allows us to take better account of the fact that some texts, such as epitaphs or inscriptions in sacred space, do not suggest any meaning-defining authorship at all. Finally, this also brings into view the fact that if actions are constitutive of meaning, then so too is the act that we ourselves as scholars perform when investigating inscribed artefacts. Text culture is thus the temporally unfinished context of understanding that encompasses inscribed artefacts and that must be taken into account in order to understand them.

The theory of material text cultures thus assumes that the meaning of a text is not fixed, but rather emerges on the side of reception, whereby 'reception' encompasses a multitude of possible activities with reference to the inscribed artefact in question and its presence. The focus on the emergence of textual meaning and of the cultural significance of textual artefacts in acts of reception also requires a concentration on practices. For this reason, our research approach is praxeologically oriented.[17] The cultural meaning of writing is thus by no means to be understood in a subjectivistic way. The praxeological turn of the hermeneutically de-essentialised theory of material text cultures consists in reconstructing the meaning of what is written from those practices in which the writing was probably embedded. In doing so, the premise that meaning is assigned 'from without' does not contradict the fact that certain such assignments are relatively stable in routinised contexts of action (= practices). Furthermore, not every conceivable practice is equally plausible, so that the assignment of textual meaning and cultural significance is by no means arbitrary. The reconstruction of plausible reception practices via material(s), traces of use, spatial location, and contemporary texts on the handling of texts or pieces of writing plays a central role in the application of the theory of material text cultures.

---

17 This praxeological shift to the reception-side production of textual meaning and the cultural significance of inscribed artefacts, which are both thus strongly dependent on specific material presence, is what Markus Hilgert has called "text anthropology" (Hilgert 2010 and 2016).

To describe these practices, the theory of material text cultures takes into account the action-structuring effect ('agency') of the material condition of writing as an element of a network-like interrelationship between human actor and inscribed artefact ('actant'). As in most theories of the material turn, this interrelation can be described with the help of the above-mentioned actor-network theory (ANT) in order to capture accurately the relationship of inscribed artefacts to the persons acting on or in conjunction with them. However, talking about things as 'actants' implies an often too strong assumption, especially for praxeologically oriented research. Our conception of the 'agency' of things as an action-structuring effect, rather than as a direct form of agency, draws the necessary conclusions from this. Moreover, Latour's ANT is based on a very precise description of empirically accessible relationships of cause and effect and on comprehensive data sets that are simply no longer available for past cultures.

The interrelation of inscribed artefacts and human actors can therefore be better understood as a 'material arrangement'.[18] Schatzki understands a material arrangement as a "set of interconnected material entities" that can include people and things. They "can be segregated into four types: humans, artefacts, organisms, and things of nature".[19] In contrast to Latour's ANT, Schatzki complements the social phenomenon of 'material arrangements' with the social phenomenon of practices.[20] All "human coexistence [...] inherently transpires as part of nexuses of practices and material arrangements";[21] Schatzki then names four such nexuses: "causality, prefiguration, constitution, and intelligibility",[22] assuming a primary connectedness of human practice and materiality and thus regarding materiality as being originally constitutive and irreducibly formative for social life. The agential character of the material can be considered on a case-by-case basis in this model, but in contrast to the network-like connectedness in material arrangements of people with things, it need not be considered as a determining factor for all contexts of practice. With this methodological correction, we can make fewer presuppositions for the praxeologically oriented research of inscribed artefacts than is necessary for material culture studies. Material text culture theory thus becomes more accessible, especially for the study of societies and cultures that cannot be observed in as much detail as would be required by ANT, which was originally developed for the analysis of modern science.

We have thus linked into the theories of the material turn by taking up its focus on the materiality of writing and its premise of the de-essentialisation of writing's meaning, together with the concomitant praxeological orientation and a non-subject-centred form of the interplay of inscribed artefacts and human actors. Nevertheless,

---

18 Cf. Schatzki 2003 and 2010.
19 Schatzki 2010, 129.
20 He defines practices as "organized spatial-temporal manifolds of human activity [, e. g., ...] cooking practices" (Schatzki 2010, 129).
21 Schatzki 2010, 129.
22 Schatzki 2010, 139.

we have reshaped the premises (which at this point have already undergone change in comparison with material turn theories) by attempting to give them the overall form of a specific theory of material text cultures: namely, one that decidedly encompasses (and restricts itself to) inscribed artefacts. This theory approaches the meaning of texts and the cultural significance of inscribed artefacts with an 'extended hermeneutics' in mind. This approach retains a special feature compared to the material turn, because material text culture theory always refers to *inscribed* artefacts, and thus specifically to artefacts in which the tense, sometimes contradictory relationship between the meaning of a given text and the respective meaning assigned to the artefact as a whole in the various practices of reception must be dealt with.

The theory of material text cultures assumes that the materiality of texts and the presence associated with it are themselves constitutive of meaning. This applies both to the meaning of the text as well as to the cultural-historical significance of an inscribed artefact. Materiality and presence are intertwined with the actions in which the artefacts are involved. For the reconstruction of meaning, then, the determination of this context of action is of paramount importance, with the result that the hermeneutic effort to find a pure textual meaning intended by a given author tends to take a back seat. Material text culture theory can thus also deal with practices in which inscribed artefacts play a role, but where the semantics of the text is not accessible to the actors (or the majority of them). In such cases, what is written acquires a cultural-historical meaning independent of the textual semantics. For the theory of material text cultures, the documenting of arrangements and personal networks in which writing is integrated is at least as relevant as the philological analysis of the text found on the material. In order to understand the meaning of writing in a given culture, material text culture theory also methodically includes texts in which writing per se and the specific written word(s) are discussed ('metatexts', see below).

The theory of material text cultures, and its application presented here, was initially developed especially for the subject area of pre-modern text cultures, the reason being that the absence (or deliberate non-practice) of techniques of mass reproduction of writing influenced both the latter's specific valence and presence as well as writing-related practices more generally. Yet, while the theory may be more adequate for pre-modern text cultures, it is not without value for modern or post-modern digital text cultures, since even under the conditions of ubiquitous writing or digital information processing, the materiality of what is written—perhaps precisely in its fleeting character and in the individual worthlessness of the specific artefact—develops its own forms of presence and associated practices. These, too, can be understood by a theory of material text cultures.

Concepts and Elements of a Theory of Material Text Cultures

In order to avoid repetitive definitions of terms in the individual chapters and theses, we explain here briefly the most important terms and elements of a theory of material text cultures.

Text / What is written

For the discussion of a theory of material text cultures, a fundamental decision was made not to talk about cultures of *writing*, but about *text* cultures. The theory of material text cultures is not concerned with research on writing in general, if we understand this as the totality of referential, present, and operational signs (i. e., disjunctive signs that are basically applied in accordance with a rule-based system).[23] Nor is it concerned with investigating the specific characteristics of different 'cultures' shaped by writing in the sense of a comparative analysis of one or more cultures possessing a writing system with other, purely oral societies. Rather, material text culture theory is concerned with researching the relationships between what is written, the materiality of this writing, and its specific presence within a historical constellation. Writing and written scripts should be seen as only one part of the cultural practice and reception of the act of writing, which also includes writing implements, materials, areas for writing, scenarios of writing, texts, text producers, scribes, people reading to audiences and people reading just to themselves, etc.[24] Concentrating on scripts and writing per se against the backdrop of this diversity of text-related practices would be too narrow a focus; furthermore, doing so would not enable us to answer the question of determining the materially composed cultural meaning of what is written.

At the same time, we have taken pains in our studies not to have too broad a concept of the term 'text'; we have been exclusively concerned with materially present texts on (material) artefacts and thus we have not taken into account instances of (to a certain extent mentally present) 'repeated speech' in different situations, which could also be meaningfully described as a 'text'.[25] To clarify this distinction conceptually, we often speak of 'the written', 'what is written', 'written things', or 'the written word' as opposed to 'writing(s)' in a more general sense. Compared to a detemporalised, dematerialised concept of text, this set of expressions has the advantage of conceptually representing the action on the artefact: the material production of the texts, the preparation of the material to be inscribed, the act of writing itself, etc. As 'written

---

[23] Cf. Grube/Kogge 2005.
[24] Cf. Zanetti 2012.
[25] Ehlich 1994; Lieb 2015, 3; Lieb/Ott 2016.

things', texts become recognisable as both the result of and participant in various practices. In this way, a praxeologically oriented theory can already conceptually depict an expanded spectrum of textual functions.

By 'text culture', we mean: the specific context of the materials, places, and practices pertaining to what is written; the inscribed artefacts themselves; and the prevailing attitudes towards writing and written things, such as they can be reconstructed in texts and actions. Text cultures can be reconstructed for historical spaces and times and thus help to determine the (purely semantic) meaning of texts through their significance as forming part of a text culture—a culture which for its part can be very diverse and not always aligns smoothly with the content of the text itself.

Artefact

Since all things on which something is written exist as *made* things *inasmuch* as they are inscribed, we call these things **'artefacts'**. This is immediately obvious for text supports such as clay tablets or pieces of parchment that entail labour-intensive means of production requiring the use of specific skills or crafts (Lat. *artes*). But even etched stones or tree bark have an artefactual character in their capacity as text supports, and in this way, the cultural moulding of the objects under study is emphasised.[26] We also use the term 'artefact' instead of 'object', which—mainly due to its counter-term 'subject'—establishes an asymmetrical relation between human actors and things, both from the outset as well as after the production process. The concept of artefact also points to the material arrangements in which text-bearing things, and the people who act on and in conjunction with them, are located: these can be producers, recipients, archivists, etc.; or even actors in magical practices that imply inscribed artefacts.

As already stated above, one of the most important methodological decisions made by the CRC has been that of a kind of hermeneutic restraint. The texts from past cultures that have come down to us as artefacts, and the presence of such texts, are *not first* subjected to a textual hermeneutic analysis of the meaning of the text at the level of the textual content. Rather, our first step is to analyse and describe a given text with a view towards its material, topological, and praxeological dimensions. Consequently, this means that the artefacts are not understood as being random, interchangeable, and ultimately insignificant bearers of writing, but rather are taken seriously as essential components of an interaction that takes place between artefacts, texts, and people. Even the respective material quality of the stuff and matter intended for inscription that has not yet been processed and shaped can lend itself conspicuously to human actors to this very end ('affordance'). The same applies to

---

26 Cf. Reckwitz 2006 and 2008; Lueger 2000; Hurcombe 2007; Margolis/Laurence 2007; Eggert 2014.

the processed artefact, which also has its own affordances due to its materiality.[27] Artefacts are more than just material remnants on which traces of past action can be discerned or 'read'. According to theories of praxeology, such artefacts form a constitutive component of practices.

For this reason, we have also decided against predominantly using terms like 'media', 'written media', and the like. It has long been clear in the field of media theory that media are not merely empty vehicles that simply transmit messages unaltered from sender A to receiver B; rather, media themselves communicate, bear intrinsic meaning, and leave indelible traces in the transmitted content. Nevertheless, the concept of medium evokes a primacy of communication, of transmission intentions on one side and reception on the other. For a theory of material text cultures, this fixation on the communicative functions of inscribed artefacts falls short, since it does not take into account the numerous other functions such artefacts have: the practice of magic; the commemoration of people, places, things, and events; the wielding of power and/or authority; the ability to injure or harm; the manifestation of various kinds of presence; etc. Even if a sender-receiver structure can be identified in a certain sense for every use of writing and for every inscribed artefact, the message is by no means always identical with the textual content: a single word carved in huge letters in marble—a name, for instance—does not 'mean' its textual content, but rather the artefact as a whole has a culturally ascertainable meaning. Talking about written media obscures the fact that the artefact itself, in its entirety—in terms of production, material, installation, accessibility, etc.—has a meaning within a given culture, of which the meaning of the textual content can in no way be detached.

By speaking of inscribed artefacts, we wish to indicate the materially and praxeologically oriented dimension of our studies. The generalised (albeit not dogmatic) decision against using such terms as 'object' and 'medium' thus goes hand in hand with this theoretical framework, given our view that artefacts serve as action-guiding positions in arrangements. Furthermore, we also hold that in order to understand such artefacts, one can never only take the textual content into account, but must also always bear in mind the interrelation of the artefacts' material and semantic aspects.

Materiality – Topology – Presence – Metatexts

In order to explore the cultural meaning of inscribed artefacts and their specific presence in a given historical situation, we have developed a heuristic for the reconstruction of text cultures. The methods include describing the materiality as precisely as possible and, in connection to this, describing the spatial situation, insofar as it is still recognisable or able to be reconstructed. From both perspectives ideally (usually

---

27 Cf. Gibson 1977.

this means: with sufficient historical records), it is possible to draw conclusions about practices in which the artefacts played a role. In doing this, we are not primarily concerned with one-off actions of individuals on inscribed artefacts. Rather, the cultural significance of what is written is derived from practices, i. e., from actions that occur with relative frequency and regularity. Since material and spatial analysis in itself is often only fragmentarily possible, and since the pertinent actions (whether one-time or routine) cannot be observed by us (anymore), we consult texts about writing in general and specific instances of the written word that originate from, or were demonstrably received by, the culture under consideration. We call these texts 'metatexts' (in a departure from the usual literary and scientific usage of this term). Such metatexts are of great help in identifying probable text-related practices and consequently in understanding a text, a text-bearing artefact, and the text culture associated with both.

Materiality is best explained in the context of, and in distinction to, the terms 'matter' and 'material'.[28] 'Matter' is the physical substance of which a thing is made. In the theoretical framework presented here, 'material' also denotes the physical substance, but from a different perspective: namely, matter insofar as it has been culturally shaped and/or changed by humans. This altering and shaping takes place when an artefact is produced; material is matter that has been made available to and for cultural ends. Materiality, in turn, refers to the concept that an artefact (or the writing on an artefact) has physical matter and that this matter determines the artefact in a specific way. The concept of materiality draws attention to this feature, to the 'madeness' from matter on the part of artefacts and what is written, and to the possibilities and practices of matter-related manipulation and the attribution of meaning.

In order to adapt to one's specific research topic, it makes sense to further differentiate between two aspects of 'materiality'. A narrower meaning of the term has in mind the artefacts' 'matter': this could be clay, stone, parchment, etc.—that is, whatever type of matter that has been culturally (trans)formed into 'material'. By contrast, a broader understanding of the term, also allows for the description of the formal arrangement of external elements—e. g. format, layout conventions, text-image arrangement, etc.—or the aesthetic dimension of an artefact as genuine component of its material agency.

Topology focuses less on the materiality of an artefact than on the latter's spatial dimensions. This could be the location of a text within an ensemble of other texts, artefacts, and spaces surrounding it; architectural arrangements that make specific practices and perspectives possible; and so on. Topologies thus serve to capture artefact arrangements as well as provide clues for further specifying the kind of presence accorded to the artefacts and what effects were believed to emanate from this presence. Since the so-called spatial turn in cultural studies, the aspect of space itself has also come increasingly to the fore in historical analyses. Space is considered both

---

28 Cf. Appadurai 1986; Benne 2015; Miller 2005; Reckwitz 2002; Schatzki 2010; also Meier/Focken/Ott 2015, 19–26.

as a topographically measurable quantity as well as something which can be non-topographical in meaning (for instance, when we speak of 'virtual space' or of the 'liturgical space' evoked by a text).

In many ways, the space in which inscribed artefacts are present determines their reception practices. The surrounding space defines how people perceive such artefacts, whether via reading or merely by looking or gazing at them; and at times it incorporates the artefacts into the practices that take place within it. In case of restricted accessibility, space determines the group of people who alone can see the artefacts or even who has them at their disposal. Furthermore, space may transfer its own character and status to the inscribed artefacts located in it.[29] Conversely, however, these artefacts can also participate in the constitution and characterisation of the space in which they are present. Thus, writing—for example, in or on churches—can secure the sacred status of a space as well as internally differentiate and structure it. Or, in the case of ancient sanctuaries, writing can mark such places' boundaries and formulate rules of appropriate behaviour in and around them. Through the progressive accumulation and concentration of mutually referential inscriptions, ancient and medieval urban spaces can even acquire the memorial and authoritative character of a public 'archive'. Finally, topology can also be used to look at the spatial dimension of what is written on the artefact itself. Inscriptions on buildings or statuary monuments can 'guide' users and viewers in their perception of, and movement within, space. If the inscribed artefact has the manageable dimensions of a leaf of parchment or an inscribed stele, the writing's topology touches on aspects of layout as well.

By **presence**, we mean the way in which an inscribed artefact was 'at hand' as an element of material arrangements and integrated into practices. Our concept of presence thus does not aim at mere localisation, but rather at the praxeological dimension of inscribed artefacts. It is important to note that presence does belong to an artefact *sui generis*, but is often intended and consciously produced.[30] This aspect comes into its own particularly when considering both the material of artefacts and their spatial situation. In describing inscribed artefacts, we try to capture the way in which the artefact was visible or tangible for actions on and with it, or how the artefact functioned within the material arrangement. For the presence of an inscribed artefact, then, both its affordances—its inherent offers or invitations to action—and its topological integration are decisive. We can note in this context a particularly interesting borderline case of presence: namely, that of restricted accessibility. Some inscribed artefacts were deliberately withdrawn from the sphere of action and often even from the realm of the visible. Even this (non-)relationship to (a given) space and the people in that space is central to how we understand an artefact or a text culture. Quite often,

---

29 Cf. Frese/Keil/Krüger 2014.
30 Cf. Allgaier et al. 2019, 194–197.

the spatial location (if it can be reconstructed at all) defies easy explanation. We find inscriptions placed so high up that no one can read them; sealed lead tablets in wells and fountains; precious manuscripts accessible to only a very select group of people. Such examples—where what is written resists simple explanations of its use—pointedly demonstrate the integration of inscribed artefacts into their own text cultures and thus bear for us special heuristic value.

Describing the presence of an inscribed artefact is explicitly not an anti-hermeneutic strategy for us, as it is in the case of Hans Ulrich Gumbrecht, who has played presence and hermeneutics off each other.[31] According to Gumbrecht, Western intellectual history—with its fixation on intelligible meaning—must be counterbalanced by taking into account what comes into view (the 'Präsentisch-sich-Ereignende') in its aesthetic and sensual qualities. With regard to the specific case of inscribed artefacts, by contrast, material text culture theory emphasises that the experience of presence and the hermeneutic search for textual meaning usually occur simultaneously and mutually influence one another. This is because the meaning of a text also only 'comes into view' ('ereignet sich') in the reception situation and in the recipient, and therefore cannot be separated from the presential effects of the material and spatial givenness of the text.

Since it is often no longer possible to ascertain the historical placement of inscribed artefacts, the topological description, and thus the reconstruction of the intended or actual effect(s) and practice(s) of such artefacts, is a particularly sensitive methodological point. A prominent role in this context is played not least by **metatexts** ("writings about the written"),[32] which we define following the common use of the term (albeit slightly differently) in literary studies.[33] For us, 'metatexts' are texts in which inscribed artefacts and the human actors and practices associated with them are described, narrated, or discussed. Such metatexts—where extant—often offer insights into precisely those aspects no longer accessible in the physically preserved artefacts. Metatexts help us to reconstruct the practices carried out on and with writing. It can be observed time and again though that the metatextual representation of inscribed artefacts and the practices connected to them do not necessarily reflect historical reality. Yet in any case, the depictions preserve and reflect practices and (conceivable) possibilities that can be very valuable for understanding the text cultures to which such metatexts belong. In this context, self-referentiality should be mentioned as an important form of metatextuality, which is of special interest to the CRC's central question of the constitution or reconstruction of meaning when reflection on the production and nature of the writing is made in the very same text. Last but not least, the analysis of fictional, at times fantastic or unreal writings, offers an important complement and sometimes even a corrective to artefact-centred research,

---

31 Cf. Gumbrecht 2003.
32 Cf. Hilgert 2010, 95–95, our translation, German text: "Geschriebenes über Geschriebenes".
33 On this, cf. Focken/Ott 2016b.

because it can show what kinds of meaning and possibilities were generally attributed to writing within a given culture.[34]

Overview of Thematic Fields and Theses

The synthesis of the research at the CRC 933 was carried out in a concentrated fashion within six interdisciplinary thematic field groups. More theoretically fundamental questions were bundled in the thematic fields 'Reflecting on Writing and Writtenness' (Chapter 1), 'Layout, Design, Text-Image' (Chapter 2) and 'Memory and Archive' (Chapter 3). These thematic areas deal with basic questions concerning the function and effect of writing in its material constitution as well as such writing's associated design, spatial location, and evoked presence. These sections are also where the relationship of a theory of material text cultures to recent theory formation is outlined. Writing in its own effectiveness beyond functions of communication is the subject of Chapter 1. Chapter 2 gathers thesis-like considerations on the material design of writing and its relationship to other elements on an artefact's surface and/or surrounding area; here, the relationship between text and image, as well as the iconic quality of writing ('Schriftbildlichkeit'), also play a role. Chapter 3 deals with the commemorative and archival function of writing, since the frequently intended (but often, also accidental) survival of writing over time is so fundamentally connected with its materiality that these functions also play an important role in cases where an inscribed artefact was not produced specifically as a storage medium.

The thematic field of 'Material Change' (Chapter 4) deals with the (dis)appearance of material text supports, of new technologies, and the cultural practices related to such technologies: that is, the processes that lead to a medium- to long-term change in the material presence of inscribed artefacts within a culture. The initial hypothesis of the CRC was that in societies in which techniques for the mass reproduction of texts are not (yet) available, specific ways of handling what is written—and thus specific text cultures—develop. The latter display specific connections between text, materiality, spatiality, presence, and related practices: connections that can be understood quite well, for instance, in historical situations of change. Especially vivid examples of these historical changes are the transition in material from parchment to paper, or the change in format from the scroll to the codex. This is even truer since these changes never happened suddenly, but rather often took place only partially or were completely rejected at first.

The thesis-like reflections of the four thematic fields of a more general nature are followed by two thematic fields dealing with specific concentrations of cultural and social functions of writing: namely, 'Sacralisation' (Chapter 5) and 'Political Rule and

---

34 Cf. Focken/Ott 2016a; Wagner/Neufeld/Lieb 2019.

Administration' (Chapter 6). The theses have been brought forward in a cross-cultural comparative manner on definable areas of social practice pertaining to the cultic/religious and political/administrative spheres, respectively. In so doing, it has not been our intent to level the enormous cultural-historical differences between cultures, nor have we sought to deny the fact that the modern concept of 'religion' was not at all realised as such in many cultures, or that in some cultures, the political sphere cannot be meaningfully separated from that of the religious/sacred. Nevertheless, there are areas in every culture that can be addressed more specifically with regard to practices of administration or to matters pertaining to the realm of the sacred. The comparative research on text cultures belonging to different social spheres is to be understood as heuristic in nature. Not only does this section of the present work show that the social spheres diverge strongly when compared across times and cultures, but also that different text-related practices prevail in different spheres within a society. Be that as it may, pre-modern text cultures can be studied comparatively in this way, with similarities and differences in text-related practices and attitudes identifiable in similar social spheres.

The bundled theses of these thematic fields are comprehensive neither in terms of the quantity of possible social spheres nor in terms of the multiple historic text cultures. Nevertheless, the studies presented here are meant to be paradigmatic in nature and can demonstrate the productivity of a theory of material text cultures in a comparative cultural perspective. This research programme is not complete, nor is it intended to be.

As mentioned above, we list at the end of this introduction all the theses in the order in which they appear in the present volume. They do not present a completely uniform picture, since the individual chapters address material text culture(s) quite differently: not only from a thematic viewpoint, but also in terms of their respective methodological approaches. This heterogeneity shows that the collected theses are not intended to represent a closed or finite theory. It also reflects the diversity of the research that has been included in the theses: text- and matter-analytical approaches, historical-descriptive and transhistorical-theoretical research, postmodern cultural studies and basic research into material as defined above and as conducted during the existence of the CRC spanning more than a decade. Often, these different approaches have intertwined with one another; sometimes, they have merely stood side by side as findings of different kinds. It should also be taken into account that the theses in this volume cover neither the entire research and labour of the CRC nor the topic of material text cultures in its fulness. Yet in them, the CRC's research is condensed in form. The theses bring together aspects and underlying principles of material text cultures that have proven pivotal over the past twelve years. Formulated as theses, these findings do not claim to be indisputable and universally valid, but rather invite us to wrestle with them, to think them through further, to supplement them, to differentiate them and, if necessary, to revise them at one point or another.

Chapter 1
Reflecting on Writing and Writtenness

Thesis 1 Writing cannot be reduced to its representational function, but has an aesthetic presence and effectiveness in and of itself. —— 33

Thesis 2 The materiality and presence of what is written produce their own semantic content. —— 40

Thesis 3 If what is written is not thought of in terms of communication between subjects, it itself takes on corporeality and agency. —— 44

Thesis 4 The dimensions of what is written are explicitly or implicitly reflected in pre-modern texts. —— 48

Thesis 5 The aisthetic permanence of what is written, i. e., its (long- or short-term) temporal permanence as perceived by the senses, is constitutive for the meaning and effect of writing. —— 52

Thesis 6 The spatial realisation is constitutive for the meaning and effect of what is written. —— 56

Chapter 2
Layout, Design, Text-Image

Thesis 7 Layout and writing supports are mutually dependent. In non-typographic writing cultures, the influence of the writing support is more diverse. —— 69

Thesis 8 The layout of what is written and the design of its characters always carry a potential for meaning. —— 74

Thesis 9 The layout of what is written can be significantly determined by the communicative intentions of the producers. —— 83

Thesis 10 Layout offers different reception practices. —— 92

Thesis 11 On multiple levels, layout and text type stand in a close connection that can be influenced from various sides. —— 96

Overview of Thematic Fields and Theses — 23

Chapter 3
Memory and Archive

Thesis 12 Memory and archive are always dynamic and never concluded. — 120

Thesis 13 Artefacts experience 'memory biographies' that can be modified during production and reception. — 125

Thesis 14 The intentions of the 'archons' are manifested in the archives' location and conditions of access. — 127

Thesis 15 The material composition and organisation of archival records reveal information about their 'archons'. — 132

Thesis 16 In archives, inscribed artefacts are filtered, coded, and transformed. — 136

Thesis 17 There is a direct correlation between the materiality of memory media, their target groups, and their chances of survival. — 140

Thesis 18 Writing on memory media can shape memory and permanently bridge the gap between intention and reception. — 142

Chapter 4
Material Change

Thesis 19 The materiality of text cultures changes not in leaps and bounds, but in processes of a continual nature. — 161

Thesis 20 The affordance and function of inscribed artefacts, as well as practices of production and reception, change asynchronously along with processes of material change. — 165

Thesis 21 Material change sparks ambivalent reactions. — 173

Thesis 22 Taking recourse to traditional techniques of production leads to a re-evaluation of traditional materials, ways of production, and formats, as well as to changes in the attribution of meaning and practices of use. — 180

Thesis 23 Changes in actors in the course of material change coincides with shifts in power relations and social contexts. — 184

Chapter 5
Sacralisation

Thesis 24 Writing has hierographic potential. —— 205

Thesis 25 Writing opens up possibilities for the separation of profane and sacred space, thus creating spaces of liminality. —— 214

Thesis 26 The status of sacrality is always endangered. The demonstrative use of writing serves to authenticate, legitimise, and stabilise sacrality. —— 224

Thesis 27 Sacred places (temples, churches, altars) attract writing: inscribed artefacts partake there of the sacred, while simultaneously contributing to sacralisation themselves. —— 231

Chapter 6
Political Rule and Administration

Thesis 28 Rulers and administrators of multilingual realms consciously chose which languages and writing systems were materialised in writing. Inscribing a text in multiple languages on a monument almost always served primarily to visualise authority. —— 258

Thesis 29 Geographical or geopolitical space may contribute to the prestige and authority of a rulership text by associating the agent behind the text with the authority of the place. —— 267

Thesis 30 A change in the materiality of a particular text often signals a shift in the function of the document. —— 271

Thesis 31 Layout can considerably alter the significance of texts and allows for a distinction between rulership writing and administrative writing. From the layout, one can gauge the degree of sophistication and standardisation of an administration. —— 278

Thesis 32 Simplified cursive handwriting, shorthands, or abbreviations are characteristic of basic forms of administrative writing. Rulership writing tends to use scripts that can convey care, durability, and faithfulness, which often leads to 'monumental' applications of script. —— 280

Thesis 33 Images can reinforce the message of rulership writing, visualise the ideological framework of societal order, and address larger, less literate audiences, but they are not always an integral part of rulership writing. —— 283

Thesis 34 Rulership or administrative texts, particularly those written on portable media, often required some means of material authentication in order to prove the validity of the artefact. —— 286

Thesis 35 Administrative writing included some of the most interactive forms of inscribed artefacts, whereas rulership communication was usually intended to be unidirectional. —— 288

Bibliography

Allgaier, Benjamin/Bolle, Katharina/Jaspert, Nikolas/Knauber, Konrad/Lieb, Ludger/Roels, Evelien/Sauer, Rebecca/Schneidereit, Nele/Wallenwein, Kirsten (2019), "Gedächtnis – Materialität – Schrift. Ein erinnerungskulturelles Modell zur Analyse schrifttragender Artefakte", in: *Saeculum* 69/2, 181–244.

Appadurai, Arjun (1986), *The Social Life of Things. Commodities in Cultural Perspective,* New York.

Aronin, Larissa/Hornsby, Michael/Kiliańska-Przybyło, Grażyna (eds.) (2018), *The Material Culture of Multilingualism,* Cham (CH).

Barsch, Sebastian/Norden, Jörg van (eds.) (2020), *Historisches Lernen und Materielle Kultur. Von Dingen und Objekten in der Geschichtsdidaktik,* Bielefeld.

Benne, Christian (2015), *Die Erfindung des Manuskripts. Zu Theorie und Geschichte literarischer Gegenständlichkeit,* Frankfurt (Main).

Bennett, Tony/Joyce, Patrick (2010), "Material Powers. Introduction", in: Tony Bennett and Patrick Joyce (eds.), *Material Powers. Cultural Studies, History and the Material Turn,* London/New York, 1–21.

Caroll, Timothy/Walford, Antonia/Walton, Shireen (eds.) (2021), *Lineages and Advancements in Material Culture Studies. Perspectives from UCL Anthropology,* London/New York.

Daston, Lorraine (ed.) (2004), *Things That Talk. Lessons from Art and Science,* Princeton.

Eggert, Manfred K. H. (2014), "Artefakt", in: Stefanie Samida, Manfred K. H. Eggert, and Hans Peter Hahn (eds.), *Handbuch Materielle Kultur. Bedeutungen, Konzepte, Disziplinen,* Stuttgart/Weimar, 169–173.

Ehlich, Konrad (1994), "Funktion und Struktur schriftlicher Kommunikation", in: Hartmut Günther and Otto Ludwig (eds.), *Schrift und Schriftlichkeit. Ein interdisziplinäres Handbuch internationaler Forschung,* vol. 1, Berlin/New York, 18–41.

Elias, Friederike/Franz, Albrecht/Murmann, Henning/Weiser, Ulrich Wilhelm (eds.) (2014), *Praxeologie. Beiträge zur interdisziplinären Reichweite praxistheoretischer Ansätze in den Geistes- und Sozialwissenschaften* (Materiale Textkulturen 3), Berlin/Boston, https://doi.org/10.1515/9783110370188.

Focken, Friedrich-Emanuel/Ott, Michael R. (eds.) (2016a), *Metatexte. Erzählungen von schrifttragenden Artefakten in der alttestamentlichen und mittelalterlichen Literatur* (Materiale Textkulturen 15), Berlin/Boston, https://doi.org/10.1515/9783110417944.

Focken, Friedrich-Emanuel/Ott, Michael R. (2016b), "Metatexte und schrifttragende Artefakte", in: Friedrich-Emanuel Focken and Michael R. Ott (eds.), *Metatexte. Erzählungen von schrifttragenden Artefakten in der alttestamentlichen und mittelalterlichen Literatur* (Materiale Textkulturen 15), Berlin/Boston, 1–9, https://doi.org/10.1515/9783110417944-002.

Frese, Tobias/Keil, Wilfried E./Krüger, Kristina (eds.) (2014), *Verborgen, unsichtbar, unlesbar – zur Problematik restringierter Schriftpräsenz* (Materiale Textkulturen 2), Berlin/Boston, https://doi.org/10.1515/9783110353587.

Gibson, James J. (1977), "The Theory of Affordances", in: Robert Shaw and John Bransford (eds.), *Perceiving, Acting, and Knowing: Toward an Ecological Psychology,* Hillsdale, 67–82.

Glassie, Henry (1999), *Material Culture,* Bloomington, IN.

Goll, Tobias/Keil, Daniel/Telios, Thomas (eds.) (2013), *Critical Matter. Diskussionen eines neuen Materialismus,* Münster.

Grube, Gernot/Kogge, Werner (2005), "Zur Einleitung: Was ist Schrift?", in: Gernot Grube, Werner Kogge, and Sybille Krämer (eds.), *Schrift. Kulturtechnik zwischen Auge, Hand und Maschine,* Munich, 9–19.

Gumbrecht, Hans Ulrich (2003), *Production of Presence: What Meaning Cannot Convey,* Stanford, CA.

Haasis, Lucas/Rieske, Constantin (eds.) (2015), *Historische Praxeologie. Dimensionen vergangenen Handelns,* Paderborn.

Hahn, Hans Peter (2005), *Materielle Kultur. Eine Einführung,* Berlin.

Hahn, Hans Peter (2015a), "Der Eigensinn der Dinge – Einleitung", in: Hans Peter Hahn (ed.), *Vom Eigensinn der Dinge. Für eine neue Perspektive auf die Welt des Materiellen,* Berlin, 9–56.

Hahn, Hans Peter (2015b), "Lost in Things. Eine kritische Perspektive auf Konzepte materieller Kultur", in: Philipp W. Stockhammer and Hans Peter Hahn (eds.), *Lost in Things. Fragen an die Welt des Materiellen,* Münster/New York, 9–23.

Hedreen, Guy Michael (ed.) (2021), *Material World. The Intersection of Art, Science, and Nature in Ancient Literature and its Renaissance Reception,* Leiden/Boston.

Hicks, Dan/Beaudry, Mary C. (eds.) (2010), *Material Culture Studies,* Oxford.

Hilgert, Markus (2010), "Textanthropologie. Die Erforschung von Materialität und Präsenz des Geschriebenen als hermeneutische Strategie", in: *Mitteilungen der deutschen Orient-Gesellschaft zu Berlin* 142, 87–126.

Hilgert, Markus (2016), "Materiale Textkulturen. Textbasierte historische Kulturwissenschaften nach dem *material culture turn"*, in: Herbert Kalthoff, Torsten Cress, and Tobias Röhl (eds.), *Materialität. Herausforderungen für die Sozial- und Kulturwissenschaften,* Paderborn, 255–268.

Hilgert, Markus/Hofmann, Kerstin P./Simon, Henrike (eds.) (2018), *Objektepistemologien. Zur Vermessung eines transdisziplinären Forschungsraums,* Berlin.

Hodder, Ian (1986), *Reading the Past. Current Approaches to Interpretation in Archaeology,* Cambridge.

Hurcombe, Linda M. (2007), *Archaeological Artefacts as Material Culture,* New York.

Kalthoff, Herbert/Cress, Torsten/Röhl, Tobias (eds.) (2016), *Materialität. Herausforderungen für die Sozial- und Kulturwissenschaften,* Paderborn.

Keupp, Jan (2017), "Die Gegenstandslosigkeit des Materiellen: Was den material turn zum Abtörner macht", in: *Mittelalterblog* (26. Juni 2017), https://mittelalter.hypotheses.org/10617 (accessed 6/9/2018).

Keupp, Jan/Schmitz-Esser, Romedio (2015), "Einführung in die 'Neue alte Sachlichkeit'. Ein Plädoyer für eine Realienkunde des Mittalters in kulturhistorischer Perspektive", in: Jan Keupp and Romedio Schmitz-Esser (eds.), *Neue alte Sachlichkeit. Studienbuch Materialität des Mittelalters,* Ostfildern, 9–46.

Knorr Cetina, Karin/Schatzki, Theodore (2001), *The Practice Turn in Contemporary Theory,* New York.

Kotrosits, Maia (2020), *The Lives of Objects. Material Culture, Experience, and the Real in the History of Early Christianity,* Chicago/London.

Lake, Crystal B. (2020), *Artifacts. How We Think and Write about Found Objects,* Baltimore.

Latour, Bruno (1996), "On Actor-Network Theory. A Few Clarifications", in: *Soziale Welt* 47, 369–381.

Latour, Bruno (2005), *Reassembling the Social: An Introduction to Actor-Network Theory,* Oxford/New York.

Lieb, Ludger (2015), "Spuren materialer Textkulturen. Neun Thesen zur höfischen Textualität im Spiegel textimmanenter Inschriften", in: Beate Kellner, Ludger Lieb, and Stephan Müller (eds.), *Höfische Textualität. Festschrift für Peter Strohschneider* (GRM-Beiheft 69), Heidelberg, 1–20.

Lieb, Ludger/Ott, Michael R. (2016), "Schnittstellen. Mensch-Artefakt-Interaktion in deutschsprachigen Texten des 13. Jahrhunderts", in: Friedrich-Emanuel Focken and Michael R. Ott (eds.), *Metatexte. Erzählungen von schrifttragenden Artefakten in der alttestamentlichen und mittelalterlichen Literatur* (Materiale Textkulturen 15), Berlin/Boston, 265–280, https://doi.org/10.1515/9783110417944-014.

Lueger, Manfred (2000), "Artefaktanalyse", in: Manfred Lueger (ed.), *Grundlagen qualitativer Feldforschung. Methodologie – Organisierung – Materialanalyse,* Vienna, 140–163.

Margolis, Eric/Laurence, Stephen (eds.) (2007), *Creations of the Mind: Theories of Artifacts and Their Representation,* New York.

Meier, Thomas/Focken, Friedrich-Emanuel/Ott, Michael R. (2015), "Material", in: Thomas Meier, Michael R. Ott, and Rebecca Sauer (eds.), *Materiale Textkulturen. Konzepte – Materialien – Praktiken* (Materiale Textkulturen 1), Berlin/Munich/Boston, 19–31, https://doi.org/10.1515/9783110371291.19.

Meier, Thomas/Ott, Michael R./Sauer, Rebecca (eds.) (2015), *Materiale Textkulturen. Konzepte – Materialien – Praktiken* (Materiale Textkulturen 1), Berlin/Munich/Boston, https://doi.org/10.1515/9783110371291.

Miller, David (1987), *Material Culture and Mass Consumption,* Oxford.

Miller, David (ed.) (2005), *Materiality,* Durham/London.

Olsen, Bjørnar (2003), "Material Culture after Text: Re-Membering Things", in: *Norwegian Archaeology Review* 36, 87–104.

Olsen, Bjørnar (2010), *In Defense of Things. Archaeology and the Ontology of Objects,* Lanham, MD/Plymouth (UK).

Reckwitz, Andreas (2002), "The Status of the 'Material' in Theories of Culture: From 'Social Structure' to 'Artefacts'", in: *Journal for the Theory of Social Behaviour* 32 (2), 195–217.

Reckwitz, Andreas (2006), *Die Transformation der Kulturtheorien. Zur Entwicklung eines Theorieprogramms,* Weilerswist.

Reckwitz, Andreas (2008), "Der Ort des Materiellen in den Kulturtheorien. Von sozialen Strukturen zu Artefakten", in: Andreas Reckwitz, *Unscharfe Grenzen. Perspektiven der Kultursoziologie,* Bielefeld, 131–156.

Reckwitz, Andreas (2012), "Affective Spaces. A Praxeological Outlook", in: *Rethinking History. The Journal of Theory and Practice* 16 (2), 241–258.

Samida, Stefanie (2016), "Materielle Kultur und dann? Kulturwissenschaftliche Anmerkungen zu einem aktuellen Trend in der Zeitgeschichtsforschung", in: *Zeithistorische Forschungen / Studies in Contemporary History* 13, 506–514.

Samida, Stefanie/Eggert, Manfred K. H./Hahn, Hans Peter (eds.) (2014), *Handbuch Materielle Kultur. Bedeutungen, Konzepte, Disziplinen,* Stuttgart/Weimar.

Schatzki, Theodore (1996), *Social Practices. A Wittgensteinian Approach to Human Activity and the Social,* New York.

Schatzki, Theodore (2002), *The Site of the Social. A Philosophical Account of the Constitution of Social Life and Change,* Pennsylvania.

Schatzki, Theodore (2003), "A New Societist Social Ontology", in: *Philosophy of the Social Sciences* 33 (2), 174–202.
Schatzki, Theodore (2010), "Materiality and Social Life", in: *Nature and Culture* 5 (2), 123–149.
Schreiber, Stefan/Hofmann, Kerstin P./Meier, Thomas/Mölders, Doreen (eds.) (2016), *Massendinghaltung in der Archäologie. Der material turn und die Ur- und Frühgeschichte,* Leiden.
Schulz-Schaeffer, Ingo (2000), "Kapitel VIII. Akteur-Netzwerk-Theorie. Zur Koevolution von Gesellschaft, Natur und Technik", in: Johannes Weyer (ed.), *Soziale Netzwerke. Konzepte und Methoden der sozialwissenschaftlichen Netzwerkforschung,* Munich/Vienna, 187–211.
Schüttpelz, Erhard/Bergermann, Ulrike/Dommann, Monika/Stolow, Jeremy/Taha, Nadine (eds.) (2021), *Connect and Divide. The Practice Turn in Media Studies,* Zürich.
Tacke, Andreas/Münch, Birgit Ulrike/Augustyn, Wolfgang (eds.) (2018), *Material Culture. Präsenz und Sichtbarkeit von Künstlern, Zünften und Bruderschaften in der Vormoderne,* Petersburg.
Tilley, Christopher (1990), *Reading Material Culture: Structuralism, Hermeneutics and Poststructuralism,* Oxford.
Tilley, Christopher (1991), *Material Culture and Text: The Art of Ambiguity,* London.
Wagner, Ricarda/Neufeld, Christine/Lieb, Ludger (eds.) (2019), *Writing beyond Pen and Parchment. Inscribed Objects in Medieval European Literature* (Materiale Textkulturen 30), Berlin/Boston, https://doi.org/10.1515/9783110645446.
Woodward, Ian (2007), *Understanding Material Culture,* London et al.
Zanetti, Sandro (ed.) (2012), *Schreiben als Kulturtechnik. Grundlagentexte,* Berlin.

Chapter 1
Reflecting on Writing and Writtenness

Stephanie Béreiziat-Lang, Nele Schneidereit, Dennis Disselhoff, Robert Folger, Marina Aurora Garzón Fernández, Jonas Grethlein, Ludger Lieb, Christina Schulz, Sarina Tschachtli, Laura Velte

Chapter 1
Reflecting on Writing and Writtenness

Stephanie Béreiziat-Lang, Nele Schneidereit, Dennis Disselhoff, Robert Folger, Marina Aurora Garzón Fernández, Jonas Grethlein, Ludger Lieb, Christina Schulz, Sarina Tschachtli, Laura Velte

Our focus in this chapter is on the premises of material text culture theory that touch on the phenomenon of writing itself. While much research has been carried out and much ink spilt on writing and its history, our interest here by contrast lies not so much in a cultural differentiation of various writing systems or their historical development, but rather in the general aspects of writing as a material and presentic phenomenon. Thus, this chapter is not a contrastive study of, say, Egyptian hieroglyphics and Mesopotamian cuneiform—although a great deal could be said about the material conditions of both writing systems, as has in fact been done by some of the researchers involved in the CRC 933. Rather, we focus here more on writing in a general sense, understood as being interrelated systems of signs that enable communication across time and space. Connected to the notion of an 'extended hermeneutics' as presented in the introduction to this volume, we are also primarily interested in writing's own efficacy beyond its communicative functions. Writing refers to a semantics beyond itself, yet through its material presence—according to Thesis 1 below—it generates meaning that expands or counteracts this very semantics. The notion of authorship and intention are thus secondary to our inquiry, since writing—like language itself—is also based on generalisation and conventionalisation, so that a supposedly individual statement is always overwritten by sign-like conventions and transferred to a new situational (textual) context.

Writing as the totality of signs of a referential, presentic and operational character—that is, disjunctive signs whose application is generally rule-governed[1]—makes communication at once possible and impossible, insofar as what is meant by someone cannot be written down as such, as the specific thing an individual had in mind. In communication that stretches across space and time (something which writing is supposed to enable), the semantic decoding of what is individually meant is jeopardised by the absence of sender and receiver. Writing can stand the test of time and thereby transcends the semantic level of its meaning; it appears still as 'writing' even when there is no one left who can receive and interpret its semantic message as such.

The first thesis of this volume deals with this expanded perspective on the meaning of the written and its dimensions: "Writing cannot be reduced to its representational function, but has an aesthetic presence and effectiveness in and of itself." In principle, all further observations are based on this initial thesis. This is because

---

[1] Cf. Grubbe/Kogge 2005.

it is only at the level of the *meaning* of writing as something that goes beyond the semantics of what has been written that the aspects of textual materialisation and the concomitant effects of presence first come into view. The materiality and presence of writing are themselves, deliberately or not, carriers of meaning. They can support what is meant in the text, but they can also ignore or even counteract such meaning. Every written text therefore becomes polyphonic in a certain sense due to its materiality and presence, and this complex web of meaning requires an 'extended hermeneutics', which is explained in more detail in Thesis 2: "The materiality and presence of what is written produce their own semantic content."

Following this, we engage with two chains of thought on the characteristics of writing that occur more frequently in intellectual history. Thesis 3 touches on the intrinsic corporeality of writing and the subject-independent agency that goes hand in hand with such embodiment: "If what is written is not thought of in terms of communication between subjects, it itself takes on corporeality and agency." Thesis 4 explores the self-reflexive power of writing, which often refers especially to the corporeality or materiality of such writing: "The dimensions of what is written are explicitly or implicitly reflected in pre-modern texts." Admittedly, these theses emphasise examples from European discourse in particular. This circumstance is to be understood as purely exemplary and in no way excludes the application of these observations to other cultural spheres. Writing's enduring character beyond the lifetime of any single individual is something that has apparently led cultures across the centuries and around the world to ascribe special power to it.

In some cases, writing itself becomes the subject—it has its own physicality and can act. Writing is present and draws our gaze, whether that be graffiti in large letters on a wall or building or tiny lettering scrawled on a tabletop. Its presence 'means' something, even if no specific significance can be inferred automatically. Sometimes, this agency of writing is particularly emphasised in the imagination of a particular culture. This is the case, for example, when writings that have been assigned special ('magical') agency are staged, write themselves (as in literatures of the European Middle Ages, for example), or intervene as actors in a story (of sacred nature, for example) and determine it (on 'writing magic', cf. Chapter 5, Thesis 24). Such a living character and even sacred potency is ascribed to writing, for example, in rituals still performed today on Bali, in the course of which writing drawn on palm leaves is not permitted to be read, but rather exists as a kind of 'pure' writing, autonomous and bearing meaning only inasmuch as it is recognisable and effective in its materiality as 'writing'. European Antiquity and the Middle Ages, on the other hand, know of 'speaking' objects, on which inscriptions in the first-person initiate a complex game involving the notions of authorship and the self-efficacy of writing.[2]

This power of writing is reflected time and time again in philosophical and literary texts. Such metatextual passages can appear as explicit comments on cultural practices

---

2 Cf. Edelmann-Singer/Ehrich 2021.

in relation to the material design of what is written, or as implicit, even fictionalised, references (letters that do not arrive, writings that cannot be deciphered, etc.) that allow conclusions to be drawn about the cultural potential of what is written. At times, these commentaries are also self-reflexive in a narrower sense in that the text refers to its own textual materiality and its own status as a written composition. While notions of the special efficacy of what is written on account of its material form or corporeality are more common in pre-modern cultures than in modern ones, the self-reflexivity of writing(s) is not, strictly speaking, a phenomenon specific to pre-modernity. Nevertheless, the pre-modern era especially abounds with instances in which writing refers to its own materiality and writtenness, both explicitly and implicitly, and analysing these instances enables us to gain access to the text cultures of this period.[3]

Finally, Theses 5 and 6 address the fundamental fact that writing—no matter how long- or short-term its duration, or how big or small its appearance—can only be realised in time and space. (Thesis 5: "The aisthetic permanence of what is written, i. e., its [long- or short-term] temporal permanence as perceived by the senses, is constitutive for the meaning and effect of writing"; Thesis 6: "The spatial realisation is constitutive for the meaning and effect of what is written.") The meaning of a piece of writing is not only shaped and determined by its presence in space (monumental or restricted[4]), its arrangement in the wider visual context, or its (intentional or accidental) illegibility, but also by the endurability of such writing in the field of vision, or by the permanence or ephemerality of its material, respectively. Viewed thus, we can focus on how what is written interacts with potential recipients in ever new encounters, all of which are nonetheless already conceivable by the initial act of writing. The way in which this encounter actually happens can run counter to how it was initially envisioned: for example, when the spatial configuration of a piece of writing shifts over time, or when the cultural practices surrounding what is written undergo change or become obsolete. In any case, as already outlined at the beginning, the problem (but also the accompanying creative potential) once again comes to light here of a semantic polyphony determining all writing, when we regard it as autonomous and in its efficacy independent of any specific communication situation.

Thesis 1
Writing cannot be reduced to its representational function, but has an aesthetic presence and effectiveness in and of itself.

Writing is materially realised and thus has an immediate presence and concomitant effectiveness. We lose sight of this property if writing is primarily understood as a

---

3 Cf. Focken/Ott 2016a.
4 Frese/Keil/Krüger 2014a.

representational system. In what follows, we trace out an understanding of writing in which it essentially goes beyond being merely a vehicle for conveying thought, which is deemed controllable by the writing subject. When we speak here of 'writing' as a cultural technique, we always understand this term in a general way without any specificity with regard to cultures and writing systems. Considerations of the conceptual and practical writing differences that exist amongst, for example, phonographic alphabetic scripts, syllabic scripts, or logographic writing systems such as Chinese characters or Egyptian hieroglyphs are left aside. In order to reflect on the theoretical content of such a general perspective, however, we shall first approach it from the cultural tradition of alphabetic scripts, since they quite clearly illustrate the argument against the representational character of writing.

In most modern-era and present-day European theories of writing—not to mention in everyday life—writing has been understood from the point of view of (spoken) language: namely, writing has been regarded as language that has been written down primarily for the purpose of overcoming the temporal and/or spatial distance between sender and receiver. In such logocentric models, what is written represents oral speech, which in turn is merely the vehicle of a prior inner world of thoughts, the expression of intentions.

Every epistemic and cultural formation constructs narratives on the respective status, genesis, and function of 'writing'. It is crucial to consider these narratives not as absolute, but rather as culturally dependent conceptions,[5] and to keep in mind the implications of such narratives for power politics.[6] In theoretical discourse on the subject of writing, for example, the dominant European narrative in modern times has been decidedly teleological. It has portrayed writing as a secondary cultural technique, chronologically subsequent to language and—depending on the epistemological perspective—increasing the latter's complexity (Condillac, Rousseau) while at the same time implying a loss of 'authenticity' and of the individuality of the immediate expression of language (this 'phonocentrism', according to Derrida, has pervaded the whole of Western philosophy since Plato[7]). A model for establishing a hierarchy between language and writing is then argumentatively sought in human phylogeny and ontogeny (and thus assumed to be quasi-natural), according to which human beings come into the world without language and writing, but with the ability to speak. The acquisition of a specific language develops in a given culture without any instruction at the end of the first year of life; literacy develops only with instruction, and is thus seen as a cultural achievement in contrast to language acquisition. This development of the

---

5 We mean here 'narratives' in the sense of a *meta-récit*, cf. Lyotard 1986. On narratives of 'writing' in different cultural contexts, see also Gumbrecht/Pfeiffer 1993.
6 The implications of narratives on 'writing' for power politics tend to deny the status of 'writing' to other writing systems, cf. Greek views on the scriptless *barbaroi* or the views of colonial powers with regard to Mesoamerican cultures (cf. Mignolo 2003; Errington 2008). Certeau 1990 also posits that generally speaking, writing is an epistemic instrument (of power) of an all-encompassing character.
7 Derrida 1967. The critique of writing in Certeau 1975 proceeds in a similar vein.

individual would then roughly correspond to a history of the development of humankind in which cultures first have language and then—possibly, but also not all cultures—acquire writing as a regulated system of disjunctive signs that can be used for variable content in variable situations and that can express verbal utterances. This perspective allows historical theories of writing to establish cultural (and in effect, Eurocentric) hierarchies not only between language and writing, but also between different writing systems, as seen for example when such theories posit a path of positive development progressing from mere gestures to pictograms to hieroglyphs, thence to syllabic forms of writing, and finally reaching the apex of alphabetic scripts (Condillac, Rousseau, Hegel). Alphabetic writing is seen in such lines of thought to be the highest level of writing development, since it is said to render the pictorial character of the signs secondary and allows them to become paradoxically invisible, the plainly seen but mainly ignored means for transporting and transmitting verbal utterances.[8]

By contrast, ever since Plato's *Phaedrus,* the traditional critique of writing has established a quite different view for interpreting the connection between language and writing in terms of writing and media theory. With the critique of the mere externality of form (writing) as opposed to the actual internality of content (direct linguistic expression), the teleological perspective becomes a tipping point. Precisely because writing replaces the human voice, Plato considers the former to be ambivalent: as a *pharmakon,* it can be useful, but also poisonous, thus becoming a dehumanising, merely apparent simulacrum. Plato's critique of writing is radicalised by Derrida and Certeau into a necessity: writing and all signs in general (including gestures, pictograms, and ultimately even words, i.e., language itself) are understood as being the condition of the possibility of expression and understanding, and as making it simultaneously impossible to convey what is originally meant and thought. Every written expression, every sign is always subsequent to what is supposed to be expressed and is never 'authentic' with regard to it. The uniqueness of the meaning or thought that is intended to be expressed is always absent in the sign (be it writing, a linguistic sign, or a gesture).[9]

Building on this theoretical foundation, Derrida developed a concept of writing that deduces a reversal in the relationship between writing and language from the absence of the signified in the signifier: Derrida's provocation consists in placing writing *before* language. At first glance, he would seem to contradict not only the historical sequence of the historical development of language and writing as outlined above, but also the sequence of how individuals learn language and writing, as well as ulti-

---

[8] On historical theories of writing, cf. e.g. the handbook *Schrift und Schriftlichkeit,* edited by Günther/Ludwig 1994, vol. 1. These assumptions of a cultural-historical development are in line with the framework of teleological conceptions of history and are only based in part on historical studies of writing systems. Moreover, they do not sufficiently take into account the fact that writing can also fulfil non-referential functions distinct from speech communication.

[9] On the "dangerous supplement" *(dangereux supplément)* of the written and the category of absence, cf. Derrida 1967. On dehumanisation as the de-voicing of writing vis-à-vis the authenticity of speech and bodily performance, cf. also Certeau 1975.

mately the common-sense notion that writing is merely a retrospective record of linguistically composed thought. Derrida's *archi-écriture* is in a certain sense even prior to thinking, in that it prescribes fundamental structures.[10] This 'priorness' of writing is, of course, not meant in historical or temporal terms, but rather refers to the general primordiality of the sign before the concrete intention of communication. Derrida's considerations are based on the absence of the signified in the signifier—a central point already in Plato's critique of writing—and on the physical absence of sender and receiver in the situation of written communication (which can be extended over space and time). In this communication between absent persons, however, the sign remains present when the sender is gone and even in cases where it never reaches its recipient. The permanent (present) character of the written sign and the possibility of its use in infinite contexts are the very condition of the possibility of written communication.

The premise here is that writing is 'iterable', i.e., not bound to particular senders or particular contexts, but applicable by all competent users. It can be 'grafted' into ever new contexts by connecting the signs of a specific script to form infinite quantities of text. Writing must thus be completely independent of specific communication intentions in order to be able to function in the absence of sender and receiver. However, this leads to the assumption of a general impossibility of communication—that is, if we understand the latter to be the accident-free transport of an intention from sender to receiver. Derrida therefore understands the core properties of writing to be the "break with the horizon of communication as communication of consciousnesses or of presences and as linguistical or semantic transport of the desire to express oneself *(vouloir-dire)*", as well as the "disengagement of all writing from the semantic or hermeneutic horizons".[11] This has implications for the textual hermeneutics that are discussed anew in the context of (post-)structuralism: even from the point of view of their respective contexts, texts as distinct, meaning-bearing units of signs cannot be understood in a simple way and with certainty (with regard to authorial intent).[12]

As is well known, Derrida's theory of absence as being essential to writing leads to a clearly expanded concept of writing, since what has been said about writing also applies to all "orders of 'signs' and [...] [to] all languages in general but moreover, beyond semio-linguistic communication, [...] [to] the entire field of what philosophy would call experience", even to the "experience of being".[13] It is not necessary to accept the epistemological expansion of the concept of writing (especially since the philosophy of mind offers more epistemological models than that of the external world's representation by ideas as its internal signs) in order to work with Derrida's analysis of the classical concept of writing and the consequences of his thinking.

---

10 On the concept of *archi-écriture* as an element of the unconscious and the psychoanalytical implications that follow from this, cf. Derrida 1967.
11 Derrida 1988, 8–9.
12 Cf. Haß/Noller 2015.
13 Derrida 1988, 9.

Besides, Derrida's concept of writing is too expansive for a meaningful theory of material text cultures in terms of its epistemological or even ontological consequences.

What is fruitful, however, is the premise of separating writing from the communication situation if we assume that all written expression, in fact any linguistic expression, is only possible through systems of signs (characters, words) that exist before us and before a given desire for expression. These signs, along with the code that regulates them, enable expression and communication; yet at the same time, they render individual expression as such impossible. In order to be understandable, we have to employ systems of signs that must be fundamentally independent of any individual desire for expression and any specific communicative context. Communication, understood as the undamaged transport of intentions, is just as impossible in the here and now as it is over long distances of space and time.

Derrida's concept of writing can thus be understood as a basis for reflecting on the autonomy of materially present signs in an infinite number of contexts with their very own efficacy. This concept can thus also serve to put the representational character of writing into perspective with regard to language. Reflecting on the autonomy of writing vis-à-vis intentions, thoughts, and language can explain numerous writing practices better than theories of writing can, which understand writing as pure representation, as a repository of the linguistic.

In today's theoretical debates, as well as in the wake of new media configurations, there have been repeated calls not to reduce the phenomenon of writing simply to the linguistic and communicative processes that precede the act of writing. The range of phenomena broadly termed 'writing' also includes notational and arithmetical writing, for example, which cannot be understood in terms of spoken language. Furthermore, the realm of the written has its own practices that are detached from spoken language, such as highlighting, cutting up, and reassembling a text, among others. Moreover, ideas regarding the magical effects of writing or other cultural practices that presuppose the very materiality or ephemerality of writing (such as cultic practices) and play with the categories of (il)legibility or (in)visibility become more comprehensible when the independence and self-efficacy of writing is taken into account. A "meaningful concept of writing" must therefore no longer be considered a "derivative of speech"[14] and must not be thought of solely in terms of the "order of the discursive".[15] Gernot Grube, Werner Kogge, and Sybille Krämer call for a triadic structural model of writing—a kind of *via media* opposed to both an exceedingly narrow concept of writing and the exceedingly broad one espoused by Derrida—which regards the categories of reference, aisthetic presence, and operativity as essential features of the phenomenon of writing.[16]

---

14 Krämer 1998, 82, our translation, German text: "Derivat der Rede".
15 Grube/Kogge 2005, 11, our translation, German text: "Ordnung des Diskursiven".
16 Cf. the publications resulting from the DFG Research Training Group 1458 'Notational Iconicity: Materiality, Perceptibility and Operativity of Writing', which was active from 2008–2013 at the Free University of Berlin.

When we speak of the "aisthetic presence" of writing,[17] we mean that characters are visually perceptible—or at least must have been for a short period of time in order for such characters to be considered as writing. In this context, the enduring quality inherent in something written unfolds its own potential for meaning alongside the meaning that is proper to what is written (see Thesis 5). Scholars have noted that the presence of writing stands in tension between the poles of visibility and invisibility.[18] On the one hand, this alludes to the spatial foundation of writing, which always presupposes an already "formatted space".[19] On the other hand, writing is always a "pictorial phenomenon",[20] and as such must also be perceived in its creative expression.

The pictoriality of writing indicates that the aisthetic presence of writing (that is, such as it stands in relation to sense perception) is always also an *aesthetic* presence: namely, one related to a particular quality of perception (beautiful or ugly, easy or hard to recognise, large or small, etc.) with its own particular effect. Inscribed artefacts, whether they be manuscripts, books, or screens in the context of historical development, must deal with this fundamental tension between writing's quality as image on the one hand and as character(s) on the other. In doing so, they can stress either quality to a greater extent in different ways. While some artefacts allow the materiality of the writing to play second fiddle in the act of reception, in hopes that the content of the writing might appear all the more prominently, other artefacts can prevent precisely such a reception and emphasise the materiality and pictoriality, which in turn can 'block'[21] semantic reception or at the least force it to compete against other dimensions of meaning that are transmitted by the artefact's materiality.

If the pictoriality of the writing is very prominent—as is the case in the ornamental use of writing, the creation of images with writing, or the rich decoration of initials (cf. Fig. 4 in Chapter 2 and Fig. 5 in Chapter 5)—the content of what is written (its meaning, its reference) fades into the background, and the dimensions of what the pictorial element itself means must also be taken into account in the act of reading. For example in medieval art this back and forth of written and pictorial elements with regard to legibility shifts away referentiality from the level of the sign to that of the textual environment of the written characters, whereby such characters posit a pictorial meta-commentary that either increases or ironically undermines levels of meaning. In the interplay between writing and image, legibility moves along a spectrum of ostentatious display, of moments of concealment and even of pretence.[22] In iconoclastic contexts, for example, writing takes on a complex role as a 'hybrid' formation,

---

17 Kogge/Grube 2005, 14, our translation, German text: "aisthetischer Präsenz".
18 Cf. Frese/Keil/Krüger 2014a.
19 Krämer 2005, 28, our translation, German text: "formatierten Raum".
20 Rehm 2019, our translation, German text: "Bildphänomen". On the 'pictoriality of writing', cf. the explanations in Chapter 2, pp. 78–83.
21 Cf. Lieb 2015, 3–4, who also provides further bibliography, especially n. 11 on Gumbrecht; see also Gumbrecht/Pfeiffer 1993.
22 Cf. Horstmann 2024.

in which iconic and discursive elements are united:[23] writing stands in "competition with other visibilities",[24] while at the same time always itself remaining an image and thus subverting the actual critique of images that is fixated on the written form.[25]

It nevertheless remains relevant that the 'pictoriality of writing' (or 'notational iconicity', cf. Chapter 2, pp. 78–83) represents a specific rather than pure kind of iconicity, since the sign-like quality is over-coded here by means of pictorial and semantic elaboration. The effect of the pictoriality of writing is based on the fact that the reference of what is written can be pushed aside by its particular material presence—a possibility (following Derrida) that is always inherent in writing. Notably, a potential sign character can here itself be denoted as a 'reference'; in other words: an image of writing can refer rather to its own inherent possibility of being sign-like than to any external content. The function of writing as a means of communication (the primacy of which is to be questioned here) thus becomes more complex: even the suspension of the linguistic referential function of what is written could be described as a communicative act, since the strategies of the "restricted presence", invisibility, and illegibility of the written word can for their part be "essentially involved in the production of social meaning" precisely beyond referentiality.[26] In this respect, the communicative function of writing could be expanded, such that writing could communicate itself as a possible means of communication, with the pictorial dimension also remaining part of the communication process.

The operational aspect of the triadic structural model[27] distinguishes writing from images; writings are "built up of elements which are in principle distinguishable and definite", and with which "one *can* in principle operate according to unambiguous rules".[28] Consequently, the operationality of writing can be detached from individual communication situations and can form its own systems. For example, the binary code of 1 and 0 or a computer programme has no (or at least, no simple) reference in an individual desire for expression; it is not based on anything linguistic. Because of their contextual independence, written characters and writing systems can become self-dynamic and completely independent of semiotic orders. This is also where a self-generative aspect of writing comes into play.

Furthermore, if we broaden the concept of writing to include computer-based media, this basic premise leads to an "auto-operativity" in which signs themselves have the capacity to act,[29] being self-generating within their own system of reference. Fol-

---

23 Cf. Krämer 2018, 210.
24 Strätling/Witte 2006, 8, our translation, German text: "Konkurrenz zu anderen Sichtbarkeiten".
25 Strätling/Witte 2006, 9.
26 Frese/Keil/Krüger 2014b, 234, our translation, German text: "restringierte[ ] Präsenz", "an der Produktion von sozialem Sinn wesentlich beteiligt". Cf. also Chapter 2, pp. 78–83.
27 Grube/Kogge 2005.
28 Grube/Kogge 2005, 15, our translation, German text: "aus prinzipiell unterscheidbaren und definiten Elementen aufgebaut", "[und mit dem] grundsätzlich nach eindeutigen Regeln operiert werden kann".
29 Krämer 2005, 46; Grube 2005.

lowing Luhmann, writing can also be considered as an "autopoietic system" which in the network of its own operations is itself able to reproduce, further develop, and reflect on structures. "By condensing and confirming writing", writes Luhmann, "a written text [...] generates a tremendous potential for texts yet unwritten".[30] Here again, neither aisthetic presence nor referentiality are criteria for a basic system-internal legibility of the code, which can be increasingly detached from human actors and the code's primordial sense of a communicative act.

But writing also unfolds its own capacity for action outside its own system. If writing can be described as a medium that need not be preceded by any (linguistic or) mental concept, then its own dynamic and constructive character becomes clear. Thus, we find an echo of the operational aspect of writing in Derrida's concept of writing. As a "visualisation of the cognitive", writing enables a haptic way of dealing with epistemic objects so to speak, which lets these objects emerge into being and makes them tangible.[31] Writing's status as mere object vis-à-vis a subject who writes, then, is also itself called into question, and the act of writing, as White and Barthes have noted, could be considered as a 'mediopassive' form or voice between the active and the passive in which the act of writing itself shapes the writer's status as subject[32] (one finds examples for this in some Indo-European language grammars). On the surface of the material writing support, the possibility emerges for the constitution of subjectivity in the act of writing, a field of operation that makes the production of the subject possible in the first place and underlines the active dimension of the practice of writing, in its function which does not serve merely to represent, but also to create entire worlds and systems of logic.[33]

Thesis 2
The materiality and presence of what is written produce their own semantic content.

At the heart of the first thesis lies the claim that meaning is not simply represented by what is written; indeed, meaning is rendered in some ways impossible. This does not mean, however, that we cannot strive for the meaning produced by what is written via hermeneutic procedures. The unavoidability of materiality and presence, and thus the efficacy, of written signs or what is written is accompanied by the production of further meaning. This additional meaning, however, is just as much beyond the control

---

[30] Cf. Luhmann 1993, 351 and 356, our translation, German text: "Indem er die Schrift kondensiert und bestätigt", "erzeugt ein geschriebener Text [...] ein ungeheures Potential für noch ungeschriebene Texte".
[31] Krämer 2005, 42, our translation, German text: "Visualisierung des Kognitiven".
[32] Cf. White 1993.
[33] On the problem of the *page blanche* cf. Certeau 1990, 199; Foucault 1994.

of a writing subject (or 'authorial intent') as is the semantic meaning represented by the signs. This has consequences for the extended hermeneutic approach, which is not concerned solely with the semantics of texts, but also with the meaning of what is written inasmuch as it supplements, overlaps with, negates, or ignores the semantics of the text. In the following, we consider this surplus production of meaning along with the writing-related practices that are associated with and effected by it. In doing so, we also link motifs from media theory to the 'extended hermeneutics' proposed here.

The referential aspect of writing—which can become secondary in the overly strong presence of the pictorial aspect or of the operationality of writing systems that can only be read by machines and are devoid of meaning for a human reader—nevertheless remains the vanishing point of our everyday concept of writing. We deal with writing in such a way that we understand it as conveying meaning even when we have no way of deciphering what has been written; we simply assume that it makes sense. We cannot imagine another way of dealing with what is written in everyday life other than as something that can be read and thus ultimately understood—even if its understanding eludes some. Referential means that writing stands as signs for something. This can be, among other things, generic ideas, syllables, or sounds, which usually stand for comprehensible content (meaning) as elements of a natural language.

Hermeneutics deals with the referentiality of texts as a 'doctrine of interpretation', which is only necessary because the reference(s) of texts, their semantics, is problematic. Reference can be problematic because the interpreter is insufficiently able to understand what is meant, or because what is meant—or the text—deliberately or inadvertently blocks an interpretation; or because what is written is illegible or the inscribed artefact is damaged; or because the writing system is unknown (e. g., the medieval Voynich manuscript, which to date has not been deciphered). It is also problematic for the illiterate and for children, who nevertheless understand writing in the sense of a (potential) sign code that bears meaning. We cannot deal here with the history and critique of hermeneutics as an assumption of the possible elevation of an inner meaning from its merely external and accidental form, even though the criticism has lost none of its polemical potential in the course of overcoming post-structuralism and the latter's supposed arbitrariness of meaning.[34] It should be noted, however, that a hermeneutics extended to materiality, presence, and efficacy is not concerned with reconstructing an original meaning along the lines of authorial intent.[35] What is meant here is that in the understanding of the written word, which is always tied to culture and context, it is not *only* the semantics of the written word which must be included, but that a large number of other elements that carry meaning enter into the hermeneutic endeavour. The materiality and specific presence of an inscribed artefact

---

34 On this, cf. Haß/Noller 2015.
35 On (the history of) hermeneutics and its critique, cf. the instructive short article by Aleida Assmann, in which she traces the path from a triple configuration (text-reader-pathfinder) via a double one (text-reader) to a single one (text) (A. Assmann 1996).

have their own potential meanings that expand or modify the understanding of what is written. Some are intentional, such as the particular value of the material used; some are accidental, such as the careless scrawl on a clay shard. Even the safekeeping of a piece of writing 'bestows' meaning, e. g. the display of a relic authentic in a modern exhibition space as well as the hiding of a secret message or the sinking of a lead tablet inscribed with a curse into a well. The practices in which a given inscribed artefact were involved are often not easy to reconstruct, but nonetheless relevant to its meaning. They too form an essential component of the artefact's specific presence and are thus part and parcel with its cultural and semantic meaning, which extended hermeneutics enables us to grasp.

The 'decoding' of the elements of an inscribed artefact that provide meaning, as well as of—more broadly speaking—its 'text culture', can only ever be approximate, since each reception situation comes with its own patterns of interpretation. In a way, the procedure incorporating the materiality and presence of what is written into the hermeneutic endeavour expands the degrees of uncertainty by asking about the meaning of an inscribed artefact that is situated and integrated into a text culture. Such an 'extended' hermeneutics also does not establish any instances of authorial intent for the text culture: only in rare cases is there a clear indication of the intent(ion) with which the design or placement of an inscribed artefact was undertaken in the way it was found. In most cases, the historical meaning must be reconstructed provisionally and cautiously. Metatexts, but also the textuality or materiality reflected in a text itself, can provide us with clues to this end (cf. Thesis 4), although the inherent dynamics of any given instance of writing resist being completely 'decoded', even with the aid of such metatexts.

What is particularly relevant here, then, is that writing not only transmits a possible semantic meaning, but that it also generates meaning through its specific materiality, presence, and the practices in which it is/was integrated. The generation of this meaning can occur both consciously and unconsciously, and can in fact also undermine the meaning of what is written. Likewise, twentieth-century media theory has not only criticised the assumption that media are mere vehicles of meaning, but has also already identified them as a "source of meaning" of their own, in the sense of McLuhan's dictum that the medium is the message.[36] Especially in the case of disruption, the veil of the medium's supposedly simple function as content bearer is parted and the medium becomes visible as such. What we see, however, is nothing other than what was already there: the materiality of the medium always generates a trace of its own efficacy, which can be completely opposed or parasitic to the intended transmission. Materiality produces a 'surplus', an 'added value' of meaning, which is mostly neither intended nor even within the control of writing subjects. Paul Zumthor has described this in terms of the voice as the medium of speech, which—like an

---

36 McLuhan 1964.

'unintentional trace'—always bears meaning on its own, often deviating from what is intended to be said.[37] Here, the medium itself is not only the bearer of a meaning; "rather the trace of the medium is preserved in the message".[38]

Gumbrecht has already argued that media (and thus also writing) produce their own 'surplus' of meaning and do not refer deictically to some extrinsic meaning, but rather appear themselves with their aisthetic qualities.[39] On "this side of hermeneutics"[40], the medium's materiality offers phenomena of presence that elude and run counter to the interpretive gesture—at least insofar as this gesture refers solely to the semantics of a text. The very materiality of the medium thus changes the latter's status from being an object of investigation to being a subject that determines its own parameters for how to be read. The intrinsic efficacy of materiality is reflected above all in the perceptibility and durability of what is written (cf. Theses 5 and 6), but it also has an influence on semantic content of the written word and can even contradict it under certain circumstances.

Media—and this is equally valid for writing—thus not only condition the possibility of meaning, but are themselves accorded agency in the course of a "crossing, shifting, i. e. subversion" of meaning.[41] Therefore, neither writing in general nor specific instances of the written word can be regarded as an "instrument".[42] Writing is not simply a vehicle bearing the meaning with which it has been charged, but rather can enrich what is meant as a source of meaning in itself, or even supply a completely different meaning. As mentioned before, neither this critique of an instrumental understanding of writing nor a general critique of hermeneutics (like Gumbrecht's, for instance) entail that the reference to meaning should be abandoned altogether. What is problematised is the monosemy and absolutisation of meaning in general, along with the idea that meaning could be detached from its medial forms of expression without them generating meaning on their own. Likewise, the reader is urged to make an effort to understand the text, but is also made aware by the critique of hermeneutics of the fact that references can be infinite and that a clear deduction of them all is impossible. Moreover, from a historical perspective, we see that it is not only the contexts of medial preconditions and thus the 'messages' of the media themselves (McLuhan) that are subject to change, but also the practices and forms of reception in the contexts of different cultural systems of knowledge.

---

37 Cf. Krämer 1998, 79.
38 Krämer 1998, 81, our translation, German text: "vielmehr bewahrt sich an der Botschaft die Spur des Mediums".
39 Cf. Gumbrecht 2003.
40 Here we pun on the title of the German translation of Gumbrecht's work *Production of Presence: What Meaning Cannot Convey*, which first appeared in English; Schulte's translation into German is entitled *Diesseits der Hermeneutik: Über die Produktion von Präsenz* (Gumbrecht 2004).
41 Krämer 1998, 90, our translation, German text: "Durchkreuzung, Verschiebung, eben Subversion".
42 Krämer 1998, 90, our translation, German text: "Instrument".

This sensitisation to contexts of meaning as infinite is, in a certain sense, a first prerequisite for dealing with pre-modern instances of writing, since the cultures from which surviving written testimonies originate stand at a great temporal, and thus cultural, remove from the present. However, the caution necessary in comprehension, as well as the reference to the presence of inscribed artefacts, their topographies, and the practices related to them as sources of meaning in their own right when dealing with pre-modern societies, applies equally to the present day due to the critical engagement with a structural model of writing (see Thesis 1 above). At the same time, it often seems to have been the case historically that in cultures without techniques for the mechanical reproduction of writing, the intrinsic efficacy of the presence of written characters was virtually staged, presupposed for magical practices and often reflected on in the texts themselves. It often is with particular clarity that the specific epistemological situation of pre-modern and 'non-typographic' writing cultures allows for the material and somatic dimension of what is written and its own efficacy to show (cf. Thesis 3).[43]

Thesis 3
If what is written is not thought of in terms of communication between subjects, it itself takes on corporeality and agency.

As stated in Thesis 1, most modern theories of writing, and the self-evident notion of the written word that dominates everyday life today, assume that what is written is essentially a vehicle for communicating the thoughts and intentions of subjects. These subjects, viewed as minds juxtaposed to the world of things, have bodies that provide the material basis for the production and transmission of meaning via sounds, writing, or other signs. If one assumes that writing produces meaning—that is, that writing takes the place of the subject as the origin of meaning and intention—then writing becomes its own body able to act on its own surroundings. The physicality of what is written[44] at once implies and presupposes agency.

In relation to the 'Western world', by which we mean here predominantly Eurocentric cultures regardless of actual geographical location, the corporeality of writing has above all a historical dimension. In the course of technological advancement, especially with the increasing spread of typography and the emergence of hegemonic models of 'strong' subjectivity in the fifteenth to eighteenth centuries (emblematic in the Cartesian subject),[45] this corporeality is increasingly replaced by the notion of 'spiritual

---

43 Cf. Hilgert 2010 and 2016.
44 Cf. Béreiziat-Lang/Folger/Palacios Larrosa 2020.
45 On the formation of modern forms of subjectivity at the beginning of the modern era, cf. Folger 2009. 'Strong' subjectivity is characterised by the categorical opposition of subject and environment; cf. Dünne 2003, 59.

communication' through the vehicle of immaterial or only incidentally material writing, although retaining some residual significance in modern 'Western' societies (for example, in the religious sphere). Although the assumption of a disembodied writing has become globally relevant with the history of colonial expansion and the concomitant hegemony of 'Western' epistemologies, notions of a corporeality of the written word can be more or less prevalent in other cultures. The corporeality of writing is historically and culturally determined and cannot be detached from specific epistemologies and models of subjectivity. In what follows, we explain this thesis on the basis of Western medieval epistemology, whose roots lie in Greco-Roman philosophy.

The critique of the logocentric concept of writing made by the post-structuralists and found in more recent work that takes into account not only the semiotic dimension of such writing, but also the pragmatics and materiality of the same, shows that how one understands writing changes historically and is based on different epistemologies (Theses 1 and 2). The study of writing in pre-modern cultures must not only take into account explicit reflections of writtenness in metatexts, but also the epistemological presuppositions of writing, since these are essential for understanding historical writing practices.

In pre-modern European epistemology, writing had a very special and privileged relationship with the body or the somatic. There was neither the Cartesian separation of mind and matter, nor was there a sundering of the body from its environment. The body was not merely an instrument for the creation of written or inscribed artefacts. Rather, there existed a special relationship of writing to the body, a relationship that imbued artefacts with somatic qualities—in contrast to the Cartesian perspective, in which they were considered inanimate and without any agency of their own.

Before we return to the materiality of writing, however, a few remarks on materiality in medieval conceptions of thought and cognition are necessary. A cornerstone of pre-modern epistemology is the notion that there is no thinking without images.[46] This principle is affirmed by Thomas Aquinas in his commentary on Aristotle's *On Memory and Recollection* (90–91).[47] In another text, his commentary on the Greek philosopher's *On the Soul* (432a3–10), Aquinas writes: "Instead, when one actually contemplates *(speculatur)* anything, one must at the same time form a phantasm for oneself. Phantasm are likenesses of sensible things, but they differ from them in that they exist outside of matter."[48] In his *Summa*, he emphasises the somatic character of

---

46 Cf. Aristotle, *De memoria et reminiscentia*, 449^b, 48–49. For a description of the basic model of pre-modern Western psychology (as a synthesis of terminologically-speaking, frequently heterogeneous accounts) and its epistemological basis, see Folger 2009, 42–71.
47 Cf. Thomas Aquinas, *In Aristotelis libros De sensu et sensato, De memoria et reminiscentia commentarium*, 311–315.
48 Thomas Aquinas, *A Commentary on Aristotle's De Anima*, 391 (transl. by R. Pasnau). Cf. Thomas Aquinas, *In tres libros Aristotelis De Anima præclariβima Expositio*, liber III, lectio XIII, col. 237: *Sed cum speculetur, necesse simul phantasma aliquod speculari. Phantasmata enim sicut sensibilia sunt præterquam quod sunt sine materia.*

mental processes: "The body is necessary for the activity of the intellect, not as the organ through which it acts, but in order to supply it with its object; for images stand in relation to the intellect as color in relation to the sight."[49]

The material body is the foundation of intellectual processes. The *phantasmata* relate to the intellect, just as colour does to the sense of sight. The principle of the fundamental role of images and their phantasmatic quality in all processes of perception and cognition (which led Giorgio Agamben to speak of a "pneumophantasmology"[50]) was the foundation not only of Aristotelian-Thomistic philosophy in particular, but also of European epistemology in general. This manifested itself in and established the medical and psychological theories of the Aristotelian-Galenic school of thought with very practical implications. The *phantasmata* that are mentioned are neither mental images in the contemporary sense nor are they mere representations. Pre-modern epistemology postulated that *formae, phantasmata,* and *species* all emanate from things, moving through a medium (usually the air) towards the eye and being transported through the eye to the inner senses of the *anima sensibilis*.[51] The perceptual and cognitive process was said to culminate in the storage of such images at the back of the brain, the seat of memory. These stored images are then said to be the material basis of the operations of the intellect, i. e., the *anima rationalis*.

What is decisive here is that the *species* are to be understood as the physical basis of mental processes, because these are based on Aristotelian hylomorphism. Regardless of the Aristotelian differentiation between matter (ὕλη) and form (μορφή), one cannot speak of any dualism. Just as material objects always have a form, *species* always have a material basis. Because form always requires matter, this explains why a *species* cannot exist without a 'medium', even if this be something as 'insubstantial' as air. Even the *spiritus* or *pneuma*—which is the medium of all mental processes, especially of the *phantasmata*—is considered to be no more than the most refined product of digestion, that is, matter in its highest sublimation.[52] 'Thinking in images' should thus be understood as an essentially material form of thinking, with this epistemology implying that there was no ontological difference between the physical environment and body and the realm of the mental or psychical. As Suzannah Biernoff notes, "medieval theories of perception and knowledge often employed tripartite, not binary schemata; frequently making a sharper distinction between levels of soul than between soul and body."[53] There is no sharp distinction between *mens*, body, and world. From a Cartesian perspective, this means that in the pre-modern era, the *res*

---

49 Thomas Aquinas, *Summa Theologiae*, Ia. 75,2 (p. 12–13) (transl. by T. Suttor). Cf. ibid.: *Dicendum quod corpus requiritur ad actionem intellectus, non sicut organum quo talis actio exerceatur, sed ratione objecti; phantasma enim comparatur ad intellectum sicut color ad visum.*
50 Cf. Agamben 1977.
51 Cf. Tachau 1982.
52 Thus depicted, for example, by the personal physician of the Catholic monarchs, Francisco López de Villalobos, in his comedy *Anfitrion*, 487–489; cf. also Folger 2002, 44–45.
53 Biernoff 2002, 25.

cogitans is either an integral part of the *res extensa* or inherent to it. Thus, when we speak of pre-modern materiality, we must take into account that matter, things, and even human artefacts have a spiritual dimension, because spirituality is necessarily material, even if this materiality is minimal and the prevailing ideology of our day disdains this to the privileging of what is intellectual.

What does this mean for the materiality of writing? First of all, it means that the materiality of written characters in the epistemology described above cannot be understood as a combination of two physical, neutral materials: namely, the means of writing and the writing support (e. g., ink and paper). Writing has an extremely reduced material basis, the extreme case of which being when writing is applied to paper and even more so in letterpress printing, in which the illusion of immateriality can arise. At the same time, writing is highly formed and therefore approaches the spiritual. Thus, it possesses an agency *sui generis* that transcends writing subjects and their intentions. In this respect, writing is an image, but as 'pictorial writing' ('Schriftbild', cf. Chapter 2, pp. 78–83) it has a particular efficacy.

An interesting variation on this negotiation between a material basis of writing and its inherent spiritual dimension can be found in the Jewish and Islamic traditions of the late medieval Mediterranean. Here, the approach to the spiritual finds its physical representation in the creation of decidedly 'immaterial' writings. Letters cut into paper, for example, in which the characters are precisely not applied to the material but consist rather of the empty spaces thus created therein, were described in the fourteenth century by the Castilian rabbi Shem Tov (also known as Sem Tob or Santob) de Carrión as "form without matter"[54]. The corporeal nature of this writing is explicitly stressed and emphasised in the first person, which also lends a subjective agency to this 'immaterial' writing: "[M]y body is made of nothingness. I am pure spirit (רוּחַ)".[55] The negation here of the corporeal and material dimension of writing refers once again to the somatic quality otherwise attributed to conventional writtenness—and to the special quality of writing whose matter is 'immaterial'. Shem Tov highlights this incorporeality as a miraculous quality, likening these immaterial letters to God's own writing on the tables of the law: "Make [with scissors] rows, words cut like the engravings on a seal, like the writing of God engraved on the tablets, standing as a miracle for the peoples".[56] Although the tablets of Moses have a heavy, solid, and three-dimensional physical materiality, Jewish tradition describes the writing of these tablets as a miraculous form of writing that was "to be read on both sides"—just like the letters cut into the paper could be.[57]

---

[54] Sem Tob, *Maʿaśeh ha-rav*, 61; English transl. by Colahan 1979, 287.
[55] Sem Tob, *Maʿaśeh ha-rav*, 61; English transl. by Colahan 1979, 287.
[56] Sem Tob, *Maʿaśeh ha-rav*, 54; English transl. by Colahan 1979, 281.
[57] Sem Tob, *Maʿaśeh ha-rav*, 69; English transl. by Colahan 1979, 295. In comparison with this perspective, which emphasises the negativity of the signs in the midst of a material writing support, see also the reflections on the tables of the law in Thesis 5, section 3).

Light also belongs to this dimension of the (im)materiality of the spiritual. In the late medieval Islamic world, glass lamps in Mamluk mosques were decorated with so-called 'light writing', often with the corresponding Qur'ān verse, "God is the light of the heavens and the earth" (24:35).[58] Similar to the blank spaces of letters in calligraphy cut into paper, blank spaces in painted glass can be left out in the form of characters drawn in reverse, allowing light to shine through and projecting 'words of light'. Likewise, light can be seen as a property of writings having divine origins in Christian medieval literature. This is the case in Meister Otte's *Eraclius* (ca. 1200), where a letter coming directly from heaven is "written with luminous letters" *(geschriben von liehten buochstaben)*.[59] The fact that light is immaterial yet visible places it in direct connection with the dimension of the spiritual. Such writings of light and letters cut into paper, which are said to "blossom in the air",[60] are two examples of writing as a 'form without matter' that illustrate the pre-modern epistemology of writing while at the same time rendering it more complex.

Under the auspices of pre-modern 'Western' epistemology, including the variations on the (im)materiality of writing from the Jewish or Islamic tradition that circulate there, one cannot speak of a representational function of writing, but rather of the 'formal' co-presence of the signified in such writing. Writing is thus not a vehicle for the intentions of writing subjects, but is in a powerful sense the embodiment of a spiritual content that is not limited to the dimension of semantics. In the sense of the physicality of writing, spatiality—understood as the integration into an arrangement of other more or less spiritual environments endowed with agency, or as mobility (cf. Thesis 6)—and permanence—understood as 'lifespan' (cf. Thesis 5)—are essential parameters of the efficacy of writing and its concomitant practices.

Thesis 4
The dimensions of what is written are explicitly or implicitly reflected in pre-modern texts.

In many respects, pre-modern texts are concerned not only with the written word itself, but also with the practices associated with writing (such as reading and the act of writing) and with the materiality of text supports. After some introductory remarks, we identify metatextual reflections on these and other dimensions pertaining to what is written, according to their degree of explicitness.

By 'dimensions of what is written', we mean here the properties that are inherent in the presence of the written and which allow for instances of the written word to be

---

58 Graves 2018, 238.
59 Cf. Ernst 2006, 116, our translation.
60 Sem Tob, *Ma'aśeh ha-rav*, 68; English transl. by Colahan 1979, 294.

further qualified: in addition to materiality itself, these are, for example, the physicality of what is written (cf. Thesis 3), its aisthetic permanence (cf. Thesis 5), and its spatiality (cf. Thesis 6).

In this thesis, we focus on corresponding reflections of pre-modern texts. Such texts, which we refer to as 'metatexts' in relation to the specific research interests of the CRC 933 (see Introduction, p. 19), play an important methodological role, both in terms of the concrete reconstruction of actual pre-modern practices (in the sense of written sources) and as a reflection of pre-modern thinking on writtenness and practices related to written material.[61] Different academic disciplines tend to have respective aspects on which they focus in the study of metatexts. While explicit metatextual reflections are often good at inferring real practices, metatextual reflections of an implicit nature, and especially those found in fictional, literary texts, are often broader in comparison to actual instances of writing and do not necessarily depict actual writing practices with accuracy.

Explicit reflections on what is written can be found, for example, in pre-modern treatises that deal with literary criticism, although the focus of such treatises is usually less on the practices of writing and reading themselves than on questions of content or style with regard to the composition of literature in certain genres. Corresponding reflections on the drafting of historiographical texts can be found, for example, in Lucian's work *How to Write History (Quomodo historia conscribenda sit)*. Explicit reflections on the production and reception of what is written in general have been the subject of pre-modern philosophical texts ever since Plato's *Phaedrus*. It is not only in this dialogue that writtenness is reflected in opposition to oral speech; this juxtaposition is emblematic of pre-modernity insofar as the beginnings of ancient literature at least emerge from a culture of performance. This culture did not lose its significance in subsequent centuries, as is shown, for example, by imperial-era epideixis and individual reading practices. Perhaps this is why this performance is evoked at least *ex negativo* in many pre-modern reflections on writtenness. And literature in the vernacular languages of the Middle Ages also has its origins in such a culture of performance.

The term 'what is written' or 'the written word', however, by no means refers only to literary pieces of writing in the broader sense. Rather, pre-modern texts of European antiquity (for example, within the framework of methodological asides) reflect precisely on the extent to which literary texts differ from other types of the written word. Thus, in literary texts themselves, the practices of literary and epigraphic writing are juxtaposed one to another, as well as the characteristics attached to the inscribed products resulting in each case. Depending on the writing support that is usually used in the respective writing process, the respective degree of material longevity and of free circulatability of what is written varies, for example (cf. Theses 5 and 6).

---

61 See here especially the volume of conference proceedings, *Metatexte. Erzählungen von schrifttragenden Artefakten in der alttestamentlichen und mittelalterlichen Literatur* (Focken/Ott 2016a), as well as Gertz et al. 2015 on 'metatext(uality)'.

The dimensions mentioned here of what is written are reflected, for example, in the historiographical works of Herodotus and Thucydides (for instance, in their respective methodological chapters and in Thucydides's funeral oration of Pericles). When different writing practices are discussed—for example, the historiographical writing that emerged with these works or more traditional inscriptional writing—this is partly done implicitly through epigraphic semantics (i.e., through the transferred use of vocabulary that (more) literally refers to inscriptions and the practices associated with them). In these methodological chapters, by contrast, comment is made more explicitly on the functions of what is written, including above all the suitability of one's own written medium for the creation of a lasting *memoria*. Thucydides, for example, describes his work as a "possession for all time" (κτῆμά ἐς αἰεὶ), distinguishing it from a "prize-essay to be heard for the moment",[62] a juxtaposition that aims at the contrast between the permanence of what is written and the transience of what is spoken.

In the literature of European antiquity, however, there are also implicit reflections on the dimensions of what is written, with the result that literary texts in which inscriptions are mentioned or quoted can be interpreted as inscription-related metatexts.[63] This does not apply only to historiographical texts such as Herodotus's *Histories*, in which even real inscriptions and the artefacts inscribed with them are mentioned; in rare cases, like the so-called Serpent Column (Herodotus, *Histories*, 8.82.1), these artefacts and inscriptions still exist today, and thus modifications (here by Herodotus) compared to what is really inscribed can be recognised.[64] Fictional novels, such as Heliodorus's *Aethiopica*, can also be understood as metatexts, since they speak, among other acts of writing, of the affixing of inscriptions to herms, stones, and temples (*Aethiopica*, 5.5.1). At the same time, the way in which inscribed *memoria* and its concomitant material conditions are staged suggests a certain perspective on the "memorial culture profile"[65] of the metatext itself. Metatexts can thus draw attention both to similarities and to differences between the two writing practices involved, while simultaneously bringing other dimensions of what is written into focus: besides the respective intended acts of reception themselves, for example, the conditions of these acts in the form of spatial realisation or the aisthetic permanence of what is written can also come into view (see Theses 5 and 6).[66]

However, the kind of metatextuality discussed here thus far is only one possible way in which pre-modern texts can implicitly reflect on the dimensions of what is

---

62 Thucydides, *The Peloponnesian War*, 1.22.4, transl. by C. F. Smith.
63 Cf. Allgaier et al. 2019, 200; cf. also Allgaier 2022.
64 On the discrepancies between the actual column and the inscribed artefact as depicted by Herodotus, see in detail Allgaier 2022 with reference to, among others, West 1985, 280.
65 Allgaier et al. 2019, 200, our translation, German text: "erinnerungskulturelle[s] Profil".
66 On this, cf. also Focken/Ott 2016b, 7.

written — and the different practices of writing and inscribing represent only one of the many aspects of the written word that could be considered here in contrast. Metatextuality can be understood not only as a certain relationship of one text to another (following Gérard Genette), but also (according to Zoran Kravar) as a reflection of a text on itself, either with regard to its entirety or to individual aspects.[67] Thus, to stay with the example above of text production, pre-modern literary texts not only present by way of contrast alternative writing practices in their plot — e. g., the chiselling of inscriptions into stone or the embroidering of a textile fabric with a text, such as we see in Heliodorus's *Aethiopica*, by means of which a mother communicates across spatial and temporal distance with her daughter who was abandoned years ago — but they also stage literary writing itself. Such a representation can then be interpreted as *mise-en-abyme* and thus as an implicit, self-referential reflection on the dimensions of what is written, especially if there are further signals for such self-referentiality.[68]

Other definitions take metatextuality even further: for example, Markus Hilgert's definition of a metatext as being "what is written about what is written" ("Geschriebenes über Geschriebenes").[69] However, the arbitrariness resulting from such a definition is heuristically problematic, since "almost every piece of writing is likely to be characterised, at least in terms of its genre, by certain features of other pieces of writing that are incorporated or transformed in it".[70] Such a broad definition of metatextuality is thus difficult to put into practice; regardless of any fixed criteria, exegesis can proactively interpret any texts as metatexts in the above sense. In this case, the process of reflection on what is written no longer takes place within the text itself, but is undertaken by the text's recipients. In terms of how research is carried out, it therefore makes more sense to restrict the concept of metatextuality to those texts in which what is written plays a role on the level of plot. Particularly when a text belongs to a genre in which plot does not play a major role, it also makes sense to speak of metatextuality when what is written is present on the level of the imagination (e. g., on the level of metaphor).

In the explanations so far, we have concentrated primarily on those dimensions of the written word that are dependent on the materiality of the respective writing supports: the practices of writing and inscribing; the function or suitability of what is written as a memory support; and aisthetic permanence and spatial realisation, as will be dealt with in the theses below. With regard to this thesis, however, the aspects mentioned here of what is written should be understood as exemplary and not as

---

[67] Genette 1993, 13; Kravar 1994, 274. On this, cf. also Focken/Ott 2016b, 2.
[68] Cf. also Focken/Ott 2016b, 3–4.
[69] Focken/Ott 2016b, 3, who refer to Hilgert 2010, 98, our translation.
[70] Focken/Ott 2016b, 3, our translation, German text: "fast jedes Schriftstück dürfte zumindest seiner Gattung nach von bestimmten Merkmalen anderer Schriftstücke geprägt sein, die in ihm aufgenommen oder transformiert sind".

exhaustive. Metatexts, for example, also reflect other preconditions of text reception, such as the necessity of competence in a certain language or literacy on the part of the recipient. However, if the targeted use of writing systems is presented, whose mastery is reserved for certain social groups, epistemic aspects of power relations emerge as a dimension of what is written.[71]

> **Thesis 5**
> The aisthetic permanence of what is written, i. e., its (long- or short-term) temporal permanence as perceived by the senses, is constitutive for the meaning and effect of writing.

The written word always has the function of standing the test of time. This time span, i. e., its temporal permanence, can be of different lengths, ranging along a scale between the long-term and persistent to the short-term and ephemeral. Its (intended, assumed, or actual) length has a lot to do with the material permanence of what is written. The sensual perception of this materially conditioned duration often results in a specific effect on the recipient and a specific attribution of meaning to what is written.

Writing is always linked to some kind of material and to this material's physical properties: it is what we term *aisthetically permanent*,[72] whereby a sensual perceptibility of its permanence (gradually scalable between the poles of persistence and ephemerality) is meant. Amongst its physical properties, the actual temporal permanence of the material in question (or one assumed by the writers and recipients) is often particularly relevant to what is written. This is fundamentally connected to the fact that the written word usually has the function of enabling communication in situations that are temporally separated from one another: the producer (writer, client, author, sender) and the recipient (reader/addressee, either silently or aloud; receiver) of what is written are usually not at the same place at the same time. Therefore, a minimum of material permanence is required on the part of what is written. We can often observe that there is a natural correlation between the (believed, desired, assumed, or actual) relevance of the writing to possible recipients in the distant future on the one hand, and the material permanence of what it written that is generated in the production process on the other. For example, what is important for future generations (or con-

---

[71] Cf. Focken/Ott 2016b, 7 with a list of further aspects of communicative configurations that metatexts can reflect.
[72] Here we are setting a "substantial material concept as a foundation [...] as outlined by the meanings 'material' and 'raw material'" (Meier/Focken/Ott 2015, 25), our translation, German text: "substantiellen Material-Begriff zu Grunde [...], wie er mit den Bedeutungen 'Rohstoff' und 'Werkstoff' umrissen ist".

sidered to be such) is set in stone so that it can be received by future generations for as long as possible. By contrast, concrete information and instructions for action, which only need to last for a few hours or days and are only relevant to specific individual short-term recipients, are written—if at all—on transitory supports such as post-its or wax tablets,[73] i. e., such writing is only recorded ephemerally and (as a rule) is soon destroyed or lost.

In this kind of correlation between materiality and writing, where the relationship between the two is thus held to be purely functional, the material takes on a necessary, albeit subsidiary role, serving merely as an instrument for the communication made possible by the written word. This approach, however, leaves aside a whole gamut of aspects that go hand in hand with the sensual perceptibility of the written word's permanence, but which do not fit into its communicative functionality. If these aspects are emphasised, we see effects come into view that go beyond the pure communication of information as transmitted by means of the written text:

1) *The perception of a correlation between texts considered of permanent importance and their persistent materiality.* Some inscriptions are intended for a permanent reception, e. g., those that are affixed to monuments (gravestones) and serve the permanent *memoria* (or the visualisation of the deceased in such a *memoria*). They are primarily affixed to writing supports made of stone precisely because "materially immanent properties […] such as hardness, durability, permanence (longevity) and resistance" allowed for an "expectation of significant permanence with regard to the continued existence of the inscribed content".[74] Written content of a legally valid nature (in the context of permanent legitimation efforts), such as can be found on boundary stones, at city gates, or on other public buildings (think here of length measurements on a medieval parish church, for instance), is also usually engraved into writing supports made of stone.[75] The perception of the persistence derived from the material results in the attribution of authority and power to the author of the writing, and of temporal validity to what is written.

2) *The attribution of (auratic) meaning due to the perception of a large quantity of permanently preserved written material.* The abundance of codices consisting of a plethora of parchment pages tightly bound together and stored on solid shelves or in massive chests in a medieval library can be perceived as an example of the persistence and consolidation of knowledge and the texts that contain such learning. This aisthetic permanence then evokes wonder and admiration at the pres-

---

[73] Wagner 2019.
[74] Cf. Balke et al. 2015, 248–249, our translation, German text: "materialimmanente[ ] Eigenschaften […] wie Härte, Beständigkeit, Dauerhaftigkeit (Langlebigkeit) und Widerstandsfähigkeit [lassen] signifikante Dauerhaftigkeit im Hinblick auf den Fortbestand des verschrifteten Inhalts erwarten".
[75] The permanence or ephemerality *ex negativo* of materiality can be coded iconologically (or semiologically) in these contexts; cf. Raff 2008, 49–60.

ence of knowledge in this one place (as an outstanding nexus of past and future practices of thinking and writing), engendering reverence for those who know the practices that pertain to the management of this intellectual abundance. And this permanence ascribes a very specific meaning to what is written: namely, that it is part of a nucleus, a consolidation of knowledge, and can thus lay claim to an inherent relevance.

3) *The perception of ephemeral materiality and ephemeral writing as a marker of meaning.* It is true that the choice of a writing support characterised by material ephemerality can affirm the 'ephemeral' meaning of the written word and express the expectation of its very limited effect, e. g., because only a single, clearly delimited situation of use is anticipated for its reception (a shopping list, for example). But the opposite can also be the case: particularly in the religious sphere, ephemerality quite often correlates to maximum meaning and effect.[76] This is the case, for instance, with the word *menetekel*, which is written (painted?) on a white wall as though by the hand of some spirit and which passes devastating judgement on King Belshazzar, who dies the same night (Dan 5); or in the episode with the adulteress, when Jesus writes with his finger on the ground while the scribes and Pharisees insist on the law written (!) by Moses, according to which the woman is to be stoned to death (John 8:1–11): the ephemerality of what is written in dust or sand (the wording of which is not even mentioned) paradoxically points precisely to the eternal validity of the message, the *logos*, which is a message of grace and of not imputing, of not writing down sin: "Go, and from now on sin no more!" With the ephemeral writing on the ground, Jesus causes the persistent stone writing of the tables of the law of Moses to be crushed to dust and itself to be blown away.

4) *The accidental persistence of ephemeral materiality and ephemeral writing as a recoding of meaning.* When a piece of writing that was once ephemerally recorded is later found, reused, or newly charged with meaning, persistence occurs rather accidentally.[77] The aisthetic permanence of what is written can, as it were, be recoded from one (former) present to another (later) present in such a way that, depending on the parameters of reception, the meaning and efficacy of the writing also changes. The graffiti and dipinti, for example, which can still be found in great numbers today both inside and outside the houses in Pompeii and Herculaneum were often ad hoc creations, components of current-affairs communi-

---

76 Cf. Lieb 2017.
77 An artefact biography can then be written with a view to the different situations of historical reception, which helps "to neatly separate the different layers of function and meaning chronologically, locate them in their respective cultural contexts, and determine transcultural processes" (Meier/Tsouparopoulou 2015, 50–51), our translation, German text: "die unterschiedlichen Funktions- und Bedeutungsschichten chronologisch sauber zu trennen, in ihren jeweiligen kulturellen Kontexten zu verorten und transkulturelle Prozesse zu bestimmen"; on this with examples, cf. Allgaier et al. 2019.

cation or else ephemeral 'scribblings', which as a rule were intended to have a very limited effect in time and space and were only intended for a specific group of addressees.[78] Nevertheless, they enjoy special attention today because they are evidence of ancient communication and writing culture, with a historically conscious present-day therefore ascribing significant testimonial value to them. A similar situation can be seen in written evidence that is secured as part of a criminal case: such instances of writing no longer serve their initial, perhaps ephemeral, purpose, but are made persistent for the purpose of later evidence. Another prominent example of such a historically conditioned reinterpretation or new attribution of meaning is the so-called *titulus*, which according to the account of John the Evangelist (19:19–20) was written on Pilate's own behalf in Hebrew, Greek, and Latin before being affixed to the cross of Christ so that its admonitory and provocative content could be received by the Jews passing by: "Jesus Christ, king of the Jews".[79] It is true that the biblical tradition does not provide any information about the material nature of the writing or the writing support here. Yet due to its reference to the crucified Christ, whom the tablet was intended to identify to the addressed Jews as their 'king', we can assume that the inscribed tablet was originally produced rather ephemerally: it only had to serve its purpose until Jesus should be taken down from the cross. However, the medieval tradition of legends surrounding the finding of the cross by Saint Helena, the mother of Constantine the Great, reinterpret the persistence of the *titulus*. In this interpretation, the *titulus* is not preserved by chance: it must cede its original, merely ephemeral efficacy as intended by Pilate in favour of the long-term identificatory function as seen in the finding of the cross by the emperor's mother, something said to be predetermined by God. Ambrose, who can be regarded as the author of the oldest known and oft-quoted account of the cross's *inventio*, thus takes care to report that Helena, guided by the Holy Spirit, was only able to distinguish the true cross of Christ from the other two crosses of the thieves crucified alongside him by means of the still-preserved and still-legible *titulus*.[80]

---

78 Cf. Lohmann 2018 and Opdenhoff 2021.
79 The Greek and Latin wordings of the *titulus* text have come down to us in the respective recensions of the New Testament: *Iesus Nazarenus rex Iudaeorum (Biblia Sacra Vulgata)*; Ἰησοῦς Ναζωραῖος ὁ βασιλεὺς τῶν Ἰουδαίων *(Novum Testamentum Graece)*. While no ancient copies of the New Testament have survived in Hebrew, the Aramaic/Syriac Peshitta renders the text thus: ܗܢܐ ܝܫܘܥ ܡܠܟܐ ܕܝܗܘܕܝܐ *(Syriac-English New Testament)*, and the translation of the text into Biblical Hebrew by the Jewish convert Ezekiel Margoliouth (d. 1894) and published in 1923 reads: יֵשׁוּעַ הַנָּצְרִי מֶלֶךְ הַיְּהוּדִים *(Hebrew New Testament)*. See also the parallel passages in Mark 15:26, Luke 23:38 and Matt 27:37.
80 Heussler 2006, 76. The *Oration on the Death of Theodosius*, attributed to Ambrose, was given in 39 CE.

Thesis 6
The spatial realisation is constitutive for the meaning and effect of what is written.

Characters unfold spatially and can be read from right to left, from left to right, or from top to bottom (in rare cases also from bottom to top). In order for characters to be identifiable as such, there must be a certain amount of space between them.[81] What is written thus always encompasses space, regardless of the support it is on. Inscriptions not written on parchment or paper, but rather carved into wood, chiselled into stone, engraved or etched into metal, sewn onto textiles, or cast into or applied to a substrate, also reveal a tangible three-dimensional 'height difference' vis-à-vis the writing support.[82]

The development of inscribable materials, styles and types of writing, and reproduction processes has always been accompanied by a specific treatment of the spatiality of writing. In cultures that did not yet possess standardised reproduction processes for writing, striking interactions between the appearance of the writing and the support material come to the fore more frequently. The angular shapes of runes, for example, facilitated carving into solid materials such as wood, stone, or bone,[83] while conversely, rounded characters such as those found in many scripts from India and Southeast Asia enabled the use of palms leaves as a writing support, which otherwise could be torn through more easily by angular letters.[84] The genuine spatiality of writing also plays an important role in terms of text layout. Not only do the positioning of what is written and the relationship between the inscribed and non-inscribed surface areas guide one's perception of an artefact; the size of the script also plays a role in this process. While minuscule scripts or types of writing that form ligatures (such as cursive) are generally space-saving, majuscule scripts take up a relatively large amount of space. They are therefore also suitable for drawing attention to certain informational content.

What is written, however, occupies space not only through its own spatial expansion, but also in its potential mobility. Here, too, the materiality of the artefact plays an important role: small and light objects such as amulets, papyri, scarabs, and gems[85] lend themselves particularly well to being carried and moved. Such artefacts, "which carry the writing they 'bear' by virtue of their materiality from one place to another", we call 'locomobile', while we term spatially bound writing 'locostatic'.[86]

---

[81] Cf. Krämer 2018, 210.
[82] Lieb/Ott 2015, 17.
[83] Schulz 2019, 43–44. On the correspondences between writing support, layout and characters, see also Chapter 2, p. 67 and Thesis 7.
[84] Cf. Steever 1996, 426; Kuipers/McDermott 1996, 480.
[85] Theis 2015.
[86] The terminology here follows Ehlich 1994, 30; quotation from Lieb/Ott 2015, 16, our translation, German text: "die jene Schrift, die sie kraft ihrer Materialität 'halten', von einem Ort zu einem anderen bringen".

The portability and concomitant mobility of what is written is often a prerequisite for its function and meaning; it determines the practices that deal with writing. Inherently mobile writing supports such as letters or epistles, for example, enable interpersonal exchange. The practices of transmission are decisive for the function of the written word, and epistolary networks can be more precisely deduced from them.[87] Conversely, small inscribed artefacts such as amulet scrolls enable a physical relationship of proximity. What is written can be touched and kept close to the body, and it is precisely these practices that are determinative for the protective function attributed to the written word in such cases, regardless of whether the text is actually read or not.[88] Furthermore what is written is wearable when it enters into a particularly close relationship with the human body: writing interwoven into or embroidered onto textiles can be worn,[89] while human skin itself can also become inscribed, as in the case of tattoos or stigmata.[90]

The special significance of the mobility of inscribed artefacts can only be adequately described by the relational spatial concept of topology.[91] The paths that the written word can take, the relationships of proximity and distance that it can enter into, cannot be described in terms of topography, but only by means of the interactions between people and things that constitute this spatiality in the first place.

By contrast, the spatial arrangement of locostatic inscribed artefacts—such as inscriptions on buildings, tombstones, walls, gates, columns, or statues—is much more stable. Such writing is usually addressed to a larger community, tends to be designed so as to be visible in the public arena,[92] and as a rule is created from durable materials suitable for commemorative occasions. Of course, what is written can also be involved in various other practices besides simply providing information: it can offer orientation, impress, politicise, commemorate, call to action, or even codify a status quo. A legal text, for example, gains authority when it is fixed on stone in the centre of an administrative unit. This is even more clearly the case if the plaque is located in the physical vicinity of a court, for example.

For the hermeneutic endeavour to reconstruct the original meaning of a (possibly heavily damaged) inscription, the spatial arrangement (position, size, visibility, interrelationships with other artefacts, etc.) therefore offers important clues. Conversely, inscriptions on static artefacts can also provide information about the (planned) semanticisation of space. Writing on bridges, doors, and gates, for example, has a liminal function and serves to indicate the transition between adjacent spaces. By occupying the threshold between here and there, inside and outside, public and pri-

---

[87] Hamouda 2020.
[88] Hindley 2020.
[89] Lieb 2019.
[90] Béreiziat-Lang/Ott 2019.
[91] Dickmann/Witschel/Keil 2015, 113.
[92] On the phenomenon of the restricted presence of writing, cf. Frese/Keil/Krüger 2014a.

vate, sacred and profane, etc., inscriptions have a normative effect on the delimitation of spaces—indeed, they cause us to become aware of the border that is crossed between different areas in the first place. In this respect, locostatic inscribed artefacts can also be profitably included in the analysis of the social constitution of space, the scope of which has become visible in the evolving theoretical frameworks in recent decades of cultural studies.

Finally, interactions with (mobile as well as immobile) inscribed artefacts, such as can be observed especially in urban space, can extend over long periods of time and encompass different stages of cultural development. Their temporality, however, is not necessarily linear but can also become interrupted and broken. Inscribed artefacts have a kind of inherent temporality. With regard to the function of inscriptions in medieval Italian municipalities, for instance, Armando Petrucci has noted that the rediscovery of the civic and political function of open urban space took place by means of a more or less conscious recourse to ancient epigraphic models.[93] In this way, inscriptions can be recombined palimpsestically, piled up and layered on top of one another. Wide-ranging historical configurations can become embodied in them—spanning, for example, between the late Middle Ages and antiquity—whether this be due to a purely practical reuse of inscribed artefacts, or whether it be as a conscious 'invention of tradition' or an expression of a historical self-localisation on the part of those who use them.

The longevity of solid inscribed artefacts, but also the various historical decisions to preserve, relocate, supplement, or restore written testimonies, is due today to a material sedimentation of what is written, the original spatial realisation of which can often be reconstructed only with great difficulty.

---

93 Petrucci 1986, 5: "Tale situazione [sc. of the Middle Ages] venne a modificarsi in Italia, fra XI e XIII secolo, in corrispondenza della rivoluzione urbanistica delle città e della conseguente riscoperta della funzione civile e politica dello spazio urbano aperto, che fu segnata anche da un più o meno consapevole ritorno al confronto (se non proprio all'imitazione) con i modelli epigrafici antichi"; on this, cf. also von der Höh 2019.

Bibliography

Sources

Aristotle, *De Memoria et reminiscentia / On Memory,* transl. by Richard Sorabij, Providence, RI, 1972.
Biblia Sacra Vulgata. Lateinisch-deutsch, vol. V: *Evangelia – Actus Apostolorum – Epistulae Pauli – Epistulae Catholicae – Apocalypsis – Appendix,* ed. by Andreas Beriger, Widu-Wolfgang Ehlers, and Michael Fieger (Sammlung Tusculum), Berlin/Boston 2018.
Hebrew New Testament (הַבְּרִית הַחֲדָשָׁה), transl. by Ezekiel Margoliouth, London 1923.
López de Villalobos, Francisco, *Anfitrion, Comedia* (Biblioteca de Autores Españoles 36), Madrid 1950 [reímp. 1855].
Novum Testamentum Graece, based on the work of Eberhard and Erwin Nestle, ed. by Barbara and Kurt Aland, Johannes Karavidopoulos, Carlo M. Martini, and Bruce M. Metzger, 28th rev. ed., Stuttgart 2012.
Sem Tob, *Ma'aśeh ha-rav: (Milḥemet ha-'eṭ yeha-misparayim),* ed. by Yehuda Nini and Maya Fruchtman, Tel Aviv 1980.
Syriac-English New Testament / ܗܥܦܛܐ ܕܐܗܐ ܕܡܪܢ ܝܫܘܥ ܡܫܝܚܐ. *The Traditional Syriac Peshitta Text and the Antioch Bible English Translation,* ed. by George Anton Kiraz, transl. by Jeff W. Childers, J. Edward Walters, Daniel King, and Robert A. Kitchen, Piscataway, NJ, 2020.
Thomas Aquinas, *A Commentary on Aristotle's De Anima [Sentencia libri De anima],* transl. by Robert Pasnau, New Haven, CT, 1999.
Thomas Aquinas, *In Aristotelis libros De sensu et sensato, De memoria et reminiscentia commentarium,* ed. by Raymund M. Spiazzi, Rome 1949.
Thomas Aquinas, *In tres libros Aristotelis De Anima præclariβima Expositio,* Venedig: Hieronymus Scotus 1570. Online facsimile: https://mdz-nbn-resolving.de/details:bsb11199040 (accessed 9/3/2023).
Thomas Aquinas, *Summa Theologiae,* vol. 11: *Man (Ia. 75–83),* ed. and transl. by Timothy Suttor, New York 1970.
Thucydides, *History of the Peloponnesian War,* vol. 1: *Books I and II,* transl. by Charles Foster Smith, Cambridge, MA, 1956.

Research Literature

Agamben, Giorgio (1977), *Stanze: La parola e il fantasma nella cultura occidentale,* Torino.
Allgaier, Benjamin (2022), *Embedded Inscriptions in Herodotus and Thucydides* (Philippika 157), Wiesbaden.
Allgaier, Benjamin/Bolle, Katharina/Jaspert, Nikolas/Knauber, Konrad/Lieb, Ludger/Roels, Evelien/Sauer, Rebecca/Schneidereit, Nele/Wallenwein, Kirsten (2019), "Gedächtnis – Materialität – Schrift. Ein erinnerungskulturelles Modell zur Analyse schrifttragender Artefakte", *Saeculum* 69/2, 181–244.
Assmann, Aleida (1996), "Im Dickicht der Zeichen. Hodegetik – Hermeneutik – Dekonstruktion", in: *Deutsche Vierteljahrsschrift für Literaturwissenschaft und Geistesgeschichte* 70, 535–551.
Balke, Thomas E./Keil, Wilfried E./Opdenhoff, Fanny/Stroth, Fabian (2015), "Stein", in: Thomas Meier, Michael R. Ott, and Rebecca Sauer (eds.), *Materiale Textkulturen. Konzepte – Materialien – Praktiken* (Materiale Textkulturen 1), Berlin/Munich/Boston, 247–267, https://doi.org/10.1515/9783110371291.247.

Béreiziat-Lang, Stephanie/Folger, Robert/Palacios Larrosa, Miriam (eds.) (2020), *Escritura somática. La materialidad de la escritura en las literaturas ibéricas de la Edad Media a la temprana modernidad,* Leiden.

Béreiziat-Lang, Stephanie/Ott, Michael R. (2019), "From Tattoo to Stigma: Writing on Body and Skin", in: Ricarda Wagner, Christine Neufeld, and Ludger Lieb (eds.), *Writing Beyond Pen and Parchment. Inscribed Objects in Medieval European Literature* (Materiale Textkulturen 30), Berlin/Boston, 193–208, https://doi.org/10.1515/9783110645446-010.

Biernoff, Suzannah (2002), *Sight and Embodiment in the Middle Ages,* New York.

Certeau, Michel de (1975), *L'écriture de l'histoire,* Paris.

Certeau, Michel de (1990), *L'invention du quotidien,* vol. 1: *Arts de faire,* Paris.

Colahan, Clark (1979), "Santob's Debate: Parody and political Allegory. Conclusión", in: *Sefarad: Revista de Estudios Hebraicos y Sefardíes* 39.2, 265–308.

Derrida, Jacques (1967), *De la grammatologie,* Paris.

Derrida, Jacques (1988), "Signature Event Context", transl. by Jeffrey Mehlman and Samuel Weber, in: Jacques Derrida, *Limited Inc,* ed. by Gerald Graff, Evanston, IL, 1–24.

Dickmann, Jens-Arne/Witschel, Christian/Keil, Wilfred E. (2015), "Topologie", in: Thomas Meier, Michael R. Ott, and Rebecca Sauer (eds.), *Materiale Textkulturen. Konzepte – Materialien – Praktiken* (Materiale Textkulturen 1), Berlin/Munich/Boston, 113–128, https://doi.org/10.1515/9783110371291.113.

Dünne, Jörg (2003), *Asketisches Schreiben: Rousseau und Flaubert als Paradigmen literarischer Selbstpraxis in der Moderne,* Tübingen.

Edelmann-Singer, Babett/Ehrich, Susanne (eds.) (2021), *Sprechende Objekte. Materielle Kultur zwischen Antike und Früher Neuzeit,* Regensburg.

Ehlich, Konrad (1994), "Funktion und Struktur schriftlicher Kommunikation", in: Hartmut Günther and Otto Ludwig (eds.), *Schrift und Schriftlichkeit. Writing and Its Use. Ein interdisziplinäres Handbuch internationaler Forschung. An Interdisciplinary Handbook of International Research* (Handbuch zur Sprach- und Kommunikationswissenschaft 10,1), Berlin/New York, 18–41.

Ernst, Ulrich (2006): *Facetten mittelalterlicher Schriftkultur. Fiktion und Illustration. Wissen und Wahrnehmung,* Heidelberg.

Errington, Joseph (2008), *Linguistics in a Colonial World. A Story of Language, Meaning, and Power,* Malden/Oxford.

Focken, Friedrich-Emanuel/Ott, Michael R. (2016a), "Metatexte und schrifttragende Artefakte", in: Friedrich-Emanuel Focken and Michael R. Ott (eds.), *Metatexte. Erzählungen von schrifttragenden Artefakten in der alttestamentlichen und mittelalterlichen Literatur* (Materiale Textkulturen 15), Berlin/Boston, 1–9, https://doi.org/10.1515/9783110417944-002.

Focken, Friedrich-Emanuel/Ott, Michael R. (eds.) (2016b), *Metatexte. Erzählungen von schrifttragenden Artefakten in der alttestamentlichen und mittelalterlichen Literatur* (Materiale Textkulturen 15), Berlin/Boston, https://doi.org/10.1515/9783110417944.

Folger, Robert (2002), *Images in Mind: Lovesickness, Spanish Sentimental Fiction and Don Quijote,* Chapel Hill, NC.

Folger, Robert (2009), *Escape from the Prison of Love: Caloric Identities and Writing Subjects in Fifteenth-Century Spain,* Chapel Hill, NC.

Foucault, Michel (1994), *L'écriture de soi,* in: Michel Foucault, *Dits et écrits,* vol. 4, ed. by Daniel Defert and François Ewald, Paris, 415–430.

Frese, Tobias/Keil, Wilfried E./Krüger, Kristina (eds.) (2014a), *Verborgen, unsichtbar, unlesbar – zur Problematik restringierter Schriftpräsenz* (Materiale Textkulturen 2), Berlin/Boston, https://doi.org/10.1515/9783110353587.

Frese, Tobias/Keil, Wilfried E./Krüger Kristina (2014b), "Zur Problematik restringierter Schriftpräsenz – Zusammenfassung dieses Bandes", in: Tobias Frese, Wilfried E. Keil, and Kristina Krüger (eds.), *Verborgen, unsichtbar, unlesbar – zur Problematik restringierter Schriftpräsenz* (Materiale Textkulturen 2), Berlin/Boston, 233–242, https://doi.org/10.1515/9783110353587.233.

Genette, Gérard (1993), *Palimpseste. Die Literatur auf zweiter Stufe,* Frankfurt (Main).

Gertz, Jan Christian/Krabbes, Frank/Noller, Eva Marie/Opdenhoff, Fanny (2015), "Metatext(ualität)", in: Thomas Meier, Michael R. Ott, and Rebecca Sauer (eds.), *Materiale Textkulturen. Konzepte – Materialien – Praktiken* (Materiale Textkulturen 1), Berlin/Munich/Boston, 207–218, https://doi.org/10.1515/9783110371291.207.

Graves, Margaret S. (2018), "The Lamp of Paradox", in: *Word & Image* 34. 3, 237–250.

Grube, Gernot (2005), "Autooperative Schrift – und eine Kritik der Hypertexttheorie", in: Gernot Grube, Werner Kogge, and Sybille Krämer (eds.), *Schrift. Kulturtechnik zwischen Auge, Hand und Maschine,* Munich, 81–114.

Grube, Gernot/Kogge, Werner (2005), "Zur Einleitung: Was ist Schrift?", in: Gernot Grube, Werner Kogge, and Sybille Krämer (eds.), *Schrift. Kulturtechnik zwischen Auge, Hand und Maschine,* Munich, 9–22.

Gumbrecht, Hans-Ulrich (2003), *Production of Presence: What Meaning Cannot Convey,* Stanford, CA.

Gumbrecht, Hans Ulrich (2004), *Diesseits der Hermeneutik. Die Produktion von Präsenz,* transl. by Joachim Schulte, Frankfurt (Main).

Gumbrecht, Hans Ulrich/Pfeiffer, K. Ludwig (eds.) (1993), *Schrift* (Materialität der Zeichen, series A, vol. 12), Munich.

Günther, Hartmut/Ludwig, Otto (eds.) (1994/1996), *Schrift und Schriftlichkeit. Ein interdisziplinäres Handbuch internationaler Forschung,* 2 vols., Berlin/Boston.

Hamouda, Fatma E. (2020), *Communication and the Circulation of Letters in the Eastern Desert of Egypt during the Roman Period* (Dissertation), https://archiv.ub.uni-heidelberg.de/volltextserver/28289/.

Haß, Christian David/Noller, Eva Marie (eds.) (2015), *Was bedeutet Ordnung – was ordnet Bedeutung? Zu bedeutungskonstituierenden Ordnungsleistungen in Geschriebenem* (Materiale Textkulturen 10), Berlin/Boston, https://doi.org/10.1515/9783110419665.

Heussler, Carla (2006), *De Cruce Christi. Kreuzauffindung und Kreuzerhöhung. Funktionswandel und Historisierung in nachtridentinischer Zeit,* Paderborn.

Hilgert, Markus (2010), "'Text-Anthropologie'. Die Erforschung von Materialität und Präsenz des Geschriebenen als hermeneutische Strategie", in: *Mitteilungen der Deutschen Orient-Gesellschaft* 142, 87–126.

Hilgert, Markus (2016), "Materiale Textkulturen. Textbasierte historische Kulturwissenschaften nach dem *material culture turn*", in: Herbert Kalthoff, Torsten Cress, and Tobias Röhl (eds.), *Materialität. Herausforderungen für die Sozial- und Kulturwissenschaften,* Paderborn, 255–268.

Hindley, Katherine Storm (2020), "The Power of Not Reading: Amulet Rolls in Medieval England", in: Stefan G. Holz, Jörg Peltzer, and Maree Shirota (eds.), *The Roll in England and France in the Late Middle Ages. Form and Content* (Materiale Textkulturen 28), Berlin/Boston/Munich, 289–306, https://doi.org/10.1515/9783110645125-011.

Höh, Marc von der (2019), "Einleitung", in: Katharina Bolle, Marc von der Höh, and Nikolas Jaspert (eds.), *Inschriftenkulturen im kommunalen Italien. Traditionen, Brüche, Neuanfänge* (Materiale Textkulturen 21), Berlin/Boston/Munich, 305–324, https://doi.org/10.1515/9783110642261.

Horstmann, Lisa (2024), "Die Darbringung Christi im Gronauer Glasfenster. Zum ikonischen Bedeutungspotential von Pseudoinschriften", in: Tobias Frese, Lisa Horstmann, and Franziska Wenig (eds.), *Sakrale Schriftbilder. Zur ikonischen Präsenz des Geschriebenen im mittelalterlichen Kirchenraum* (Materiale Textkulturen 42), Berlin/Boston, 163–184, https://doi.org/10.1515/9783111304496-007.

Krämer, Sybille (1998), "Das Medium als Spur und als Apparat", in: Sybille Krämer (Ed.), *Medien – Computer – Realität. Wirklichkeitsvorstellungen und Neue Medien,* Frankfurt (Main), 73–94.

Krämer, Sybille (2005), "Operationsraum Schrift: Über einen Perspektivenwechsel in der Betrachtung der Schrift", in: Gernot Grube, Werner Kogge, and Sybille Krämer (eds.), *Schrift. Kulturtechnik zwischen Hand und Maschine,* Munich, 23–57.

Krämer, Sybille (2018), "Bild in der Schrift. Über 'operative Bildlichkeit' und die Kreativität des Graphismus", in: Boris Roman Gibhardt and Johannes Grave (eds.), *Schrift im Bild. Rezeptionsästhetische Perspektiven auf Text-Bild-Relationen in den Künsten,* Hannover, 209–222.

Kravar, Zoran (1994), "Metatextualität", in: Dieter Borchmeyer and Viktor Žmegač (eds.), *Moderne Literatur in Grundbegriffen,* 2nd rev. ed., Tübingen, 274–277.

Kuipers, Joel C./McDermott, Ray (1996), "Insular Southeast Asian Scripts", in: Peter T. Daniels and William Bright (eds.), *The World's Writing Systems,* New York, 474–484.

Lieb, Ludger (2015), "Spuren materialer Textkulturen. Neun Thesen zur höfischen Textualität im Spiegel textimmanenter Inschriften", in: Beate Kellner, Ludger Lieb, and Stephan Müller (eds.), *Höfische Textualität. Festschrift für Peter Strohschneider* (GRM-Beiheft 69), Heidelberg, 1–20.

Lieb, Ludger (2017), "Von Gottes Glanz und Schrift. Flüchtige Texte als Zeichen des Ewigen", in: *Schein & Sein – Ruperto Carola Forschungsmagazin* 11, 79–85, https://doi.org/10.17885/heiup.ruca.2017.11.23756.

Lieb, Ludger (2019), "Woven Words, Embroidered Stories: Inscriptions on Textiles", in: Ricarda Wagner, Christine Neufeld, and Ludger Lieb (eds.), *Writing Beyond Pen and Parchment. Inscribed Objects in Medieval European Literature* (Materiale Textkulturen 30), Berlin/Boston, 209–220, https://doi.org/10.1515/9783110645446-011.

Lieb, Ludger/Ott, Michael R. (2015), "Schrift-Träger. Mobile Inschriften in der deutschsprachigen Literatur des Mittelalters", in: Annette Kehnel and Diamantis Panagiotopoulos (eds.), *Schriftträger – Textträger. Zur materialen Präsenz des Geschriebenen in frühen Gesellschaften* (Materiale Textkulturen 6), Berlin/Munich/Boston, 15–36, https://doi.org/10.1515/9783110371345.15.

Lohmann, Polly (2017): *Graffiti als Interaktionsform. Geritzte Inschriften in den Wohnhäusern Pompejis* (Materiale Textkulturen 16), Berlin/Boston, https://doi.org/10.1515/9783110574289.

Luhmann, Niklas (1993), "Die Form der Schrift", in: Hans Ulrich Gumbrecht and Ludwig Pfeiffer (eds.), *Schrift,* Munich, 349–366.

Lyotard, Jean-François (1986), *Das postmoderne Wissen. Ein Bericht,* ed. by Peter Engelmann, transl. by Otto Pfersmann, Graz/Vienna.

McLuhan, Marshall (1964), *Understanding Media: The Extensions of Man,* New York.

Meier, Thomas/Focken, Friedrich-Emanuel/Ott, Michael R. (2015), "Material", in: Thomas Meier, Michael R. Ott, and Rebecca Sauer (eds.), *Materiale Textkulturen. Konzepte – Materialien – Praktiken* (Materiale Textkulturen 1), Berlin/Munich/Boston, 19–32, https://doi.org/10.1515/9783110371291.19.

Meier, Thomas/Tsouparopoulou, Christina (2015), "Artefakt", in: Thomas Meier, Michael R. Ott, and Rebecca Sauer (eds.), *Materiale Textkulturen. Konzepte – Materialien – Praktiken* (Materiale Textkulturen 1), Berlin/Munich/Boston, 47–61, https://doi.org/10.1515/9783110371291.47.

Mignolo, Walter D. (2003), *The Darker Side of the Renaissance: Literacy, Territoriality, and Colonization,* 2nd ed., Ann Arbor, MI.

Opdenhoff, Fanny (2021): *Die Stadt als beschriebener Raum: Die Beispiele Pompeji und Herculaneum* (Materiale Textkulturen 33), Berlin/Boston, https://doi.org/10.1515/9783110722758.

Petrucci, Armando (1986), *La scrittura. Ideologia e rappresentazione,* Turin.

Poole, Kevin R. (2013), "On the Figure of Voxmea in Gonzalo de Berceo's Poema de Santa Oria", in: *Modern Philology* 110.3, 289–312.

Raff, Thomas (2008), *Die Sprache der Materialien. Anleitung zu einer Ikonologie der Werkstoffe,* Münster et al.

Rehm, Ulrich (2019), "Schrift/Bild. Die Inscriptio aus der Perspektive kunsthistorischer Mediävistik", in: Ulrich Rehm and Linda Simonis (eds.), *Poetik der Inschrift,* Heidelberg, 75–97.

Schulz, Katja (2019), "Inscriptions in Old Norse Literature", in: Ricarda Wagner, Christine Neufeld, and Ludger Lieb (eds.), *Writing Beyond Pen and Parchment. Inscribed Objects in Medieval European Literature* (Materiale Textkulturen 30), Berlin/Boston, 41–62, https://doi.org/10.1515/9783110645446-003.

Steever, Sanford B. (1996), "Tamil Writing", in: Peter T. Daniels and William Bright (eds.), *The World's Writing Systems,* New York, 426–430.

Strätling, Susanne/Witte, Georg (eds.) (2006), *Die Sichtbarkeit der Schrift,* Munich.

Tachau, Katherine (1982), "The Problem of the *Species in medio* at Oxford in the Generation after Ockham", in: *Mediaeval Studies* 44, 349–443.

Theis, Christoffer (2015), "Mobile und immobile Schriftträger", in: Thomas Meier, Michael R. Ott, and Rebecca Sauer (eds.), *Materiale Textkulturen. Konzepte – Materialien – Praktiken* (Materiale Textkulturen 1), Berlin/Boston/Munich, 611–618, https://doi.org/10.1515/9783110371291.611.

Wagner, Ricarda (2019), "Tablets and the Poetics of the Premodern Post-It", in: Ricarda Wagner, Christine Neufeld, and Ludger Lieb (eds.), *Writing Beyond Pen and Parchment. Inscribed Objects in Medieval European Literature* (Materiale Textkulturen 30), Berlin/Boston, 239–254, https://doi.org/10.1515/9783110645446-013.

West, Stephanie (1985), "Herodotus' Epigraphical Interests", in: *Classics Quarterly* 35, 278–305.

White, Hayden (1993), "Schreiben im Medium", in: Hans Ulrich Gumbrecht and K. Ludwig Pfeiffer (eds.), *Schrift,* Munich, 311–318.

―――
Chapter 2
Layout, Design, Text-Image

Nikolaus Dietrich, Lisa Horstmann, Andrea Bernini, Susanne Börner, Sarah Braun, Johannes Fouquet, Tobias Frese, Adrian Heinrich, Rebecca Hirt, Carina Kühne-Wespi, Giuditta Mirizio, Rebecca Müller, Gustavo Fernández Riva, Anett Rózsa, Anna Sitz, Friederike Stahlke, Chun Fung Tong, Sebastian Watta

Chapter 2
Layout, Design, Text-Image

Nikolaus Dietrich, Lisa Horstmann, Andrea Bernini, Susanne Börner, Sarah Braun, Johannes Fouquet, Tobias Frese, Adrian Heinrich, Rebecca Hirt, Carina Kühne-Wespi, Giuditta Mirizio, Rebecca Müller, Gustavo Fernández Riva, Anett Rózsa, Anna Sitz, Friederike Stahlke, Chun Fung Tong, Sebastian Watta

A text can be spoken, heard, or even just thought. Its wording can be determined in detail down to the letter; or it can also be malleable. If the text is written down, its wording becomes fixed. While in our current digital age, writing down a text is no safeguard against changes being made in how such a text is represented, under the conditions of a material culture of writing, the act of writing something down inevitably entails a second 'fixing', as it were: the text takes on a *concrete form*. This is determined by a wide array of factors: for instance, by the writing support, the writing technique, the letters/characters used, possibly the combination of the latter with non-linguistic signs on the same writing support, and the spatial arrangement of all these elements on the writing support.[1] This last point, in which we see the various aspects mentioned here converge, is what we understand and analyse in the following as 'layout'.[2]

The abovementioned aspects are interrelated in many ways and determine collectively, in a complex web of interdependency, the phenomenon of layout in a comprehensive understanding of the term. The specific stylisation of the letters of Gothic script thus not only depends on individual scribes working within the framework of the typical scribal aesthetics of their time, but is also connected to the ductus of the quill (as a writing tool) on parchment (as the writing support).[3] The way in which the layout of a text comprises more than just characters depends, among other things, on the type and material of the writing support. Thus, the layout of writing in a magnificent liturgical codex may integrate pictorial elements of various kinds, while monumental stone inscriptions chiselled onto building façades may appear in combina-

---

[1] For this definition of layout, we have taken as our basis the normal case of an inscribed support of manageable dimensions: papyrus scrolls, book pages, stone stelae, and the like. Cases in which the writing support goes far beyond such dimensions, as well as multi-part inscribed monuments (e. g., the stone surfaces of a public square with the assemblage of inscriptions there), where the question of layout would touch on that of topology, are not included in what follows.
[2] On the conceptualisation of writing as an arrangement, see the foundational work by Cancik-Kirschbaum/Mahr 2005.
[3] See Enderwitz/Opdenhoff/Schneider 2015, esp. 475–480 on writing with the pen in Arabic calligraphy and European book illumination; and Becker/Licht/Schneidmüller 2015, 337–348 on parchment as a writing material.

Open Access. © 2024 the authors, published by De Gruyter. This work is licensed under the Creative Commons Attribution-NonCommercial-NoDerivatives 4.0 International License.
https://doi.org/10.1515/9783111325514-003

tion with similarly chiselled ornamentation. If the object described is itself already an image, as in the case of a statue covered with inscriptions, the layout arising from the combination of linguistic and non-linguistic signs is again of a different kind. By contrast, if the act of writing is performed on an arbitrary object that serves the purpose of inscription but is otherwise worthless (such as a pottery shard or ostracon), then what is written usually ends up lacking any non-linguistic embellishments. But even in this supposedly simplest case of textuality subject to pragmatic aspects, the question arises as to how the writing is designed, and this perhaps even more intensively so in such a case, since the writer must find a way of dealing with the random specifications presented by the object used as the writing support in order to attain a desirable graphic text form. Even without the use of figurative elements, the pragmatic act of writing inevitably results in a certain appearance on the part of the writing that could always have turned out differently. The basis of the following analysis is therefore the realisation that *there is no writing without layout.*

In addition to the material factors already mentioned, it is not surprising that the content of a text also proves to be an essential factor in the layout of writing. The relevance of content for our analysis is evidenced not only by the *semantic dimension of the arrangement* of the text on its support, which can be ascertained in many cases and through which, as it were, mental arrangements become crystallised in material writing; it is also made clear by the seemingly banal correlation between *layout and text type*, which can often be observed across cultures and epochs, but is also multi-layered and sometimes deliberately undermined. In many cases, we see the emergence (for individual text types) of standardised layouts that are valid for a wide variety of cultural spheres and eras. The immediate recognisability of a text type that is thus provided can decisively influence the attribution of meaning in the subsequent reading process. Moreover, this recognition factor can define the epistemic status of the statements made in the text (as in the case of a scientific text with its footnote apparatus), or even be indispensable for the successful attribution of meaning, as in the case of a list, which as mere text results in a grammatically meaningless juxtaposition of words, but in the specific layout of a list conveys precise informative content.

The relevance of content-related points of view in the analysis of laid out text also applies to borderline cases of material writing, such as the occasionally encountered nonsense inscriptions found for instance in Greek vase painting[4] or on Indo-Scythian coinage, whose meaningless sequences of letters only imitate 'normal' inscriptions in the layout and letter forms used. Insofar as they still hint at some inherent content, even though their wording is meaningless, these instances of writing invite their respective recipients to ascribe meaning. Another borderline case of material writing (albeit a much more common one) is when the meaning of the text is present, but the text itself is no longer legible for a variety of reasons: for example, because

---

4 See recently Chiarini 2018; some remarks in Dietrich 2018, 188–192.

the inscribed artefact has been permanently removed from its context of use through being stored or deposited elsewhere, or because the writing is still visible as such on account of its location and/or graphic design, but is no longer legible per se as text.[5] In addition to both text content and the initially mentioned material factors that determine layout, such borderline cases of material writing bring up another factor of essential importance in the following analysis of layout as a necessary property of all writing: namely, reception. As we shall show, under the conditions of material text culture, there is less of a clear-cut distinction between the categories of reception and production. It is neither the case that layout in material text cultures is mechanistically derived from the conditions of the production of writing, nor that layout is unilaterally subservient to the reception of material writing, but rather that layout breaks through this dichotomy. The multifaceted phenomenology of the graphic design of writing in material text cultures can be explained much better *if layout is situated between production and reception* in the analysis.

The following analysis of layout (including the particularly interesting special case of when writing and images come together) is structured according to the aspects mentioned here: layout and writing support; the semantics of layout; layout between production and reception; layout and text type. As different as layout practices may be between writing cultures and epochs, these aspects nevertheless mark out fundamental problem areas, and it is the critical engagement with these problems that has given rise to the layout conventions that individual academic fields and disciplines have been able to describe and ascertain.

Thesis 7
Layout and writing supports are mutually dependent. In non-typographic writing cultures, the influence of the writing support is more diverse.

If layout is understood as a spatial arrangement on the writing support, then it is first necessary to examine how the latter co-determines the layout through its own form, material, and affordances for writers and readers. The fact that a writing support, with its specific materiality profile, can be highly prescriptive for the layout of what is written on it does not appear at all to be self-evident if we look at the main writing support in typographic societies, i. e., a sheet of paper—be that in loose leaf form, as a page in a book, a printout of a digitally created text document, etc. When it comes to the layout conventions we tend to take for granted—the fact that we usually present texts in

---

[5] On the restricted presence of writing, see Frese/Keil/Krüger 2014 and some contributions in Keil et al. 2018.

parallel lines, divide them into paragraphs, leave a certain margin around the central text block, supplement these texts with headings and subheadings, etc. — are these really contingent upon the fact that the text in question is printed or written on paper, and not on other material? Are not criteria such as the clear presentation of the meaning of the text and the facilitation of fluent reading more decisive by far in this regard?

In non-typographic societies, it is not difficult to find examples of material writing in which the correspondence between layout and writing support is immediate. One such case is presented by scrolls made of narrow bamboo or wooden strips that are bound together, among the oldest known Chinese writing materials and used in early imperial administration.[6] The vertical alignment of the 'lines' — the characteristic 'superposition' rather than 'juxtaposition' of characters — results directly from the affordances of the writing material, where the narrow vertical strips provide just enough space for one character, almost forcing one to position the next character below it, rather than beside. This example, in which the nature of the writing support proves to be strongly prescriptive for the layout of the writing, could be cited as a paradigmatic case of a theory of the layout of writing that would emphasise material factors. However, it would be just as easy at once to proffer counter-examples in which the nature of the writing support has been adapted to existing layout conventions, albeit ones that primarily facilitate reading. Thus, the simplest explanation for the portrait format — more common diachronically and transculturally in non-typographic societies than the landscape format for written book pages — would be that the former gives rise to relatively short lines that make reading easier. This in turn could serve as the basis for a theory of the layout of writing that would prioritise the reception of the text's meaning and subordinate the material writing support to this meaning of the text. Whether the cases of adapting the writing support to the layout should be given theoretical priority or vice versa is a bit like asking what came first, the chicken or the egg. Rather, what determines the phenomenology of material writing cultures in the most diverse ways — and what we present here via a few examples — is the *mutual conditionality* of formal layout and the material writing support. Nevertheless, in the non-typographic writing cultures studied, the writing support is generally given much greater weight in this mutual conditionality, and this material dimension of a writing culture often penetrates more deeply into the realm of formal layout than would correspond to modern intuitions.

A marble Attic inscription stele from the late sixth century BCE, on which the wording of an Athenian public decree was carved for its public installation in the sanctuary, may illustrate the latter point (Fig. 1).[7] Although the artefact was made solely to accommodate this inscription, and the perfectly smoothed surface and

---

6 Tsien 1962, 183–184. The vertical alignment of lines is nevertheless possible even without such a material explanation. On Egyptian papyri, the oldest (and later abandoned) method was also to write in vertical columns, although papyrus certainly lends itself to a horizontal orientation of text.
7 Dietrich 2020, 177–179.

Fig. 1: Attic inscription stele with a decree concerning Salamis (IG I³,1 1), late 6th century BCE. Athens, Epigraphic Museum 6798, 6798a, 6825, and 12 936. Reproduction from Kirchner 1935, pl. 6.13.

extremely neatly carved letters guarantee good visibility and legibility for the text, the layout—with its long, vertically running lines of script—is oriented towards the highly rectangular shape of the inscribed object rather than to the text's need for fluent readability, which short horizontal lines could better facilitate. Instead of emancipating itself from its material base by taking advantage of some of the empty marginal strips to 'free up' a block for writing, the inscription begins in the upper right corner of the stele, following the edges closely and filling the surface of the front side evenly and comprehensively with lettering. There is no distinction between the text field and the background of the inscription; both are fused together into one. In order to realise this fusion of text and material carrier perfectly, a great amount of additional planning was required. Since the inscription stele tapers slightly towards the top in accordance with the usual shape of such stelae, the vertical lines of lettering had to be arranged ever so slightly in radial fashion: while the letters at the beginning of the lines almost touch each other at the top, they move apart almost imperceptibly towards the bottom.

Writing, though, can of course also use as writing supports already existing artefacts that have not (or not exclusively) been produced for the purpose of being inscribed. Several examples come to mind: sculptural works of art can be inscribed;[8] inscriptions can be applied to buildings;[9] and even casually discarded pottery shards can be recycled as writing supports.[10] In such cases, the question of the mutual conditionality of layout and writing support arises in a different way. After all, in these instances, only the writing can be adapted to the already existing material support, which has (at least primarily) been produced to other ends. Greek inscriptions carved into the fluting of columns, for example, are an example of how the writing (or the writers) 'searches' for a suitable writing surface on an artefact that was not intended per se for to be written on. As much as the inscriptions in such cases respect the specifications of the artefacts used as the writing surface instead of demonstratively disregarding them à la modern urban graffiti, there nevertheless remains an element of mutual conditionality here in the relationship between what is written and the writing surface, since the chiselling of the inscription also *turns* the fluting into a line of writing. The inscription not only 'seeks out' a writing surface for itself, it also 'creates' it. This principle can be seen, for example, in the well-known votive statue of the Nike of Kallimachos from the Athenian Acropolis, which was placed on a column. The column was only double fluted—which was all that was needed for the engraving of the dedicatory inscription—while the rest of the column shaft was left rough.[11]

The same principle of the mutual conditionality of writing and the writing surface is found much more frequently at the level of everyday culture. The shard of a broken, useless clay vessel from the middle of the Roman Imperial era depicted here (Fig. 2) only became an 'active' artefact of human culture again when it became the writing support for a letter. The characteristic porosity of fired clay, which in the shard's earlier existence as an intact clay vessel was still an unexploited material affordance in this respect, now makes the shard an ideal writing surface for ink. Writing with ink, in turn, entails the use of other letter forms: Greek cursive, which differs significantly from the majuscules of chiselled Greek inscriptions.

---

8 Dietrich 2017, 298–316 (Greek); Berti/Keil/Miglus 2015, 506 (Akkadian).
9 On monumental inscriptions in general: Berti et al. 2017; Bolle 2020 (late antiquity). The case of Pompeii (graffiti, among other things): Lohmann 2017; Opdenhoff 2020.
10 On the so-called ostraca: Caputo/Lougovaya 2021.
11 Fouquet 2020, 107–108.

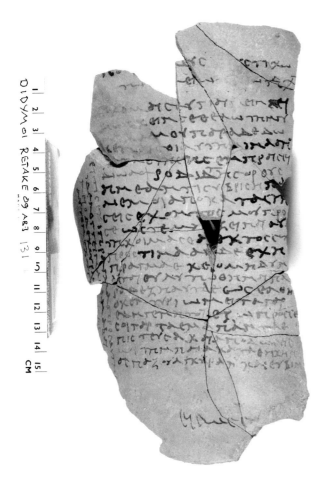

Fig. 2: Private letter on ostracon with *versiculus transversus* from the eastern Egyptian desert (Didymoi [present-day Khashm el-Menih]), ca. 115–140 CE. Original size: 17 × 21.5 cm, made of clay. O. Did. 406 (inv. no. D131 – CSA 131); Qift, Archaeological storeroom Did. 131; © Adam Bülow-Jacobsen.

This artefact, extreme in its simplicity, highlights another important phenomenon in the relationship between layout and writing support. As arbitrary as the shape of the shard may be, the layout of what is written on it nevertheless reflects the characteristic elements of epistolary layout in this period, with a salutation offset at the top, a text block, and closing greetings offset at the bottom: a layout found analogously in private letters on specially produced writing supports such as papyrus.[12] Instead of making full use of the available writing space for each line from one edge of the shard to the other, care was taken to begin the line at the same height. The area left free by this was then filled with additional vertically running lines *(versiculi transversi)*, but in the end this did not impinge upon the then typical layout of a letter, used here despite the support's adverse characteristics. For all the material writing support's importance for the concrete form of what is written, a certain autonomy is retained for the layout, which reveals here the text type independently of the writing surface.

---

12 Sarri 2018, 112–113.

Thesis 8
The layout of what is written and the design of its characters always carry a potential for meaning.

Writing can be conceptualised as the arrangement of characters on the physical surface of an object. Writers select signs from a repertoire, give them concrete shape, and place them in spatial relationships to one another.[13] The potential meaning of a configuration of inscriptions set up step by step in this way arises essentially from its two-dimensionality and its synoptic perception as a structured surface,[14] since writing uses spatial relationships to represent contexts that are not spatial in nature: for instance (to cite the obvious, but by no means only, example), when the immediate superimposition or juxtaposition of written characters corresponds to the temporal succession of linguistic signs in spoken speech. From an aesthetic perspective of reception, writing thus has less in common with spoken language than with the image, because even though writing and reading, as the basic—although not necessarily the only!—modes of production or reception of what is written, occur in temporal succession, writing as a simultaneously perceivable two-dimensional arrangement is subject to preconditions with regard to its perception that are attributed to the image, at least according to Lessing's classic juxtaposition of image and text.[15] The transition from image to writing would thus not be essential, but rather situational and functional, i. e., a question of use and perspective.[16]

When a written text is interpreted, the referential value of individual signs and their topologically signified relation to each other are primary, but not alone decisive, with regard to the meaning attributed to the text in question.[17] The same text is interpreted differently when it is presented in a different layout, and specific information about the genre and status of the artefact, as well as relative hierarchies of its compositional elements, can be determined from the layout alone. With regard to the genre and function of an inscribed artefact, the alleged lack of a particular design can also be informative in this context. The design of characters and their arrangement in a

---

13 See here the foundational work by Cancik-Kirschbaum/Mahr 2005.
14 Krämer 2005, 32; Krämer/Totzke 2012, 16–17; from the perspective of textual linguistics: Steinseifer 2013.
15 Cancik-Kirschbaum/Mahr 2005, 101, 114. Other aspects of the spatiality of writing, such as that of "interspatiality" ("Zwischenräumlichkeit") (Krämer/Totzke 2012, 17, our translation), are by contrast suitable for distinguishing between writing and image, with 'interspatiality' referring to the discrete organisation of a writing system's signs. From this perspective, the distinction thus sets writing apart from the "continuous 'density'" (ibid., our translation, German text: "kontinuierliche 'Dichte'") of the image. See also Grube/Kogge 2005, 14–16.
16 On the aspect of the pictoriality of writing ("Schriftbildlichkeit"), see in detail pp. 78–83, as well as Chapter 1, pp. 38–39.
17 Cf. Cancik-Kirschbaum/Mahr 2005, 99–101.

particular layout are thus significant and have the same capacity for representation[18] as do individual characters when they conventionally stand for sounds, words, language-independent terms, or mathematical concepts.

The whole of the visually perceptible text inevitably unfolds its own potential for meaning in any interpretation as a formed and fashioned body in conjunction with the tangible and perceptible materiality of the inscribed artefact: the very physiognomy of the writing has signifying power. This potential for meaning is independent of the textual content, yet it also stands in a relationship of tension with the latter, since it can support and reinforce the text, but also undermine it. The relationship between writing and images, as well as other graphic elements, is also characterised by a reciprocal dynamism. New features can be emphasised in this interaction where images and writing complement, contrast with, or even negate each other. The ways in which the layout of writing and the design of the writing's characters represent something else—that is, how they function as signs and mean something—can be classified according to the theory of signs under the umbrellas of index, icon, and symbol.[19]

As an index, the written word refers back to the body of the person writing and the sequence of his or her movements. The signifying power of layout and design *qua* index is based on the fact that both—as effect or symptom—play an essential role in the process to which they point back.[20] Anyone who pays attention to the specific appearance of upward and downward strokes in an example of handwriting and who tracks the succession, overlapping, and interweaving of its characters will find that the concrete materiality of what is written indicates a past writing scene and allows for conclusions to be drawn about such different aspects as the direction of writing, revision steps, tools used, textual templates, the practical knowledge and ability of the person writing, but also issues such as haste or concentration and thus also the purpose of the act of writing.[21] Here, we can think for instance of the obvious differ-

---

[18] Aleida Assmann understands the "ability to represent" ("Fähigkeit zur Repräsentation") as "signifying power" ("Zeichenkraft") (A. Assmann 2015, 53, our translations) and establishes this as the *definiens* of the sign.

[19] For this classic tripartite theory of signs according to Charles S. Peirce, see A. Assmann 2015, 54–56. This is not the place to elaborate a comprehensive semiotics of the design and layout of writing in non-typographic text cultures. The remarks may merely demonstrate via a rough outline—in the sense of the thesis—that there is no interpretation for which the layout and design of writing are devoid of meaning. On the semiotics of typography from a systematic and historical perspective, see Wehde 2000.

[20] The decision to speak of 'the written word' ('Geschriebenes') here rather than of text or writing more generally ('Schrift') emphasises the indexical potential for meaning inherent to the materiality of inscribed artefacts and the design and layout of what is written, respectively; cf. Ott/Kiyanrad 2015, esp. 157–158.

[21] For such an analysis based on the design of what is written, cf. Dietrich 2020 (dedicatory inscription of the early Greek statue of Nikandre on Delos). On the literary concept of the writing scene, cf. Campe 1991; Stingelin 2004 as well as other volumes of the book series *Zur Genealogie des Schreibens* edited by D. Giuriato, M. Stingelin, and S. Zanetti.

ences between a completely ephemeral list of incoming goods quickly jotted down by a shipping dock overseer and an inventory of a temple's treasure that is executed and kept with great care in list form.

For the semantics of the spatial arrangement of what is written, the iconic qualities of layout and character design are decisive. Here, their signifying power arises from a formal or metaphorical similarity to the subject matter they are supposed to express or to the thing they refer to. That elaborately designed initials, a *carmen figuratum,* or even the figures of the *masora figurata*[22] formed from rows of letters have an iconic quality, hardly requires detailed discussion. This may be more the case with ordinary section headings, whose semantic function is based on the metaphorical relationship of similarity between larger font size and superior (i. e., greater) meaning, as can also be observed in this present volume.[23] A relationship of similarity can also be posited, figuratively speaking, wherever a linear spatial arrangement of characters represents the temporal sequence of spoken speech, as is the case with theatrical texts such as the so-called late medieval and early modern *Dirigierrollen*, on which the directors of theatrical productions had both the text of a play and other staging information in one continuous scroll rather than a codex or book. The iconic positionality of characters here encodes the temporal dimension of another medial event. In the case of the headline, it expresses the qualification of a relationship between signs or of the knowledge represented by them.

The layout and design of written characters attain symbolic significance above all in special cases of scriptal marking, such as the use of colour codes, the marking of foreign-language words via italicisation, or the use of special (e. g., archaising) character forms as well. In all these cases, the specific semantics of the marking of selected groups of signs does not draw on any similarity between the type of emphasis and the intended distinction of meaning, as in the above example of the larger headline: there is neither a metonymic nor a metaphoric relationship between the Antiqua script/font and the Latin language. In such cases, the signifying power is based solely on a common convention or a valid rule, i. e., an ultimately arbitrary assignment, which is characteristic of symbols as a basis for meaning.

Now that we have derived our general thesis on the potential for meaning inherent in layout and the design of characters, we provide more concrete examples of this potential in the following by taking a look at the conventionality of layout, the intermedial encounter of writing and image, and pictoriality as an essential quality of the written word.

---

22 Cf. Attia 2015, as well as more generally the research of the CRC's subproject B04 'Scholarly Knowledge, Drollery or Esotericism? The Masora of the Hebrew Bible in its Various Material Properties'.
23 The same could be said, for example, about footnotes, whose marginal position on the page, together with the smaller font size, marks the discourses conducted in them as secondary to the main text; cf. on this the remarks in Krämer 2005, 36–38, as well as the self-ironic essay by Rieß/Fisch/Strohschneider 1995.

Meaningful Conventionality: In medieval manuscript culture, we find numerous examples of the potential for meaning in the layout of writing. Meaning is not only generated via extraordinary design, but also by largely inconspicuous layouts. Such meaningful conventionality already exists by virtue of the fact that the genre and function of an artefact can often be recognised by its layout, provided one understands the conventions of the respective historical context. These conventions are sometimes even explicitly presented in contemporary texts, as in the case of English administrative scrolls, the design of which was set out in detail by Fitz Neal in the twelfth century.[24] These scrolls were prescribed to be single-columned, unlike most books of the time. Fitz Neal even describes the characteristics of the ruling and line spacing.

Meaningful conventionality is also found in the design of individual layout elements in medieval manuscripts. Initials were often used for the purpose of marking the beginnings of a text section. Sentences that introduced or summarised a section of text were often written in red ink, while other embellishments and instances of rubrication contained certain elements that stood out in other ways. Particularly complex and expressive layout conventions are found in the frequently glossed manuscripts from the High Middle Ages. The middle of the page is occupied by the main text split over two columns, with the commentary being arranged around the main text in a smaller-sized lettering. Trained readers could immediately recognise the text type and the hierarchies of the individual elements from this widespread format, while even those who did not know these conventions in detail knew at a glance that this was the layout of a scholarly text. These examples show that one can recognise text type and function, as well as the hierarchies of the elements, without having to decipher the text's content.

Writing and Image: Questions about the layout's potential for meaning also apply to artefacts where writing and image come together, and can thus also be included in a general area of research that can already look back on a certain tradition. The perspective of a mutually stimulating interaction of textual *content* and (figurative) images—René Magritte's famous pipe, which is avowedly not a pipe at all[25]—has been part of the methodological toolbox of image and literary studies research in the field of *word and image studies* for quite some time.[26] For example, the term 'iconotext', co-coined by the literary scholar Peter Wagner, points to the reciprocal referential character of both media, which can only be understood comprehensively.[27] Beyond

---

24 Clanchy 2013, 135.
25 Cf. Foucault 1973.
26 See, e. g., Newby/Leader-Newby 2007; Squire 2009; Gibhardt/Grave 2018; as well as the individual contributions to the ancient studies conference held in Gießen *IkonoTexte – Duale Mediensituationen* (2006), https://www.uni-giessen.de/resolveuid/a124a1d394940c883a58345e21e92e31 (accessed 9/9/2021).
27 Wagner 1995; Wagner 1996. This was already noted by Montandon 1990, 6 ("une œuvre dans laquelle l'écriture et l'élément plastique se donnent comme une totalité insécable").

the analytical categories of text and image or writing *qua* image, however, the materiality of writing as a visual design element in its own right has often gone unnoticed, and specifically with regard to its graphic arrangement, such materiality can complement or modify the generation of meaning within the image.[28]

A particularly dense interweaving is shown, for example, by a fragmentary pediment stele from Tegea in Arcadia (Greece), which can be dated to the middle of the fourth century BCE. This stele depicts in its image field a ruling couple from Caria, Ada and Idrieus, and between them the god Zeus Labraundos, who was particularly significant for the Hekatomnid dynasty to which they belonged (Fig. 3).[29] The iconography leaves no doubt as to the distribution of roles: the hierarchical relation of mortals to deity is demonstrated by Ada's gesture of adoration and Idrieus's proffered greeting, but most clearly by the characteristic difference in size between the figures. All three figures are identified by onomastic inscriptions carved into the head of the stele shaft, whereby the placement above the respective figure ensures the correct assignment.[30] On the horizontal plane, however, a different ordering principle is revealed: by placing the inscription of Zeus's name higher than the two of the ruling couple, the layout takes up and participates in the picture's composition and its underlying concept of sacrality. Beyond this kind of production-aesthetic perspective, one can also inquire into the interaction of the layout of the writing *in* the image in the process of reception with specific attributions of meaning.[31]

The Pictoriality of Writing *(Schriftbildlichkeit)*: As we have just seen, scripts and characters can enter into an exciting dialogue with figurative images in layout; but every script also has a characteristic appearance and is therefore to be understood as an 'image' in the full sense of the term. Layout proves to be a means for generating meaning not only with regard to writing *and* image, but also with regard to writing *as* image (the pictoriality of writing). Whether the iconicity of a script is highlighted or instead downplayed in the sense of a standardised layout of writing does not change this fundamental observation: every script is always also an image.[32]

---

28 As counter-examples, see for example Lorenz 2010; Gerleigner 2016; Dietrich/Fouquet/Reinhardt 2020; various contributions in Dietrich/Fouquet 2022.
29 London, British Museum, Inv. 1914,0714.1; cf. Waywell 1993; Keesling 2017, 64.
30 IG V,2 89: "Ἄδα. | Ζεύς. | Ἰδριεύς." On ancient epigraphs, see for example Feraudi-Gruénais 2017.
31 For an aesthetic perspective on the reception of writing in images, see for example Gibhardt/Grave 2018; Lorenz 2010, esp. 133–135; as well as the contributions by K. Lorenz and J. Fouquet in Dietrich/Fouquet 2022.
32 J. Assmann 2012; Watts 2013; Bedos-Rezak/Hamburger 2016; Debiais 2017; Hamburger 2011 and 2014; Krämer/Cancik-Kirschbaum/Totzke 2012; Mersmann 2015; Riccioni 2008; Roth 2010; Rehm/Simonis 2019; Frese/Horstmann/Wenig 2024. Cf. also the work and projects of the interdisciplinary DFG Research Training Group 'Notational Iconicity' ('Schriftbildlichkeit') at the Free University of Berlin (2008–2013).

Fig. 3: Pediment stele with depictions of Zeus Stratios and the Carian rulers Ada and Idrieus, middle 4th century BCE, Tegea (Greece). Width 43.2 cm, height 44.5 cm. London, British Museum, inv. 1914,0714.1 © The Trustees of the British Museum (CC BY-NC-SA 4.0).

In some cultures and religions, the pictoriality of writing is explicitly called for as an aesthetic norm and cultivated in practice, as can be seen for example in East Asian or Arabic 'calligraphy'. In other cultural contexts, however, the pictoriality of writing can be virtually ignored or denied: the latter is especially true of iconoclastic discourses, in which writtenness has been (and still is) weaponised as an argument against proscribed images, the rebellious use of images, or ostentation more generally speaking.[33]

---

[33] Strätling/Witte 2006, 8–9. On the Christian-influenced discourse of the Western Middle Ages: Feld 1990; Frese 2006.

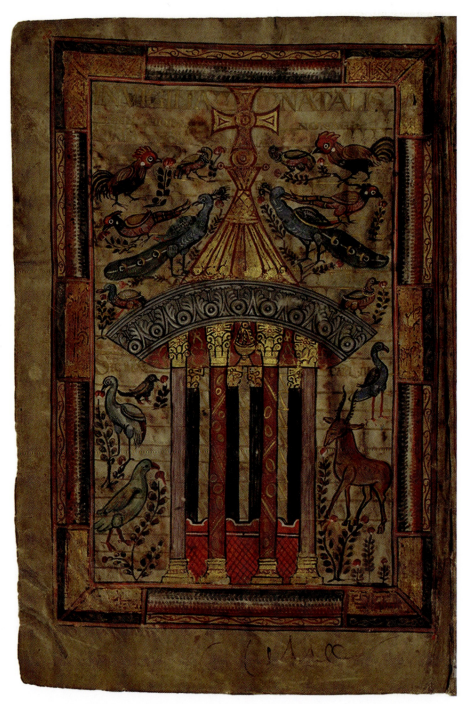

Fig. 4 (double page): Godescalc Evangelistary, Fountain of Life, and the beginning of the Christmas pericope according to Matthew (Matt 1:18–19). Paris, Bibliothèque nationale de France, Ms. nouv. acq. lat. 1203, fol. 3v–4r. Worms (?), 781–783, parchment, 310 × 210 mm. Source: http://gallica.bnf.fr.

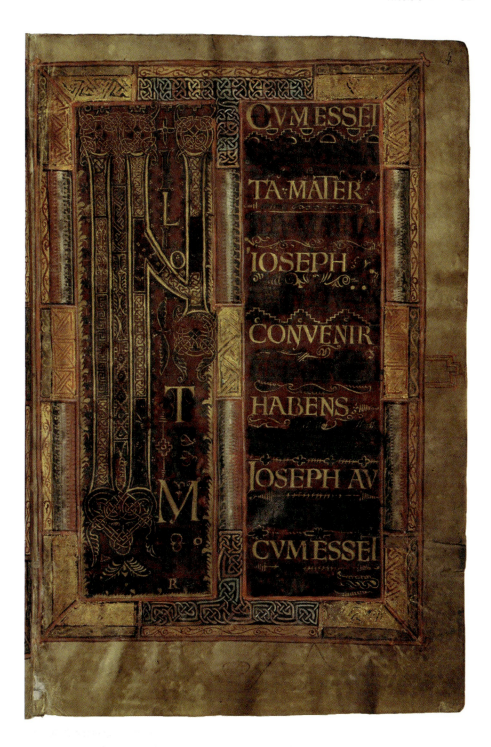

Of particular interest in the history of writing, however, are historical configurations in which the respective ideological position stood in tension with concrete writing praxis. This was the case, for example, at the court of the Frankish king Charlemagne (d. 814). In a famous treatise (the so-called *Libri Carolini*), the court scholar Theodulf of Orléans eloquently defended the superiority of writing over images.[34] In Theodulf's view, none of the great figures of scripture—Moses, David, the prophets, the apostles, even Christ himself—had ever painted; instead, they had written.[35] Therefore, only writing—and not images—could adequately represent the divine law. At the same time, however, splendid liturgical manuscripts were being produced at Charlemagne's court, such as the early Godescalc Evangelistary, which were adorned with pages of writing that had the appearance of magnificent paintings due to their rich colouring (gold and silver ink, purple background) and their specific layout (framing) (Fig. 4).[36] In this sense, it was only logical that the scribe Godescalc should emphasise in the final dedicatory poem of the aforementioned gospel lectionary that the golden letters had been "painted" *(pinguntur)* on the purple pages.[37]

Now, it can be assumed that differences in the perception and evaluation of the pictoriality of writing in the early Middle Ages can also be traced back to differences in the percipients' respective fields of activity or profession (bishop, theologian, scribe, painter, etc.). These differences themselves, however, have to do with the tension between the character of image and sign: a tension which is fundamentally inherent in every script and which especially comes to the fore in its reception. One could simply say that in terms of their pictoriality, scripts are *seen* or *beheld,* while in terms of their being a sequence of signs, they are *read.* In this sense, research has also emphasised that in the acts of reading and decoding, the specific materiality of the information support is hidden or absorbed and that the sign-like nature of the script educates us in principle to 'look beyond' the form to the meaning. In its function as a medium, script can be said in an ideal manner to vanish and to refer to what is invisible.[38] At the same time, however, the materiality and thus the visibility of the script cannot be said to vanish, but rather remains ever present and is "resistant to a complete injection into programmes of coding and decoding".[39]

---

34 *Libri Carolini*; Haendler 1958; Saurma-Jeltsch 1994; Saurma-Jeltsch 1997; Mitalaité 2007.
35 *Libri Carolini* II, 30, p. 303–322; cf. Haendler 1958, 81.
36 Most recently: Embach/Moulin/Wolter-von dem Knesebeck 2019. On the Godescalc Evangelistary: Crivello/Denoël/Orth 2011; Reudenbach 1998; Winterer 2013, 79–85.
37 *Poetae Latini aevi Carolini* 781 (vol. 1, 94–95).
38 Strätling/Witte 2006, 9; Krämer 2006, 75.
39 Strätling/Witte 2006, 7, our translation, German text: "resistent gegenüber einer restlosen Einspeisung in Programme des Codierens und Decodierens". Susanne Strätling and Georg Witte speak here of a "tension between the sign-transcending comprehension and the perceptual resistance of the material" (again our translation, German text: "Spannung zwischen zeichentranszendierendem Verstehen und perzeptorischer Resistenz des Materials").

This tension between visibility and invisibility is undoubtedly an essential characteristic of scripts and writing. From the perspective of visual studies and textual anthropology, however, it should be stressed that the specific pictoriality of writing not only remains 'resistant' to the sense of the text, but can also fundamentally co-determine and modify it. Thus, the precious colours and the ornamental splendour of the letters in the Godescalc Evangelistary should not be overlooked, nor is their effect exhausted in 'pure' aisthetic presence. Rather, the specific shapes and colours suggest meanings of their own that reinforce, complement, and soteriologically specify the textual meaning of the Gospel according to Matthew (lordly dignity, cosmology, transcendence, vitality, etc.).[40] Once again, layout as a means of ostentatiously emphasising the iconicity that fundamentally befits writing thus turns out to be the bearer of potential meaning.

Thesis 9
The layout of what is written can be significantly determined by the communicative intentions of the producers.

So far, layout has been discussed as the arrangement of writing on a given writing support. Doing so, however, has reduced the complexity of the matter by an essential element. After all, every example of writing is the result of an act of writing, and the inscribed artefact that arises through this act of production in turn gains its presence and relevance essentially through practices of reception. When production (Thesis 9) and reception (Thesis 10) are brought into the discussion of layout in what follows, we can first state that the layout of writing allows for conclusions to be drawn about the conditions of its production and the intended reception. The fact that we first pay attention to the production side of things takes into account the fact that under the conditions of non-typographic text cultures that lack mechanised reproduction techniques, each individual piece of writing is based on its own act of production, in which the layout of the writing and the design of the characters can and must always be determined anew.

This becomes clear when looking at medieval codices and the practice behind copying.[41] The creation and thus the appearance of a manuscript are directly dependent on the actors involved in the production process—the commissioners, scribes, painters, rubricators and/or proofreaders—and conclusions about the intentions of these various agents can be drawn from the layout of such a book. This can be seen particularly well in different copies of the same work, if they are largely similar in

---

40 Cf. the corresponding notes on the Hillinus Codex (also called the Hillinus Evangelistary) in Cologne, by Rehm/Simonis 2019, 10–11.
41 Gertz et al. 2015.

the wording of what is written, but differ greatly in their layout. The layout decisions made by the producers of each individual copy have a guiding effect on the reception process by communicating to the recipients *how* the text is supposed to be read and *as what*.

One Middle High German text on behaviour and etiquette, *Der Welsche Gast* ('The Italian Guest'), for example, survives today in 24 manuscripts,[42] all of which can be traced back in varying degrees of relationship to a single manuscript that is now lost.[43] In the work, written in 1215/16 by the Italian cleric Thomasin von Zerklaere and copied and distributed for almost 250 years, the text remains nearly the same across all extant copies, but these copies differ considerably in size, material, layout, and character/script design.[44] In the oldest and at the same time smallest surviving manuscript (A), the text was written in Gothic minuscule in a single column (Fig. 5a). The coloured pen drawings of the picture cycle accompanying the text are located in the margins and are mostly rotated 90 degrees with respect to the writing. Book beginnings are marked with simple red headings and split-bar initials. Although it was also written in Gothic minuscule (albeit in two columns), the manuscript (E), one hundred years younger than A, contains much richer and more ambitious decoration (Fig. 5b).[45] The miniatures are painted in opaque colours, decorated with gold, and framed by ornamental borders. In contrast to manuscript A, these are inserted in E into planned recesses in the body of the text, so that they are assigned to fixed passages therein. Accordingly, the copyists do not allow any leeway in the text-image relationship through the page design, as is the case with the rather loose connection in manuscript A. Different types of major and minor initials, as well as the presence of *litterae florissae* and *litterae notabiliores*, result in a hierarchising, clearly more stringent visual structure of the text.[46] Based on layout and design, the manuscript can be attributed to the workshop of Kuno of Falkenstein, whose skills are exemplified in this magnificent codex.[47] The paper manuscript (b), produced in the fifteenth century, has a completely different appearance with the same content (Fig. 5c). The text is written in two columns in bastarda, with the wash pen drawings being fitted unframed into the text column, partly reduced in terms of the objects or figures in the individual motifs for reasons of space

---

[42] All surviving manuscripts of *Der Welsche Gast* can be found as digital copies at: https://digi.ub.uni-heidelberg.de/wgd/ (accessed 6/3/2023). For the following, cf. also the publications of the CRC's subproject B06 'Material Presence of the Scriptural and the Practice of Iconographic Reception in Mediaeval Didactic Poetry. Text-Image Edition with Commentary of *Der Welsche Gast* by Thomasin von Zerklaere', https://thomasin.materiale-textkulturen.de/publikationen.php (accessed 6/3/2023), most recently Schneider et al. 2022.
[43] Manuscript stemmata providing information about the relationships can be found in Kries 1985, 154 (https://doi.org/10.11588/diglit.52821#0168) and Horstmann 2022, 315.
[44] Ott 2002.
[45] Ott 2002, 35.
[46] Wolf 2018.
[47] Ronig 1984; Roland 1991.

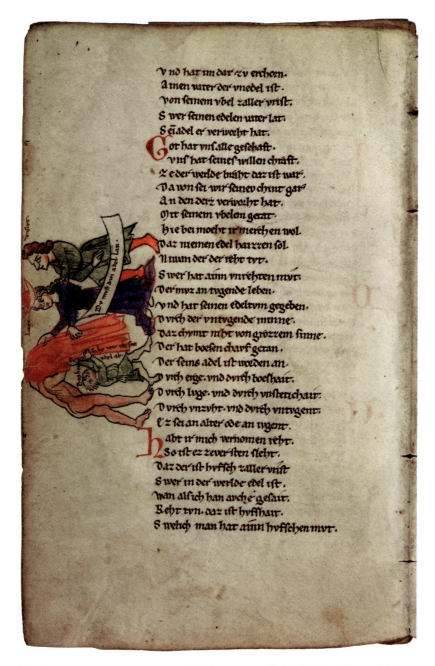

Fig. 5a: Thomasin von Zerklaere, *Der Welsche Gast*. Motif 69: 'The vices strip a nobleman of his nobility like a dress'. Heidelberg, University Library, Cod. Pal. germ. 389, fol. 61v. Carinthia, ca. 1256, parchment, 225 leaves, 18.1 × 11.5 cm. Text in Gothic minuscule, one hand; 106 coloured pen-and-ink drawings, three illustrators, two illuminators. Single column, structured by rubricated highlight initials. Miniature at the page margin, rotated 90 degrees to the text.

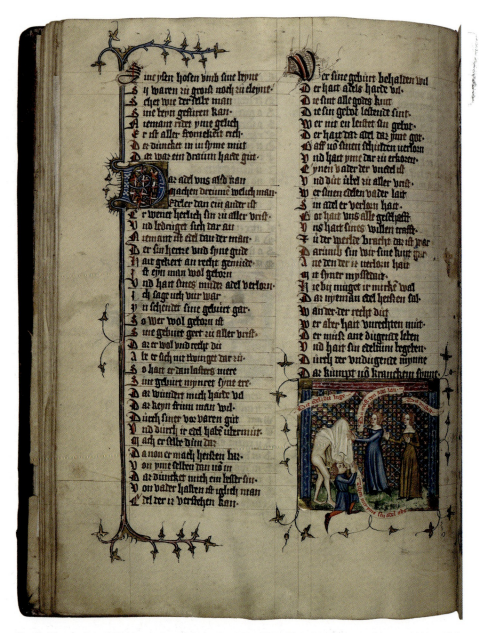

Fig. 5b: Thomasin von Zerklaere, *Der Welsche Gast*. Motif 69: 'The vices strip a nobleman of his nobility like a dress'. New York, The Morgan Library & Museum, Ms. G. 54, fol. 24v. Trier (?), workshop of Kuno von Falkenstein, ca. 1380, parchment, 74 leaves, ca. 35.4 × 25.6 cm. Text in Gothic minuscule, one hand; 72 miniatures framed by ornamental borders, presumably one illustrator and one illuminator. Two columns, structured by a colour field initial (D) with a golden background, floral interior field fillings and vine-like extensions flanking the text area, decorative initials at the top of the page with cardels and human profile. Miniature in a reserved space in the text field, golden frame with red and blue filling and vine-like extensions.

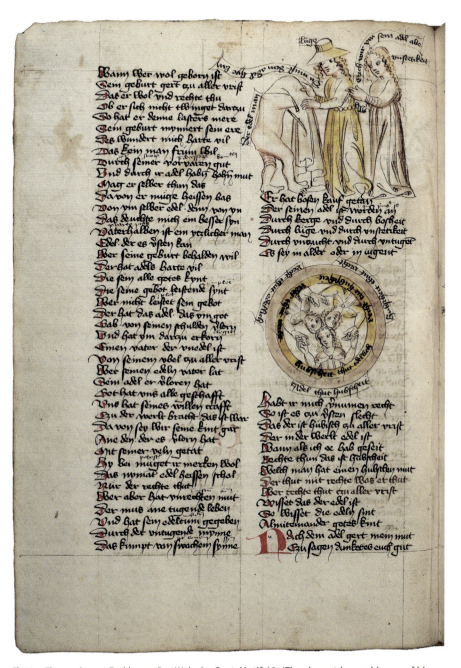

Fig. 5c: Thomasin von Zerklaere, *Der Welsche Gast*. Motif 69: 'The vices strip a nobleman of his nobility like a dress' and motif 70: 'Interconnectedness of law, nobility and courtliness'. Heidelberg, University Library, Cod. Pal. germ. 330, fol. 33v. Eichstätt (?), ca. 1420, paper, 104 leaves, ca. 31.2 × 21.8 cm. Text in bastarda, one hand, Latin and Czech interlinear glosses; 113 wash pen drawings, probably by one hand. Two columns, structured by rubricated highlight initials, miniatures inserted into the text column without frames.

compared to the other manuscripts, and with the text proper being accompanied by interlinear glosses in Latin and Czech. The fleeting, probably incomplete execution of the picture cycle and the addition of the selective translation of the text indicate an intended use in the production as a textbook for German lessons.

The copyists thus adapted the appearance of the respective manuscript to changing circles of recipients, styles, workshop conventions, client wishes, etc. Layout and design can therefore render visible changes in the situations of use and design demands.[48] One could say that the producers communicate with the recipients by means of the layout, for example, by showing off their abilities or by suggesting a certain way of reception that is different from that of the original.

In manuscript production, processes of standardisation can also be observed within workshop circles. Such processes usually serve to increase efficiency but can also lead to layout and design becoming the distinguishing feature of a production site. Regardless of the texts passed down in them, the manuscripts of such workshops then appear quite uniform in layout. Manuscripts from the workshop of Diebold Lauber in the fifteenth century, for example, show a uniformity in design that includes a representative format, standardised text structure and layout, indices of numbered chapters, and red chapter headings as well as large-format, mostly full-page illustrations, all of which serves to increase the recognition of the responsible producers. This standardised layout becomes the hallmark of the workshop and the manuscripts produced there become recognisable 'name-brand merchandise' for the recipients.[49] In this way, the producers use the layout and design to communicate to the recipients or potential buyers of the books that they were produced in a capable workshop.

These considerations lead to our thesis set out above: The layout of what is written can be significantly determined by the communicative intentions of the producers.[50] This begins in part already with the selection of the audience addressed in the layout: the person or group of persons who affixes a text to a writing support (or has it affixed) can use the layout to deliberately enigmatise and encrypt the content in such a way as to exclude those recipients who do not command the corresponding specialist knowledge. This applies, for example, to the late antique figure poems *(carmina figurata)* in the form of lattice poems, which render a second text legible through the arrangement of the letters of the first one *(versus intexti)*.[51] Such attempts at encoding can also be found in some Ashkenazic manuscripts up to the thirteenth century.[52] From here, the

---

48 Horstmann 2022, 2. The different use of text-structuring elements in the manuscripts of *Der Welsche Gast*, i. e., different initials, script design, headings, and other special features in the text that provide a visual framework and direct the reader's eye, is described by Starkey 2022.
49 Saurma-Jeltsch 2014.
50 For the premises of communication, see Chapter 1, p. 35–37.
51 Squire/Wienand 2017. On figure poems of classical antiquity: Pappas 2012.
52 See Attia 2015; Liss 2018 and 2021; Halperin 2021.

transition to a layout that is an expression of virtuosity and is intended to impress both viewer and reader is a smooth one. Emphatically artistic layouts, such as those found in the figure poems of late antiquity or the *Masora Figurata* illustrations of later Ashkenazic and Sephardic biblical manuscripts from the fourteenth century onwards (and which clearly stand out from standard productions of the same period), presuppose that the poets or visual artists have thought about the layout ahead of time and make clear their intention to communicate their own technical and artistic abilities to the recipients via the layout.

A self-reflexive moment of layout can come into play especially when a scribe or painter designs his or her own name. For example, Jan van Eyck's signature in his *Portrait of a Man* demonstrates that he is able to imitate various types of writing on different materials or create them himself (Fig. 6).[53] The writing support in the painting is an old and chipped stone parapet. On it, the painter writes his name in white paint in what looks to be a kind of handwriting, a chancery script typically written with a pen in documents. He thus evokes a legal act, just as he does with the unusual formulation "Actum […] a […]" instead of the more commonly encountered term *fecit* in signatures.[54] Another French inscription in Gothic majuscule ("LEAL SOVVENIR") simulates chiselled letters. Finally, above it, in the centre of the parapet in white paint and Greek capital letters, is the inscription TYM. ⲰΘEOC, which has been interpreted by some as the name of an ancient musician or sculptor, and thus referring to the sitter's profession, or as a combined Latin-Greek text but written solely with Greek letters ('TUM OTHEOS' = 'then God').[55] Oil painting, at once both a technique and a medium, and the brush as instrument, are pushed to the creative limits here in the imitation of different types of material and script. The expectations associated with the layout are simultaneously raised and dashed by the painter's virtuosity. The sculpted inscription is painted, and via the fictitious material, it creates the impression of a name having been inscribed onto a monument. This association is contrasted with the expression,

---

[53] London, National Gallery, oil on wood, 33.3 × 18.9 cm. The signature reads: "Actu(m) an(n)o d(omi)ni 1432 10 die octobris a ioh(anne) de eyck". The elaborate staging of the signature is particularly striking here, since Jan van Eyck was one of (if not *the*) first painter in the Netherlands to sign panel paintings; see Gludovatz 2005, esp. 118. Writing is additionally thematised in this portrait by the scroll (?) that the sitter holds in his hand: Surprisingly, the writing—fictitious (Campbell 1998, 218), and in any case illegible—is applied to the outside. On the inscriptions of the painting, see Fruhstorfer 1987 (with the correct observation that the white inscriptions are independent of the painted damage to the stone; the temporal course of the application would thus also have to be considered); Paviot 1995; Harbison 2012, 246–247.

[54] Among others: Wood 1978, 653.

[55] Alluding to the musician Timotheos of Miletus, Panofsky among others identified in 1949 the man in the painting as the musician and composer Gilles Binchois, a member of the Burgundian court chapel. Wood 1978, 650, agreed that 'Timotheus' did not directly name the sitter and argued with the layout: the writing was too inconspicuous compared to the artist's signature, being small and devoid of embellishment. For an overview of the numerous attempts at identification, see Campbell 1998, 220 (see here 222 for the reading as Latin words).

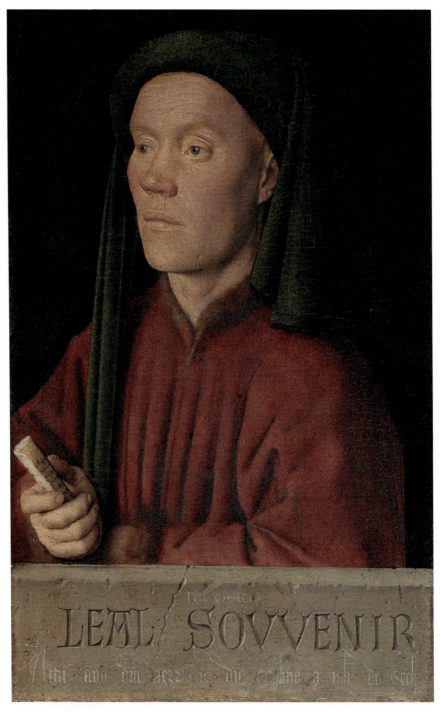

Fig. 6: Jan van Eyck, Portrait of a Man (so-called Timotheos). London, National Gallery, 1432. Oil on wood, height 33.3 cm, width 18.9 cm. © The National Gallery, London.

which could be a motto or a specific call to 'faithful remembrance'. There is no real deception here—the viewer is not left in the dark about the fact that he or she is standing in front of a painting—but the painter plays with perception, expectations, and knowledge via the layout.[56] While the individual bits of textual content remain hazy in their meaning and seem almost enigmatic, the painter uses the layout and the multitude of script forms on display, together with the writing implements and the material writing support suggested by them, to communicate very clearly to the recipients his level of ambition and his expectations vis-à-vis an educated audience.

Not only on the part of the executing artist, but also on that of the client, is it possible for a special level of aspiration to be manifested through layout and conveyed to the recipients, with this being the case both independently of the content of the recorded text and in tandem with the aim of underscoring certain references to meaning. Precious materials, contrasting colours, and the underlining of text were chosen not only to emphasise individual names, but also to create visually meaningful references that suggested—in addition to an element of prestige—not only human interaction, but also a proximity to the divine. In the medium of ancient and late antique mosaic inscriptions, for example, this could be accomplished with glass tesserae (small glass cubes or cuboids) covered with gold foil. They were rarely used for floor mosaics because of their fragility and cost-intensive production, so it was all the more conspicuous when they were in fact used in such settings. In the Church of St Paul in Philippi, Macedonia, built in the fourth century, an inscription in the eastern section of the nave refers to the activity of Bishop Porphyrios, who had outfitted the church with mosaics in the name of Christ.[57] Gold glass tesserae against a grey background were used to emphasise in striking manner the names of Christ, Paul, and Porphyrios. They make visible to the viewer the decorative cost and effort, but also visually connect the person of the donor with the sphere of the sacred, represented by the apostle as well as Christ himself. The remaining words of the inscription were set in stone tesserae of blue colour against a white background, with only the word ἐν ('in') appearing in red, probably in order to emphasise the donation's reference to Christ.[58]

The sheer size and length of inscriptions also convey a special claim on the part of the client via their good visibility and the physical effort required to read them. The five inscriptions on the church of San Matteo and the palace facing opposite in Genoa, which celebrate the battle victories of admirals hailing from the Doria family, obviously involved a great deal of financial and organisational planning and effort:[59]

---

56 How all this is to be connected with the person of the sitter remains controversial; see among others Dhanes 1980, 182–184; Rehm/Simonis 2019, 12–13.
57 Philippi, Archaeological Museum, Δ 15.265; SEG 27, 304: "Πορ[φύ]ριος ἐπίσκο- | πος τὴ[ν κ]έντησιν τῆς βασιλικῆ- | ς Παύλο[υ ἐπ]οίησεν ἐν Χρ(ιστ)ῷ" ('Bishop Porphyrios made the mosaic of the Basilica of Paul in Christ'). See also Pilhofer 2009, 394–396 n. 329/G472; Leatherbury 2020, 42, 44, 46; Dadaki 2011; Pelekanides 1975, 101.
58 Leatherbury 2020, 42.
59 Müller 2002, 126–133.

each inscription runs along layers of Carrara marble in only three lines of text, but these lines are more than nine metres long. It would have been simpler from the point of view of both the planning and the execution—not to mention the cost—to place the inscriptions (as was otherwise customary in Genoa) on a few higher stone slabs and to use smaller letters. The low but long inscriptions are likely not only to have attracted attention due to their unusual layout, but they can also be seen from every vantage point on the facing piazza due to their coursing across the entire façade of the church or palace, respectively. The claim fundamentally associated with the medium of monumental inscription[60]—in this case, that of the noble Doria family vying for leadership in Genoa—is thus conveyed to a wide gamut of people, while only a laborious and time-consuming walk along the façade makes the content of the texts intelligible. The aisthetic guidelines, which are clearly controlled here by the client, thus broaden the spectrum of perception and appear to be situated entirely in the service of the family and its agenda.

Thesis 10
Layout offers different reception practices.

As shown in the last thesis, the producer determines through the layout and design of what is written the reception and thus also the form of such text to a decisive extent.[61] The layout and design can increase the legibility of a text, direct the reader's eye, and offer up interpretations, but they can also obscure such readability to the point of illegibility.

In the course of the eighth-century Carolingian educational reforms, for example, a large number of codices were produced that reveal a striving for clarity and unambiguity in their design. In addition to the introduction of a general script—namely, the Carolingian minuscule, which replaced the regional scripts of individual writing centres—how folios were designed also bears witness to these aspirations for uniformity.[62] Copied texts were transferred into a new layout that visually structured the text for the reader and was legible across regional borders. In addition to the Carolingian minuscule as a script for text, ancient majuscule scripts were used for writing especially emphasised words or lines of text. A fixed hierarchy of scripts even emerges:[63] for book and chapter titles, text incipits, and colophons, a regular ranking of *capitalis quadrata*, uncial, and semi-uncial scripts is evident, with *capitalis rustica* also being

---

60 Foundational here are Petrucci 1986; Bartoli Langeli/Giovè Marchioli 1996.
61 Ast/Attia/Jördens/Schneider 2015.
62 Further characteristics of the new Carolingian aesthetics in design are provided by Tino Licht, who cites the example of the scriptorium at the imperial abbey in Lorsch (present-day Germany) near Worms, cf. Licht 2013.
63 Job 2013.

used for incipits, explicits, and running titles. In the Carolingian Renaissance, the correct understanding of Holy Scripture and other texts was a prerequisite for correct faith: whoever did not understand the words of Scripture and reproduce them correctly opened themselves up to the danger of heresy. In this context, the understanding of the content of the text already takes as its starting point the text's legibility.[64]

Moreover, a specific layout can also facilitate specifically intended copying processes.[65] The so-called Pipe Rolls or Great Rolls of the Exchequer, in use since the twelfth century for recording administrative audits in England, are individual parchment rotuli that were tied together at the heads and rolled up. The horizontal arrangement of the text on the rolls follows the logic of accounting. In this context, the large spacing left by the scribe not only testifies to an intended clarity of these documents, but also facilitated copying by dividing the documents into individual sections.[66]

However, an increase in legibility is not the only effect layout can have on text; it can also lead to textual illegibility. Accordingly, the design can suggest a reception that obviously does not see an actual 'reading' as the first and most important possibility of reception. The presence of writing that is restricted by different means of design or spatial arrangement can obscure the recognisability of the characters themselves. For example, the golden writing on an ornamental page of the Guntbald Gospels, produced at the beginning of the eleventh century, is hidden behind vine-like ornamentation that is likewise in gold and resembles the shapes of the letters.[67] Effortless reading was not intended in this case: the page was simply meant to be looked at first.[68] The famous Chi-Rho page of the Book of Kells from around 800 also impressively shows[69] that the design of the writing on the purely visual level illustrates invisible Christian mysteries through the visible and at once inseparable entanglements of script, image, and ornament in the masterful way the Christ monogram is decorated almost beyond recognition.[70] For the recipient, such splendid pages in a manuscript seem visually impressive at first; the text can only be read out from within the image(ry) on closer inspection. Beholding the page, marvelling at what one sees, looking closely and gazing at the sight are all reception practices provoked above all by the design of what is written.[71]

Finally, one of the reception practices that laid-out text can encourage is also the act of writing. Such practices are already taken into account in the layout when deter-

---

[64] Scholz 2015, 280–281.
[65] Kypta 2015 explicitly examines the uses of the Pipe Rolls based on their layout.
[66] Kypta 2015, 281.
[67] Dom- und Diözesanmuseum Hildesheim, inventory no. DS 33, fol. 88v; see also: Frese 2014, 4–5. On 'Enigmatic Calligraphy' in early medieval gospels, see Reudenbach 2021.
[68] Becht-Jördens 2014 shows different modes of how medieval characters were received.
[69] Dublin, Trinity College, Ms. 58. A digitised copy of the manuscript can be viewed online at: https://doi.org/10.48495/hm50tr726 (accessed 4/11/2022).
[70] Lewis 1980.
[71] Becht-Jördens 2014.

mining the typeface. The often astonishingly wide margins left around the central text block in medieval codices, despite parchment being an expensive writing material, fall in line with the usual practice of writing commentary.[72] The blind ruling of the blank page already determines its division into spaces allocated for the text proper, pictorial elements, and commentary (Fig. 7),[73] with the actual text only taking up part of the page. Both the columns surrounding the text as well as the enlarged line spacing provide space for comments and interlinear glosses. The layout of early modern writing calendars is explicitly intended for the addition of handwritten notes: these were annual calendars that emerged in the printing age with the invention of letterpress printing with movable type (sixteenth century).[74] They consist of a calendar for the twelve months of the year, with each calendar page juxtaposed with a blank one on which handwritten notes can be made. Within the calendar, knowledge of an astrological and medical nature together with everyday know-how for practical living is correlated to the individual days of the month, so that the best dates for bloodletting, haircuts, or marriage can be identified, for example.[75] On the pages for writing, which are either simply blank[76] or else marked out by the layout with a specific field for writing, the calendar writer can record personal experiences, plan appointments, or reflect on what he or she has experienced. Writing calendars are therefore equipped with a specific affordance through their print layout: handwritten notes are explicitly anticipated and taken into account.

However, layout specifications can also be undermined, whether by contemporaries or via new uses and re-uses at a later point in time, such that the approach of the history of reception can prove fruitful. This approach focuses less on the recipients conceived during production than on the historical audience, the users of an artefact and how they have dealt with and handled it.[77] This shows that intended modes of reception were not always realised. The users of the writing calendars, for example, sometimes had a very idiosyncratic way of dealing with the writing fields provided. In some surviving copies, one can observe how the designated writing fields remain empty and handwritten entries are only present at the bottom of the page, below the text field.[78] The relationship between handwriting and printing, or the constraint of the handwriting to the space indicated by the printing, varies both quantitatively and qualitatively.

---

[72] Different types of books can be provided with wide margins for such a productive reception: glossed Bible manuscripts (de Hamel 1984), legal codices (L'Engle/Gibbs 2001), encyclopaedic manuscripts (Meier 1997), or codices used in teaching (Wimmer 2018).
[73] On lining and page division, see also: Schneider 2014, 128–139.
[74] Cf. Tersch 2008, 19–21.
[75] Cf. Landwehr 2014, 22.
[76] On the subject of blank space, cf. Brendecke 2005, 91–105.
[77] See the overview under 'Rezeptionsgeschichte' (history of reception) in the *Metzler Lexikon Kunstwissenschaft* (ed. by Pfisterer 2011) as well as in the anthology of Bell et al. 2021.
[78] E.g., the calendar with the shelfmark 4° Nw 2404 [1571] from the library of the Germanisches Nationalmuseum, writing page for April.

Fig. 7: Aristotle, *Opera varia. Metaphysica cum glossis,* Berlin State Library—Prussian Cultural Heritage Foundation (SBB-PK), Departement of Manuscripts and Early Printed Books, Ms. lat. fol. 286, 1300, 111 leaves, fol. 37r. Public Domain Mark 1.0.

The layout and design of writing can increase legibility and thus facilitate the reading, understanding, or copying of a text in its reception. Yet these elements can also evoke reception practices that do not suggest reading as the first and most important task: inscribed artefacts, through their design, encourage successive decoding upon intensive viewing, in which potential meanings are not confined to the textual level alone but may also be grasped through a different kind of reception. Furthermore, layout and design can influence how an artefact is handled, in that the recipient must follow a certain procedure in order to grasp what is written. Finally, the layout of inscribed artefacts can also invite additional writing: as a mode of reception intended by or independent from production, and in ways conforming to the layout or undermining it.

Thesis 11
On multiple levels, layout and text type stand in a close connection that can be influenced from various sides.

When we look at layout, we can often immediately identify the type of text we are dealing with: a receipt with goods and prices listed; a poem with line divisions; a scholarly book (like this one) with a table of contents, section headings, and bibliography. In fact, layout sometimes defines text type: the specific formatting together with certain paratexts may indicate that a text is a letter, for instance. But what exactly is meant by 'text type'? Whereas the term 'genre', as it has traditional been understood, refers to a group of texts from a specific cultural and epochal context with certain common characteristics (for example, ancient Greek funerary inscriptions), 'text type' as a transcultural term is not related to any specific time or culture (for example, funerary inscriptions from antiquity to the present day).[79] The scientific, text-linguistic classification of texts into text types is fluid, broader, and ascertainable by a variety of criteria: characteristics and styles (descriptive, normative, informative, cognitive, aesthetic, etc.); the entities that produce the texts (individuals or institutions); the classes to which texts are assigned from an emic or etic perspective (letters, dedications, lists, administrative documents, poems, etc.); or even the medium itself.[80] These different criteria by which text types are classified can help to differentiate some of the content-based categories commonly used in the study of historical texts: a 'letter' may be written by an administrative, commercial, or religious institution; it may be informative as a personal communiqué, descriptive as a piece of administrative correspondence, or normative as an order from a superior. It can be an entirely fictional letter embedded

---

[79] Fricke 1981, 132–138; Kubina 2018, 151–152.
[80] Gansel/Jürgens 2009.

in a narrative, or a real letter containing a poem. Even though all these representatives of the text type 'letter' differ fundamentally according to content criteria, they can all emulate the same basic layout.

The process of developing a standardised layout associated with a particular type of text can be gradual or rapid, the result of institutional requirements ('top-down') or a self-propelled process ('bottom-up'). The standardised layouts that result from this process depend on a variety of factors: the nature of the writing supports, usability issues, or even the writing system itself (left-to-right, top-to-bottom, logographic or alphabetic, etc.).[81] For example, texts on coins, seals, and gems are typically short and/or closely associated with images due to the limited space available. In the case of scholarly texts, it is the user orientation that led to the development of layout elements such as large headings, rubrication, numbering, and the offsetting of section beginnings in the European Middle Ages. Decisions about layout are often not made by the authors of the texts themselves, but may be at the discretion of scribes, stonemasons, artists, patrons, or intermediaries. For example, the decision to leave large blank spaces in a manuscript could be made by a client or administrator who wanted to write extensive marginal notes in the book or fill in the gaps deliberately left in an administrative account (cf. Chapter 6 'Political Rule and Administration'), or it could be the decision of a scribe who wanted to show the importance of the text by means of this valuable 'wasted' space. As different as the actors involved and the driving factors of development may be, at a certain point a conventional layout, if not indeed a normative arrangement, emerges that is expected of a particular text type within a cultural group regardless of any further developments.

Some text types have had consistent layouts across wide geographical and temporal expanses. Postal arrival notices in Chinese administrative records written on the back of bamboo or wooden slat scrolls from the third century BCE to the first century CE had a fixed layout (Fig. 8).[82] In later copies of such notes, the arrival notes were prescribed as cloze text, or never even filled in. One of the possible reasons for this practice could have been the efforts to make the writing recognisable as an official document. However, this layout would only have had signal value for the staff who were familiar with the practice of such arrival notices. This information contained in the standardised layout would thus be exclusive, but not personal.

In other cases, this extra-textual information from the layout was accessible to the general public within a cultural area. Ancient Roman laws and decrees were often publicly displayed engraved on bronze tablets. The layout of such public copies was highly standardised, which required central organisation of the drafting process.[83] A consistent and orderly layout suggests institutional control over the materials and

---

[81] Ast/Attia/Jördens/Schneider 2015.
[82] For the image of Juyan no. 506.9b, see *Juyan Han jian*, 155; for Wuyiguangchang no. 412b, see *Changsha Wuyiguangchang Dong Han jiandu*, 88.
[83] Decorte 2015, 253.

Fig. 8a (left): Chinese wooden strip from Juyan, with the inscription: 十月壬戌卒周平以來；即日嗇夫尊發尉前 ('In the first year of the Yuanyan reign, in the tenth month, which began with a *jiawu* day, on the *wuwu* (twenty-ninth) day, soldier Zhou Ping presented this document; on the same day, overseer Zun opened this document in front of the commander.'). 12 BCE, 21.9 × 2.4 cm. Juyan, no. 506.9B (inv. no. H11678). © Courtesy of the Institute of History and Philology, Academia Sinica, Taiwan; Academia Sinica Centre for Digital Cultures (CC BY-NC-ND 3.0 TW).

Fig. 8b (right): Chinese wooden strip from Wuyi Square, with the inscription: 正月 日 郵人以來；史 白開 ('On [gap] day of the first month, the postman presented this document; the scribe [gap] reported and opened this document.'). 110 CE, 23.4 × 3 cm. Wuyiguangchang, no. 412B (inv. no. 2010CWJ1③:201-21), © Changsha Municipal Institute of Cultural Relics and Archaeology.

methods of textual production, thus conveying authority. The case of the *Res Gestae* of the first Roman emperor Augustus illustrates these ideas. Augustus's autobiographical account of his achievements was carved into a temple wall in a mainly Greek-speaking city, in both the original Latin text and a Greek translation. The question arises as to why the effort was made to also make a copy of the Latin text available to a Greek-speaking audience. Even if the inscription appeared as a kind of *lorem ipsum* or nonsensical text to the viewers, the inscription written in the language of the Roman centre of power nevertheless conveyed authority through the presence of a heading in large letters and the division of the text into columns, both characteristics of official government documents in this period.[84] The layout of magical writings (curses, prayers, fortune-telling, etc.) by private individuals or ritual specialists often has a comparable signal character, albeit working with contrary means. Here, traditional layouts are often almost entirely avoided, in accordance with the alterity of the texts and their intended readers, namely (according to modern understanding) supernatural powers.[85] Magical texts found on a multitude of artefacts from the ancient Mediterranean, for example, often used curved lines, changes in writing direction, and texts in 'image form' to communicate with the beyond.[86]

However, the correspondence that can frequently be observed between text type and layout does not apply without exception. This is the case, for example, with a demotic wisdom text that has been preserved in several manuscripts containing identical texts but different layouts, including the Insinger papyrus from the first century BCE (Fig. 9). The text consists of a series of maxims grouped into numbered chapters, each of which has an overarching theme, although the individual maxims contained therein rarely refer to one other. On the Insinger papyrus, this content structure is also reflected in the layout: each maxim is written on a single line.[87] This makes it possible to identify individual maxims quickly and structure the flow of reading. But not every manuscript in which this text has been preserved has this same layout. In the Carlsberg 2 papyrus, for example, the individual maxims are partly separated from each other by empty spaces and are not always accorded a single designated line. In this manuscript, however, the chapter numbers are highlighted in red ink, which makes it much easier to find where each chapter begins.[88]

The lack of correspondence between text type and layout is of particular interest when the typical layout of *another* text type has been deliberately followed. In the Han period in China (202 BCE–220 CE), for example, ritual texts such as the *Letter to the Underworld* sometimes adopted the form of administrative writings by imitating their

---

[84] Roels 2018; Sitz 2019.
[85] Kiyanrad/Theis/Willer 2018. See also Chapter 5 'Sacralisation'.
[86] Faraone 2012.
[87] Lichtheim 1983, 109–112.
[88] Quack 2019, 422–429; on the use of red ink in Egyptian texts, see Ast/Jördens/Quack/Sarri 2015, 310–311; on the influence of visual form on legibility, see Berti/Haß/Krüger/Ott 2015, 641–642.

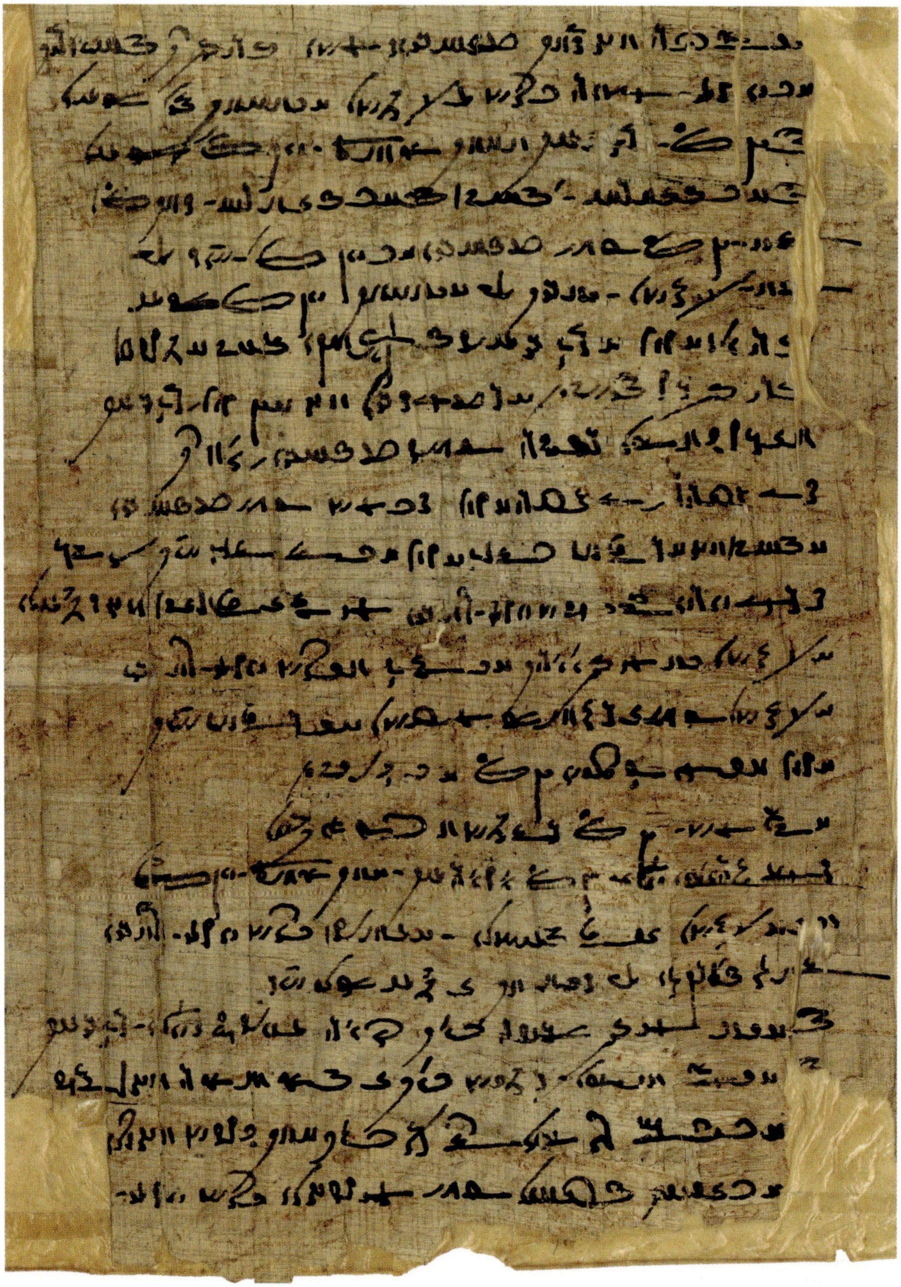

Fig. 9: Papyrus Insinger, a manuscript of the 'Great Demotic Book of Wisdom', recto col. 5; 1st century BCE, Akhmim, 18.5 × 24.9 cm (detail). Rijksmuseum van Oudheden, Leiden, F 95/5.1 vel 2.

layout and other material features. However, this does not mean that these two texts function in the same way or were composed in a similar context.[89] Similarly, if the text type is the same, the influence of the writing material on the layout may be evident, one such example being Latin military lists written on ostraca.[90] Although standardised in principle, such documents also show a tendency in various cases to adapt the layout to the writing surface. This can be seen in the differences between the standard layout of the military list Ch.L.A. I 7 I (written on papyrus) versus the irregular layout of the list O.BuNjem 8 (written on an ostracon), where the last lines do not follow the semi-columnar layout. In other cases, the layout remains basically the same, and it is the smaller writing frame of the ostracon that influences the text instead: the grid scheme in O.Claud. II 308 (ostracon) corresponds to that of Ch.L.A. I 7 V, but the words written in the small squares are altogether more abbreviated in the former than those in the latter. In still other cases, different layouts in the same type of text are due to different cultural imprints rather than to different materiality. Thus, the palaeographic background of scribes may be reflected in the layout of their letters. A random example of this would be the Latin letter SB XXVIII 17 098, which is characterised by a structured layout, as opposed to the Greek letter O.Krok. II 203, where the layout does not display any particular format.[91]

Finally, the actors engaged in writing the texts could consciously play with the layout. A Latin inscription found in Rome advertises the services of a stonemason's workshop.[92] However, the inscription begins with the letters *DM*: an abbreviation for the phrase *dis manibus* ('to the spirits of the dead'), a common beginning of Roman funerary texts. These letters 'D' and 'M' are usually arranged in grave inscriptions with a certain distance between them in a separate line. In such a layout, they produced a characteristic image of script that could be immediately recognised as such without actually reading a text. The layout of the inscription from Rome corresponds exactly to this layout and thus presents the inscription as an epitaph, and it is only on closer inspection/reading that we see the content specified as an advertisement of sculptors offering their services—for example, for the erection of a tomb.[93] This 'visual pun' shows in a unique way how aware stone sculptors were of the importance of text layouts and associated text types.

In summary, we can state the following about the relationship between layout and text type. Instances of writing that belong to the same text type are often linked together through the similarity of their respective layouts, sometimes across cultural

---

89 Lai 2015.
90 Bagnall 2011, 117–137; Sarri 2018, 77–79; Caputo/Lougovaya 2021.
91 For images of the mentioned artefacts, see: Ch.L.A. I, 15–16 (for Ch.L.A. I 7 I and Ch.L.A. I 7 V); O.BuNjem, 126 (for O.BuNjem 8); O.Claud. II, pl. 39 (for O.Claud. II 308); Bülow-Jacobsen 2003, 425, fig. 223 (for SB XXVIII 17 098); Bülow-Jacobsen/Fournet/Redon 2019, 92 (for O.Krok. II 203).
92 CIL VI 9556.
93 Kruschwitz 2008.

and epochal boundaries. In this way, the layout acquires a signal character for the recipient with regard to the expected content, type, and character of the respective text, even without any actual reading process taking place. The processes of standardisation responsible for such correspondences are partly the result of the institutionally prescribed setting of norms (for example, in the case of ruling and administrative writings), and partly the result of their own dynamics in the interaction of the various actors involved in the production of what is written. But the material nature of the writing supports—for example, their small format in the case of coin or gem inscriptions—can also be responsible for correspondences between layout and text type. Admittedly, a correspondence between layout and text type does not apply without exception; but individual actors are able to use the (for the most part) not strictly prescriptive character of this correspondence in order to exploit the standardised character of the layouts of certain text types, the expectation horizon set by this, and the opened-up fields of connotation pertaining to layouts typical of text types as a special means of design: design marked by a certain playful quality, and sometimes characterised by the deliberate thwarting of these same correspondences.

Bibliography

Abbreviations and Sigla

Ch.L.A. I — *Chartae Latinae Antiquiores I*, ed. by Albert Bruckner and Robert Marichal, Olten/Lausanne, 1954.

CIL VI — *Corpus Inscriptionum Latinarum VI: Inscriptiones Urbis Romae Latinae*, ed. by Wilhelm Henze, Giovanni Battista de Rossi, Eugen Bormann, Christian Huelsen, and Johann Martin Bang, Berlin 1876–2000.

IG I^3,1 — *Inscriptiones Graecae*, vol. I, ed. 3: *Inscriptiones Atticae Euclidis anno anteriores*, fasc. 1: *Decreta et tabulae magistratuum*, ed. by David Lewis, Berlin 1981.

IG V,2 — *Inscriptiones Graecae*, vol. V: *Inscriptiones Laconiae Messeniae Arcadiae*, fasc. 2: *Inscriptiones Arcadiae*, ed. by Friedrich Hiller von Gaertringen, Berlin 1913.

O.BuNjem — *Les Ostraca de Bu Njem*, ed. by Robert Marichal (Libya Antiqua, Suppl. VII), Tripolis 1992.

O.Claud. II — *Mons Claudianus. Ostraca graeca et latina II*, ed. by Jean Bingen, Adam Bülow-Jacobsen, Walter E. H. Cockle, Hélène Cuvigny, François Kayser, and Wilfrid Van Rengen, Cairo 1997.

O.Krok. II — *Ostraca de Krokodilô II: La correspondance privée et les réseaux personnels de Philoklès, Apollôs et Ischyras*, ed. by Adam Bülow-Jacobsen, Jean-Luc Fournet, and Bérangère Redon (Fouilles de l'Ifao 81), Cairo 2019.

SB XXVIII — *Sammelbuch griechischer Urkunden aus Ägypten*, vol. XXVIII, ed. by Andrea Jördens, vol. ed. by Rodney Ast, Wiesbaden 2013.

SEG 27 — *Supplementum Epigraphicum Graecum*, vol. XXVII (1977), ed. by H. W. Pleket and R. S. Stroud, Amsterdam 1980.

Sources

Changsha Wuyi Guangchang Dong Han jiandu 長沙五一廣場東漢簡牘 (The Eastern Han Ledgers and Tablets from Wuyi Square in Changsha), vol. 2, ed. by Changsha shi wenwu kaogu yanjiusuo 長沙市文物考古研究所 (Changsha City Institute for Cultural Antiquities and Archaeology) et al., Shanghai 2018.

Juyan Han jian 居延漢簡 (The Han Ledgers of Juyan), vol. 4, ed. by Jiandu zhengli xiaozu 簡牘整理小組 (Ledger and Tablet Editorial Team), Taipei 2017.

Libri Carolini: Opus Caroli regis contra synodum (Libri Carolini), ed. by Ann Freeman with the assistance of Paul Meyvaert (Monumenta Germaniae Historica: Concilia, vol. 2, Suppl. 1), Hannover 1998.

Poetae Latini aevi Carolini, vol. 1, ed. by Ernst Dümmler (Monumenta Germaniae Historica: Poetae Latini medii aevi 1), Berlin 1881.

Research Literature

Assmann, Aleida (2015), *Im Dickicht der Zeichen,* Berlin.

Assmann, Jan (2012), "Schriftbildlichkeit. Etymographie und Ikonographie", in: Sybille Krämer, Eva Cancik-Kirschbaum, and Rainer Totzke (eds.), *Schriftbildlichkeit. Wahrnehmbarkeit, Materialität und Operativität von Notationen* (Schriftbildlichkeit 1), Berlin, 139–145.

Ast, Rodney/Attia, Elodie/Jördens, Andrea/Schneider, Christian (2015), "Layouten und Gestalten", in: Thomas Meier, Michael R. Ott, and Rebecca Sauer (eds.), *Materiale Textkulturen. Konzepte – Materialien – Praktiken* (Materiale Textkulturen 1), Berlin/Munich/Boston, 597–609, https://doi.org/10.1515/9783110371291.597.

Ast, Rodney/Jördens, Andrea/Quack, Joachim Friedrich/Sarri, Antonia (2015), "Papyrus", in: Thomas Meier, Michael R. Ott, and Rebecca Sauer (eds.), *Materiale Textkulturen. Konzepte – Materialien – Praktiken* (Materiale Textkulturen 1), Berlin/Munich/Boston, 307–321, https://doi.org/10.1515/9783110371291.307.

Attia, Élodie (2015), *The Masorah of Elijah ha-Naqdan. An Edition of Ashkenazic Micrographical Notes* (Materiale Textkulturen 11), Berlin/Boston, https://doi.org/10.1515/9783110417920.

Bagnall, Roger S. (2011), *Everyday Writing in the Graeco-Roman East* (Sather Classical Lectures 69), Berkeley/Los Angeles.

Bartoli Langeli, Attilio/Giovè Marchioli, Nicoletta (1996), "Le scritte incise della Fontana Maggiore", in: Carlo Santini (ed.), *Il linguaggio figurativo della fontana maggiore di Perugia,* Perugia, 163–195.

Becht-Jördens, Gereon (2014), "Schrift im Mittelalter – Zeichen des Heils", in: Joachim Friedrich Quack and Daniela Christina Luft (eds.), *Erscheinungsformen und Handhabung Heiliger Schriften* (Materiale Textkulturen 5), Berlin/Munich/Boston, 245–310, https://doi.org/10.1515/9783110371277.245.

Becker, Julia/Licht, Tino/Schneidmüller, Bernd (2015), "Pergament", in: Thomas Meier, Michael R. Ott, and Rebecca Sauer (eds.), *Materiale Textkulturen. Konzepte – Materialien – Praktiken* (Materiale Textkulturen 1), Berlin/Munich/Boston, 337–347, https://doi.org/10.1515/9783110371291.337.

Bedos-Rezak, Brigitte/Hamburger, Jeffrey F. (eds.) (2016), *Sign and Design. Script as Image in Cross-Cultural Perspective (300–1600 CE)* (Dumbarton Oaks Symposia and Colloquia), Washington D. C.

Bell, Peter/Fehrmann, Anje/Müller, Rebecca/Olariu, Dominic (eds.) (2021), *Maraviglia. Rezeptionsgeschichte(n) von der Antike bis in die Moderne,* Vienna/Cologne/Weimar.

Berti, Irene/Bolle, Katharina/Opdenhoff, Fanny/Stroth, Fabian (eds.) (2017), *Writing Matters. Presenting and Perceiving Monumental Inscriptions in Antiquity and the Middle Ages* (Materiale Textkulturen 14), Berlin/Boston, https://doi.org/10.1515/9783110534597.

Berti, Irene/Haß, Christian D./Krüger, Kristina/Ott, Michael R. (2015), "Lesen und Entziffern", in: Thomas Meier, Michael R. Ott, and Rebecca Sauer (eds.), *Materiale Textkulturen. Konzepte – Materialien – Praktiken* (Materiale Textkulturen 1), Berlin/Munich/Boston, 639–650, https://doi.org/10.1515/9783110371291.639.

Berti, Irene/Keil, Wilfried E./Miglus, Peter A. (2015), "Meißeln", in: Thomas Meier, Michael R. Ott, and Rebecca Sauer (eds.), *Materiale Textkulturen. Konzepte – Materialien – Praktiken* (Materiale Textkulturen 1), Berlin/Munich/Boston, 503–518, https://doi.org/10.1515/9783110371291.503.

Bolle, Katharina (2020), *Materialität und Präsenz spätantiker Inschriften. Eine Studie zum Wandel der Inschriftenkultur in den italienischen Provinzen* (Materiale Textkulturen 25), Berlin/Boston, https://doi.org/10.1515/9783110633566.

Brendecke, Arndt (2005), "'Durchschossene Exemplare'. Über eine Schnittstelle zwischen Handschrift und Druck", in: *Archiv für Geschichte des Buchwesens* 59, 50–64.

Bülow-Jacobsen, Adam (2003), "The Traffic on the Road and the Provisioning of the Stations", in: Hélène Cuvigny (ed.), *La route de Myos Hormos. L'armée romaine dans le désert Oriental d'Égypte. Praesidia du désert de Bérénice I* (Fouilles de l'IFAO 48), Cairo, 399–426.

Campbell, Lorne (1998), *The Fifteenth Century Netherlandish Schools: National Gallery Catalogues*, London.

Campe, Rüdiger (1991), "Die Schreibszene. Schreiben", in: Hans Ulrich Gumbrecht and Karl Ludwig Pfeiffer (eds.), *Paradoxien, Dissonanzen, Zusammenbrüche, Situationen offener Epistemologie*, Frankfurt (Main), 759–772.

Cancik-Kirschbaum, Eva/Mahr, Bernd (2005), "Anordnung und ästhetisches Profil. Die Herausbildung einer universellen Kulturtechnik in der Frühgeschichte der Schrift", in: Birgit Schneider (ed.), *Diagramme und bildtextile Ordnungen* (Bildwelten des Wissens 3,1), Berlin, 97–114.

Caputo, Clementina/Lougovaya, Julia (eds.) (2021), *Using Ostraca in the Ancient World. New Discoveries and Methodologies* (Materiale Textkulturen 32), Berlin/Boston, https://doi.org/10.1515/9783110712902.

Chiarini, Sara (2018), *The So-Called Nonsense Inscriptions on Ancient Greek Vases between Paideia and Paidiá,* Leiden.

Clanchy, Michael T. (2013), *From Memory to Written Record. England 1066–1307,* Chichester.

Crivello, Fabrizio/Denoël, Charlotte/Orth, Peter (2011), *Das Godescalc-Evangelistar. Eine Prachthandschrift für Karl den Großen,* Darmstadt.

Dadaki, Stavroula (2011), "Part of a Mosaic Floor", in: Anastasia Lazaridou (ed.), *Transition to Christianity: Art of Late Antiquity, 3rd – 7th Century AD* (Exhibition Catalogue, Onassis Cultural Center, New York City, 7. Dezember 2011 – 14. Mai 2012), New York, 135, Kat. Nr. 96.

Debiais, Vincent (2017), *La croisée des signes: L'écriture et les images médiévales (800–1200),* Paris.

Decorte, Robrecht (2015), "Publishing Laws: An Investigation of Layout and Epigraphic Conventions in Roman Statutes", in: *Zeitschrift für Papyrologie und Epigraphik* 195, 243–254.

Degler, Adam (2017), "Aureus of Postumus with the Owner's Graffito (Gounthiou)", in: Maria Caccamo Caltabiano (ed.), *XV International Numismatic Congress. Taormina 2015. Proceedings, vol. II,* Rome/Messina, 723–726.

Dhanens, Elisabeth (1980), *Hubert und Jan van Eyck,* Königstein.

Dietrich, Nikolaus (2017), "Framing Archaic Greek Sculpture: Figure, Ornament and Script", in: Michael S. Squire and Verity J. Platt (eds.), *The Frame in Classical Art: A Cultural History,* Cambridge, 270–316.

Dietrich, Nikolaus (2018), *Das Attribut als Problem. Eine bildwissenschaftliche Untersuchung zur griechischen Kunst,* Berlin/Munich/Boston.

Dietrich, Nikolaus (2020), "Überlegungen zum Layout griechischer Statueninschriften ausgehend von der Nikandre-Weihung", in: Nikolaus Dietrich, Johannes Fouquet, and Corinna Reinhardt, *Schreiben auf statuarischen Monumenten. Aspekte materialer Textkultur in archaischer und frühklassischer Zeit* (Materiale Textkulturen 29), Berlin/Boston, 147–195, https://doi.org/10.1515/9783110645422-004.

Dietrich, Nikolaus/Fouquet, Johannes (eds.) (2022), *Image, Text, Stone. Intermedial Perspectives on Graeco-Roman Sculpture* (Materiale Textkulturen 36), Berlin/Boston, https://doi.org/10.1515/9783110775761.

Dietrich, Nikolaus/Fouquet, Johannes/Reinhardt, Corinna (2020), *Schreiben auf statuarischen Monumenten. Aspekte materialer Textkultur in archaischer und frühklassischer Zeit* (Materiale Textkulturen 29), Berlin/Boston, https://doi.org/10.1515/9783110645422.

Embach, Michael/Moulin, Claudine/Wolter-von dem Knesebeck, Harald (eds.) (2019), *Die Handschriften der Hofschule Kaiser Karls des Großen. Individuelle Gestalt und europäisches Kulturerbe*, Trier.

Enderwitz, Susanne/Opdenhoff, Fanny/Schneider, Christian (2015), "Auftragen, Malen und Zeichnen", in: Thomas Meier, Michael R. Ott, and Rebecca Sauer (eds.), *Materiale Textkulturen. Konzepte – Materialien – Praktiken* (Materiale Textkulturen 1), Berlin/Munich/Boston, 471–484, https://doi.org/10.1515/9783110371291.471.

Faraone, Christopher A. (2012), *Vanishing Acts on Ancient Greek Amulets: From Oral Performance to Visual Design*, London.

Feld, Helmut (1990), *Der Ikonoklasmus des Westens* (Studies in the History of Christian Thought 41), Leiden.

Feraudi-Gruénais, Francisca (2017), "Das synaktive Potential von Beischriften", in: Irene Berti, Katharina Bolle, Fanny Opdenhoff, and Fabian Stroth (eds.), *Writing Matters. Presenting and Perceiving Monumental Inscriptions in Antiquity and the Middle Ages* (Materiale Textkulturen 14), Berlin/Boston, 43–76, https://doi.org/10.1515/9783110534597-004.

Foucault, Michel (1973), *Ceci n'est pas une pipe. Deux lettres et quatre dessins de René Magritte*, Montpellier.

Fouquet, Johannes (2020), "Dekorative (Un)fertigkeit. Zum Prozess des Beschreibens auf einer Gruppe von spätarchaisch-frühklassischen Statuenbasen aus Athen", in: Nikolaus Dietrich, Johannes Fouquet, and Corinna Reinhardt, *Schreiben auf statuarischen Monumenten. Aspekte materialer Textkultur in archaischer und frühklassischer Zeit* (Materiale Textkulturen 29), Berlin/Boston, 103–146, https://doi.org/10.1515/9783110645422-003.

Frese, Tobias (2006), *Die Bildkritik des Bernhard von Clairvaux. Die Apologia im monastischen Diskurs*, Bamberg.

Frese, Tobias (2014), "'Denn der Buchstabe tötet' – Reflexionen zur Schriftpräsenz aus mediävischer Perspektive", in: Tobias Frese, Wilfried E. Keil, and Kristina Krüger (eds.), *Verborgen, unsichtbar, unlesbar – zur Problematik restringierter Schriftpräsenz* (Materiale Textkulturen 2), Berlin/Boston 2014, 1–16, https://doi.org/10.1515/9783110353587.1.

Frese, Tobias/Horstmann, Lisa/Wenig, Franziska (eds.) (2024), *Sakrale Schriftbilder. Zur ikonischen Präsenz des Geschriebenen im mittelalterlichen Kirchenraum* (Materiale Textkulturen 42), Berlin/Boston, https://doi.org/10.1515/9783111304496.

Frese, Tobias/Keil, Wilfried E./Krüger, Kristina (eds.) (2014), *Verborgen, unsichtbar, unlesbar – zur Problematik restringierter Schriftpräsenz* (Materiale Textkulturen 2), Berlin/Boston, https://doi.org/10.1515/9783110353587.

Fricke, Harald (1981), *Norm und Abweichung: Eine Philosophie der Literatur*, Munich.

Fruhstorfer, Martin (1987), "Fiktionssprünge in Van Eycks Bildnis des sogenannten Timotheos", in: *Oud Holland* 101 (4), 277–279.

Gansel, Christina/Jürgens, Frank (2009), *Textlinguistik und Textgrammatik. Eine Einführung,* 3rd ed., Göttingen.
Gerleigner, Georg S. (2016), "Tracing Letters on the Eurymedon Vase. On the Importance of Placement of Vase-Inscriptions", in: Dimitrios Yatromanolakis (ed.), *Epigraphy of Art. Ancient Greek Vase-Inscriptions and Vase-Paintings,* Oxford, 165–184.
Gertz, Jan Christian/Schultz, Sandra/Šimek, Jakub/Wallenwein, Kirsten (2015), "Abschreiben und Kopieren", in: Thomas Meier, Michael R. Ott, and Rebecca Sauer (eds.), *Materiale Textkulturen. Konzepte – Materialien – Praktiken* (Materiale Textkulturen 1), Berlin/Munich/Boston, 585–595, https://doi.org/10.1515/9783110371291.585.
Gibhardt, Boris R./Grave, Johannes (eds.) (2018), *Schrift im Bild. Rezeptionsästhetische Perspektiven auf Text-Bild-Relationen in den Künsten* (Ästhetische Eigenzeiten 10), Hannover.
Gludovatz, Kathrin (2005), "Der Name am Rahmen, der Maler im Bild. Künstlerselbstverständnis und Produktionskommentar in den Signaturen Jan van Eycks", in: *Wiener Jahrbuch für Kunstgeschichte* 54, 115–175.
Grube, Gernot/Kogge, Werner (2005), "Zur Einleitung: Was ist Schrift?", in: Gernot Grube, Werner Kogge, and Sybille Krämer (eds.), *Schrift. Kulturtechnik zwischen Auge, Hand und Maschine,* Munich, 9–19.
Haendler, Gert (1958), *Epochen karolingischer Theologie. Eine Untersuchung über die karolingischen Gutachten zum byzantinischen Bilderstreit,* Berlin.
Halperin, Dalia-Ruth (2021), "Micrography Mounted Falconers: An Exegetic Text and Image", in: Hanna Liss (ed.), *Figurative Masorah in Western European Manuscripts,* Frankfurt (Main) et al., 59–101.
Hamburger, Jeffrey F. (2011), *The Iconicity of Script. Writing as Image in the Middle Ages* (Word & Image 27.3), Abingdon et al.
Hamburger, Jeffrey F. (2014), *Script as Image* (Corpus of Illuminated Manuscripts 21), Paris et al.
Hamel, Christopher de (1984), *Glossed Books of the Bible and the Origins of the Paris Booktrade,* Woodbridge.
Harbison, Craig (2012), *Jan van Eyck: The Play of Realism,* 2nd ed., London.
Horstmann, Lisa (2022), *Ikonographie in Bewegung. Die Überlieferungsgeschichte der Bilder des Welschen Gastes,* Heidelberg 2022, https://doi.org/10.11588/heibooks.1004.
Job, Jon (2013), [Art.] "Karolingische Schriftenhierarchie", in: *Wörterbücher zur Sprach- und Kommunikationswissenschaft (WSK) Online,* https://www.degruyter.com/database/WSK/entry/wsk_id_wsk_artikel_artikel_21970/html (accessed 10/9/2021).
Keesling, Catherine (2017), *Early Greek Portraiture. Monuments and Histories,* Cambridge.
Keil, Wilfried E./Kiyanrad, Sarah/Theis, Christoffer/Willer, Laura (eds.) (2018), *Zeichentragende Artefakte im sakralen Raum. Zwischen Präsenz und UnSichtbarkeit* (Materiale Textkulturen 20), Berlin/Boston, https://doi.org/10.1515/9783110619928.
Kemmers, Fleur/Scholz, Markus (2017), "Ein spezifischer Wert: Ein republikanischer Denar mit Graffiti aus Groß-Rohrheim (Lkr. Bergstraße)", in: Udo Reker (ed.), *Iucundi acti labores. Festschrift für Egon Schallmayer anlässlich des 65. Geburtstags* (Jahrbuch für Archäologie und Paläontologie in Hessen, Sonderbd. 5), Wiesbaden, 124–128.
Kirchner, Johannes (1935), *Imagines inscriptionum Atticarum. Ein Bilderatlas epigraphischer Denkmäler Attikas,* Berlin.
Kiyanrad Sarah/Theis, Christoffer/Willer, Laura (eds.) (2018), *Bild und Schrift auf 'magischen' Artefakten* (Materiale Textkulturen 19), Berlin/Boston, https://doi.org/10.1515/9783110604337.
Kneißl, Peter (1969), *Die Siegestitulatur der römischen Kaiser. Untersuchungen zu den Siegerbeinamen des ersten und zweiten Jahrhunderts* (Hypomnemata 25), Göttingen.

Krämer, Sybille (2005), "'Operationsraum Schrift'. Über einen Perspektivwechsel in der Betrachtung von Schrift", in: Gernot Grube, Werner Kogge, and Sybille Krämer (eds.), *Schrift. Kulturtechnik zwischen Auge, Hand und Maschine,* Munich, 23–57.

Krämer, Sibylle (2006), "Zur Sichtbarkeit der Schrift oder: Die Visualisierung des Unsichtbaren in der operativen Schrift. Zehn Thesen", in: Susanne Strätling and Georg Witte (eds.), *Die Sichtbarkeit der Schrift,* Munich, 75–84.

Krämer, Sybille/Cancik-Kirschbaum, Eva/Totzke, Rainer (2012), *Schriftbildlichkeit. Wahrnehmbarkeit, Materialität und Operativität von Notationen* (Schriftbildlichkeit 1), Berlin.

Krämer, Sybille/Totzke, Rainer (2012), "Einleitung: Was bedeutet Schriftbildlichkeit?", in: Sybille Krämer, Eva Cancik-Kirschbaum, and Rainer Totzke (eds.), *Schriftbildlichkeit. Wahrnehmbarkeit, Materialität und Operativität von Notationen* (Schriftbildlichkeit 1), Berlin, 13–35.

Kries, Friedrich Wilhelm von (1985), *Thomasin von Zerclaere. Der Welsche Gast,* vol. 4: *Die Illustrationen des Welschen Gasts: Kommentar mit Analyse der Bildinhalte und den Varianten der Schriftbandtexte. Verzeichnisse, Namenregister, Bibliographie* (Göppinger Arbeiten zur Germanistik 425/IV), Göppingen, https://doi.org/10.11588/diglit.52818.

Kruschwitz, Peter (2008), "Patterns of Text Layout in Pompeian Verse Inscriptions", in: *Studia Philologica Valentina* 11 (8), 225–264.

Kubina, Krystina (2018), "Manuel Philes – A Begging Poet?", in: Andreas Rhoby and Nikos Zagklas (eds.), *Middle and Late Byzantine Poetry: Texts and Contexts,* Turnhout, 147–181.

Kypta, Ulla (2015), "Selbstreproduzierende Abrechnungen. Was das Layout der englischen Pipe Rolls des 12. Jahrhunderts über ihren Zweck verrät", in: Gudrun Gleba and Niels Petersen (eds.), *Wirtschafts- und Rechnungsbücher des Mittelalters und der frühen Neuzeit. Formen und Methoden der Rechnungslegung: Städte, Klöster, Kaufleute,* Göttingen, 273–293.

L'Engle, Susan/Gibbs, Robert (2001), *Illuminating the Law. Legal Manuscripts in Cambridge Collections* (Ausstellungskatalog), London/Turnout.

Lai, Guolong (2015), *Excavating the Afterlife: The Archaeology of Early Chinese Religion,* Seattle.

Landwehr, Achim (2014), *Geburt der Gegenwart. Eine Geschichte der Zeit im 17. Jahrhundert,* Frankfurt (Main).

Leatherbury, Sean V. (2020), *Inscribing Faith in Late Antiquity. Between Reading and Seeing,* New York.

Lewis, Susanne (1980), "Sacred Calligraphy: The Chi Rho Page in the Book of Kells", *Traditio* 36, 139–158.

Licht, Tino (2013), "Beobachtungen zum Lorscher Skriptorium in karolingischer Zeit", in: Julia Becker, Tino Licht, and Stefan Weinfurter (eds.), *Karolingische Klöster. Wissenstransfer und kulturelle Innovation* (Materiale Textkulturen 4), Berlin/Munich/Boston 2014, 145–162, https://doi.org/10.1515/9783110371222.145.

Lichtheim, Miriam (1983), *Late Egyptian Wisdom Literature in the International Context,* Freiburg (Breisgau)/Göttingen.

Liss, Hanna (2018), "Aschkenasische Bibelcodices als Träger exegetischer und theologischer Geheimnisse", in: Ursula Schattner-Rieser and Josef M. Oesch (eds.), *700 Jahre jüdische Präsenz in Tirol. Geschichte der Fragmente, Fragmente der Geschichte,* Innsbruck, 203–223.

Liss, Hanna (2021), "Negation oder Transformation? Illustrative Auflösung masoretischer Listen in einem mittelalterlichen hebräischen Manuskript", in: Şirin Dadaş and Christian Vogel (eds.), *(Nicht)Wissen – Dynamiken der Negation in vormodernen Kulturen,* Wiesbaden, 313–330.

Lohmann, Polly (2017), *Graffiti als Interaktionsform. Geritzte Inschriften in den Wohnhäusern Pompejis* (Materiale Textkulturen 16), Berlin/Boston, https://doi.org/10.1515/9783110574289.

Lorenz, Katharina (2010), "'Dialectics at a Standstill': Archaic Kouroi-cum-Epigram as I-Box", in: Manuel Baumbach, Andrej Petrovic, and Ivana Petrovic (eds.), *Archaic and Classical Greek Epigram,* Cambridge, 131–148.

Meier, Christel (1997), "Illustration und Textcorpus. Zu kommunikations- und ordnungsfunktionalen Aspekten der Bilder in den mittelalterlichen Enzyklopädiehandschriften", in: *Frühmittelalterliche Studien* 31, 1–31.

Mersmann, Birgit (2015), *Schriftikonik. Bildphänomen der Schrift in kultur- und medienkomparativer Perspektive,* Paderborn.

Mitalaité, Kristina (2007), *Philosophie et théologie de l'image dans les Libri Carolini* (Collection des études augustiniennes: Série Moyen Âge et temps modernes 43), Paris.

Montandon, Alain (ed.) (1990), *Iconotextes. Colloque international à l'Université Blaise Pascal du 17 au 19 mars 1988,* Paris.

Müller, Rebecca (2002), *Sic hostes Ianua frangit. Spolien und Trophäen im mittelalterlichen Genua,* Marburg 2002.

Newby, Zahra/Leader-Newby, Ruth (eds.) (2007), *Art and Inscriptions in the Ancient World,* Cambridge.

Opdenhoff, Fanny (2021), *Die Stadt als beschriebener Raum. Die Beispiele Pompeji und Herculaneum* (Materiale Textkulturen 33), Berlin/Boston, https://doi.org/10.1515/9783110722758.

Ott, Michael R./Kiyanrad, Sarah (2015), "Geschriebenes", in: Thomas Meier, Michael R. Ott, and Rebecca Sauer (eds.), *Materiale Textkulturen. Konzepte – Materialien – Praktiken* (Materiale Textkulturen 1), Berlin/Munich/Boston, 157–168, https://doi.org/10.1515/9783110371291.157.

Ott, Norbert H. (2002), "Mise en page. Zur ikonischen Struktur der Illustrationen von Thomasins 'Welschem Gast'", in: Horst Wenzel and Christina Lechtermann (eds.), *Beweglichkeit der Bilder. Text und Imagination in den illustrierten Handschriften des 'Welschen Gastes' von Thomasin von Zerclaere* (Pictura et poesis 15), Cologne, 33–64.

Panofsky, Erwin (1949), "Who is Jan Van Eyck's 'Tymotheos'?", in: *Journal of the Warburg and Courtauld Institutes* 12, 80–82.

Pappas, Alexandra (2012), "The Treachery of Verbal Images: Viewing the Greek Technopaegnia", in: Jan Kwapisz, David Petrain, and Mikolaj Szymanski (eds.), *The Muse at Play: Riddles and Wordplay in Greek and Latin Poetry,* Berlin/Boston, 199–224.

Paviot, Jacques (1995), "The Sitter for Jan van Eyck's 'Leal Sovvenir'", in: *Journal of the Warburg and Courtauld Institutes* 58, 210–215.

Pelekanides, Stylianos M. (1975), "Ἀνασκαφή Φιλίππων", in: *Πρακτικά της εν Αθήναις Αρχαιολογικής Εταιρείας* 130, 91–102.

Petrucci, Armando (1986), *La scrittura: Ideologia e rappresentazione,* Turin.

Pfisterer, Ulrich (ed.) (2011), *Metzler Lexikon Kunstwissenschaft,* 2nd ed., Stuttgart.

Pilhofer, Peter (2009), *Philippi,* vol. II: *Katalog der Inschriften von Philippi* (Wissenschaftliche Untersuchungen zum Neuen Testament 119), 2nd ed., Tübingen.

Quack, Joachim Friedrich (2019), "Neue Fragmente des großen demotischen Weisheitsbuches mit einer Kollation der bereits publizierten Fragmente", in: Joachim Friedrich Quack and Kim Ryholt (eds.), *Demotic Literary Texts From Tebtunis and Beyond* (The Carlsberg Papyri 11), Copenhagen, 421–469.

Rehm, Ulrich/Simonis, Linda (2019), "Formen und Wirkungsweisen der Inschrift in epochen- und fächerübergreifender Perspektive. Umrisse eines Forschungsprogramms", in: Ulrich Rehm and Linda Simonis (eds.), *Poetik der Inschrift,* Heidelberg, 7–23.

Reudenbach, Bruno (1998), *Das Godescalc-Evangelistar: Ein Buch für die Reformpolitik Karls des Großen,* Frankfurt (Main).

Reudenbach, Bruno (2021), "Enigmatic Calligraphy: Lettering as Visualized Hermeneutic of Sacred Scripture", in: Jörg B. Quenzer (ed.), *Exploring Written Artefacts. Objects, Methods, and Concepts,* vol. 2 (Studies in Manuscript Cultures, vol. 25), Berlin/Boston, 773–794.

Riccioni, Stefano (2008), "Épiconographie de l'art roman en France et en Italie (Bourgogne/Latium). L'art médiéval en tant que discours visuel et la naissance d'un nouveau langage", in: *Bulletin du entre d'études médiévales d'Auxerre* 12, 1–12.

Rieß, Peter/Fisch, Stefan/Strohschneider, Peter (1995), *Prolegomena zu einer Theorie der Fußnote*, Münster.

Roels, Evelien (2018), "The Queen of Inscriptions Contextualized. The Presence of Civic Inscriptions in the Pronaos of Ancient Temples in Hellenistic and Roman Asia Minor (4th cent. BCE – 2nd cent. CE)", in: Emilie van Opstall (ed.), *Sacred Thresholds. The Door to the Sanctuary in Late Antiquity,* Leiden, 221–253.

Roland, Martin (1991), *Illustrierte Weltchroniken bis in die zweite Hälfte des 4. Jahrhunderts,* Vienna.

Ronig, Franz (1984), "Die Buchmalerei-Schule des Trierer Erzbischofs Kuno von Falkenstein. Ein Forschungsbericht", in: Michael Berens, Claudia Maas, and Franz Ronig (eds.), *Florilegium artis. Beiträge zur Kunstwissenschaft und Denkmalpflege, Festschrift für Wolfgang Götz,* Saarbrücken, 111–115.

Roth, Michael (ed.) (2010), *Schrift als Bild* (Ausstellungskatalog Kupferstichkabinett Staatliche Museen zu Berlin 29.10.2010 – 23.1.2011), Petersberg.

Sarri, Antonia (2018), *Material Aspects of Letter Writing in the Graeco-Roman World,* (Materiale Textkulturen 12), Berlin/Boston, https://doi.org/10.1515/9783110426953.

Saurma-Jeltsch, Lieselotte (1994), "Karolingische Bildtheologie. Zur karolingischen Haltung gegenüber dem Bilderstreit", in: Johannes Fried, Rainer Koch, Lieselotte E. Saurma-Jeltsch, and Andreas Thiel (eds.), *794 – Karl der Große in Frankfurt am Main. Ein König bei der Arbeit* (Ausstellungskatalog zum 1200-Jahre Jubiläum der Stadt Frankfurt am Main im Historischen Museum Frankfurt am Main, 18.5. – 28.8.1994), Sigmaringen, 69–72.

Saurma-Jeltsch, Lieselotte (1997), "Das Bild in der Worttheologie Karl des Großen. Zur Christologie in karolingischen Miniaturen", in: Rainer Berndt SJ (ed.), *Das Frankfurter Konzil 794. Kristallisationspunkt karolingischer Kultur,* vol. 2: *Kultur und Theologie* (Quellen und Abhandlungen zur mittelrheinischen Kirchengeschichte 80/2), Mainz, 635–675 and 1069–1079.

Saurma-Jeltsch, Lieselotte (2014), "Der Einzelne im Verbund. Kooperationsmodelle in der spätmittelalterlichen Buchherstellung", in: Armand Tif (ed.), *Wege zum illuminierten Buch. Herstellungsbedingungen für Buchmalerei in Mittelalter und früher Neuzeit,* Böhlau, 177–201.

Schneider, Christian/Schmidt, Peter/Šimek, Jakub/Horstmann, Lisa (eds.) (2022), *Der 'Welsche Gast' des Thomasin von Zerklaere. Neue Perspektiven auf eine alte Verhaltenslehre in Text und Bild* (Kulturelles Erbe: Materialität – Text – Edition 2), Heidelberg, https://doi.org/10.17885/heiup.545.

Schneider, Karin (2014), *Paläographie und Handschriftenkunde für Germanisten. Eine Einführung,* 3rd ed., Berlin/Boston.

Scholz, Sebastian (2015), "Bemerkungen zur Bildungsentwicklung im Frühen Mittelalter. Zusammenfassung", in: Julia Becker, Tino Licht, and Stefan Weinfurter (eds.), *Karolingische Köster. Wissenstransfer und kulturelle Innovation* (Materiale Textkulturen 4), Berlin/Munich/Boston 2014, 275–289, https://doi.org/10.1515/9783110371222.275.

Sitz, Anna M. (2019), "Beyond Spolia: A New Approach to Old Inscriptions in Late Antique Anatolia", in: *American Journal of Archaeology* 123 (4), 643–674.

Squire, Michael J. (2009), *Image and Text in Graeco-Roman Antiquity,* Cambridge.

Squire, Michael/Wienand, Johannes (eds.) (2017), *'Morphogrammata' / The Lettered Art of Optatian. Figuring Cultural Transformations in the Age of Constantine* (Morphomata 33), Paderborn.

Starkey, Kathryn (2022), "Die Entstehung eines Nachschlagewerks?", in: Christian Schneider, Peter Schmidt, Jakub Šimek, and Lisa Horstmann (eds.), *Der 'Welsche Gast' des Thomasin von Zerklaere. Neue Perspektiven auf eine alte Verhaltenslehre in Text und Bild* (Kulturelles Erbe: Materialität – Text – Edition 2), Heidelberg, 151–177, https://doi.org/10.17885/heiup.545.c13908.

Steinseifer, Martin (2013), "Texte sehen – Diagrammatologische Impulse für die Textlinguistik", in: *Zeitschrift für germanistische Linguistik* 41 (1), 8–39.

Stingelin, Martin (ed.) (2004), *"Mir ekelt vor diesem tintenklecksenden Säkulum." Schreibszenen im Zeitalter der Manuskripte* (Zur Genealogie des Schreibens 1), Munich.

Strätling, Susanne/Witte, Georg (2006), "Die Sichtbarkeit der Schrift zwischen Evidenz, Phänomenalität und Ikonizität. Zur Einführung in diesen Band", in: Susanne Strätling and Georg Witte (eds.), *Sichtbarkeit der Schrift,* Munich, 7–20.

Tersch, Harald (2008), *Schreibkalender und Schreibkultur. Zur Rezeptionsgeschichte eines frühen Massenmediums,* Vienna.

Tsien, Tuen-Hsuin (1962), *Written on Bamboo and Silk. The Beginnings of Chinese Books and Inscriptions,* Chicago.

Wagner, Peter (1995), *Reading Iconotexts: From Swift to the French Revolution,* London.

Wagner, Peter (1996), "Introduction: Ekphrasis, Iconotexts, and Intermediality – the State(s) of the Art(s)", in: Peter Wagner (ed.), *Icons – Texts – Iconotext. Essays on Ekphrasis and Intermediality* (European Cultures 6), Berlin/New York, 1–40.

Watts, James (ed.) (2013), *Iconic Books and Texts,* Sheffield.

Waywell, Geoffrey, B. (1993), "The Ada, Zeus and Idrieus Relief from Tegea in the British Museum", in: Olga Palagia and Wiliam D. Coulson (eds.), *Sculpture from Arcadia and Laconia. Proceedings of an International Conference Held at the American School of Classical Studies at Athens, April 10–14, 1992* (Oxbow Monograph 30), Oxford, 79–86.

Wehde, Susanne (2000), *Typographische Kultur. Eine zeichentheoretische und kulturgeschichtliche Studie zur Typographie und ihrer Entwicklung* (Studien und Texte zur Sozialgeschichte der Literatur 69), Tübingen.

Werz, Ulrich (2004), *Gegenstempel auf Reichs- und Provinzialprägungen der römischen Kaiserzeit. Katalog der Sammlung Dr. Konrad Bech, Mainz* (Schriftenreihe der Numismatischen Gesellschaft Speyer 45), Speyer.

Wimmer, Hanna (2018), *Illustrierte Aristotelescodices. Die medialen Konsequenzen universitärer Lehr- und Lernpraxis in Oxford und Paris* (Sensus. Studien zur mittelalterlichen Kunst 7), Vienna/Cologne/Weimar.

Winterer, Christoph (2013), "'Das Wort Gottes in ruhmvollem Glanz blinkend'. Kunst im Umkreis Karls des Großen", in: Michael Imhof and Christoph Winterer: *Karl der Große. Leben und Wirkung, Kunst und Architektur,* 2nd ed., Petersberg, 76–117.

Wolf, Jana (2018), *Das Überführen des Welschen Gastes in ein französisches Layout-System. Die New Yorker Handschrift E,* https://archiv.ub.uni-heidelberg.de/artdok/5861/ (accessed 19/7/2022).

Wood, Wendy (1978), "A New Identification of the Sitter in Jan van Eyck's 'Timotheus' Portrait", in: *The Art Bulletin* 60 (4), 650–654.

Woytek, Bernhard (2010), *Die Reichsprägung des Kaisers Traianus (98–117),* vol. 1 (Moneta Imperii Romani 14), Vienna.

Chapter 3
Memory and Archive

Nikolas Jaspert, Kirsten Wallenwein, Barbara Frenk, Matthias Kuhn, Solvejg Langer, Tino Licht, Joachim Friedrich Quack, Loreleï Vanderheyden, Franziska Wenig, Wolf Zöller

Chapter 3
Memory and Archive

Nikolas Jaspert, Kirsten Wallenwein, Barbara Frenk, Matthias Kuhn, Solvejg Langer, Tino Licht, Joachim Friedrich Quack, Loreleï Vanderheyden, Franziska Wenig, Wolf Zöller

The digital age's de-spatialisation and de-materialisation of large bodies of knowledge has brought into focus that in contrast to the present day, written materials were regularly collected at specific, localisable places in earlier epochs. Institutions, associations, groups, or even individual persons were responsible for such collections and, through specific practices, they stored and permanently secured artefacts bearing all kinds of information so that these could be used at a later date.

Against this backdrop, in what follows we analyse non-typographic societies and their handling of knowledge repositories. By way of introduction, two essential forms of storage—memory and archive—are examined in their relationship to each other, before we proceed to address the ways in which relevant research has been spurred on by recent impulses in the field of cultural studies. Since the perspective of the CRC 933 'Material Text Cultures', on which this publication is based, focuses in particular on the physical supports of writing, we reflect in a third step on the specific epistemological value of analysing memory and archives in ways that are sensitive to materiality. Finally, we expand our analytical framework to include 'writing' itself as a factor and the implications thereof. This introduction is based on seven theses which are presented, discussed, and exemplified below.

Both archive and memory can be described as storage facilities, i. e., as systems where something can be deposited after undergoing a process of selection for possible (re)use. What is deposited there is saved as a result of filtering practices[1] (cf. Thesis 16) and is thus itself a trace of previous selection processes. Here, we must distinguish between storage planned for the short term, for an indefinite amount of time, or for the long term (comparable to short-term and long-term systems in human memory). Long term storage requires certain forms of organisation and a particularly differentiated handling of the stored material. Likewise, prospective short-term storage can turn into long-term or even permanent storage due to external circumstances: for example, when memories or archives end up being lost due to external factors and only return to use after much time has elapsed.[2] In the case of archives, these external factors can be the effects of warfare or burial through natural disasters; in the case of human memory,

---
[1] On storage practices, cf. Ast et al. 2015.
[2] Cf. Markowitsch 2009; Pritzel/Markowitsch 2017. On the transience and complete loss of archives, see Filippov/Sabaté 2017.

Open Access. © 2024 the authors, published by De Gruyter. This work is licensed under the Creative Commons Attribution-NonCommercial-NoDerivatives 4.0 International License.
https://doi.org/10.1515/9783111325514-004

we can think here of the superimposition of memories as a result of traumatic experiences. Individual human memory is understood here as a dynamic and changeable system created through filtering processes, with people cognitively accessing the past on the basis of this system.[3] The respective processes are cognitive performances, which are generally referred to as 'remembering': What is experienced is recorded and stored by memory, while at the same time being further processed in order to be modelled anew in a practical manner in the very moment of remembering.[4] As stated in Thesis 12, this momentum and changeability is a common feature of both human memory and the archive. This dynamic variability must be emphasised because common notions of memory are strongly marked by metaphors of static storage. We must distinguish individual human memory from the memory of a social group ('collective memory', 'cultural memory'), which can be understood as that shared 'knowledge' of the past that acquires familiarity and validity due to collective communication processes.[5]

The 'archive' (from the Greek ἀρχεῖον or Latin *archium/archivum*), a term that in recent times has been semantically extended in various ways, functions as a special form of storage. In the ancient sense of the word, it denotes an official building in which certain documents were stored for future use, and by extension also refers to institutions or authorities (e. g., a state archive) that received artefacts after a process of selection and organisation.[6] In both cases, the archive predominantly fulfils political and administrative functions.[7] Archives are similar to collections in that both can be said to form ensembles of objects: They bring things together or 'socialise' them in one place.[8] For earlier periods, libraries and treasuries are typical examples of collections,[9] while the museum can be seen as a representative case for the modern era.[10] For the

---

[3] On the term 'memory' as well as its materialisation in 'memory media', cf. Allgaier et al. 2019, 185–186 (with further bibliography), as well as the information below in notes 46 and 47.
[4] Cf. Markowitsch 2009.
[5] Cf. A. Assmann 1999; J. Assmann 2018; Ernst 2000; Donk 2009; Erll/Nünning/Young 2010; Erll 2017.
[6] On the history of European archives in particular, see the lecture transcripts of Brenneke 1953, 107 ff., in whose estate there was an 'archive article' for a *Dictionary of German History, 1943–1946* (ed. by Dietmar: Brenneke 2018, 7–137); on the Latin designation of the archive in Antiquity and the Middle Ages: ibid., 9; Corens/Peters/Walsham 2016, who pursue a socio-historical account of archives in their edited collection of essays, focus on the early modern period; Jungen/Raymond 2012 follow an anthropological approach; on the cultural history of the archive, cf. Vismann 2011, especially 91–100 (English translation: Vismann 2008, 57–61).
[7] Horstmann/Kopp 2010. See also Chapter 6 'Political Rule and Administration'.
[8] On the practice of collecting, cf. Wilde 2015; Schmidt 2016. On socialisation, cf. Ehmig 2019.
[9] Medieval collections of interest to museums or antiquarians are known for their coins: Petrarch gave Charles IV gold and silver coins bearing the portraits of ancient emperors from his own treasured holdings *(quas in deliciis habebam)*, see: *Petrarcas Briefwechsel mit deutschen Zeitgenossen*, 185. The case of Stephan Matthias von Neidenburg (1480–1495), the bishop of Kulm who is described in the *Prussian Chronicle* as a manic collector crazy for coins, is famous: Waschinski 1968.
[10] So as to be comprehensive, we should recall here that such collections can in turn generate their own administrative archival records: Bödeker/Saada 2007.

pre-modern era, it is not always possible to clearly distinguish an archive from a collection.[11] The papal *scrinium,* for example, was both an archive and a library, and the archives of the French kings were kept together with the royal treasury in the High Middle Ages.[12] Finds from the Neo-Babylonian period document that archival material and literary texts were housed together.[13] A clear demarcation of the two is also difficult to discern in Han-period China, where documents pertaining both to rulers and to administration were stored and presented alongside other objects.[14] In Japan, the *zushoryō*, established at the beginning of the eighth century, is considered to be the first state library, although it also served simultaneously as both a scriptorium and an archive.[15]

In principle, however, both ways of socialising objects can be separated analytically. Collections generally consist of things brought together from different locations to a single place. While it may well be the case that these ensembles were designed to be used or consulted at a later date, in a great many instances they served primarily for display and representation. The archive, on the other hand, was marked in the non-typographic age less by the fact that its contents had been sought out, found, and gathered together than by the fact that these items had been deposited, handed over, or stowed away with later use or consultation in mind. They are thus less the result of a determined search and the acquisition than the consequence of storage with the prospective aim of later use.[16] The artefacts socialised in archives are generally speaking of a predominantly administrative nature and pertain to the political or economic sphere rather than being cultural or representative in character. Consequently, archives rarely acquired a specific aura, as can occasionally be observed with famous collections. However, being situated at a prominent locale—at a ruler's residence, for example, or at a place of worship, temple, or monastery regarded as being especially suffused with sanctity—and being directly linked to political power could imbue archives with increased prestige and representativity.

Since both collections and archives are meant to be used, they are in principle accessible, even if this accessibility is reserved to a chosen few. This accessibility distinguishes them fundamentally from deposits whose contents are withheld from people, either completely (genizot, grave deposits, etc.) or for an indefinite period (granaries, buried hoards). In earlier times, access to archives and collections was usually extremely

---

11 Cf. J. Assmann 2001; Ast et al. 2015; Friedrich 2016; Ryholt/Barjamovic 2019. A careful attempt to uncover the arrangement of archives between late Antiquity and the early Middle Ages in Europe is provided by Krah 2016.
12 Cf. Barret 2013, 305.
13 Cf. J. Assmann 2001; Brenneke 1953, 107; Pedersén 2005.
14 Cf. Fölster 2018.
15 Cf. Kornicki 1998, 365; Sommet 2011, 14.
16 Cf. Wellmann 2012, 392. Collections present knowledge, while archives, through their order and arrangement, also consider future use and thus control the reality they precede: cf. Ebeling 2016, 129. On the distinction between politics and archives, see the contributions in Bausi et al. 2018 and therein programmatically: Fölster 2018, 201–230.

restricted, but the modern era has seen such ensembles become permanent institutions that have been opened to the public more frequently than was previously the case.[17]

Two broader notions connected to the concept of archives are primarily encountered in the field of ancient studies. On the one hand, typologically related finds originating from a secure find context are grouped together into what are termed 'dossiers' or 'corpora'.[18] Sometimes, specialist literature also refers to these as 'archives', even if the artefacts collected there were not originally located together in the same place—a fact that can give rise to misunderstandings. In this case, scholars effectively turn into retroactive founders of archives in that archaeological discoveries are clustered together for later use according to established scientific practices.[19] On the other hand, even those artefact ensembles are considered as archives whose holdings were indeed deposited together in one place and discovered there by archaeologists, although the latter were by no means originally stored in the abovementioned sense, i. e. with the intention of enabling a possible later use.[20] The common element essential to these different understandings of the terms 'archive' and 'collection' is the 'socialisation' of artefacts in one place, whether originally intended or subsequently encountered.[21]

The Concept of the Archive through the Lens of Cultural Studies

The concept of an archive thus shows a broad semantic spectrum, one that has recently been expanded due to the driving force of cultural studies. Research in the humanities that has focused on materiality, such as that conducted in the CRC 933 'Material Text Cultures', necessarily requires distancing oneself from recent Foucauldian uses of the term 'archive' in cultural studies. Michel Foucault understood the archive as the law of

---

17 On the institutionalisation of the European archive in the early modern period, see Friedrich 2013.
18 The term 'dossier', ambiguous as it is, is also often used for collections compiled by modern scholars from disparate discovered material (for example, of papyri). On the distinction between 'archives' and 'dossiers', see Martin 1994; Jördens 2001; Vandorpe 2009, 218–219. Ulrike Ehmig and Adrian Heinrich suggest replacing the term 'dossier' with the paraphrase "contextual socialisation of what is written" (Ehmig/Heinrich 2019, 1; our translation, German text: "kontextbedingte Vergesellschaftung von Geschriebenem"). For an introduction to archives and archival records in ancient studies: Boussac/Invernizzi 1996; Brosius 2003; Kehoe 2013.
19 Here, academic research becomes in retrospect the founder of an archive as it were, inasmuch as it compiles excavation finds according to scientific criteria for later evaluation. Occasionally, an extended, metaphorical use of the term 'archive' is noticeable, which builds on the idea that researchers can gain information from this context of finds just as they might from a document archive (e. g., an environmental archive, the oceans, layers of the earth): "everything is an archive" (Wellmann 2012, 391; our translation, German text: "alles ist Archiv").
20 Cf. Martin 1994, 570. Additionally, it is difficult in excavations to understand the composition of artefact arrangements perfectly, a fact that makes it difficult to determine whether they belonged to an archive or not.
21 Ehmig 2019.

what can be said and thus as a system of statements.²² This expanded, metaphorical interpretation of the term is difficult to operationalise if we attach great importance to the materiality of archives or archival holdings.²³ On the other hand, archival analyses undertaken in the field of cultural studies have also provided valuable stimuli for research on materiality in the humanities more generally.²⁴ This is especially true of Jacques Derrida's call not to understand the archive as a static storage institution, but rather to explore its changeability and the discourses and practices embedded in it.²⁵ These practices include not only the selection of archival material, but also the constant adaptation and curation of the artefact arrangements stored there. Being sensitive to the praxeological dimension of archiving invites us to inquire about its actors and the social (power-political, cultural, discursive) implications of their actions. Derrida emphasised the importance of these actors, whom he called 'archons', and highlighted their discursive power, i. e., their ability to interpret the archives.²⁶

The term 'archon', however harbours certain dangers. In a purely linguistic sense, it refers to Greek Antiquity, where the word *archōn* (plural: *archontes*) was generally used to describe a public official. Here, though, our concern is less with ancient functionaries than with the new meaning ascribed to the term by Jacques Derrida. The French philosopher used this term (in its French form, *archonte*) to refer to those who shape the discourse about what is kept in a specific archive and its organisation. These 'archons' may be the aforementioned guardians of an archive, i. e. officials comparable to the archivists of our own day. But this is only part of the term's meaning, since 'archons' in the Derridean sense also refers to any individual or group who determines the discourses associated with archives and archival records: These could be the rulers or masters over an archive, i. e., those who have founded or own it. Such persons also have a direct influence on the form, use, and interpretation of the archival material. In some cases, such as in private archives, both aspects of the 'archon' might coincide in the same individual or group of persons; in other cases, such as larger seigneurial or state archives, different persons or groups of persons fulfil the roles of archivists and archive masters, respectively. Since an essential characteristic of an archive is its dynamism and changeability, the comprehensive collective term 'archon' is particularly suitable for describing everyone who has a bearing on this changeability. It is therefore a key term for a broad, cultural studies-based understanding of the archive and will be used as such in this text.

Finally, the modification of archives—and of forms of storing knowledge in general—is conditioned not only by the multiplication and dissemination of knowledge,

---

22 Foucault 1969, 170 (English translation: Foucault 1972, 129); Gehring 2004, 54–75; Stingelein 2016, 23–24.
23 For a critique of this, cf. A. Assmann 2001, 270.
24 For an overview, see Ebeling/Günzel 2009.
25 Derrida 1995a (English translation: Derrida 1995b).
26 Derrida 1995a, 13 (English translation: Derrida 1995b, 9–10); cf. also Wirth 2005, 22–24.

but also by processes of rationalisation and streamlining. An archive not only handles storage media; it is itself a changeable medium of storage.[27] This involves changes in the cultural practices that are carried out on and with different artefact arrangements.[28] Such practices range from the production of artefacts to their use and reception, from archival selection and organisation to the destruction of such materials. This chapter therefore also interrogates the cultural practices performed by different groups of people with respect to archives and the degree to which these actions were based on the changing discourses shaped by the 'archons' in question.

Materiality as a Category of Analysis

A cultural-studies approach also proves helpful for studies focussing on the materiality of both individual and social memory, since here, too, we can observe a variability comparable to that of an archive, especially when dealing with material 'memory media'[29] (cf. Thesis 13). We understand such media as artefacts that trigger individual memory or stimulate collective communication about the past. As with other objects, their physical transience depends not only on contingent factors but also on their respective materiality.[30] They can serve quite different forms of memory: 'pragmatic' memory, designed for short-term, brief recollection; 'commemorative' memory, oriented towards regular remembrance; and the special form of social memory called 'cultural memory' following Aleida and Jan Assmann.[31] The specific forms of memory media that are selected to be archived endow an archive with the function of a 'memory agency',[32] since they specify what can be remembered, by whom, and at what time, and thereby organise not only the act of remembering, but also that of forgetting: While certain media are accepted into a specific archive, others have been discarded. The archiving of material memory media thus proves to be, in terms of memory theory, a "fact-producing act".[33]

This raises the question of the possible connections between the materiality of artefacts and their prospective use. Differences in media also reflect differences in meaning, since the support material and other external features indicate the content.[34] This leads to the assumption that there is a direct correlation between the materiality and

---

[27] Cf. Reininghaus 2008; Friedrich 2013, 125–126.
[28] Foundational here on the relationship between artefact arrangements and the practices carried out on them is Schatzki 2016, 79–81.
[29] Erll/Nünning 2004; Vedder 2012; Allgaier et al. 2019, 182–187.
[30] Cf. Wimmer 2016; Ebeling 2016, 126–127.
[31] Cf. A. Assmann 2001; J. Assmann 2018; Allgaier et al. 2019, 185–187.
[32] Cf. Wellmann 2012, 388–390 (quotation on p. 388; our translation, German text: "Gedächtnisagentur").
[33] Vismann 2011, 89 (English translation: Vismann 2008, 56). Cf. Auer 2000; Barnert/Herzberg/Hikel 2010; Ebeling 2016, 125.
[34] Cf. Erll 2004; Ebeling 2016, 126–127. On this, cf. also Chapter 2 'Layout, Design, Text-Image'.

the target groups of artefacts, especially if the latter were assembled with the intention of creating and preserving memories for a specific group of recipients (cf. Thesis 17).

A perspective that is sensitive to the issue of materiality also has implications for how we understand the term 'archive'. Picking up the impulses of cultural studies outlined above — but with a decided focus on materiality — we therefore propose defining an 'archive' as an artefact repository particularly related to the administrative sphere that is intentionally created and designed for long term usage. Through the selection, storage, and organisation of memory media, an archive thus understood forms changeable arrangements that are in turn integrated into varying discourses.

The 'archons' of these discourses decide whether the material design, the spatial arrangement, or the use of the socialised artefacts is mobilised, restricted, or even halted, which sometimes has considerable consequences for historical processes and their subsequent interpretation. Does the analysis of the changeable, material character of the artefacts and their repositories allow conclusions to be drawn about their custodians (cf. Thesis 15)? In any case, the analysis of the artefacts contained within an archive provides information about the archive's material design, arrangement, and use. The physical dimension inherent in both memory and archive thus stimulates enquiries into the relationship between space and accessibility and into the topological dimension of what is stored, i. e. how it was organised, arranged, and collected so as to enable the construction of knowledge (cf. Thesis 14).

Inscribed Artefacts as Subjects of Study

The focus of the CRC 933, on which the entire present volume is based, is not on artefacts in general, but rather more specifically on inscribed artefacts. According to Aleida Assmann, "writing" ("Schrift"), and in an extended sense, "what is written" ("Geschriebenes"), serves as the precondition for archives and archiving in non-typographic societies.[35] From the perspective of material, memory, and archive studies, the question thus arises as to what added value writing bestows on artefacts and which functions it fulfils.

A fundamental challenge in the production of artefacts that are conceived from the outset as memory media is to ensure their subsequent use as intended by their producers. The time between production and reception can sometimes be long and the medium can become exposed to various influences.[36] The changeability of the archive or changes in the cultural practices associated with it can sometimes lead to an imbalance between the original intention on the part of the producers and the actual reception of the artefacts.[37] This difference leads us to ask what role writing

---

35 Cf. A. Assmann 2001, 279. On this and what follows: Allgaier et al. 2019, 197–200.
36 Cf. Allgaier et al. 2019, 187–188.
37 Cf. Erll 2017, 145–146.

plays in mitigating this tension in accordance with the producers' intentions, despite the impossibility of wholly resolving it (cf. Thesis 18).

Writing can be applied onto its support material both during and after the production of an artefact: Objects that are already inscribed can be supplemented by further writing. In other cases, memory media lose their original material supports and are reduced to their textual content, but may continue to live or even be renewed in material form as part of an archive. Socialised artefacts are often subject to such editing and curation. The 'archons' oversee such practices and thus occupy an intermediate position between producer and recipient. This archival work on the object raises questions about its consequences for the relationship between the original artefact and its later recipient(s) (cf. Thesis 15). The reception of memory media depends not least on the 'aura' or 'presence' ascribed to them or perceived through them by actors, institutions, or practices. Thus, some objects can be charged with meaning due to their material make-up, authenticity, artistry, or contextualisation. Writing—especially of an exotic, luxurious, or otherwise unusual nature—can also trigger this effect. Such writing can already be applied to an artefact during its production, or can end up being perceived as aura-laden by recipients after a certain period of time has passed. This aura contributes to providing artefacts with an immediacy that bridges the temporal distance to the time of their creation.[38]

In what follows, the ideas of our theses, which could only be outlined briefly in this introductory part, are fleshed out, explained in detail, and clarified by examples. Our aim here is to demonstrate the potential that subjects central to the humanities, such as memory and archives, can provide when viewed from the perspective of 'material text cultures' against the backdrop of our own digital age.

Thesis 12
Memory and archive are always dynamic and never concluded.

Outside academia, one sometimes encounters the erroneous idea that what is deposited in an archive is permanently removed from the access of societies, groups, or individuals. It is supposedly robbed of its agency by being withdrawn from its usual contexts of meaning, filed away and thus 'frozen' or 'fossilised', as it were. According to this view, whatever is deposited is considered as having been laid to rest in a graveyard of written texts or, at best, as having lapsed into some kind of dormant state from which it only awakes upon being removed once again from the archive.[39]

---

[38] On the term 'aura' originally: Benjamin 1974, 479–480; cf. also Allgaier et al. 2019, 194–197.
[39] A change in this respect is noted by Ebeling 2016, 130: "Today, archives are no longer regarded as passive places and dusty sepulchres for written materials" (our translation, German text: "Archive gelten heute nicht mehr als passive Orte und verstaubte Schriftfriedhöfe").

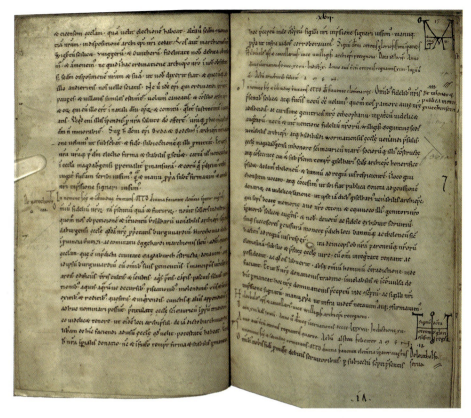

Fig. 1a: Documents and monogram tracings transmitted in copy form via a cartulary in the *Liber Privilegiorum S. Mauritii Magdeburgensis*. Magdeburg, Landeshauptarchiv Sachsen-Anhalt, Cop. Kopiare und andere Amtsbücher, No. 1a, fol. 16v–17r.

It is true that such a loss of vitality and action can be observed. A family archive can expire as such when the family in question dies out, is exiled, or the like. Documents safely deposited in advance can remain permanently hidden by being buried. This situation is plausible for Ancient Egypt, for instance, as demonstrated by the fact that some collections of family documents cease after the suppression of a native uprising against Persian rule.[40]

However, the field of classical archival studies (archivology)[41] has long known that such forms of fossilisation by no means occur regularly. The processing of archival material does not have to end with its selection and storage. This is precisely the difference between a deposit (in the sense described above) and an archive. In the former, the focus is on securing and locking objects away; in the latter, the change of what is

---

[40] Thus in Vleeming 1991 and Pestman 1994.
[41] Ebeling/Günzel 2009.

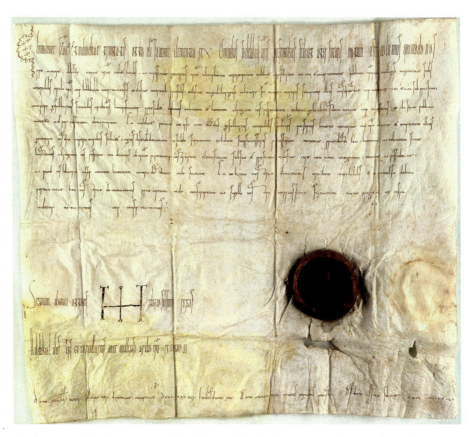

Fig. 1b: Original charter of Otto III, dated 20 May 987. Magdeburg, Landeshauptarchiv Sachsen-Anhalt, Rep. U 1, Erzstift Magdeburg I, 52.

deposited is systemic, since archival material can undergo changes through inventorisation, registration, compilation, and other administrative interventions, and can sometimes even lose its material support through transcription and thus be reduced to its textual content. In the European Middle Ages, for example, documents were copied or their textual contents incorporated into another document. Furthermore, entire manuscripts of copied deeds—so-called cartularies—were often produced in non-typographic societies (Fig. 1a and 1b).[42] In these processes, the material of the inscribed artefact could change (e. g., from papyrus to parchment, from parchment to paper). In other cases, artefacts remained physically intact, but underwent a change of form: for example, by being complemented with inscriptions or other additions, reduced in size by cutting or other actions, discarded or even destroyed (cancellation)

---

[42] Cf. Kosto/Winroth 2002. An impressive example of this form of archival differentiation is examined by McCrank 1993.

Fig. 2: Archival processing of written material: the rebinding of parchment documents into codices. Arxiu i Biblioteca Episcopal de Vic (photo: Nikolas Jaspert).

as a result of withdrawal, or altered in their physical presence by folding, smoothing, unrolling, buckling, or the like (Fig. 2).

Finally, archival materials can also undergo change when the spatial context of their storage shifts—for example, when an archive is restructured or when new document series are introduced, thus leading to re-compilations of artefact arrangements. In addition to this immediate physical re-contextualisation in one place, indirect changes in the spatial framework can also be observed: for example, when archives are divided up or change their location.[43] The transfer of the papal archives from Rome to Paris in 1810 at the behest of Napoleon Bonaparte, as well as their return in 1815–1817, is an impressive example of the dislocation and changeability of an archive. During this process, many documents were lost, while others were altered (for example, through the removal or replacement of bindings). In such new arrangements, the topology of the artefacts changes, which in turn can have an impact on their use and their praxeological dimension.

---

43 Such changes are, among other things, the subject of separate 'archive histories'; cf. note 27 above.

Even without any translocation, the physical framing of the archive is usually dynamic: An archive is set up and initially grows by incorporating more texts of the intended kind, i. e., by following the founders' intentions. This is true, for example, of a seignorial archive housing documents considered important over decades or even centuries, or of a private archive accumulating important legal documents from a single family over several generations. An example of the latter are the multi-part Dioskoran archives discovered in the ancient town of Aphrodito (the present-day village of Kūm Išqāw in Egypt). These document three successive generations: the archives of the eponymous Dioskoros, those of his father before him, and those of his own children; all three archives were probably collected and arranged by his wife Sophia and end shortly after the death of the aforenamed Byzantine functionary.[44] Comparable family archives can be identified in large numbers in the late Middle Ages in Europe.[45] Finally, an archive can also change insofar as it moves from being an actively growing repository of an administration to a self-contained collection of sources for historical research. These dynamic processes raise the question of the agents involved, inviting us to distinguish between the various functions of different 'archons' (cf. Thesis 15).

The memory and the use of memory media also display comparable dynamics. Neuroscience has long proven that what people experience is not unchangeably 'imprinted' onto human memory; rather, there is a fundamental difference between the acts of experiencing and remembering. 'Remembering' should be understood less as the retrieval of information than as an ad hoc performance of cognitive construction.[46] At the very moment when we remember something, the experience is always cognitively modelled, undergoing modifications and adaptations in the process. External influences such as new experiences, but also images, narratives, etc., can be responsible for this in a variety of ways: by implanting notions of what is presumed to have happened into the human memory; by closing gaps in memory; and by transforming the cognitive modelling of what has been experienced. Talking about past events, experiences, or actions also changes our cognitive construction of the past.[47] Who or what the agents of these processes of change are is a question that has been intensively researched and discussed—not without controversy—in the cognitive and neurosciences.

Adaptability and changeability are characteristics not only of individual memory, but also of collective communication about the past, i. e., social memory. Such communication is inherently dynamic,[48] since those who enjoy discursive authority in terms of interpreting the past—the 'archons of social memory', so to speak—can

---

[44] Cf. Fournet 2008.
[45] For example: Gifre/Matas/Soler 2002; Czaja 2009; Piñol 2014; Head/Rosa 2015.
[46] On what follows, cf. Markowitsch/Welzer 2005; Markowitsch 2009; Zierold 2006, 27–58; Donk 2009, 18–21; Welzer 2017, 19–25.
[47] Cf. Schacter 2001; Fried 2004.
[48] Cf. Donk 2009, 20–25; Welzer 2017, 70–110.

use their influence to update, control, or functionalise the act of remembering: through *damnatio memoriae*,[49] historical narratives, the creation of legends, and so on. Depending on the historical and cultural context, this function can be fulfilled primarily by the apparatuses of power, religious or cultural authorities, public media, or other opinion-forming forces.

This power over interpretation and memory can also extend to material memory media, whose effect on social memory is considerable. They condense and materialise historical narratives, thus triggering individual memories and facilitating collective communication about the past.[50] These constructed memories are also regularly subject to processes of change. Against this backdrop, inscriptions on artefacts are of great importance and can serve two primary purposes. When applied at the time of production, they are an attempt at securing the use of an artefact according to the creator's intent and thus seek to control or minimise the future dynamics of the inscribed artefact. When applied retrospectively, writing in turn significantly clarifies the respective writer's intentions: In this special case, the inscription becomes a momentous turning point in an artefact's biography with the ability to steer its reception in completely new directions.[51]

Thesis 13
Artefacts experience 'memory biographies' that can be modified during production and reception.

Artefacts can be created specifically to serve as future memory supports or—sometimes after phases when they have completely fallen into oblivion—end up as such only in retrospect. While the production of memory media is often occasioned by concrete intentions and geared towards a very specific kind of interaction, ensuring that these media will actually have their intended effect can only be warranted to a limited extent. Failures can occur in their production and in their ability to store the contents meant to be remembered, which is primarily due to the unpredictable, changing conditions of reception or to discrepancies between the motivations of producers and recipients.[52]

In the interplay alluded to above between divergent attributions, modifications, and changes of function, artefacts can undergo genuine careers and even veritable

---

49 On *damnatio memoriae*, see the relevant work by Varner 2004; Scholz/Schwedler/Sprenger 2014; Schwedler 2021.
50 Cf. Ebeling 2016, 126–127.
51 Cf. Allgaier et al. 2019, 197–200.
52 On the concept of memory and memory research, especially from the perspective of the CRC 933 and with a view to inscribed artefacts, see Allgaier et al. 2019; on the interplay between production and reception, cf. ibid., 187–188.

'memory biographies'. The conservation, archiving, restoration, and changes to the materiality of artefacts should also be understood and treated as part of such a 'life cycle'. The concept of a memory biography can be applied to the diachronic inscriptive, creative, intentional, physical, and receptive processes that can create, stabilise, change, wear out, or destroy an inscribed artefact. The congruence between intention and reception is a common experience in non-typographic societies and cultural formations. That tombstones are inscribed with memorial information, thus controlling and stabilising the commemoration of the deceased, can be considered as a normal case of such alignment, one that is shared by the past and the present. However, in this instance we have to be cautious when speaking about guiding or controlling reception. For in essence such a case equates to nothing else than the execution or repetition of a process of production and reception that has been collectively established and agreed upon beyond the level of the individual. An example of this kind of pattern for the inscription of artefacts, repeated countless times and requiring no innovation once it has been invented and established, is the inscription for a relic that is enshrined within an altar and hence invisible. By contrast, the use of special forms or high-quality materials, the prominent placing, intensified reproduction or protected storage—all of which can be discerned from the artefacts and their application—can all reflect attempts on the part of producers at controlling how the artefacts are to be understood and used.[53]

Why is this so? This is because reception is a complex, autonomous process that cannot be pinned down exactly in accordance with some 'original intention'. Therefore, we find manifold instances where there is an opposition between intention and reception. Rough drafts intended to be discarded can end up being preserved as autographs and become the object of public veneration. One such case is that of the working notes of Thomas Aquinas, which were venerated as relics in a convent at Saragossa.[54] Sometimes, drafts remain lying around and are considered unpublishable by an author, yet after his or her death, they appear in print, are reproduced in artefacts, and enjoy widespread reception; the late antique poet Sedulius achieved such unintended public success with his *Carmen Paschale*.[55] The reuse of ancient material as spolia in medieval buildings is another example of this widespread phenomenon.[56] Processes such as these (or similar ones) can attain a considerable degree of complexity. As they undergo processes of transformation, archives—or archival extracts—are transferred into artefacts, which themselves go through independent and diverse artefact biographies that can lead to social changes.

---

[53] On early medieval relic labels, see Licht 2017 and Wallenwein/Licht 2021.
[54] Gils 1970.
[55] On this process, which is witnessed to by *subscriptiones* on several manuscripts, cf. Wallenwein 2017, 29–32, 255–260. On correction notes in general, ibid., 5–8.
[56] Esch 1969; Wiegartz 2004; Altekamp/Marcks-Jacobs/Seiler 2013/2017; Bolle/von der Höh/Jaspert 2019, as well as the information below in note 129.

Such a path out of the archive and into the artefact, and from thence to extensive influence, can be prominently observed in the case of the Codex Florentinus of the *Digest*, the only collection of model cases of Roman law preserved on stable writing material and prepared under Emperor Justinian in sixth-century Constantinople. Due to political changes, this codification of Roman legal archives initially had no widespread effect. The codex experienced a phase of low reception while housed in southern Italy (Amalfi?) and was then brought to Pisa at the beginning of the twelfth century (as booty of war?). From then on, it was studied as part of the growing field of civil law in Italy and particularly in Bologna, before finally being carried off as a trophy in 1406 to Florence, where it is currently kept.[57] The *Digest* acted as a reference text for civil law until modern times.

The example above draws attention to the fact that concentrations of information in individual artefacts are a widespread phenomenon of historical archival transmission. Since institutional continuity is often lacking or has been markedly interrupted, traces of historical archives are often preserved only in specific deposits (e. g., Qumran, the archive of Theophanes at Hermopolis, the Villa dei Papiri, genizot) or in the form of codifications (e. g., cartularies, collections of letters). Against this background, an expanded concept of archives allows us to regard analogous codifications of various nature — legal (the *Sachsenspiegel*), commemorative (the Fraternity Book of Reichenau Abbey), administrative (conciliar acts), and liturgical (sacramentary) — as reflections and traces of archival contexts in which processes of transformation can commence once again and form the core of new archives.

Thesis 14
The intentions of the 'archons' are manifested in the archives' location and conditions of access.

Nowadays, public archives must be made accessible for everybody in accordance with current law.[58] In Antiquity and the Middle Ages, however, a very different ideal surely prevailed, since in these time periods, 'public' archives were not so much meant for the public, but rather for seignorial or economic administration. The *aerarium populi Romani* of the Roman Republic, to which is often attributed archival function, fulfilled the function of a public archive only insufficiently, if indeed at all. Although resolutions of the Senate and the people as well as lists of judges and jurors were kept as written artefacts in the Temple of Saturn on the Roman Forum, their use was practically

---

57 On this, along with further bibliography: Licht 2018, 81–88.
58 On the role of the archivist in older societies, see Thesis 15. The functions of the modern archivist are described in detail in the *Principles of Access to Archives* of the International Council on Archives (ICA) 2014.

impossible, since neither the broad mass of Romans had access to the archive, nor could authorised officials use the *aerarium* effectively. This is shown by the attempts of Cicero and Cato to specifically search for texts in the Temple of Saturn. In this sense, the *aerarium* was more like a non-public archive for state administration.[59]

But we must make a distinction here. On the one hand, we encounter archives in which documents were kept that were needed by the state in order to demonstrate its own claims (or the fulfilment thereof), such as tax lists or documents on compulsory labour. For such documents, it was important that they be kept beyond the public's unfettered reach (and thus away from the risk of falsification or even destruction). On the other hand, there existed copies of private legal documents that could be referred to in the event of legal disputes. A very well-known hieroglyphic inscription from Ramesside Egypt (thirteenth century BCE)[60] reports how a state archive was consulted in a major dispute involving property rights, and the Roman administration in Egypt had copies of private documents in two different public archives to ensure their availability for consultation.[61]

In contrast to later periods (when they are in the majority), public archives are very rarely represented in the papyrological record, in which we find a majority of the 'private' archives described above[62] that pertained to individuals,[63] families,[64] or large estates and inheritances.[65] A family or a taxpayer had a vested interest in keeping its 'papers' in a safe place so that they could be presented in case of some legal challenge. The simple act of depositing one's documents in a wall niche, for example,[66] is already a first step towards archiving them for later use. Access by people other than the family members themselves would have been problematic and would have entailed at best the risk of the documents being falsified. One example of this can be seen in a papyrus from a family archive in Egypt dating to the period of Persian rule. Sections of the text were erased at a later point in time, possibly in the course of a rivalry between two branches of the family.[67]

---

[59] Cf. Culham 1989, 113–115.
[60] Gardiner 1905.
[61] Cf. Anagnostou-Canas 2009, as well as the bibliography ibid., 169, n. 1; Jördens 2010.
[62] Cf. Jördens 2001.
[63] See, for example, the accidental discovery of the so-called 'Zenon Archive' from the period between 270–240 BCE in Clarysse/Vandorpe 1995, 10–35.
[64] For example, the archive of a family from Thebes, dated to the period between 317–217 BCE, was found in two clay jars. El-Amir 1959, 21–41 describes the general circumstances of the find and mentions that the documents of the head of the family and his possessions—"though possibly a coincidence"—were kept in the first jar, while those of his family and other relatives were found in the second jar (ibid., 40–41).
[65] On the Apion family archive, see among others Mazza 2001.
[66] A 'house of the archives' is known from Dura Europos (third century CE on the central Euphrates), in which a graffiti-covered cellar room served as an office for a certain Nebuchelos, who probably kept his documents in a kind of built-in cupboard; cf. Rostovtzeff/Welles 1931, esp. 169–170 (with illustrations) and 184.
[67] Cf. Korte 2019, 251–257.

The prerequisite for access to an archive is competence in writing. In ancient and medieval societies, for example, this was a limited skill, with literate persons writing primarily for themselves or their peers. The question as to where archives were stored is thus fundamentally linked to that of who could access them.[68] Here, we can distinguish between places for consulting documents that are not freely accessible and require the presence of an archivist, and those that are freely accessible, such as today's (mostly) free consultation of public documents via the Internet. Access to an archive (of one's own) could be managed restrictively for competing groups of 'archons', such as in the case of a dispute over archival documents between a bishop and the cathedral chapter. In such situations, permanently appointed archivists had to ensure compliance with the restrictions on access that applied to the buildings for which they were responsible. Another example is that of jointly-used archives. In the late Middle Ages in Europe, several branches of a family would sometimes share an archive. The branches jointly regulated the archive's use and symbolically demonstrated this fact via several locks on chests, letter vaults, other objects, or places that served to store the archived documents. Accordingly, the consent of all users—as well as their keys to the locks of the respective family branches—was required to use the archive.[69]

Today, both public (federal and municipal) and private archives are increasingly moving towards additionally storing documents in digital form, as this is more secure than the physical storage of originals alone. Our ancestors guarded their most precious records as best they could. Therefore, the choice of where to store archival records has been a central issue since ancient times and one conditioned by various factors.

The location of an archive was generally considered to be 'secure' by those who were able to select it as a storage place. This may have been a site regarded as being safe, unaffected by climatic changes and protected from natural disasters such as wildfires or landslides. Naturally shielded locales, such as a rocky grotto or cave, could be possible locations, although archives were more likely to be hidden in them as a deposit, as in the case of the archives hidden in a 'grotto of letters' in the Judaean Desert, where refugees from the Bar Kokhba revolt in 132 CE found shelter.[70] Yet man-made containers, such as jars or boxes, could also be used (and are more likely when the intended use is that of a consultable archive). Consider, for example, the demotic archive of Totoes discovered at Deir el-Medina in two sealed jars (Fig. 3)[71] or three monastic contracts dating to the fifth–sixth century CE from Labla that were deliberately wrapped in cloth and then stowed in a large jar.[72]

Other man-made containers that were able to house an archive, however, could be much larger, as in the case of a building deliberately erected for the optimal preserva-

---

68 On the restricted presence of writing cf. Frese/Keil/Krüger 2014.
69 Cf. Morsel 1998, 294.
70 Cf. Yadin 1962; Cuvigny 2009, 49–50, 51–52, and tables 2.6–2.7.
71 Cf. Botti 1967.
72 Cf. McGing 1990, 67.

Fig. 3: Two clay jars in which the papyrus scrolls of the Totoes archive, discovered in 1905, were kept. Turin, Museo Egizio, C01790.

tion of such holdings. We see this in the archives of secular princes from the late Middle Ages, which were often stored within fortified castles. Protection of a completely different kind was offered in cases where medieval rulers entrusted their archives to monasteries: Here, security was supposed to be provided not only by literate experts, but also by the locations' special sanctity.[73] Late Antiquity and subsequent eras also bear witness to similar patterns of storing archival materials in places of worship symbolically charged with a protective aura.[74] Already in Ptolemaic and Roman Egypt, we find public archives in which private law documents were kept, with the associated contracts concluded before local notaries. One such archive is the temple of Isis Nanaia (the so-called Nanaion), which already served as an archive in the first century.[75] Another example is formed by the five archives of Nessana in Palestine (sixth–seventh century CE), which were found in two adjoining rooms of the churches of St Mary and of Ss Sergius and Bacchus.[76] The circumstances of the discovery of the archive of Theodore, the son of Obodianos, were similar: A large number of charred papyrus scrolls were discovered in Petra in the ruins of the main church (hence their current moniker, the Petra Papyri).[77]

---

[73] One of many examples is the archive of the Aragonese kings at the Royal Monastery of Santa María de Sigena, which housed a convent of nuns connected to the Knights Hospitaller: López Rodríguez 2007, esp. 426–434.
[74] The military archives and the base of the auxiliary troops of Dura Europos (third century CE, central Euphrates) were discovered in a temple dedicated to Artemis; cf. Rostovtzeff 1933, 310–315, esp. 312.
[75] Cf. Jördens 2010.
[76] Cf. Sijpesteijn 2013; Gascou 2009, 480–481; Stroumsa 2008, 4.
[77] Cf. Gascou 2009, 480; Jördens 2021.

In his work *On the Magistracies of the Roman State (De magistratibus reipublicanae Romanae)*, John the Lydian (*De mag.* 3.19) makes mention of an archive of court records located in the substructure of the Hippodrome in Constantinople. The premises are said to have extended from the area under the emperor's loggia (the *kathisma*) all the way to the curved tribune of the track (the *sphendonē*), and — according to the author — could be consulted by anyone who requested to see them. In 1927, archaeological excavation works led to the discovery of five small rectangular rooms under the south-eastern half of the Hippodrome (i. e., the section described by John the Lydian) that opened onto a common corridor. In addition to their close proximity to the Great Palace, which was directly connected to the Hippodrome on the north-east, the substructures under the spectator tiers of the racetrack offered plenty of storage space, a constant cool temperature, and protection against external influences and damage by fire, for instance.[78]

Throughout the European Middle Ages, kings moved from one place to another in what is known as itinerant kingship. Their archives (or portions thereof) also moved with them, often stored in chests, and therefore also needed to be mobile,[79] which raises the following questions: Is the archival material housed in a small container that corresponds to it in size, or is it situated in a special room that affords the storage of additional documents? Is the container mobile and therefore able to be taken by its owner on journeys, or is it fixed in place? There is evidence that Pipe Rolls were consciously used in fief administration in England because they were easier to transport than codices. During journeys from one fief to the next, scribes would write the levies on the rolls, and the sums received would in turn be transferred to other rolls and archived after their return to the central seat of power.[80]

Public archives, by contrast, were stored near an administrative or ruling centre. During the Roman period in Egypt, the central archives for depositing public documents were known to be housed in what were called 'libraries' (one example being the library of the Patrika district in Alexandria). Later, the archives of the council of Hermopolis were created, which contained valuable data on the city between the years 266–268 CE;[81] the list could be extended.[82] In late medieval Europe, the development of fixed residences for rulers led to the creation of archives in or at the rulers'

---

[78] Cf. Haensch 2013, 334–335; Grünbart 2018, 322–323; Kelly 1994.

[79] From the twelfth century onwards, however, the use of registers as a substitute for archives can be determined with increasing frequency. Registers are the actual beginning of portable, mobile units of stored knowledge in the style of archives. On this, see Vismann 2011, 134–135 (English translation: Vismann 2008, 76–77).

[80] Cf. Zanke 2017; Holz/Peltzer/Shirota 2019; Holz 2022, 193.

[81] Cf. Drew-Bear 2009.

[82] Similarly, the aforementioned *aerarium* in Rome, which served as a repository of important state documents, was housed not only in a sacred space (the Temple of Saturn), but also in the political heart of the Roman Republic, since the temple stood between the Capitol and the Roman Forum; on this, cf. Culham 1989, 102.

palaces, while the establishment of municipal town halls led to the creation of municipal archives, mirroring a development that had already been accomplished by less mobile rulers such as bishops. We thus see that location and access are essential to archives.

> **Thesis 15**
> The material composition and organisation of archival records reveal information about their 'archons'.

The 'archive' should not be thought of apart from its custodians or masters, whom we refer to by the generic term 'archons'. These persons control the archive in political and/or administrative terms and fulfil two important tasks: protecting archival materials against the physical decay of their material forms; and adapting them to new needs, contemporary discourses, and presumed future uses.[83] Within the group of 'archons', we can distinguish two subgroups defined by the responsibilities and rights each subgroup enjoys vis-à-vis the archive. Authorities—such as kings, princes, bishops, abbots, etc.—should be understood as seigneurial 'archons': They act as sovereigns over archival holdings and significantly shape an archive's fate through their foundation of or later intervention in it. Distinct from the preceding group are the administrative 'archons': people who are responsible for the administration of an archive, but who can also wield considerable power in terms of their agency. An example of this latter kind of 'archon' is an archivist in his or her role as guardian of an official archival building, who would first of all be responsible for the archive's physical security and integrity, as well as for the storage and conservation of its holdings. Quite often, this person was appointed as a scribe and thus responsible not only for the preservation, but also for the production of documents.[84]

These 'archons' and the inscribed artefacts within an archive maintain relationships with one another via certain practices. The 'archons' possess competencies in terms of power politics,[85] and as the creators of the archives, it is they who decide—whether individually or as a group—who has access to the archives; what is to be recorded and thus handed down; and what is to be culled and consigned to oblivion.[86] In addition to the political dimension just mentioned, this filtering process within an archive can also reflect religious, financial, ideological, and aesthetic interests (cf. Thesis 16). The visible result of this exercise of power is both the archive *qua* building and the artefacts contained therein. An example of the foregoing can be

---

[83] Derrida 1995a (English translation: Derrida 1995b); cf. Wellmann 2012, 386; Wirth 2005, 22–23.
[84] For the European Middle Ages, cf. here: Hermand/Nieus/Renard 2019.
[85] Cf. Wirth 2005, 22–23.
[86] Cf. Wellmann 2012, 388–389; Esch 1985; Auer 2000.

found in the *Codex Theodosianus* (XV 14,8), where a decree on the removal of documents from an archive has been preserved. According to the decree, the verdicts pronounced by the *iudices* appointed by Magnus Maximus—a usurper whom Theodosius I defeated in 388 CE—were to be rendered invalid and removed from the *scrinia* (their original place of safekeeping).[87]

The 'archon' is also responsible for expanding and updating the archive, charged as he is with the task of building up the latter's holdings. Such acquisition work includes, above all, the collection and selection of inscribed artefacts, a task which brings the 'archon' into close contact with the guardians of such compilations (libraries, museums, etc.).[88] Other important functions such as the organisation, indexing, and analysis of archival material—not to mention making all this available to intended or authorised audiences—indicate that the 'archon' is no mere collector.[89] He must also react to technical and material developments, guarantee the ongoing preservation of archival materials, and ensure their future legibility. Later 'archons' followed the respective practices of their own times in the material reworking of written, preserved materials. Thus, medieval manuscripts sometimes contain marginalia such as reading notes, indications of order, or drawings, which allow conclusions to be drawn about the 'archons' themselves.[90] Archives (in the sense of artefact arrangements) often display a diversity of content and material hailing from diverse cultures, to which the respective 'archon' must be sensitive. One obstacle can be the removal of collected items from their original contexts. The 'archon' must first determine the artefacts' provenance, then situate them within the archive, and finally prepare them for future use. It is his task to assign both structural meaning (through registration, etc.) and cultural significance to the artefacts and to construct plausible reception practices. Furthermore, he must guarantee their accessibility and use. In this way, the 'archon' becomes the intermediary between producers and archive users (i. e., the recipients of the archival materials) (cf. Thesis 13).

After the artefacts have been assembled in one place and a decision has been made—according to specific criteria—as to whether they should join the archive's col-

---

87 Cf. Haensch 2013, 336.
88 Cf. Wellmann 2012, 385.
89 Cf. note 8 above.
90 On this, cf. Traube 1910, 6: "Even the copying of any given text by a writer is a small historical fact. Everything that this and each subsequent scribe deliberately or unconsciously adds of his own—his mistakes and corrections; his marginalia down to the simplest notice to the reader, the sign for *nota* and *require*, or the pointing hand—all these brief, almost silent intimations and signs can be interpreted as historical evidence" (our translation, German text: "Schon die Abschreibung irgend eines Schriftstellertextes ist eine kleine historische Tatsache, all das, was dieser und jeder folgende Schreiber von Eigenem absichtlich oder unbewußt hinzutut, seine Fehler und Verbesserungen, seine Randbemerkungen bis herab zum einfachsten Avis au lecteur, dem Zeichen für *nota* und *require* oder der weisenden Hand—all diese kurzen, fast stummen Winke und Zeichen können als geschichtliche Zeugnisse gedeutet werden").

lection or be discarded, they are subject to yet a further process of organisation (cf. Thesis 16). Caution, though, is required here, as the effectiveness of modern bureaucracy and systematisation can distort our view of the archives of non-typographic societies. Thus, we find evidence for different kinds of central archives in the European Middle Ages. The most important in this respect were probably those of the papacy. Furthermore, there were also a number of highly developed archival holdings, such as the fifteenth-century treasure vault in the castle of the dukes of Savoy at Chambéry, the documents of which were distinguished by extensive classification and inventorisation. At the same time, however, numerous sacks of archival materials are documented as being kept in the same 'vault', but they remained unregistered, merely bearing the curt label "of no value" *(nullius valoris)*.[91] In rare cases—as evidenced by the example of the oldest archive directory of the Austrian dukes from Baden, dating to the end of the fourteenth century—schemes of archival organisation with collocation notes have survived. The directory in question shows the beginnings of a systematic ordering of the holdings, which were divided according to subject areas and dominions and housed in twenty-eight drawers specially marked with letters and shelf marks that included images.[92]

Archive holdings can be classified according to their content, use, location, material composition, and other criteria, including legal content, document type or genre, and so on. Artefacts archived in this way allow conclusions to be drawn about the motivations and priorities of the 'archon'. Through material processing—such as the affixing of seals, stamps, and other signs of authentication—the material can be changed and either increase or decrease in significance. Additionally, changes in format, layout, or standardisation can be made—for example, by applying identical book bindings—in order to mark the assembled artefacts as the property of a specific institution (Fig. 4). The transformation of the text document itself is also possible. For example, 'archons' could bind individual pages together in volumes for conservational reasons (Fig. 2) or cut rotuli into sections in order to store them better and insert them into the archive's classification scheme.[93] Such persons thus had a very concrete bearing on the artefacts and the way they were socialised. At the same time, however, the artefacts themselves dictated how they were to be stored and preserved in terms of their affordances.[94] Scrolls, for example, were stored differently from codices in the royal administration of medieval England.[95] Clay tablets necessitated different

---

[91] Cf. Widder 2016, 107–108; Rück 1971, 49–67; on the handling of paper cf. Meyer-Schlenkrich 2018.
[92] Cf. Lackner 2002, 261–262.
[93] This happened, for example, with the so-called Salisbury Roll, a genealogical roll of the Earls of Salisbury, which was cut up and bound into a codex at a later date, presumably in the eighteenth century (Payne 1987, 189). Cf. also note 111 below. A further example of archival editing and the transformation of textual documents placed in archives are volumes containing texts that have been pasted together, so-called *tomoi synkollēsimoi*; on this, see among others Clarysse 2003.
[94] On the practice of organisation, cf. Ast et al. 2015, 698–699.
[95] While the royal administration stored rolls in bags and sacks, they did not do the same with codices, which along with rolls were stored in chests for long-term archiving. Cf. Holz 2019, 186.

Fig. 4: Material and formal unification of a historically evolved archive from the European Middle Ages. Arxiu i Biblioteca Episcopal de Vic (photo: Nikolas Jaspert).

storage conditions than did papyri. To a certain extent, the support material determined the artefacts' chances of survival.[96] Besides the inscribed material itself, the shape and number of artefacts conditioned their topological arrangement. Small, rare (and therefore highly valuable) ivory tablets, important legal documents, and similar items could be stored in wooden chests or cabinets, for example; letters on papyrus could be collected into bundles,[97] while files or large quantities of archival material in general were deposited in special storerooms or even kept jumbled together in bags or sacks without being registered at all. An exciting example of the storage of archival documents that were considered to be particularly valuable or significant in terms of their content can be found in the inventory of the Abbey of Herzogenburg in Lower Austria from 1781. It reports that while indexing the archived documents, someone came across the chapter letter of foundation from the year 1112, which had theretofore been presumed lost. After its surprising rediscovery, the document was placed in a crafted metal case with golden decoration in 1779 and subsequently kept in the archives with special care.[98]

Furthermore, the frequency and intensity of an artefact's use determines how it was stored and whether it was easily accessible (cf. Thesis 14). The 'archon' had to ensure that the artefact was appropriately stored and presented and, above all, that it

---

[96] Cf. Esch 1985, passim.
[97] Cf. Fournet 2007, 688; Vanderheyden 2014, 168.
[98] Stiftsarchiv Herzogenburg, H. 4.2-F.1001/2; Penz 2004, 20.

could be used in the future. The proper storage of an artefact with respect to its materiality can inform us about the practices and motives of the 'archon'. Lists compiled in the Mediterranean region at the beginning of the fourteenth century on behalf of local rulers shed light on this process of organising archival material. In the inventory of the royal chapel of Palermo from 1309, for example,[99] we find a complete commitment to the tradition of regarding the royal archives and the royal treasury as equal institutions, with the inventory thus listing *objets d'art,* vestments, documents, and books all together.[100] Within this compilation, however, the documents are listed separately and are organised according to their local affiliation (the so-called principle of pertinence) and arranged hierarchically within the respective pertinence categories into the groups *privilegia* (partly in purple), *instrumenta*, and *rescripta*. These were stored in a large chest decorated with ivory, in which the majority of the listed documents were kept together.[101] From this storage arrangement, one can determine that the listed order according to pertinence and hierarchy represented a systematisation projected onto the collection by the 'archons'. Three years earlier, in the Crown of Aragon, chancery officials had already compiled an inventory of all parchment documents that provided information about the king's patrimonial possessions and which were apparently kept together in a separate container—a large chest—for this very reason.[102] In 1345, another compilation was made of all the documents of the crown archives housed in the royal palace in Barcelona, which at that time was considered an independent institution. This inventory not only shows the organisation of the documents, but also notes how they were stored in cabinets or sacks, depending on their materiality (codices, parchment charters etc.).[103]

Thesis 16
In archives, inscribed artefacts are filtered, coded, and transformed.

Archival materials are always undergoing processes of archival treatment and handling. Before inscribed artefacts find their way into an archive, they must first undergo a process of filtering that enables a targeted use of the texts. Only through this conscious selection does a contingent collection of writings become an archive. Subsequent to this are steps of an editorial or curatorial nature that serve to process archival materials for prospective use and thus facilitate or maintain their usability.

---

[99] *Tabularium regiae*, 98–103.
[100] On the identity of treasury and archive, see Bresslau 1912, 162.
[101] *Tabularium regiae*, 100.
[102] Cf. *Catálogo de memoriales e inventarios*, 24.
[103] Cf. *Catálogo de memoriales e inventarios*, 32.

After this initial selection and collection, further processing takes place: additional selecting (sorting and determining items for potential discarding), organising (e. g., according to format or state of preservation), rationalising (compiling inventories and indices), cataloguing (applying shelf marks/call numbers, dorsal notes, uniform bindings) and finally preserving for future recipients. Moreover, there are filtering processes that are conditioned by the creation and interpretation of meaning, the written material's state of preservation, storage capacities, and translation processes.

Due to limited capacity, 'archons' usually have an interest in sorting out duplicates. In typographic societies, duplicates are sometimes hardly worth preserving simply on account of storage capacities, with such writings being filtered out upon entering the archive. Different versions of a text, however, may enter the archive or remain in the collection if they contain additional information, which is especially true for transcripts in non-typographic societies. Often, these texts are not simply copies of something said or written, but rather contain within themselves text and layout variants indicating contexts of use.[104] This is particularly common in the case of medieval narrative sources, which makes it difficult to identify and reconstruct the original text when preparing a (critical) edition.

This situation can be clearly seen in the Byzantine archive from Aphrodito, which contains several documents and poems in drafts and successive versions. For example, two papyri give two versions of the same document: One version is by an Egyptian and the other by a Constantinopolitan. The second copy provides us with a unique opportunity to compare two different cultures through instances of writing, vocabulary, and idiom, since people wrote differently on the banks of the Nile than they did on the Golden Horn in the capital of the Byzantine Empire.[105]

The intent of the 'archons' is to select and preserve, through filtering processes, those writings that fulfil the archive's purpose and can be integrated into the archive's structure. This filtering follows an inherent logic, while at the same time creating meaning, since texts are re-contextualised in this act of 'filtration'. Every archive user is therefore dependent on the selection and interpretative skills of the 'archon', who in turn discards any inscribed artefacts which he considers not (sufficiently) relevant for posterity and thus not worth preserving. In other words: The present is assembled anew in archives—'encoded', as it were—and the future is thus anticipated.[106]

---

104 On this, see Traube 1910, 7: "Even those manuscripts that seem to have lost all value because their immediate originals are still preserved and have been found can regain their own value when viewed historically" (our translation, German text: "Selbst solche Handschriften, die jeden Wert einzubüßen scheinen, da ihre unmittelbaren Vorlagen noch erhalten sind und aufgefunden wurden, können bei historischer Betrachtung ihren Wert zurückgewinnen").
105 Cf. Fournet 2018.
106 Cf. Ebeling 2016, 129.

The assessment of the relevance of inscribed artefacts changes over time. Ephemeral witnesses to everyday life that are not considered worth archiving by their contemporaries can acquire an entirely new value when the temporal distance between the past of their production and the present-day of their reception grows and they become rare witnesses to bygone practices. Today, when such accidentally preserved instances of writing that pertain to everyday life from past times are found, they are often deemed to be extraordinary and valuable cultural assets for an archive. In earlier eras, by contrast, the tendency was for 'archons' to admit only such inscribed artefacts that fitted into a specific archive's structure. Monastic archives primarily collected textual witnesses of legal acts and theological/ecclesiastical works, rather than writings that pertained to everyday life of the religious (notes, recipes, sketches, instructions). When the latter happened to end up in the archive, this was often only by chance.[107] Thus, for example, exercise texts prepared by novices in monastic scriptoria have survived only in small numbers, often hidden amongst other bound writings. An example of this is the Reichenau exercise book, which contains among other things a Greek-Latin vocabulary list together with other (educational) content.[108] We must thus distinguish between intentionally stored (selected) archival material and material that has been handed down only by accident.

In the final analysis, this means that in the world of archives, oblivion is the rule, remembrance is the exception. A special case are those things and texts that are preserved not *because of*, but *despite* their lack of textual meaning. If meaning or significance is ascribed to an artefact via its materiality, or an object is otherwise intriguing enough to merit archiving, it can most certainly end up in the archive's holdings.

Post-filtering processes of editing and curation are indispensable for the maintenance of an archive, but they can permanently modify inscribed artefacts and thus hinder the recipients' direct access to the original. Changes to text supports can be useful for a variety of reasons. Practices such as rebinding or relocating archival records alter the material nature of the written material as well as its original arrangement *qua* artefact. The example of medieval cartularies or registers shows that what was written was often reduced to the level of textual content. In some cases, seals, monograms, and other authentication marks on charters were transferred into cartularies and thus preserved in their visual form (Figs. 1a and 1b). However, the external features of the original (a charter bearing a wax seal or lead bulla, etc.) can no longer be fully discerned even here, especially since charters and cartularies were often kept separately after the transcription of text and imagery, and the originals of the former were often not handed down. Occasionally, there are even indications in manuscript compilations as to where the original documents copied in these collections were kept. Such is the case with the note, dating to around 1490, on the cover of a fief register belong-

---

107 Cf. Esch 1985, *passim*.
108 Sankt Paul im Lavanttal, Stiftsbibliothek, Cod. 86b/1.

ing to the counts of Hohenlohe: *Dise revers liegen zu Oringen im gewelbe* ("These feudal charters are located in the vault at Öhringen").[109] Usually, though, there were no explicit references to the material form of the original in such copies. If the cartulary still exists today as an archival source, it provides access to the textual content—but not the materiality—of the original artefact. The aura of the original inscribed artefact also becomes lost through this process of editing. Even the most exact copy possible cannot substitute the material presence of the original for later users, since the authenticity and biography of the original inscribed artefact cannot be duplicated.

The archives of the Papal Penitentiary in Rome may serve as an example of this kind of loss, since they contain neither the plaintiffs' petitions nor the papal missives issued in response, but only the abridged versions of successfully concluded proceedings that were recorded in the codices. The result is not only that merely a fraction of the information originally available for the proceedings remains extant, but also that the actual materiality of the texts (petitions, issued responses, dispensations, absolutions) was not archived at all. The almost palpable aura of a letter issued by the Pope himself, for example, can thus no longer be grasped in the archive.[110] The archive concentrates and transmits a selected amount of information which only allows for limited contexts of interpretation.

The material conditions of the written records of a given archive and their durability fundamentally determine the filtering and editing processes. The role an artefact's format plays for judging its relevance to the archive should not to be underestimated: Bound manuscripts have a better chance of being handed down than do loose notes or unusual formats, which are more likely to be discarded or have their textual content transferred onto other (more usual) media. Poorly preserved inscribed artefacts could be selected for discarding or, in the best case, handed down as waste paper. In this way, they are actually already removed from the archive, yet are still preserved for posterity (albeit in a misappropriated form). This temporally subordinate filtering process is irregular and often situational, but it is responsible for the fact that much information is lost on the level of both content and material as a result of archival processing. In other cases, poorly preserved documents, or documents that have been insufficiently secured for further preservation, are transcribed or transferred to new storage media. It also occurs that relevant information supports from different textual corpora are combined in new written media. Frequently, essential material information is then no longer preserved, with the transfer of information being prioritised at the expense of the materiality of the text, and material references between form and content being lost as a result. This can be seen, for example, in *Writhe's Garter Book*:

---

109 Hohenlohe-Zentralarchiv Neuenstein, GA 120, no. 5, note on the front cover of the binding. Our translation.
110 On this, cf. the volumes of the *Repertorium poenitentiariae Germanicum*: Schmugge 1996–2018; occasionally, documents of the Penitentiary, scattered across various archives throughout Europe, have nevertheless been preserved, but not in the archives of the Penitentiary itself: Schmugge 1995, 125.

The present-day codex contains not only a cut-up scroll, but also other heraldic and genealogical works in individual layers, all of which were originally not connected and only collated later in various stages of processing.[111]

The archival processing of inscribed artefacts thus leads over time to texts being preserved either in their original material form or just as textual information. Archival materials thus undergo a process of transformation that ensures that what is written remains accessible in the future to possible users. These processes can either facilitate access to the original artefact (better retrieval, use, understanding, etc.) or enhance the distance to it (e. g., spatially through transcription).

At a very basic level, selection takes place because of the limited spatial capacity of an archive. If the amount of writing that is preserved continues to increase and the archive reaches the limits of its capacity, a selection must be made as to what is to remain preserved and what is not. Even when an archive is redesigned, relocated, or rededicated, filtering processes take place and the originally established archives only continue to exist in modified form. An unintentional filter that is difficult to control is the passage of time. Materials can be completely lost due to environmental factors (fire, water, vermin); they can also become inaccessible due to negligence on the part of the 'archons' (misplacing, losing, incorrect filing of holdings) or be affected by archival use (bending, folding, cutting) as well. Older textual content—those written on parchment, for instance, and no longer deemed worth keeping at a later point in time—was sometimes erased or washed away, and the material re-inscribed with new text. In special cases, we are sometimes fortunate to be able to decipher the original text that was written. One such example is Cicero's *On the Commonwealth (De re publica)*, which has come down to us in significant fragments unintentionally preserved via a parchment palimpsest discovered in the Vatican Library.[112]

Especially in the case of the contexts of transmission in non-typographical societies, where the loss of text is already quite extensive, only a fraction of the originally available information has come down to us in this way. We must therefore consider the prior selection and processing of such texts when interpreting archival documents.

Thesis 17
There is a direct correlation between the materiality of memory media, their target groups, and their chances of survival.

Within the lively research on memory carried out in recent years in the fields of cultural studies and history, the thesis has been formulated that the analysis of the materiality and concrete physical form of memory media allow for conclusions to be drawn about

---

111 *Medieval Pageant. Writhe's Garter Book*, 1.
112 Rome, Biblioteca Apostolica Vaticana, Vat. lat. 5757 (CLA I 35).

their effects and functions.¹¹³ Following the work of the CRC 933, this postulation can be extended so as to claim that the material properties of memory media furthermore provide clues about their intended recipients. To this end, we must determine on a case-by-case basis the extent to which the intended purpose of a given memory media and the choice of its target group directly influence its design.¹¹⁴ In this context, it is useful to take into account aspects such as the size of the recipient group addressed by the memory medium and its intended duration—what has been termed its 'time index'.¹¹⁵ Following Jan Assmann, we understand this as the factor transcending the present and referring back to various layers of the past.¹¹⁶

If a given artefact has been designed with longevity in mind, the following features seem to be called for: a durable and robust material for the support; careful and elaborate design; and a prominent spatial location, especially if a regular, constant, or cyclical use is intended. Due to this configuration, an opposition can arise between the desired lifespan of the memory medium and the particular qualities of its material support. If its material value is considered to be particularly high (for example, due to its rare occurrence), the artefact stands in danger of being destroyed through refashioning. Prominent examples from non-typographic European cultures pertain to the handling of parchment or metal. Parchment—i. e., painstakingly prepared animal skins that served as inscribable material—were a precious commodity in the Middle Ages and were thus often reused, even as a kind of pre-pulp-based 'waste paper' on account of their sturdiness.¹¹⁷ Inscriptions made of bronze or even gold fared much worse because of their monetary value; it is often only the wording in copied form that has come down to us rather than the original inscribed artefact, which was usually molten down. According to the late medieval vernacular versions of the *Marvels of the City of Rome (Mirabilia urbis Romae)*, the Dioscuri (Castor and Pollux) are said to have specifically revealed that the cult statues of them that were erected on the Quirinal Hill—which in the Middle Ages were incorrectly identified as depicting Praxiteles and Phidias, sculptors who were also incorrectly described as philosophers—were not to be made of metal, lest they fall prey to the Romans' malice and greed.¹¹⁸ With regard to epigraphy, reference should be made to the *litterae aureae*, the gilded bronze letters of ancient Roman inscriptions, whose former existence is mostly only indicated by the dowel holes of the individual letters; this led to the 'development' and decipherment of a separate hole-based alphabet.¹¹⁹ Exotic ivory diptychs or works made

---

113 Cf. Erll 2004.
114 Cf. Allgaier et al. 2019, 190–193; Ebeling 2016, 127–128.
115 On the factors of the size of the recipient group and the duration of information storage, see Allgaier et al. 2019, 188–189.
116 J. Assmann 2018, 20.
117 Cf. Becker/Licht/Schneidmüller 2015; for research on fragments and waste material, see Neuheuser/Schmitz 2015.
118 *Codice topografico*, 131.
119 Cf. Alföldy 1990 and 1995; Posamentir/Wienholz 2012; Posamentir 2017.

of rock crystal, on the other hand, lent themselves to being reworked into reliquaries and (re-)inscribed because of their materiality, which facilitated their preservation, albeit in modified form.[120]

By contrast, memory media with a shorter time index are usually produced from more ephemeral materials. This category includes, for example, pragmatic memory media used on an occasional basis or only for a singular purpose, such as a notepad or shopping list, both of which function as one-time memory aids.[121] As a rule, we do not find elaborate material design here for lack of both a broad target group and a prospective future use.

The value of a physical support—which is by no means absolute, but rather tied to cultural conventions—not only points back to its target group and the meaning attributed to the artefact, but also to the social or political position of whoever commissioned the artefact and to his or her economic resources. Materiality thus builds an additional communicative bridge between the producers and recipients of memory media.

A central analytical category in all the examples discussed here is the concept of affordance, which refers to the respective options of handling the artefact which the latter offers to users on the basis of its material qualities.[122] Ideally, then, the materiality of (labelled) memory media reveals which target groups or recipients are meant to handle the artefact; where/when/how such handling should occur according to its creators; in which praxeological contexts it is to be embedded; and in which topological environment(s) it is to be integrated.

Thesis 18
Writing on memory media can shape memory and permanently bridge the gap between intention and reception.

In the context of the issues discussed in Theses 13 and 17, the labelling of memory media plays an exceptional role in helping to guarantee the producers' intended commemorative effects and in allowing for the potential shaping of memory. In this sense, writing creates unambiguity and ensures the targeted use or adequate reception of the message of memory media. While the intentions associated with the production of an unlabelled artefact sometimes remain ambiguous, writing generally facilitates the identification of an artefact-based commemorative endowment.[123]

This situation is particularly (though not exclusively) evident in the realm of funerary practices. Many cultures mark grave sites not only in purely iconic ways—e. g.,

---

[120] Cf. Gerevini 2014.
[121] Cf. Allgaier et al. 2019, 186–191.
[122] Cf. Fox/Panagiotopoulos/Tsouparopoulou 2015.
[123] Cf. Allgaier et al. 2019, 197–200.

crosses and other religious symbols—but also via explicit inscriptions that mention the name (and in some cases, other important details) of the deceased person. This can sometimes occur in a highly developed manner, such as in Ancient Egypt, where the textual genre of 'autobiography' emerged as early as the third millennium BCE and focused in particular on an individual's good personal qualities and the successful holding of office.[124] Ancient Egypt is likewise the source of the custom of 'appeals to the living', by which people who would later pass by the graves would be asked to say a prayer for those buried there, which was believed to provide the departed with useful goods in the afterlife.[125]

Similarly, even without any graphic signs, Christian tombstones and funerary slabs may, through cultural coding, inspire those who view them to pause, remember, and possibly say a prayer simply on account of their material design and location within the sacred space of a church or in special enclosed outdoor spaces, such as churchyards or cemeteries. Yet it is only through the inscribing of text that the memory is explicitly controlled in terms of how the inscriber wishes the dead to be commemorated—i.e., what ritual forms are to be used, what character traits are to be recalled, what times are to be set aside for this commemoration, etc.[126]

Inscriptions on commemorative media thus increase the likelihood that the artefacts will be recognised as bearers of memory and used in accordance with their intended purpose. What is written on commemorative media is therefore potentially suitable for bridging the gap between the intentions of the commissioners, donors, producers, or inscribers on the one hand, and the concerns of the recipients on the other hand, as discussed in Thesis 13.

In this sense, (commemorative) inscriptions secure a certain way of dealing with commemorative media, yet without necessarily preventing unintended misuse. Admittedly, compliance with the written message depended to a considerable extent on the underlying historical conditions. Secular rulers as well as ecclesiastical authorities could fall into disgrace for political or religious reasons, and their memory media could be subjected to the practice of *damnatio memoriae*.[127] But in such cases, the memory medium itself often survived in its material form, with only the name of the commemorated person being erased or removed. Additionally, after the passage of some time, both the knowledge necessary for interpreting the inscription and the social conventions indispensable for the commemoration could become lost or disappear entirely. Well into the High Middle Ages, the majority of epigraphic evidence from Roman Antiq-

---

124 Most recently, see Stauder-Porchet/Frood/Stauder 2020.
125 Cf. Desclaux 2017.
126 On the broad field of Christian memorial culture from the perspective of epigraphic studies: Kajanto 1980; Handley 2003; Treffort 2007; Dresken-Weiland/Angerstorfer/Merkt 2012; Clemens/Merten/Schäfer 2015; Jong 2019.
127 On the violent handling of written evidence, see Kühne-Wespi/Oschema/Quack 2019; on *damnatio memoriae*, see the references mentioned in note 49 above.

uity could only be understood by an educated elite of monks and clerics, as can be seen from the provenance of the majority of epigraphic sylloges from the period up to around 1200 CE. Due to the complicated administrative, onomastic, and military systems of abbreviation, further reductions in later comprehensibility must be taken into account. Above all, however, the epigraphic legacies of Antiquity were deprived of their former social and, quite often, material or architectural environments, which led to reinterpretations and recontextualisations (for example, under Christian influence).[128]

Thus, even inscriptions were not always able to prevent memory media from entering a new stage of their artefact biographies and from being reused as spolia in other semantic contexts. On the contrary: Epigraphic fragments, such as those bearing ancient names, guaranteed the material, praxeological, and topological transformation of memory media. These were suitable, for example, as tituli for saints' graves, integrated into Christian sacred spaces or re-used in complex referential systems as ornaments of medieval church façades due to their aesthetic and symbolic capacities, for which the inscribed artefacts from bygone times were sometimes even fixed upside down.[129]

Bibliography

Abbreviations and Sigla

CLA I   *Codices Latini Antiquiores. A Palaeographical Guide to Latin Manuscripts Prior to the Ninth Century*, vol. 1, ed. by Elias A. Lowe [and Bernhard Bischoff], Oxford 1934.

Sources

Catálogo de memoriales e inventarios, siglos XIV–XIX. Archivo de la Corona de Aragón, ed. by Jaume Riera i Sans, [Madrid] 1999.

Codice topografico della città di Roma, vol. 3, ed. by Roberto Valentini and Giuseppe Zucchetti (Fonti per la storia d'Italia 90), Rome 1946.

Medieval Pageant. Writhe's Garter Book: The Ceremony of the Bath and the Earldom of Salisbury Roll, ed. by Anthony Wagner, Nicolas Barker, and Ann Payne, London 1993.

Petrarcas Briefwechsel mit deutschen Zeitgenossen, ed. by Paul Piur (Vom Mittelalter zur Reformation. Forschungen zur Geschichte der deutschen Bildung 7), Berlin 1933.

Tabularium regiae ac imperialis capellae collegiatae divi Petri in regio Panormitano palatio Ferdinandi II. regni utriusque Siciliae regis iussu editum ac notis illustratum, ed. by Aloysio Garofalo, Palermo 1835.

---

128 On this phenomenon, see Greenhalgh 1989; Clemens 2003; Esch 2005; Greenhalgh 2009.
129 See the example of the cathedral of Pisa in von der Höh 2006, 386–412; on the phenomenon and practice of taking and using spolia in general, see the references mentioned above in note 56.

Research Literature

Alföldy, Géza (1990), *Der Obelisk auf dem Petersplatz in Rom. Ein historisches Monument der Antike. Festschrift für Viktor Pöschl zum 80. Geburtstag* (Sitzungsberichte der Heidelberger Akademie der Wissenschaften, Philosophisch-historische Klasse 1990.2), Heidelberg.

Alföldy, Géza (1995), "Eine Bauinschrift aus dem Colosseum", in: *Zeitschrift für Papyrologie und Epigraphik* 109, 195–226.

Allgaier, Benjamin/Bolle, Katharina/Jaspert, Nikolas/Knauber, Konrad/Lieb, Ludger/Roels, Evelien/Sauer, Rebecca/Schneidereit, Nele/Wallenwein, Kirsten (2019), "Gedächtnis – Materialität – Schrift. Ein erinnerungskulturelles Modell zur Analyse schrifttragender Artefakte", in: *Saeculum* 69 (II), 181–244.

Altekamp, Stefan/Marcks-Jacobs, Carmen/Seiler, Peter (eds.) (2013/2017), *Perspektiven der Spolienforschung* (Topoi. Berlin Studies of the Ancient World 15 und 40), 2 vols., Berlin.

Anagnostou-Canas, Barbara (2009), "Le préfet d'Égypte et le fonctionnement des archives publiques", in: Patrizia Piacentini and Christian Orsenigo (eds.), *Egyptian Archives. Proceedings of the First Session of the International Congress. Egyptian Archives / Egyptological Archives. Milano, September 9–10, 2008* (Quaderni di Acme 111), Milan, 169–186.

Assmann, Aleida (1999), *Erinnerungsräume. Formen und Wandlungen des kulturellen Gedächtnisses*, Munich.

Assmann, Aleida (2001), "Das Archiv und die neuen Medien des kulturellen Gedächtnisses", in: Georg Stanitzek and Wilhelm Voßkamp (eds.), *Schnittstelle. Medien und kulturelle Kommunikation* (Mediologie 1), Cologne, 268–281.

Assmann, Jan (2001), "Bibliotheken in der Alten Welt, insbesondere im Alten Ägypten", in: Susanne Bieri and Walther Fuchs (eds.), *Bibliotheken bauen. Tradition und Vision,* Basle/Boston/Berlin, 31–49.

Assmann, Jan (2018), *Das kulturelle Gedächtnis. Schrift, Erinnerung und politische Identität in frühen Hochkulturen,* 8th ed., Munich.

Ast, Rodney/Becker, Julia/Trede, Melanie/Wilhelmi, Lisa (2015), "Sammeln, Ordnen und Archivieren", in: Thomas Meier, Michael R. Ott, and Rebecca Sauer (eds.), *Materiale Textkulturen. Konzepte – Materialien – Praktiken* (Materiale Textkulturen 1), Berlin/Munich/Boston, 695–708, https://doi.org/10.1515/9783110371291.695.

Auer, Leopold (2000), "Zur Rolle der Archive bei der Vernichtung und (Re-)Konstruktion von Vergangenheit", in: Moritz Csáky and Peter Stachel (eds.), *Speicher des Gedächtnisses. Bibliotheken, Museen, Archive,* Teil 1: *Absage an und Wiederherstellung von Vergangenheit, Kompensation von Geschichtsverlust,* Vienna, 57–66.

Barnert, Anne/Herzberg, Julia/Hikel, Christine (eds.) (2010), *Archive vergessen* (WerkstattGeschichte 52), Essen.

Barret, Sébastien (2013), "Archiv- und Registerwesen", in: Gert Melville and Martial Staub (eds.), *Enzyklopädie des Mittelalters,* vol. 1, 2nd ed., Darmstadt, 304–307.

Bausi, Alessandro/Brockmann, Christian/Friedrich, Michael/Kienitz, Sabine (eds.) (2018), *Manuscripts and Archives. Comparative Views on Record-Keeping* (Studies in Manuscript Cultures 11), Berlin/Boston.

Becker, Julia/Licht, Tino/Schneidmüller, Bernd (2015), "Pergament", in: Thomas Meier, Michael R. Ott, and Rebecca Sauer (eds.), *Materiale Textkulturen. Konzepte – Materialien – Praktiken* (Materiale Textkulturen 1), Berlin/Munich/Boston, 337–348, https://doi.org/10.1515/9783110371291.337.

Benjamin, Walter (1974), *Das Kunstwerk im Zeitalter seiner technischen Reproduzierbarkeit <Zweite Fassung>*, in: Walter Benjamin, *Gesammelte Schriften,* vol. 1,2, ed. by Rolf Tiedemann and Hermann Schweppenhäuser, Frankfurt (Main), 471–508.

Bödeker, Hans Erich/Saada, Anne (eds.) (2007), *Bibliothek als Archiv* (Veröffentlichungen des Max-Planck-Instituts für Geschichte 221), Göttingen.

Bolle, Katharina/Höh, Marc von der/Jaspert, Nikolas (eds.) (2019), *Inschriftenkulturen im kommunalen Italien. Traditionen, Brüche, Neuanfänge* (Materiale Textkulturen 21), Berlin/Boston, https://doi.org/10.1515/9783110642261.

Botti, Giuseppe (1967), *L'Archivio demotico da Deir el-Medineh* (Catalogo del Museo Egizio di Torino 1: Monumenti e testi 1), Florence.

Boussac, Marie-Françoise/Invernizzi, Antonio (eds.) (1996), *Archives et sceaux du monde hellénistique. Torino, Villa Gualino, 13–16 gennaio 1993* (BCH supplément 29), Athens.

Brenneke, Adolf (1953), *Archivkunde. Ein Beitrag zur Theorie und Geschichte des europäischen Archivwesens*, ed. based on lecture notes and estate papers, with additions by Wolfgang Leesch, Leipzig.

Brenneke, Adolf (2018), *Gestalten des Archivs. Nachgelassene Schriften zur Archivwissenschaft*, ed. with an afterword by Dietmar Schenk, Hamburg, https://doi.org/10.15460/HUP.LASH.113.183.

Bresslau, Harry (1912), *Handbuch der Urkundenlehre für Deutschland und Italien*, vol. 1, 2nd ed., Leipzig.

Brosius, Maria (ed.) (2003), *Ancient Archives and Archival Traditions. Concepts of Record-Keeping in the Ancient World* (Oxford Studies in Ancient Documents), Oxford.

Clarysse, Willy (2003), "Tomoi Synkollēsimoi", in: Brosius, Maria (ed.), *Ancient Archives and Archival Traditions. Concepts of Record-Keeping in the Ancient World* (Oxford Studies in Ancient Documents), Oxford, 344–359.

Clarysse, Willy/Vandorpe, Katelijn (1995), *Zénon, un homme d'affaires grec à l'ombre des pyramides* (Ancorae 14), Leuven.

Clemens, Lukas (2003), *Tempore Romanorum constructa. Zur Nutzung und Wahrnehmung antiker Überreste nördlich der Alpen während des Mittelalters* (Monographien zur Geschichte des Mittelalters 50), Stuttgart.

Clemens, Lukas/Merten, Hiltrud/Schäfer, Christoph (eds.) (2015), *Frühchristliche Grabinschriften im Westen des Römischen Reiches. Beiträge zur Internationalen Konferenz "Frühchristliche Grabinschriften im Westen des Römischen Reiches", Trier, 13.–15. Juni 2013* (Interdisziplinärer Dialog zwischen Archäologie und Geschichte 3), Trier.

Corens, Liesbeth/Peters, Kate/Walsham, Alexandra (eds.) (2016), *The Social History of the Archive: Record-Keeping in Early Modern Europe* (Past & Present Supplement 11), Oxford/New York.

Culham, Phyllis (1989), "Archives and Alternatives in Republican Rome", in: *Classical Philology* 84 (2), 100–115.

Cuvigny, Hélène (2009), "The Finds of Papyri: The Archaeology of Papyrology", in: Roger S. Bagnall (ed.), *The Oxford Handbook of Papyrology*, Oxford, 30–58.

Czaja, Karin (2009), "Häuser, Truhen und Bücher. Familienarchive in der spätmittelalterlichen Stadt", in: Karin Czaja and Gabriela Signori (eds.), *Häuser, Namen, Identitäten. Beiträge zur spätmittelalterlichen und frühneuzeitlichen Stadtgeschichte* (Spätmittelalterstudien 1), Constance, 109–120.

Derrida, Jacques (1995a), *Mal d'Archive. Une impression freudienne*, Paris.

Derrida, Jacques (1995b), "Archive Fever. A Freudian Impression", transl. by Eric Prenowitz, in: *Diacritics* 25 (2), 9–63.

Desclaux, Vanessa (2017), "La syntaxe des appels aux vivants", in: *Bulletin de l'Institut Français d'Archéologie Orientale* 117, 161–202.

Donk, André (2009), "Kommunikation über Vergangenheit – Soziales Gedächtnis in kommunikationswissenschaftlicher Perspektive", in: Klaus Merten (ed.), *Konstruktion von Kommunikation in der Mediengesellschaft. Festschrift für Joachim Westerbarkey*, Wiesbaden, 13–29.

Dresken-Weiland, Jutta/Angerstorfer, Andreas/Merkt, Andreas (eds.) (2012), *Himmel – Paradies – Schalom. Tod und Jenseits in christlichen und jüdischen Grabinschriften der Antike* (Handbuch zur Geschichte des Todes im frühen Christentum und seiner Umwelt 1), Regensburg.

Drew-Bear, Marie (2009), "Contenu et intérêt historique des archives du conseil municipal d'Hermoupolis sous Gallien", in: Patrizia Piacentini and Christian Orsenigo (eds.), *Egyptian Archives. Proceedings of the First Session of the International Congress. Egyptian Archives / Egyptological Archives. Milano, September 9–10, 2008* (Quaderni di Acme 111), Milan, 187–195.

Ebeling, Knut (2016), "Archiv und Medium", in: Marcel Lepper and Ulrich Raulff (eds.), *Handbuch Archiv. Geschichte, Aufgaben, Perspektiven*, Stuttgart, 125–130.

Ebeling, Knut/Günzel, Stephan (eds.) (2009), *Archivologie. Theorien des Archivs in Philosophie, Medien und Künsten* (Kaleidogramme 30), Berlin.

Ehmig, Ulrike (ed.) (2019), *Vergesellschaftete Schriften. Beiträge zum internationalen Workshop der Arbeitsgruppe 11 am SFB 933* (Philippika 128), Wiesbaden.

Ehmig, Ulrike/Heinrich, Adrian C. (2019), "'Vergesellschaftete Schriften': Einleitende Bemerkungen", in: Ulrike Ehmig (ed.), *Vergesellschaftete Schriften. Beiträge zum internationalen Workshop der Arbeitsgruppe 11 am SFB 933* (Philippika 128), Wiesbaden, 1–6.

El-Amir, Mustafa (1959), *A Family Archive from Thebes. Demotic Papyri in the Philadelphia and Cairo Museums from the Ptolemaic Period,* Part II: *Legal and Sociological Studies,* Cairo.

Erll, Astrid (2004), "Medium des kollektiven Gedächtnisses: Ein (erinnerungs-)kulturwissenschaftlicher Kompaktbegriff", in: Astrid Erll and Ansgar Nünning (eds.), *Medien des kollektiven Gedächtnisses. Konstruktivität, Historizität, Kulturspezifität* (Media and Cultural Memory / Medien und kulturelle Erinnerung 1), Berlin/New York, 3–22.

Erll, Astrid (2017), *Kollektives Gedächtnis und Erinnerungskulturen. Eine Einführung,* 3rd ed., Stuttgart.

Erll, Astrid/Nünning, Ansgar (eds.) (2004), *Medien des kollektiven Gedächtnisses. Konstruktivität, Historizität, Kulturspezifität* (Media and Cultural Memory / Medien und kulturelle Erinnerung 1), Berlin/New York.

Erll, Astrid/Nünning, Ansgar/Young, Sara B. (eds.) (2010), *A Companion to Cultural Memory Studies,* Berlin/New York.

Ernst, Wolfgang (2000), "Im Namen des Speichers. Eine Kritik der Begriffe 'Erinnerung' und 'Kollektives Gedächtnis'", in: Moritz Csáky and Peter Stachel (eds.), *Speicher des Gedächtnisses. Bibliotheken, Museen, Archive,* Teil 1: *Absage an und Wiederherstellung von Vergangenheit, Kompensation von Geschichtsverlust,* Vienna, 99–127.

Esch, Arnold (1969), "Spolien. Zur Wiederverwendung antiker Baustücke und Skulpturen im mittelalterlichen Italien", in: *Archiv für Kulturgeschichte* 51, 1–64.

Esch, Arnold (1985), "Überlieferungs-Chance und Überlieferungs-Zufall als methodisches Problem des Historikers", in: *Historische Zeitschrift* 240, 529–570.

Esch, Arnold (2005), *Wiederverwendung von Antike im Mittelalter. Die Sicht des Archäologen und die Sicht des Historikers* (Hans-Lietzmann-Vorlesungen 7), Berlin.

Filippov, Igor/Sabaté, Flocel (eds.) (2017), *Identity and Loss of Historical Memory. The Destruction of Archives* (Identities / Identités / Identidades 7), Bern et al.

Fölster, Max Jakob (2018), "Libraries and Archives in the Former Han Dynasty (206 BCE – 9 CE): Arguing for a Distinction", in: Alessandro Bausi, Christian Brockmann, Michael Friedrich and Sabine Kienitz (eds.), *Manuscripts and Archives. Comparative Views on Record-Keeping* (Studies in Manuscript Cultures 11), Berlin/Boston, 201–230.

Foucault, Michel (1969), *L'archéologie du savoir* (Bibliothèque des Sciences humaines), [Paris].

Foucault, Michel (1972), *The Archaeology of Knowledge,* transl. by A. M. Sheridan Smith, London.

Fournet, Jean-Luc (2007), "Deux lettres inédites de la collection de Strasbourg (P. Strasb. K. 682 et 684)", in: Nathalie Bosson and Anne Boud'hors (eds.), *Actes du Huitième Congrès inter-*

national d'Études coptes. Paris, 28 juin – 3 juillet 2004, vol. 2 (Orientalia Lovaniensia Analecta 163 II), Leuven/Paris/Dudley, MA, 685–695.

Fournet, Jean-Luc (2008), "Archive ou archives de Dioscore? Les dernières années des 'archives de Dioscore'", in: Jean-Luc Fournet and Caroline Magdelaine (eds.), *Les archives de Dioscore d'Aphrodité cent ans après leur découverte. Histoire et culture dans l'Égypte byzantine. Actes du colloque de Strasbourg (8–10 décembre 2005)* (Collections de l'Université Marc Bloch – Strasbourg. Études d'archéologie et d'histoire ancienne), Paris, 17–30.

Fournet, Jean-Luc (2018), "Les Égyptiens à la capitale ou quand la papyrologie s'invite à Constantinople. Édition comparée des P. Cair. Masp. I 67 024–67 025", in: Cécile Morrisson and Jean-Pierre Sodini (eds.), *Constantinople réelle et imaginaire. Autour de l'œuvre de Gilbert Dagron* (Travaux et mémoires 22/1), Paris, 595–633.

Fox, Richard/Panagiotopoulos, Diamantis/Tsouparopoulou, Christina (2015), "Affordanz", in: Thomas Meier, Michael R. Ott, and Rebecca Sauer (eds.), *Materiale Textkulturen. Konzepte – Materialien – Praktiken* (Materiale Textkulturen 1), Berlin/Munich/Boston, 63–70, https://doi.org/10.1515/9783110371291.63.

Frese, Tobias/Keil, Wilfried E./Krüger, Kristina (eds.) (2014), *Verborgen, unsichtbar, unlesbar – zur Problematik restringierter Schriftpräsenz* (Materiale Textkulturen 2), Berlin/Boston, https://doi.org/10.1515/9783110353587.

Fried, Johannes (2004), *Der Schleier der Erinnerung. Grundzüge einer historischen Memorik,* Munich.

Friedrich, Markus (2013), *Die Geburt des Archivs. Eine Wissensgeschichte,* Munich.

Friedrich, Markus (2016), "Sammlungen", in: Marcel Lepper and Ulrich Raulff (eds.), *Handbuch Archiv. Geschichte, Aufgaben, Perspektiven,* Stuttgart, 152–161.

Gardiner, Alan H. (1905), *The Inscription of Mes. A Contribution to the Study of Egyptian Judicial Procedure* (Untersuchungen zur Geschichte und Altertumskunde Ägyptens IV,3), Leipzig.

Gascou, Jean (2009), "The Papyrology of the Near East", in: Roger S. Bagnall (ed.), *The Oxford Handbook of Papyrology,* Oxford, 473–494.

Gehring, Petra (2004), *Foucault – die Philosophie im Archiv,* Frankfurt (Main)/New York.

Gerevini, Stefania (2014), "Christus crystallus: Rock Crystal, Theology and Materiality in the Medieval West", in: James Robinson, Lloyd De Beer, and Anna Harnden (eds.), *Matter of Faith. An Interdisciplinary Study of Relics and Relic Veneration in the Medieval Period* (British Museum Research Publication 195), London, 92–99.

Gifre, Pere/Matas, Josep/Soler, Santi (2002), *Els arxius patrimonials,* Girona.

Gils, Pierre-M. (1970), "Deux nouveaux fragments autographes de Thomas d'Aquin", in: *Scriptorium* 24, 44–45 with plate 9.

Greenhalgh, Michael (1989), *The Survival of Roman Antiquities in the Middle Ages,* London.

Greenhalgh, Michael (2009), *Marble Past, Monumental Present. Building with Antiquities in the Mediaeval Mediterranean* (The Medieval Mediterranean 80), Leiden/Boston.

Grünbart, Michael (2018), "Securing and Preserving Written Documents in Byzantium", in: Alessandro Bausi, Christian Brockmann, Michael Friedrich, and Sabine Kienitz (eds.) *Manuscripts and Archives. Comparative Views on Record-Keeping* (Studies in Manuscript Cultures 11), Berlin/Boston, 319–338.

Haensch, Rudolf (2013), "Die Statthalterarchive der Spätantike", in: Michele Faraguna (ed.), *Archives and Archival Documents in Ancient Societies. Trieste 30 September – 1 October 2011* (Legal Documents in Ancient Societies 4 / Graeca Tergestina. Storia e civiltà 1), Trieste, 333–349.

Handley, Mark A. (2003), *Death, Society and Culture: Inscriptions and Epitaphs in Gaul and Spain, AD 300–750* (BAR International Series 1135), Oxford.

Head, Randolph C./Rosa, Maria de Lurdes (eds.) (2015), *Rethinking the Archive in Pre-Modern Europe. Family Archives and their Inventories from the 15th to the 19th Century,* Lisbon.

Hermand, Xavier/Nieus, Jean-François/Renard, Étienne (eds.) (2019), *Le scribe d'archives dans l'Occident médiéval. Formations, carrières, réseaux* (Utrecht Studies in Medieval Literacy 43), Turnhout.

Höh, Marc von der (2006), *Erinnerungskultur und frühe Kommune. Formen und Funktionen des Umgangs mit der Vergangenheit im hochmittelalterlichen Pisa (1050–1150)* (Hallische Beiträge zur Geschichte des Mittelalters und der Frühen Neuzeit 3), Berlin.

Holz, Stefan G. (2019), "The *Onus Scaccarii* Rolls Under Edward I (1272–1307)", in: Stefan G. Holz, Jörg Peltzer, and Maree Shirota (eds.), *The Roll in England and France in the Late Middle Ages. Form and Content* (Materiale Textkulturen 28), Berlin/Boston, 167–196, https://doi.org/10.1515/9783110645125-007.

Holz, Stefan G. (2022), *Rolle und Kodex. Die Schriftlichkeit der königlichen Finanzverwaltung Englands unter Eduard I. (1272–1307)* (Veröffentlichungen des Deutschen Historischen Instituts London 87), Berlin/Boston.

Holz, Stefan G./Peltzer, Jörg/Shirota, Maree (eds.) (2019), *The Roll in England and France in the Late Middle Ages. Form and Content* (Materiale Textkulturen 28), Berlin/Boston, https://doi.org/10.1515/9783110645125.

Horstmann, Anja/Kopp, Vanina (eds.) (2010), *Archiv – Macht – Wissen. Organisation und Konstruktion von Wissen und Wirklichkeiten in Archiven,* Frankfurt (Main)/New York.

International Council on Archives (ICA) (2014), *Principles of Access to Archives*, available at http://www.ica.org/sites/default/files/ICA_Access-principles_EN.pdf (accessed 31/7/2023).

Jördens, Andrea (2001), "Papyri und private Archive. Ein Diskussionsbeitrag zur papyrologischen Terminologie", in: Eva Cantarella and Gerhard Thür (eds.), *Symposion 1997. Vorträge zur griechischen und hellenistischen Rechtsgeschichte (Altafiumara, 8.–14. September 1997),* Cologne/Weimar/Vienna, 253–268.

Jördens, Andrea (2010), "Öffentliche Archive und römische Rechtspolitik", in: Katja Lembke, Martina Minas-Nerpel, and Stefan Pfeiffer (eds.), *Tradition and Transformation. Egypt Under Roman Rule. Proceedings of the International Conference, Hildesheim, Roemer- and Pelizaeus-Museum, 3–6 July 2008* (Culture and History of the Ancient Near East 41), Leiden/Boston, 159–179.

Jördens, Andrea (2021), "Rezension zu *The Petra Papyri V.* von Antti Arjava, Jaakko Frösén und Jorma Kaimio", in: *Gnomon. Kritische Zeitschrift für die gesamte klassische Altertumswissenschaft* 93/2, 114–118.

Jong, Mayke de (2019), *Epitaph for an Era. Politics and Rhetoric in the Carolingian World,* Cambridge.

Jungen, Christine/Raymond, Candice (eds.) (2012), *Pratiques d'archives. Fabriques, modelages, manipulations* (Ateliers d'anthropologie 36), https://doi.org/10.4000/ateliers.9004.

Kajanto, Iiro (1980), *Classical and Christian. Studies in the Latin Epitaphs of Medieval and Renaissance Rome* (Annales Academiae Scientiarum Fennicae B 203), Helsinki.

Kehoe, Dennis (2013), "Archives and Archival Documents in Ancient Societies: Introduction", in: Michele Faraguna (ed.), *Archives and Archival Documents in Ancient Societies. Trieste 30 September – 1 October 2011* (Legal Documents in Ancient Societies 4 / Graeca Tergestina. Storia e civiltà 1), Trieste, 11–20.

Kelly, Christopher M. (1994), "Later Roman Bureaucracy: Going through the Files", in: Alan K. Bowman and Greg Woolf (eds.), *Literacy and Power in the Ancient World,* Cambridge, 161–176.

Kornicki, Peter (1998), *The Book in Japan. A Cultural History from the Beginnings to the Nineteenth Century* (Handbuch der Orientalistik. Abt. 5, Japan 7), Leiden/Boston/Cologne.

Korte, Jannik (2019), "Zerreißen, Durchstreichen, Auswischen. Zerstörung von demotischen (und einer abnormhieratischen) Rechtsurkunden", in: Carina Kühne-Wespi, Klaus Oschema, and Joachim Friedrich Quack (eds.), *Zerstörung von Geschriebenem. Historische und transkulturelle*

Perspektiven (Materiale Textkulturen 22), Berlin/Boston, 229–259, https://doi.org/10.1515/9783110629040-008.

Kosto, Adam J./Winroth, Anders (eds.) (2002), *Charters, Cartularies, and Archives. The Preservation and Transmission of Documents in the Medieval West. Proceedings of a Colloquium of the Commission Internationale de Diplomatique (Princeton and New York, 16–18 September 1999* (Papers in Mediaeval Studies 17), Toronto.

Krah, Adelheid (2016), "Das Archiv als Schatzhaus? Zur Aufbewahrung von Verwaltungsschriftgut im frühen Mittelalter", in: *Francia* 43, 1–19.

Kühne-Wespi, Carina/Oschema, Klaus/Quack, Joachim Friedrich (eds.) (2019), *Zerstörung von Geschriebenem. Historische und transkulturelle Perspektiven* (Materiale Textkulturen 22), Berlin/Boston, https://doi.org/10.1515/9783110629040.

Lackner, Christian (2002), "Archivordnung im 14. Jahrhundert. Zur Geschichte des habsburgischen Hausarchivs in Baden im Aargau", in: Gustav Pfeifer (ed.), *Handschriften, Historiographie und Recht. Winfried Stelzer zum 60. Geburtstag* (Mitteilungen des Instituts für Österreichische Geschichtsforschung Ergänzungsband 42), Vienna/Munich, 255–268.

Licht, Tino (2017), "Frühe Authentiken und die Mainzer Schriftkultur im 7. und 8. Jahrhundert", in: Tino Licht and Winfried Wilhelmy (eds.), *In Gold geschrieben. Zeugnisse frühmittelalterlicher Schriftkultur in Mainz. Festgabe für Domdekan Heinz Heckwolf zum 75. Geburtstag* (Publikationen des Bischöflichen Dom- und Diözesanmuseums Mainz 9), Regensburg, 16–25.

Licht, Tino (2018), *Halbunziale. Schriftkultur im Zeitalter der ersten lateinischen Minuskel (III.–IX. Jahrhundert)* (Quellen und Untersuchungen zur Lateinischen Philologie des Mittelalters 20), Stuttgart.

López Rodríguez, Carlos (2007), "Orígenes del archivo de la Corona de Aragón (en tiempos, Archivo Real de Barcelona)", in: *Hispania. Revista Española de Historia* 67 (Nr. 226), 413–454.

Markowitsch, Hans J. (2009), *Dem Gedächtnis auf der Spur. Vom Erinnern und Vergessen*, 3rd ed., Darmstadt.

Markowitsch, Hans J./Welzer, Harald (2005), *Das autobiographische Gedächtnis. Hirnorganische Grundlagen und biosoziale Entwicklung*, Stuttgart.

Martin, Alain (1994), "Archives privées et cachettes documentaires", in: Adam Bülow-Jacobsen (ed.), *Proceedings of the 20th International Congress of Papyrologists. Copenhagen 23–29 August, 1992*, Copenhagen, 569–577.

Mazza, Roberta (2001), *L'archivio degli Apioni. Terra, lavoro e proprietà senatoria nell'Egitto tardoantico*, Bari.

McCrank, Lawrence (1993), "Documenting Reconquest and Reform: The Growth of Archives in the Medieval Crown of Aragon", in: *The American Archivist* 56, 256–318.

McGing, Brian C. (1990), "Melitian Monks at Labla", in: *Tyche. Beiträge zur Alten Geschichte, Papyrologie und Epigraphik* 5, 67–94 with plates 10–12.

Meier, Thomas/Ott, Michael R./Sauer, Rebecca (eds.) (2015), *Materiale Textkulturen. Konzepte – Materialien – Praktiken* (Materiale Textkulturen 1), Berlin/Munich/Boston, https://doi.org/10.1515/9783110371291.

Meyer-Schlenkrich, Carla (2018), *Wann beginnt die Papierzeit? Zur Wissensgeschichte eines hoch- und spätmittelalterlichen Beschreibstoffs*, Heidelberg (machine-written habilitation, forthcoming 2024 as Materiale Textkulturen 45).

Morsel, Joseph (1998), "Geschlecht und Repräsentation. Beobachtungen zur Verwandtschaftskonstruktion im fränkischen Adel des späten Mittelalters", in: Otto G. Oexle and Andrea von Hülsen-Esch (eds.), *Die Repräsentation der Gruppen. Texte – Bilder –Objekte* (Veröffentlichungen des Max-Planck-Instituts für Geschichte 141), Göttingen, 259–325.

Neuheuser, Hanns P./Schmitz, Wolfgang (eds.) (2015), *Fragment und Makulatur. Überlieferungsstörungen und Forschungsbedarf bei Kulturgut in Archiven und Bibliotheken* (Buchwissenschaftliche Beiträge 91), Wiesbaden.

Payne, Ann (1987), "The Salisbury Roll of Arms, c. 1463", in: Daniel Williams (ed.), *England in the Fifteenth Century. Proceedings of the 1986 Harlaxton Symposium,* Woodbridge, 187–198.

Pedersén, Olof (2005), *Archive und Bibliotheken in Babylon. Die Tontafeln der Grabung Robert Koldeweys 1899–1917* (Abhandlungen der Deutschen Orient-Gesellschaft 25), Saarbrücken.

Penz, Helga (2004), *Kloster – Archiv – Geschichte. Schriftlichkeit und Überlieferung im Augustiner-Chorherrenstift Herzogenburg in Niederösterreich 1300–1800,* [PhD dissertation] Vienna.

Pestman, Pieter W. (1994), *Les papyrus démotiques de Tsenhor (P. Tsenhor). Les archives privées d'une femme égyptienne du temps de Darius Ier* (Studia Demotica 4), 2 vols., Leuven.

Piñol, Daniel (2014), "Patrimonial Archives and Medieval History: The Necessary Dialogue", in: *Imago temporis. Medium Aevum* 8, 357–379.

Posamentir, Richard (2017), "Augustus und die *litterae aureae*", in: Manuel Flecker, Stefan Krmnicek, Johannes Lipps, Richard Posamentir, and Thomas Schäfer (eds.), *Augustus ist tot – Lang lebe der Kaiser! Internationales Kolloquium anlässlich des 2000. Todesjahres des römischen Kaisers vom 20.–22. November 2014 in Tübingen* (Tübinger Archäologische Forschungen 24), Rahden (Westphalia), 451–511.

Posamentir, Richard/Wienholz, Holger (2012), "Gebäude mit *litterae aureae* in den kleinasiatischen Provinzen, die Basilika von Berytus und der Jupitertempel von Baalbek", in: *Istanbuler Mitteilungen* 62, 161–198.

Pritzel, Monika/Markowitsch, Hans J. (2017), *Warum wir vergessen. Psychologische, natur- und kulturwissenschaftliche Erkenntnisse,* Berlin.

Reininghaus, Wilfried (2008), "Archivgeschichte. Umrisse einer untergründigen Subdisziplin", in: *Der Archivar* 61, 352–360.

Rostovtzeff, Michel (1933), "Les archives militaires de Doura", in: *Comptes rendus des séances de l'Académie des Inscriptions et Belles-Lettres* 77/2, 309–323.

Rostovtzeff, Michel/Welles, Bradford C. (1931), "La 'Maison des archives' à Doura Europos", in: *Comptes rendus des séances de l'Académie des Inscriptions et Belles-Lettres* 75/2, 162–188.

Rück, Peter (1971), "Die Ordnung der herzoglich savoyischen Archive unter Amadeus VIII. (1398–1451)", in: *Archivalische Zeitschrift* 67, 11–101.

Ryholt, Kim/Barjamovic, Gojko (eds.) (2019), *Libraries before Alexandria. Ancient Near Eastern Traditions,* Oxford.

Schacter, Daniel L. (2001), *The Seven Sins of Memory. How the Mind Forgets and Remembers,* Boston/New York.

Schatzki, Theodore (2016), "Materialität und soziales Leben", in: Herbert Kalthoff, Torsten Cress, and Tobias Röhl (eds.), *Materialität. Herausforderungen für die Sozial- und Kulturwissenschaften,* Paderborn, 63–88.

Schmidt, Sarah (ed.) (2016), *Sprachen des Sammelns. Literatur als Medium und Reflexionsform des Sammelns,* Paderborn.

Schmugge, Ludwig (1995), *Kirche, Kinder, Karrieren. Päpstliche Dispense von der unehelichen Geburt im Spätmittelalter,* Zürich.

Schmugge, Ludwig (ed.) (1996–2018), *Repertorium poenitentiariae Germanicum. Verzeichnis der in den Supplikenregistern der Pönitentiarie vorkommenden Personen, Kirchen und Orte des Deutschen Reiches,* 11 vols., Tübingen/Berlin/Boston.

Scholz, Sebastian/Schwedler, Gerald/Sprenger, Kai-Michael (eds.) (2014), *Damnatio in memoria. Deformation und Gegenkonstruktionen in der Geschichte* (Zürcher Beiträge zur Geschichtswissenschaft NF 4), Vienna/Cologne/Weimar.

Schwedler, Gerald (2021), *Vergessen, Verändern, Verschweigen. Damnatio memoriae im frühen Mittelalter* (Zürcher Beiträge zur Geschichtswissenschaft NF 9), Vienna/Cologne/Weimar.

Sijpesteijn, Petra M. (2013), "Nessana", in: Roger S. Bagnall, Kai Brodersen, Craige B. Champion, Andrew Erskine, and Sabine R. Huebner (eds.), *The Encyclopedia of Ancient History*, vol. 9, Chichester, 4755–4757.

Sommet, Moritz (2011), *Bibliothek und Moderne in Japan. Das wissenschaftliche Bibliothekswesen zwischen System und Kultur* (Kölner Arbeitspapiere zur Bibliotheks- und Informationswissenschaft 58), Cologne.

Stauder-Porchet, Julie/Frood, Elizabeth/Stauder, Andréas (eds.) (2020), *Ancient Egyptian Biographies. Contexts, Forms, Functions* (Wilbour Studies in Egyptology and Assyriology 6), Atlanta.

Stingelin, Martin (2016), "Archivmetapher", in: Marcel Lepper and Ulrich Raulff (eds.), *Handbuch Archiv. Geschichte, Aufgaben, Perspektiven,* Stuttgart, 21–27.

Stroumsa, Rachel (2008), *People and Identities in Nessana,* [PhD dissertation] Duke University, https://hdl.handle.net/10161/619 (accessed 31/7/2023).

Traube, Ludwig (1910), *Textgeschichte der Regula S. Benedicti* (Abhandlungen der Königlich Bayerischen Akademie der Wissenschaften. Philosophisch-Philologische und Historische Klasse 25.2), 2nd ed., Munich.

Treffort, Cécile (2007), *Mémoires carolingiennes. L'épitaphe entre célébration mémorielle, genre littéraire et manifeste politique (milieu VIIIe – début XIe siècle),* Rennes.

Vanderheyden, Loreleï (2014), "Lettre copte du dossier de Phoibadia", in: Anne Boud'hors, Alain Delattre, Catherine Louis, and Tonio S. Richter (eds.), *Coptica Argentoratensia. Textes et documents de la troisième université d'été de papyrologie copte (Strasbourg, 18–25 juillet 2010) (P. Stras. Copt.)* (Collections de l'Université de Strasbourg. Études d'archéologie et d'histoire ancienne. Cahiers de la Bibliothèque copte 19), Paris, 167–173.

Vandorpe, Katelijn (2009), "Archives and Dossiers", in: Roger S. Bagnall (ed.), *The Oxford Handbook of Papyrology,* Oxford, 216–255.

Varner, Eric R. (2004), *Mutilation and Transformation. Damnatio Memoriae and Roman Imperial Portraiture* (Monumenta Graeca et Romana 10), Leiden/Boston.

Vedder, Ulrike (2012), "Weitergeben, verlorengeben: Dinge als Gedächtnismedien", in: *Zentrum für transdisziplinäre Geschlechterstudien der Humboldt-Universität zu Berlin. Bulletin Texte* 38, 17–28.

Vismann, Cornelia (2008), *Files. Law and Media Technology,* transl. by Geoffrey Winthrop-Young, Standford, CL.

Vismann, Cornelia (2011), *Akten. Medientechnik und Recht,* 3rd ed., Frankfurt a. M.

Vleeming, Sven P. (1991), *The Gooseherds of Hou (Pap. Hou). A Dossier Relating to Various Agricultural Affairs from Provincial Egypt of the Early Fifth Century B. C.* (Studia Demotica 3), Leuven.

Wallenwein, Kirsten (2017), *Corpus subscriptionum. Verzeichnis der Beglaubigungen von spätantiken und frühmittelalterlichen Textabschriften (saec. IV–VIII)* (Quellen und Untersuchungen zur Lateinischen Philologie des Mittelalters 19), Stuttgart.

Wallenwein, Kirsten/Licht, Tino (eds.) (2021), *Reliquienauthentiken. Kulturdenkmäler des Frühmittelalters,* Regensburg.

Waschinski, Emil (1968), "Der Culmer Bischof Stephan Matthias von Neidenburg", in: *Westpreußen-Jahrbuch* 18, 5–7.

Wellmann, Annika (2012), "Theorie der Archive – Archive der Macht. Aktuelle Tendenzen der Archivgeschichte", in: *Neue Politische Literatur* 57, 385–401.

Welzer, Harald (2017), *Das kommunikative Gedächtnis. Eine Theorie der Erinnerung* (Beck'sche Reihe 1669), 4th ed., Munich.

Widder, Ellen (2016), *Kanzler und Kanzleien im Spätmittelalter. Eine Histoire croisée fürstlicher Administration im Südwesten des Reiches* (Veröffentlichungen der Kommission für geschichtliche Landeskunde in Baden-Württemberg, Reihe B: Forschungen 204), Stuttgart.

Wiegartz, Veronika (2004), *Antike Bildwerke im Urteil mittelalterlicher Zeitgenossen* (Marburger Studien zur Kunst- und Kulturgeschichte 7), Weimar.

Wilde, Denise (2015), *Dinge sammeln. Annäherungen an eine Kulturtechnik* (Edition Kulturwissenschaft 62), Bielefeld.

Wimmer, Mario (2016), "Papierorganismen: Stummes Material und verkörperte Zeit in den Archiven", in: Falko Schmieder and Daniel Weidner (eds.), *Ränder des Archivs. Kulturwissenschaftliche Perspektiven auf das Entstehen und Vergehen von Archiven* (LiteraturForschung 30), Berlin, 47–71.

Wirth, Uwe (2005), "Archiv", in: Alexander Roesler and Bernd Stiegler (eds.), *Grundbegriffe der Medientheorie* (UTB 2680), Paderborn, 17–27.

Yadin, Yigael (1962), "Expedition D – The Cave of the Letters", in: *Israel Exploration Journal* 12, 227–257 with plates 43–48.

Zanke, Sebastian (2017), "Exchequer: Das englische Schatzamt", in: Alexander Schubert (ed.), *Richard Löwenherz. König – Ritter – Gefangener,* Regensburg, 306.

Zierold, Martin (2006), *Gesellschaftliche Erinnerung. Eine medienkulturwissenschaftliche Perspektive* (Media and Cultural Memory / Medien und kulturelle Erinnerung 5), Berlin/New York.

Chapter 4
Material Change

Sylvia Brockstieger, Paul Schweitzer-Martin, Johanna Baumgärtel,
Federico Dal Bo, Friederike Elias, Rebecca Hirt, Radu Leca,
Hanna Liss, Bernd Schneidmüller, Melanie Trede

Chapter 4
Material Change

Sylvia Brockstieger, Paul Schweitzer-Martin, Johanna Baumgärtel, Federico Dal Bo, Friederike Elias, Rebecca Hirt, Radu Leca, Hanna Liss, Bernd Schneidmüller, Melanie Trede

We understand material change[1] as any diachronically observable change that affects the material nature of inscribed artefacts, whether this be in terms of the writing material itself or the tools and methods used to create this writing. The format, which determines the specific mediality and praxeology of the artefact—such as a panel, book, or scroll, for example—can also be affected by material change, but not necessarily. Material change can be understood as the disappearance or repression, as well as the emergence, of new writing materials, technologies, and their concomitant cultural practices. Examples that come to mind here, for instance, are the transition from non-typographic to typographic writing cultures, the emergence of paper as a writing material (which replaced and supplemented parchment in a process that lasted many decades[2]), or the change in format from the scroll to the codex.[3] Material change should thus be understood as a process leading to a permanent change in the material presence of inscribed artefacts within a culture over the medium- to long-term. This does not mean, however, that traditional practices must necessarily disappear during or after such change; indeed, traditional materials and practices are able to coexist alongside newly introduced ones for quite some time. Nevertheless, such coexistence often entails a redefinition and reassessment of the significance of previous materials and practices. The perspective on material change adopted in what follows is deliberately broader than the examination of how individual types of media develop would allow,[4] yet this broader perspective allows for material change to become visible in its transcultural and transhistorical relevance.

---

[1] The present chapter on the topic of material change is a continuation of the discussions that took place in the first two funding periods of the CRC 933 (2011–2019) within the context of the working group 'Situations of Material Upheaval' ('Materiale Umbruchssituationen').
[2] Cf. for example Meyer/Schneidmüller 2015; Meyer-Schlenkrich 2018; Schweitzer-Martin 2022a, 145–197.
[3] Cf. Cavallo 2016, 51. See also Peltzer 2020 on the use and function of the scroll in the Middle Ages.
[4] For a basic definition and delimitation of the concept of materiality, cf. the introduction to this volume; on the concept of media, see especially the remarks on the term 'artefact', p. 15–16. The immediate transition from the handwritten book to the printed book is described in this chapter from the perspective of material change and not from the perspective of a change in media, since initially only the production changed, but not the medium that was produced (namely, the book). In mid-fifteenth-century Europe, handwritten and printed books differed strikingly in terms of production, but not in terms of the form of the produced artefacts themselves; the communication contexts in which the medium was

Open Access. © 2024 the authors, published by De Gruyter. This work is licensed under the Creative Commons Attribution-NonCommercial-NoDerivatives 4.0 International License.
https://doi.org/10.1515/9783111325514-005

In analysing material change, our goal is to precisely describe the lasting changes in the material nature of artefacts and thereby also provide more nuanced answers to questions about the implications of these changes for media. In turn, a conceptualisation of the term 'material change' that is viable in a transhistorical sense can only be achieved in a comparative cultural perspective, i. e., by taking into account the respective cultural and historical peculiarities of material-related practices on and with inscribed artefacts. The transition from non-typographic to typographic societies is of particular importance in this context, since it allows for the specific characteristics of non-typographic societies to be cast in higher relief. This perspective of inquiry was also the particular preoccupation of the CRC 933 in its final funding phase, which subsequently directed our gaze all the more intensively back towards other phenomena of material change. The change from the manuscript culture of the Middle Ages to the print culture of the modern era is a topos of cultural memory, at least for Europe, and has accordingly been the subject of research for some time.[5] Nevertheless, a comparable phenomenon can also be observed in other societies, such as those of East Asia, in which inscribed artefacts of a printed nature had already been reproduced in great numbers since the eighth century at the latest.[6] Such societies were thus characterised by a special *longue durée* of handwritten and printed forms of writing existing simultaneously.

At present, we face great challenges in trying to manage the accelerated digital transformation in its material and discursive manifestations. On the one hand, we have to organise and manage the large quantities of data that are rapidly assuming dimensions beyond our imagination; at the same time, we know little about the durability of new writing supports, the duration of their readability, and thus the lifespan of the data stored on them. On the other hand, in the course of the multiplication of the data material, the knowledge stocks linked to this data—as well as their discursive negotiation and interpretation—are also multiplying; participants of the most diverse provenance, experts and non-experts alike, are competing over who ends up having a say in how the digital public sphere is interpreted and designed.

According to one of the guidelines behind the research design of the CRC 933, looking back in time can illuminate for us and provide perspectives on experiences

---

effective also remained the same for the time being. Only over the course of several decades did the design of the books, among other things, become more differentiated and the conditions of reception also change. It is only from this point on that one can speak of different media.

5 This change has been described teleologically in older scholarship. Questions about the manifold phenomena of overlapping and interference with regard to manuscript and print have only played a role in recent times; cf. most recently (with references to the history of scholarship here as well) the anthology of Brockstieger/Schweitzer-Martin 2023. Cf. also Augustyn 2003, 5–47; Mentzel-Reuters 2010; Schmitz 2018, 11–41; Kornicki 2019; and Dover 2021, 24–25.

6 Moments of material change can be identified in Japan, for example, with the simultaneous importing of movable wooden type by Jesuit missionaries on the one hand and metal type imported from the Korean peninsula on the other in the decades before and after 1600; cf. Sasaki 2023.

of change, acceleration, multiplication, and diversification that result from situations of material upheaval. A quantitative increase and qualitative change in the material(s) used for inscribed artefacts could also go hand in hand in the past.[7] Thus, the cross-cultural analysis of past text cultures as well as that of the present day characterised by increasing digitality complement each other in the attempt to understand better the phenomenon of material change, its preconditions, and its consequences.

If we take once again the material change that occurred in early modern Europe as a starting point, we can observe that present-day experiences of the abundance and variety of knowledge, media, and material are structurally quite similar to the experience of the dissolution of boundaries that took place at the beginning of the print era in Europe in the fifteenth and sixteenth centuries. Complaints about the number of books—and the occasional reflection of this in criticism, for example in the form of imaginary libraries or satirical book catalogues[8]—went hand in hand at the time with the conviction that people were living in a 'new age'. Through the conquest of new worlds, of either a geographical or cosmological nature, this new era also opened up new knowledge that had to be processed accordingly by means of the media of the day.[9] In new encyclopaedias, authors attempted to organise, categorise, and make manageable this newfound knowledge, yet time and time again ran up against the incompleteness of knowledge and thus also of their literary undertakings.[10]

The implications of the boom in knowledge and the flood of books—implications perceived as positive, albeit with the potential to spark a crisis—together with the intricate interdependencies of changes to media and knowledge due to the increase in and diversification of the knowledge available in early modern Europe have long been described by researchers in a nuanced way that goes beyond mere narratives of progress.[11] The much-described media revolution in the 'Gutenberg Galaxy'[12] is closely and causally linked to a specific form of material change, with this form often

---

7 The concept of the inscribed artefact for the premodern era may be only partially suitable for the analysis of the 'digital age'. However, data is also physically present, even if it cannot be directly changed by hand. Thus, one could possibly speak of digital inscribed artefacts.
8 Cf. Werle 2007; Dover 2021, 27–30; on the reorganisation of (the vast increase of) knowledge in the print era, cf. generally also Schmidt-Biggemann 1983; Seifert 1976.
9 Cf. the recent work of the DFG research unit FOR 2305 'Discursivisations of the New. Tradition and Innovation in Medieval and Early Modern Texts and Images' at the Free University of Berlin.
10 On the history of encyclopaedias, cf. Schneider 2006; Stammen/Weber 2004; on the organisation of knowledge, cf. also Blair 2020.
11 In this context, the work of the CRC 573 'Pluralisation and Authority in the Early Modern Period' from 2001–2011 at the Ludwig Maximilian University of Munich merits special mention, as it was able to show the tense way in which the authoritative dynamics of demarcation and the pluralising dynamics behind the dissolution of such boundaries shaped the political, epistemic, and literary structure of the early modern period. For an overview, cf. Dover 2021.
12 In his book of the same name, Marshall McLuhan describes the fundamental change in the social and cognitive layout of the early modern period that was triggered by the printing press, cf. McLuhan 1962; cf. fundamentally and for an introduction on the topic Garncarz 2016.

being lumped in with the concept of media and made synonymous with the problem of changes in media. In order for the book to be able to contribute qua medium to the corresponding epistemic, social, political, and cultural advances in early modern Europe, it first had to make the leap from the handwritten book—i.e., the codex— to the printed book. It had to be converted materially—i.e., via the production of paper; the manufacture of type; the development of typesetting boxes, printing ink, and the printing press; as well as via printing and distribution practices—from manuscript to print and become subject to new praxeological conditions.

The following theses describing and explaining material change are the result of the analysis of different situations of cultural upheaval that took place under disparate conditions of transmission and in very different fields of writing. It is precisely this historical, culture-specific variation that plays an important role in the presentation, as does the question as to the relationship between material change and other factors of cultural change.[13] We can only describe material change by taking into account the actors involved as well as the conditions and consequences of the given cultural context. Furthermore, in doing so, we must also consider the influence of power relations on, as well as culturally specific reactions (cultural and technological critique, but also narratives of progress) to, processes of material change. Finally, we must also be mindful of instances of non-simultaneity and the reasons behind these (Thesis 19) and must focus on the changing functions of material as well as of cultural text practices (Thesis 20).[14]

As for the present chapter: we have written this against the backdrop of material change as outlined above—namely, the current change from print culture to the digital age—which has refined our perspective on past processes of material change.[15] This leads to the critical negotiation of the processes of change or their significance for society, as is shown in Theses 21–23 (the critique of processes of change; the valorisation through recourse to traditional forms and formats; and the functionalisation of materiality in power relations).

---

13 On the relationship of technological change to social change, cf. Ogburn 1965; on cultural change, Elias 1939. Chapter 6 'Political Rule and Administration' shows that a change in the function of a text (for example, when it is transferred from an administrative context to the function of the 'pure' demonstration of power) often coincides with material change.
14 Some of the CRC 933's previous work has focused significantly on the change in meaning of materially altered artefacts and the change in practices associated with them; cf. Bolle 2020; Bolle/von der Höh/Jaspert 2019; Sarri 2017. Important reference projects for this research issue were the subprojects A01 ('Lettered and Inscribed. Inscriptions in Urban Space in the Greco-Roman Period and Middle Ages') and B09 ('Bamboo and Wood as Writing Materials in Early China').
15 Cf. Schneidmüller/Schweitzer-Martin 2020.

Thesis 19
The materiality of text cultures changes not in leaps and bounds, but in processes of a continual nature.

In cultural studies, a wide variety of thought patterns, terms, and metaphors have been used to describe processes of historical change: one finds talk of 'ruptures', 'boundaries', 'leaps', 'crises', and 'revolutions', but also of 'evolutions', 'development', 'change', and *longue durée*.[16] It is always tempting to reduce historical changes to moments of quick transition, which seems to be an easier explanation than the historically appropriate description of the inner dynamics of processual events.

The same goes for the phenomenon of material change in text cultures. It seems obvious in the course of describing such change to look for specific inventions and to trace the (planned) measures of their implementation within a given material culture; doing so would allow for a 'new approach', an innovation, to become tangible as such. The fact that innovators such as Johannes Gutenberg were stylised accordingly for purposes of cultural self-assurance seems to prove this need for a simple linear explanation. We should note, however, that this need is not only observable in modern (popular) scientific reception—Gutenberg still has a fixed place in cultural memory, even though his alleged innovation has long been the subject of critical inquiry—but can also be ascertained much earlier. The invention of typography was claimed as a particularly German achievement as early as the sixteenth century: in Nicodemus Frischlin's comedy *Iulius Redivivus* (1585), for example, the printing press, gunpowder, and the mathematical and astronomical masterpiece of the Strasbourg Cathedral clock are all mentioned in one single breath in the dialogue between Cicero and Caesar as being a triumvirate of German erudition and inventiveness. Thus, especially in the case of printing, a turning point in material cultural is cast in a patriotic light.[17] Particularly in the case of European letterpress printing, present-day observers must be aware that both the model and language of description are preformed culturally to the highest degree.

If we approach the phenomena of material change 'from below'—i.e., from the perspective of textual cultural practice—continuities become more prominent, while sudden ruptures and planned measures recede from view.[18] In the case of the transition from manuscript to print in the cultural sphere of Central Europe in the early

---

16 Cf. for example Kuhn 1976; Braudel 1977.
17 On this connection, cf. Schade 1984, 114–115. As early as 1499, the so-called Koelhoff Chronicle printed in Cologne discusses who was the inventor of letterpress printing with movable type and where it could be found locally. On this, cf. Meyer-Schlenkrich/Schweitzer-Martin 2023, 9–11; on the connection between the publishing activities of the printing houses and patriotic discourse in the early modern period, cf. Brockstieger 2018.
18 For example Needham 2015; Meyer-Schlenkrich 2018.

modern period, we can observe that we are dealing with a long-lasting process that has not yet come to an end. On the contrary, handwriting has been used to complement print in various ways (for example, in publishing or correction contexts), and can sometimes take on completely new functions (by bestowing a certain aura on a text or imbuing it with authority and/or authenticity, for instance), but has never become completely obsolete.[19] In the course of a new type of "bequest consciousness" ("Nachlassbewusstsein"),[20] autographs as well as ephemeral handwritten products came to be viewed as being material worthy of preservation and collection from the late eighteenth century onwards. Before that time, over the course of the 'long' early modern period, handwriting was used in a variety of ways. It was employed (in the publication process) to 'bring books into print'; it was also used to 'deal with' printed books—of course, by means of such long-established writing techniques as glossing or annotating. Handwriting was also used when working with and on printed materials in order to engage actively with the knowledge presented in such works and to personalise and adapt the printed text to new contexts of use. Some printed books are even intended to be adapted to personal handwritten activity via the use of leading or of specific page layouts (i. e., a corresponding affordance), such as calendrical diaries ('Schreibkalender', cf. Fig. 1) or emblem books replete with white space, which were transferred to new social and textual contexts under the moniker *alba amicorum*.[21]

In Europe, all such practices of individualising what is written testify to a new function of handwriting—one that is more dynamic and more ephemeral than was the case in previous centuries—and points ahead to modern concepts of authorship.

An even deeper form of manuscript and print existing side by side can be observed in seventeenth-century Japan. Here, too, continuity does not appear as a linear chain of events, but rather is characterised by impulses of a reciprocal nature. Even more so than is the case in Europe, the change from handwriting to printing appears in Japan as a retrospective interpretation of a historical phenomenon. For contemporaries, the change was probably not perceived as such, since the use of typography was in most cases limited to a small circle (primarily social elites). Print often remained a complementary medium to handwriting, both in terms of its intensity of use and its cultural prestige. For this reason, various printed genres usually imitate handwritten formats, merely offering a less cost-intensive alternative above a certain print runs compared to works copied out by hand.

---

19 Cf. Dover 2021, 24–25. For basic information on phenomena of interference up to ca. 1800, cf. the volume by Brockstieger/Hirt 2023. On continuities and simultaneities: Brockstieger/Schweitzer-Martin 2023.
20 Cf. Sina/Spoerhase 2017, our translation.
21 Cf. Brockstieger/Hirt 2023. On the phenomenon of leading/white space, cf. fundamentally Brendecke 2005; Feuerstein-Herz 2017.

Fig. 1: [Anonymous owner,] Georg Galgenmeyer, *Schreibkalender [...] [auf 1603]* ('Calendrical diary [...] [for 1603]'), Augsburg: Hans Schultes 1602 (Herzog August Bibliothek Wolfenbüttel, Xb 1719), pp. [2]v–[3]r. © Herzog August Bibliothek Wolfenbüttel, http://diglib.hab.de/drucke/xb-1719/start.htm?image=00004 (CC BY-SA 3.0).

In East Asia, the norm was not for prints to be made with movable type; rather, block books were made, i. e., books whose pages were each printed with wooden blocks into which images and texts were carved. Although block books appeared in Europe in the fifteenth century at about the same time as did incunabula, they were only used for certain prints. Thus, we see the block book technique being regularly used in the fifteenth and sixteenth centuries especially for lavishly illustrated genres and textbooks, which were frequently reprinted.[22] The different status and range of use of the two reproduction techniques in Asia and Europe can be attributed to various factors, ranging from the number of characters used in the respective writing systems to layout conventions and reader expectations.

Japanese block books did not simply reproduce handwriting, so they did not simply look like books written by hand. Rather, they imitated the individual hand of a single calligrapher, with print and manuscript thus being almost indistinguishable. Since the technique of woodblock printing required only a small investment, private printing with such blocks was more widespread in East Asia and often contributed significantly to enhancing the reputation of texts and their authors, as in the case of Zhang Chao or Ihara Saikaku, who self-published and distributed their texts

---

22 Cf. Wagner 2012 and 2017; Schmitz 2018, 1–11.

to a select circle of acquaintances.²³ In these cases, printing is not an autonomous practice, but rather one that reproduces the social practices of preceding manuscript cultures.

Continuities between manuscripts and printed works can also be seen in the area of content, since prints often contain allusions and references to manuscript traditions. Emerging text media such as commercially printed books benefited from the cultural prestige of famous manuscript texts by reproducing the latter. This is evident in printed versions of calligraphy miscellanea, such as the *Album of Venerable Calligraphy* (*Kohitsu tekagami* 古筆手鑑) from 1651, in which we can read the following in the preface: "I applied myself diligently to the rendering of fine brushwork, the intensity, the angle of the brush and so on. While there may be mistakes in the block printing, the shape of characters should not be doubted at all."²⁴ This admission of the limitations of the reproduction technique subordinates the printed book to the manuscripts it imitates. In this way, in a predominantly manuscript culture, the shared knowledge of readers is shaped by handwritten texts, and thus printed media often contain allusions and references to handwritten media.²⁵

This 'phenomenon of persistence' is also attested elsewhere: the advent of cheaper printing alternatives made manuscripts more desirable on account of their higher prestige. In Japan, for example, hand-painted silk scrolls enjoyed great popularity once again in the seventeenth century. Before the early modern period, only very few scrolls — just three in number have survived to our knowledge — had been painted on silk. The norm, by contrast, was to paint on *washi* (和紙, a Japanese paper that is tougher than paper made from wood pulp). In the seventeenth century, however, a newly wealthy class of merchants began to commission scrolls with hitherto unknown decoration as symbols of their social status. In truth, such artefacts were mostly intended as purely representational items, being displayed on special occasions or given as part of a dowry; they were probably not read as such. The social practice associated with the artefact was in turn replicated through printing. In the prefaces of some block book editions that contained selected illustrated stories previously reproduced in manuscript form, for example, there was a note that every bride should have this book amongst her accoutrements.²⁶

---

23 Cf. Son 2018, 53.
24 Kanai 1989, 146; English translation in Leca 2022a, 84; see also Komatsu 1972, 95–102.
25 Cf. Leca 2022a, 84.
26 Cf. Ishikawa 2020.

Thesis 20
The affordance and function of inscribed artefacts, as well as practices of production and reception, change asynchronously along with processes of material change.

The material constitution of inscribed artefacts and thus their production processes are subject to constant change, along with the expected and actual use of the artefacts. Writing and reading[27] — to name the most common, but by no means only text-related activities — are not historically and culturally constant practices. They change with the form, material, and socially assigned function of textual artefacts. At the same time, the affordance of inscribed artefacts also changes: i.e., the common use that is proffered or suggested by the material form and the knowledge 'expected' from a text about which writing-related practices are to be carried out on and with it.[28] Furthermore, as we address in the following, this change in practices does not proceed in leaps and bounds, nor does it take place synchronously with material change. Thus, practices of writing and reading can either emerge intact after an instance of material change, or such practices themselves can change and in turn influence the processes of material change with respect to writing supports or implements. The institutions responsible for the production, dissemination, or use of the artefacts (or at least those that promote them) also continue to change or even disappear, which additionally influences material change and changes in material-related practices.

When we think of text-related practices, the first thing that comes to mind today (besides writing) is reading, which has also changed fundamentally over the centuries and, as a practice, varies greatly depending on the text's intended function. Reading in religious contexts is different from reading in legal contexts; the same practice undertaken in scientific contexts differs again from that in literary contexts. And reading as a silent practice on the part of an individual, for example, has taken centuries to develop; in European antiquity, people read aloud.[29] Augustine specifically highlights the experience of reading aloud in his *Confessions* (VI.3). In the early 1990s, Ivan Illich presented his study *In the Vineyard of the Text*,[30] in which he posits the thesis that reading developed in the twelfth century from a quiet murmuring to the practice of silent reading, and that the emergence of our modern concept of a 'text' as something independent of the material of the text is connected to this. Similar processes can be

---

27 Cf. Gertz et al. 2015; Berti et al. 2015.
28 Cf. Fox/Panagiotopoulos/Tsouparopoulou 2015.
29 Fundamental here is Svenbro 1988. The general preponderance of reading done aloud in European antiquity is a point of consensus in research, even if a categorical exclusion of silent reading is controversial (see Gavrilov 1997). Cf. also Leipziger 2021.
30 Cf. Illich 1993.

found in other cultural contexts, with changes in text-related practices going hand in hand with changings to the text supports as well.[31]

Sometimes, text-related practices change and subsequently material change takes place. In other cases, text-related practices remain the same, although the material form of the texts has changed considerably. This can be observed particularly well in a typical set of reading and writing practices of contemporary culture in industrialised countries: namely, writing and reading on digital devices. Many practices of the 'analogue' era or even the manuscript age have not disappeared, but have simply been incorporated into these new developments, probably in part so as to simplify processes of adaptation. Transitions from one material to another, as well as from one medium to another, do not happen quickly, but rather slowly and discontinuously. At the same time, traditional practices flow into the design of new forms. Present-day word processing programs, for instance, include fonts that imitate handwriting. This entails either that the creators of such programs assume that the customers are interested in imitating handwriting in texts created digitally, or that they want to narrow the gap between the handwritten and the digital. Moreover, despite extensive digitalisation, traditional materials, techniques, and practices are not on their way out, much less disappearing of a sudden. Writing by hand, just like paper, remains widespread even after the vast deployment of digital techniques. Another practice that possibly refers to the material form of the scroll—or at least takes up the layout of scrolls, which we rarely deal with in everyday life—is in fact common when reading on the internet: we speak of 'scrolling' up and down a webpage. Again, the haptics of the scroll properly speaking are absent, but the notion of the material artefact of the scroll prefigures the digital practice. Other practices, such as turning pages or 'leafing' through a text, are also possible digitally (although only in a visual and not haptic sense). It seems as if this is a deliberate imitation of the practice of reading books, which contributes to the easier use of the new form.

In addition to this continuity of text-related practices after the occurrence of material change, however, we find completely new forms of text-person interaction also emerging in the digital space. Through these new forms of interaction, the formerly fixed functions of author, editor, and reader have transitioned into a more complex interrelationship. This is the case, for example, with so-called kinetic typography, which combines classical typography with animation in the form of a film, and three-dimensional typography, which has only become possible by the use of interactive Internet 2.0 technology. In his dissertation entitled *Rethinking the Book* from 1999, David Small has attempted to create a completely new, user-generated layout of the Talmud through kinetic typography (cf. Fig. 2).[32] The traditional idea

---

[31] Cf. Burnyeat 1997. For a philosophical interpretation of the concept of 'silent reading', cf. Stock 2009, 62–63. For an emotional or phenomenological reading of Augustine's Confessions, cf. the commentary on *Conf.* IV.3 in De Monticelli 1990.
[32] Cf. Small 1999.

Fig. 2: David Small, *Talmud Project*, Exhibition at the Cooper-Hewitt Museum's first National Design Triennial. © David Small.

of the book—both that of the codex as well as the 'modern book'—is expanded here to include the representation of an online hypertext and is thus able to be displayed in a 3D layout, with Small's development allowing one "to position text at any size, position and orientation in an extremely large three-dimensional space."[33] The work is experimental and brief, numbering only just over a hundred pages, yet it offers a glimpse into the possible future of texts as they break away from the traditional material form of what is written and enter digital space.

Thus far, digital representations have imitated forms for which there are established practices of use (paper, books, sometimes scrolls). With David Small's programme for reading the Talmud (cf. Fig. 2), author, editor, and reader are combined into a single figure. At the same time, this form of visualisation takes into account the complex textual form of the Talmud, which itself consists of the Mishna and the Gemara, i. e., a text and the multifaceted commentary on this text hailing from many sources. It is safe to assume that it is not by chance that Small came up with the idea of representing the Talmud through this experimental layout and of implying that such digital representations of the page were more 'suitable' for study than the traditional design of a bound book.[34]

---

[33] Small 1999, 26.
[34] Further reading: Hillner 2009, 44–45; Heller 2011; Reas/Fry 2014, 321.

The relationship of people to texts, the written word, and inscribed artefacts is part and parcel of a text culture. This is also true for cases in which we physically handle texts. Even if digitisation understood narrowly does not mean dematerialisation — since data must be physically stored, maintained, and kept available — we can still speak of an increasingly abstract relation of text to the body. Digital books are differentiated not by weight and size, but by the amount of data they contain and the computing capacity required to use them. Even before digitisation, material change was accompanied by a decrease in the use of an individual person's body. If texts had to be copied word by word in scriptoria by hand, each step towards mechanised processes — from the block book and printing with movable type to digital printing — has been accompanied by less physical work.[35]

Perhaps, then, it could be suggested that the use of the human body is becoming increasingly unnecessary in many phenomena of material change. Even though certain designs, such as the abovementioned 'leafing through' or 'scrolling', each simulate their own physicality or use of the body for different practical activities, all one needs to do to interact with or have an influence on digital products is often nothing more than swipe or press a finger. Designs in which more physical input is required, as is seen in some computer games, are not necessitated by the thing itself, but rather are the result of free design decisions. Even in mixed processes (analogue and digital together), such as the scanning of handwritten bank transfers, the number of physical activities is at least reduced. We can conclude that less material diversity results in less material experience of difference. If Niklas Luhmann once wrote that the human body had lost its significance as a locus for the perception of meaning and culture through its replacement by the book, what would he say about the development of digital writing?[36] At the very least, as Irmela Schneider argues, whenever new media emerge, the function and role of the body must be renegotiated.[37] The digitisation of text-related practices preserves the old experience of reading books and scrolls via simulation; at the same time, it changes the interaction of text, the written word, and a given person (producer/recipient) in ways that cannot yet be fully surveyed.[38]

The transition in media from manuscript to print also changes the dynamics of user responses. There is an inherent tension and feedback loop between prescribed uses (which must be more varied and general in the case of a more widespread medium such as print) and idiosyncratic ones made by individual users (which are more characteristic of manuscript cultures). After considering the interaction of persons and

---

35 At the same time, the copyists were challenged by the in part creative adaptation of written documents to specific situations, i. e., they were more intellectually involved than the typesetters of later times. Cf. Gertz et al. 2015, 585.
36 Cf. Luhmann 1990, 599.
37 Cf. Schneider 2000, 16.
38 For a comparison between 'digital natives' and 'digital immigrants' and their respective metaphors, see Günther 2007.

texts/writing, we shall now look more closely at the ways in which the material properties and social context of texts condition and enable specific reader responses. It can be shown that the form and materiality of texts are intertwined with processes of both standardisation and pluralisation of use when new content is adapted to print editions for new audiences.

To illustrate this, let us consider an example of transcultural adaptation. A group of Japanese physicians and admirers of Western scholarship set out to show that the previously held understanding of anatomy from Chinese sources was wrong by translating a Western work on the subject, namely Johann Adam Kulmus's *Anatomical Tables* (titled in Japanese *Kaitai shinsho* 解体新書 ['New Book of Anatomy']). The lengthy translation process of three and a half years involved several types of material changes.[39] This is because Japanese book culture—unlike the text's original Western context—used different book formats, printing techniques, papers, and bindings; frontispieces were not employed; and three different forms of writing (Chinese ideograms and two syllabaries) were used to write down the language. Additionally, Japanese culture described the body in terms of its involvement in the flow of energy in the universe, which meant that there was often no analogous native Japanese terminology for body parts referenced in the original Western text. The accompanying material changes are reflected in the shape of the frontispiece (cf. Fig. 3).[40] This itself is unusual for East Asian books and proclaims the book's status as a Western tome. The materiality of the page had to be adapted, both in terms of raw material (Western paper versus *washi)*, size (the Japanese edition is slightly smaller), and reproduction technique (copperplate engraving versus woodcut).[41] They were selected from another book, indicating that efforts were made to create a visuality that was adapted to the Japanese context and the intended readership there. This is reflected in the visual changes: the coats of arms are taken from another source and are symmetrical, which again is unusual for East Asian design and therefore suggests a Western origin. The man covers his pubic area, most likely the result of a publishing strategy aimed at circumventing censorship by the authorities, which included printing a sample edition with simplified content that was offered as a gift to the latter.[42]

The transformations in the text are also multi-layered. The title appears in archaic Chinese writing, and in fact, the entire book is written using only Chinese ideograms for either their phonetic or semiotic values in Japanese, the latter usage entailing the development of many new terms to describe the anatomical knowledge conveyed in Kulmus's work. Overall, this was an adaptation to standard Sinosphere format and

---

39 The following discussion is based on Lukacs 2008, 23–175. See also Proust 2002, 182–192.
40 For a detailed discussion of the frontispiece, see Lukacs 2008, 49–56.
41 The latter was a reversal of an earlier change in reproduction technique: the anatomical images used by Kulmus had already moved on from the woodcuts made by Vesalius to the latter's copperplate engravings. Cf. Lukacs 2008, 41.
42 Lukacs 2008, 47, 110.

Fig. 3: Odano Naotake, frontispiece of the engravings section of the introductory volume of *Kaitai shinsho* 解体新書 ('New Book of Anatomy'), 1774, woodcut, ink on *washi*, 26.1 × 18.1 cm, National Library of Medicine, Bethesda, MD (USA), http://resource.nlm.nih.gov/101147255X1 (accessed 27/1/2022), Public Domain.

graphics. One form of reader response was shown by Shiba Kōkan, a close associate of the group of translators. Kōkan pointed out that it was difficult for lay people to understand the ideograms and, what is more, that it was not easy to translate the text as such into maxims and commentaries (as was the case with the Confucian classics). Instead, in one of his own treatises, Kōkan attempted to adapt the content of the anatomy book for a wider Japanese audience by providing an explanation "in ordinary language and phonetic characters"[43] that also drew on the East Asian concepts of the five elements and the opposition of *yin* and *yang*.

Returning to the original translation: it should be noted that it contains yet another layer of writing. The characters for the five elements in archaic Chinese script are used as symbols for the Western books from which the illustrations were copied.[44] This bibliographical technique reflects a pluralisation of usage in the service of the Japanese scholarly community, which was familiar both with the practice of citing Chinese classics as authoritative texts and with the indexical form of knowledge classification common in Europe. By incorporating all these strategies, the book met the expectations and goals of a broad scholarly community among whom it became a 'textual institution'.[45] It thus achieved a high degree of adaptation to textual cultural practices and thus of affordance, as evidenced by the fact that three editions were printed in quick succession.[46] The expanding readership of this translation added yet another layer of text in the form of handwritten annotations, corresponding to a pluralisation of usage in didactic contexts; Koishi Genshun used the book in his Confucian Academy and glossed the printed text for this purpose. These annotations were in turn copied by his students into their own copies of the text. This shows how the culture of writing was used in conjunction with the prints to adapt the text to different uses.

In the foregoing, we can see that the tension or dynamics that arises in the course of the transition to a new written medium often leads to a rethinking of established modes of meaning-making and reading behaviour. New media allow for experimentation with different combinations of existing and emerging textual and paratextual elements. Similar phenomena can also be observed in other cultural contexts. Thus, within the complex history of the layout of early Hebrew prints, one can discern a gradual transition—certainly also due to issues of technical development—from rather simple to very complex typographical forms. One of the most striking examples is probably the printing of a Jewish code of law, written by the famous Jewish philosopher Maimonides, which is organised in an extremely complex way with many typographically interlocking columns (cf. Fig. 4). While it should be obvious that this legal text is addressed to an elite audience, it cannot be denied that consulting this volume is itself a very complex task. It is doubtful whether the editors of this text had actu-

---

43 *Dokushō bōgen*, in: Shiba Kōkan, *Shiba Kōkan zenshū*, 24–25; discussed in Screech 2002, 89.
44 Cf. Lukacs 2008, 40.
45 Cf. Marcon 2020, 137–138.
46 On the impact of *Kaitai shinsho*, see Lukacs 2008, 165–180 and Jackson 2016, 116–117.

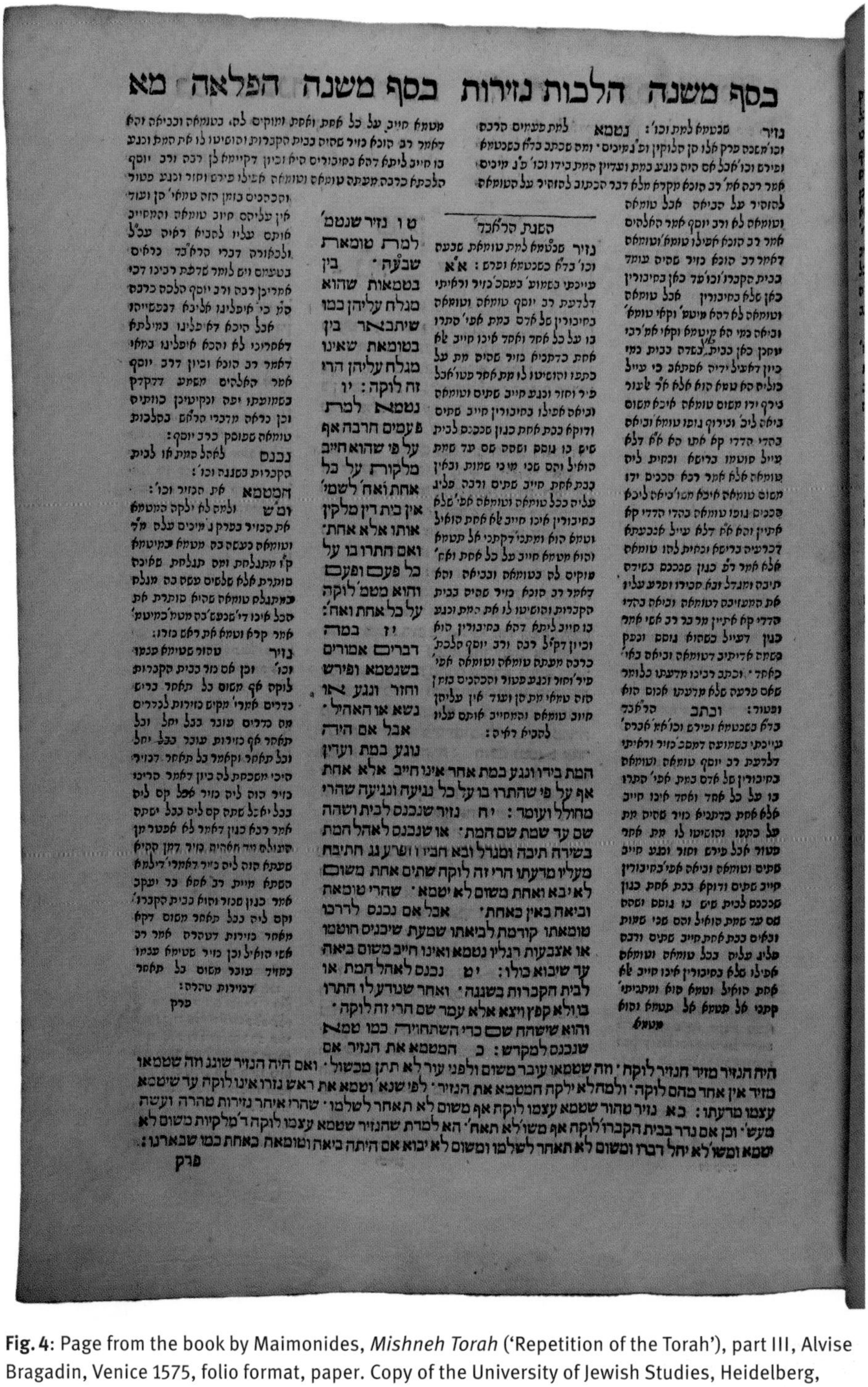
כסף משנה הלכות נזירות כסף משנה הפלאה מא

Fig. 4: Page from the book by Maimonides, *Mishneh Torah* ('Repetition of the Torah'), part III, Alvise Bragadin, Venice 1575, folio format, paper. Copy of the University of Jewish Studies, Heidelberg, call no. 296.53 VENE 1,3. © University of Jewish Studies, Heidelberg.

ally intended to compile a 'readable' book, i. e., if the volume was truly intended for practical use on the part of readers, or whether they did not also want to demonstrate the nature and organisation of knowledge, which is evident in the complex layout of a page containing several commentaries on the main text.

The analysis of the interaction between artefacts and users thus shows that text-related practices undergo change, but that this does not happen synchronously with material change, and that practices even end up being preserved that refer to forms and materials that have already become outdated. Moreover, it becomes apparent that the affordance of writing was specifically shaped in accordance with social customs.

Thesis 21
Material change sparks ambivalent reactions.

Through changes in production techniques and writing materials, reception techniques and practices also change.[47] On the one hand, such change is often emphatically welcomed as an achievement of innovation and progress, with people seeing in the material change an opportunity for changed distribution and new contexts of reception and use. On the other hand, innovations can also provoke negative reactions: concerns and reservations about the effects of these innovations might arise, especially related to fears of a loss of control and the anticipated loss of various cultural techniques. Finally, 'control fantasies', i. e., ideas of limiting or minimising the effects of material change via technical or legal means, also appear time and again as a reaction to such change.

This can be observed in medieval and early modern Europe, for example, both with regard to paper as a writing material and to printing as an innovation closely linked to this material. Printing was accompanied by enormous social upheavals that manifested themselves in disputes over whose interpretation was correct or authoritative for individual writings as well as in fundamental discussions about the value and function of entire cultural techniques. Printing books was viewed critically because some feared not only that material quality could suffer as a result of mass production, but also that one could lose the overview of printed texts and thus control over their content. As early as Gutenberg's time, people were critical of the fact that more was being printed in a day than had been previously copied in an entire year.[48]

One of the best-known contemporary reflections on early printing in Latin Europe is the 1492 treatise *De Laude Scriptorum* ('On the Praise of Scribes') by the humanist

---

[47] Cf. for example Reudenbach 2015.
[48] Cf. Widmann 1973, 8.

and Benedictine abbot Johannes Trithemius (1462–1516), in which the monk asks what difference there is between handwritten and printed material. He claims that whatever is written on parchment can last for a millennium. Yet in his argument, he questions how long printed writing might endure, since it is only something made out of paper *(res papirea)*; if a paper volume should end up lasting two hundred years, Trithemius surmises that this would already be a long time, and yet he states that many people believed they had to put their material into print.[49] In his treatise, however, Trithemius discusses not only the question of the writing material, but also that of the writing technique. In the course of his text, it becomes clear that the cultural technique of writing is important to him as a means of maintaining monastic vitality and combating listlessness or laziness *(acedia)*.[50] He is therefore not concerned with a blanket criticism of the new writing material or a different reproduction technique, but rather formulates his concern in terms of the loss of an existing cultural technique.

The assumption that paper was not of a durable nature dates back to the twelfth century in Latin Europe, the earliest time that paper was used there.[51] Often, these arguments occur in the context of administrative writings, where copies of paper documents were to be made on parchment or where the enclosure or attachment of certain documents on paper was prohibited with reference to their supposed lack of durability.[52] However, the advantages of paper were also seen, both in the quantity available and in the usually lower price compared to parchment.[53] Supply chain shortages in writing material remained a persistent problem, however, and the argument of availability and resources is encountered even in today's digital age. Although the basic raw material changed from old rags in the Middle Ages to wood pulp in the nineteenth century, the issue of the dearth of paper remains relevant up into the modern era.[54]

Trithemius's text can be understood as an ambivalent reaction to the material change that had already been perceived and reflected upon as such by his contemporaries. However, we can observe this not only in texts from Latin Europe, but also from other parts of the world. One such example is the 1684 novel by the Japanese author Ihara Saikaku, entitled *Kōshoku Nidai Otoko Shoen Okagami* 諸艶大鏡 好色二代男 ('The Great Mirror of Beauties: Son of an Amorous Man'). In the novel, which

---

49 Cf. Johannes Trithemius, *De Laude Scriptorum*, 62–65. This passage is widely cited; to name but a few instances, cf. Embach 2000; Marks 1980; Needham 2015.
50 Cf. Herweg 2010, 411–412.
51 Authoritative on the perception of paper: Meyer-Schlenkrich 2018, 198–200; on the social acceptance and social distinction of the choice between paper and parchment, cf. ibid., 213–216; for further prohibitions on paper use without explicit reference to its lack of durability, cf. ibid., 224–231.
52 Cf. Meyer-Schlenkrich 2018, 224–231.
53 Cf. Herweg 2010, 426.
54 Fulda University of Applied Sciences, for example, ran out of paper in the wake of the COVID-19 pandemic and produced its certificates digitally for a limited time: Malkmus 2020. See also Beckmann Petey 2021. After the Second World War, many newspapers in Germany could only print issues on a limited number of days per week due to the lack of paper, cf. Dussel 2004.

describes how an old man orders a copy of a novel from a chief courtesan and receives a printed copy instead of a beautifully calligraphed scroll, the criticism of the loss of time-honoured cultural techniques plays a central role. The old man's disappointment with the printed copy stands for a re-evaluation of the manuscript format, which must simultaneously be understood against Saikaku's own biographical background. Throughout his life as a poet, the author participated in a manuscript culture, albeit experimenting at times with printing techniques as well. Moreover, this criticism in the novel formulates in almost satirical fashion how a man in this situation cannot keep up with the times and that through the agency of the chief courtesan, the old man of all people receives a less valuable copy of the writing.

In the European context, besides the cultural criticism of printing, the control of the publishing sector played a central role, especially in the context of religious disputes, which could (even if not necessarily) find expression in a fundamental rejection of printing. Thus, we find amongst Jewish intellectuals in Western and Central Europe in the fifteenth and sixteenth centuries a multitude of reflections on printing with movable type.[55] The critics of printing feared above all that the writing down by hand of commentary and the individual glossing of texts would disappear as part of learning and of the transmission of knowledge from teacher to pupil(s), and that this loss would lead to an inadmissible levelling and standardisation of religious content, as is seen, for instance, in the super-commentaries on the Talmud.[56] This is because the Ashkenazi scholarly tradition did not seek to establish a closed doctrinal canon via these texts, but rather to preserve individual opinions and local traditions *(minhag ha-maqom)* by means of continuous glossing and updating in the context of learning within the yeshiva (Talmudic academy).[57]

It is therefore no coincidence that among Jewish scholars, the debate about printing was initially sparked by the discussion about the dissemination and canonisation of halakhic knowledge (i.e, legal issues, pertaining to *halakha*). This can be exemplified by the dispute over the printing of the halakhic work *Torat ha-Ḥaṭṭat* ('Teaching on the sin offering', printed in Kraków in 1569) by Rabbi Moshe ben Israel Isserles (acronym: ReMa; 1530–1572).[58] In the introduction to his work, ReMa not only ques-

---

[55] Cf. Reiner 1997.
[56] The *Talmud* (Heb. 'teaching') is a collection of rabbinical commentaries by scholars from seven generations on 36 of the 63 tractates of the Mishna, i.e., the compilation of traditional religious law made around 200 CE. It has come down in two versions: a Palestinian one with a *terminus post quem* of 400 CE (the Jerusalem Talmud or *Talmud Yerushalmi/Talmud Eretz Yisrael*), and a Babylonian one from around 500 CE (the Babylonian Talmud or *Talmud Bavli*). To this day, the *Talmud Bavli* enjoys greater authority than the *Talmud Yerushalmi*.
[57] Cf. Reiner 1997, 91–93.
[58] At the same time, ReMa was also caught up in the discussion about Maimonides's main philosophical work *Moreh ha-Nevukhim* ('The Guide for the Perplexed'), which gripped the Talmudic schools between Poland and Germany in the mid-sixteenth century; on the whole, cf. especially Reiner 1997, 93–96.

tioned the authority of the hitherto authoritative text, *Sha'arei Dura*,⁵⁹ but also its value for text criticism, and announced that he would make editorial interventions of his own. Above all, R. Ḥayyim ben Bezalel of Friedberg (ca. 1520–1588), the brother of the famous R. Yehuda Löw ben Bezalel (acronym: the MaHaRaL of Prague), comprehensively attacked the printing of *Torat ha-Ḥaṭṭat* in a retort entitled *Vikkuaḥ Mayyim Ḥayyim* ('The argument over living waters', with a pun on the author's own name): Ḥayyim held that in the Talmudic academies, one should continue to study the relevant halakhic sources⁶⁰ only with the help of a teacher on the basis of a book compiled specifically for the pupil's instruction. In this context, he especially criticised the fact that with the advent of printed halakhic compendia, an individual rabbi could henceforth base his religious practice on books rather than on a halakhic expert and adjudicator *(poseq)*. This in turn, in the MaHaRaL's view, would lead to the unnecessary loss of local customs and interpretations, which would fundamentally contradict the essence of halakhic decision-making—because, after all, there had never been a universal halakha. For Ḥayyim von Friedberg, then, it was not simply a matter of contrasting manuscript with print; rather, the book as a medium of teaching and religious/legal discourse was seen as standing against the personal authority of the teacher. Printed editions, however, were able to significantly exacerbate this fundamental dispute over teaching methods in the Talmudic academies. The rejection of learning from (printed) books and thus the rejection of any monopoly over decision-making on the part of a book's author can be interpreted as a new and canonical debate related to religious law.⁶¹

It is undisputed that the printing press permanently changed how knowledge was learnt and transmitted in the yeshivot, and it is precisely this praxeological dimension—i.e., the shattering of supposed certainties in the field of knowledge transmission and documentation—that seems to have provoked correspondingly ambivalent reactions both in the case of Jewish intellectuals in Western and Eastern Europe as well as amongst the humanists, to whom Johannes Trithemius belonged' and who can be located in a similar social field. One such reaction was the argument that printing books contributed to the multiplication of errors in large numbers.⁶² Both intentional and unintentional 'errors' go hand in hand here and play an important role in mass distribution. Unlike in a manuscript culture, where a scribe first noted an (assumed or supposed) error in a marginal gloss and thus did not immediately erase the original, printers no longer made corrections to the original manuscripts in front of them, but

---

59 Meaning 'The Gates of Düren', this is a halakhic compilation of dietary laws made in the second half of the thirteenth century by R. Isaac ben Meïr from Düren, a city in present-day North Rhine-Westphalia.
60 In addition to the Talmud, these sources were also various halakhic authorities of the eleventh to fifteenth centuries (the so-called *rishonim*).
61 Cf. Reiner 1997, 86–88; ibid., 91: "Before the coming of print, Ashkenazi culture was not based on a fixed text, and certainly had no authoritative canon."
62 Cf. Widmann 1973, 30; Wallenwein 2017, 118–120.

only while typesetting the text. This meant that tracing a reading, a turn of phrase, or even an entire textual recension was virtually no longer possible, especially since the early prints in particular did not specify their handwritten sources for the most part.[63] A classification of the manuscripts used, their provenance, and further bibliographical information beyond what was provided in the colophon would only gradually become established in the print era.

Furthermore, there was also concern that heretical content and non-approved translations of biblical texts could become disseminated. For example, the Jewish scholar Eliyyahu ben Asher ha-Levi Ashkenazi (Elia Levita; 1469–1549) wrote in a letter to the Hebraist Sebastian Münster that he was uncomfortable with some of his own works (which by then had become outdated) being reprinted without regulation either at home or abroad.[64] The protagonists of the Reformation, especially Martin Luther, were also constantly having to deal with the problem of unregulated reprints.[65] Now, the extent to which efforts at censorship could be enforced in the fifteenth and sixteenth centuries is questionable. Yet the mere attempt at censoring texts and setting normative guidelines is revealing and can be seen as a clear reaction to material change. A well-known source for this is the 1485 censorship edict of the Archbishop of Mainz, Berthold von Henneberg,[66] which forbade the printing and sale of translations from Greek, Latin, or other languages into the European vernaculars, unless they had been approved by censors. In light of the mass distribution of writing, a supervisory authority was set up in advance that sought to manipulate the printing itself.

Felix Pratensis also had the polemical and anti-Christian passages removed from R. David Qimḥi's (also referred to by the acronym RaDaQ) commentary on the Psalms in 1517 before the latter was printed as part of the first edition of the so-called *Biblia Rabbinica* (Bomberg, Venice 1515–1517) and had the former printed as an independent treatise under the title *The response of Radak to the Christians*.[67] On the other hand, as late as the end of the sixteenth century, we still find instances of retroactive censorship on the part of church authorities, which affected prints and manuscripts alike. Thus, in 1578, a commission under Cardinal Santoro was assigned with then task of establishing a Hebrew *index expurgatorius*.[68] As a result, manuscripts as well as works that had been in print up to that time began to be censored. The early prints of RaDaQ's commentary on the Psalms (Bologna 1477, censored 1595; Naples 1487) have censorship notes in the same places as do some of the manuscripts from the thirteenth and fourteenth centu-

---

63 Cf. already Tychsen 1780.
64 Cf. Peritz 1894, 263–265.
65 Cf. Kaufmann 2019, 82–83.
66 Cf. Schmitz 2018, 197–201; Widmann 1973, 43–46. On pre-censorship, cf. also Kaufmann 2019, 176–208. In Christian liturgical prints, approval notes are often found in the colophons and prefaces. Cf. GW 5464, GW M24127, GW M24229, GW M24241, GW M24388, GW M24582, GW M24660, GW M2470910, GW M24728.
67 Cf. Heller 2004, xxxvi.
68 Cf. on the whole Raz-Krakotzkin 2007, 84–94, 120–174.

Fig. 5: Psalms with commentary by R. David Qimḥi (1477) censored by Domenico Irosolimitano, p. 3r. Cambridge University Library, Inc. 3.B.74.A2[2261] © Reproduced by kind permission of the Syndics of Cambridge University Library.

ries,[69] since the censor — Domenico Irosolimitano (1555–1621), a Jewish convert[70] — censored both the prints and the manuscripts retroactively (cf. Fig. 5 and Fig. 6)[71]. For the censors, then, the change from manuscript to print was not decisive: both fell under their condemnation as equally important vectors of the ideas that were to be censored, since both material forms were still in circulation at the time.

In many cases, introductions, dedications, or colophons provide insight into the different lines of reasoning of the time and paint a contrary picture to the negative reactions.[72] Various humanists, for example, praised the fact that a multitude of works were brought to light again or anew through the printing of books.[73] In many places, the printers also boasted of their philological expertise in the colophon, which some-

---

69 Ms Parma Palatina 1872, fol. 6v (Fig. 6) and Ms Parma Palatina 2881, fol. 6v/7r, censored 1597.
70 On Domenico Irosolimitano, cf. Prebor 2007 (in Hebrew); Thomanek 2017, 236–238.
71 Ms Parma Palatina 1872 (Fig. 6) is available online: https://www.nli.org.il/en/discover/manuscripts/hebrew-manuscripts/viewerpage?vid=MANUSCRIPTS&docid=PNX_MANUSCRIPTS99000088140 0205171-1#$FL13658555 (accessed 30/6/2023).
72 A good compilation of such reactions with an appendix of sources can be found in Widmann 1973.
73 A particularly prominent representative of this position is Polydorus Vergilius, but it can also be found in other writings, including those of Johannes Trithemius. Cf. Schweitzer-Martin 2022a, 134–135.

Fig. 6: Ms Parma Palatina 1872 censored by Domenico Irosolimitano (fol. 6v) © Biblioteca Palatina, Parma.

times leaves the present-day reader rather perplexed, since the philological quality of the first prints in particular often left much to be desired. At the same time, the fact that in these prints, effusive words of dedication were addressed above all to the tomes' prospective buyers,[74] lays bare once again an important point. While on the one hand, printers of books were still seeking to address their previous clientele, who were keen on philological accuracy, on the other hand, they had long since headed to newer economic pastures, where they sought not only to win over merchants and investors to fund their book production, but also (and especially) to gain new buyers. These new purchasers were meant to establish their own libraries, but whose purpose was now to appropriately display their owners' financial means. In this way, the colophons of the incunabula in particular form a faithful mirror of the changing social and political power structure of the society from which they originate. Likewise, they depict the decline of old elites and concomitant fears of loss alongside the rise of new protagonists who knew about this shift and confronted it accordingly.

---

74 Thus the colophon of the print of the Rashi Commentary, published in 1482 in Bologna, ends with the words: "Good will be said of everyone who buys these book, and whoever immerses himself in them will see his seed [i. e., descendants], will prolong his days, and the thing [done] by his hand will prosper, and [there will be] life and peace upon Israel. Amen." (Our translation, Hebrew text: וכל הקונה מאלו הספרים טוב טוב יאמר הקונה וההוגה בהם יראה זרע יאריך ימים וחפץ ה' בידו יצלח וחיים ושלום על ישראל אמן); cf. Tychsen 1780, 65–103; cf. also Liss 2024. On the colophons see also Schweitzer-Martin 2022a, 118–127.

Thesis 22
Taking recourse to traditional techniques of production leads to a re-evaluation of traditional materials, ways of production, and formats, as well as to changes in the attribution of meaning and practices of use.

Processes of material change are often described as a new material or a new practice replacing and displacing what preceded it, with the new material taking over the functions of the old and the old becoming worthless. Processes of material change, however, are much more complex, as was made clear by the processual character of the changes described above in the first thesis of this chapter (Thesis 19). Here in Thesis 22, however, the practices of production and reception are at the centre of our considerations. Old materials and production methods are not usually discarded, but rather continue to be used, albeit often with a different function or attribution of meaning. It is precisely this re-evaluation and re-functioning of traditional materials that we exemplify in the following via the example of manuscripts and prints.

In research contributions on the early modern period and the beginning of the printing age, manuscripts and printed works—or handwriting and printed writing, as it were—are usually perceived as opponents.[75] Following this line of thought, the manuscript is said to have been gradually replaced by the invention of printing with movable type. Printing is claimed as being responsible for "the preservation and dissemination of literature per se", while manuscripts are said to belong primarily to the private sphere.[76] On closer examination, however, we see that the manuscript was not completely displaced from the field of book production. Even into the sixteenth century, handwritten and printed books competed with each other, while numerous mixed forms emerged that were characterised by the simultaneous presence of handwriting and printing that differed in each individual case (a fact we alluded to above in the introduction to this chapter and in Thesis 19).[77] If the practice of writing books by hand persists, it must be assigned a certain value or function that cannot be subsumed by printing. Holger Flachmann speaks here of a "functional differentiation"[78] between handwriting and typography: while printing allows texts to be produced and distributed cheaply, comparatively quickly, uniformly, and in large quantities, handwriting is flexible, i.e., it can be used more individually and applied more directly than printing.

This fundamental difference between the two types of production is the reason for the tendency of the manuscript to be relegated to the private sphere or to the produc-

---

75 Cf. Dover 2021, 24–25.
76 Brandis 1997, 55. (Our translation, German text: "die Bewahrung und Verbreitung der Literatur schlechthin".)
77 Cf. also Dicke/Grubmüller 2003.
78 Flachmann 2003, 138. (Our translation, German text: "funktionale Differenzierung".)

tion of autographs. In addition, handwritten methods of book production were also used where certain content was to be handed down as arcane knowledge and made accessible only to certain circles (e. g., some cabalistic traditions). Even in mixed forms—for example, in text types in which handwritten entries are anticipated and space is provided for them through a preprinted framework (e. g., calendrical diaries [Schreibkalender], genealogical books, Jewish marriage certificates [ketubbot], preprinted forms such as letters of indulgence or missives, etc.)—handwriting retains this spontaneous and individual character.

However, there are also arguments that bolster another interpretation. The difference between manuscript and print has been relativised by more differentiated studies that do not understand mixed forms as anomalies, but rather as a characteristic of premodern book production.[79] Two typical phenomena prove this. On the one hand, texts that had already been printed were typically partially reworked or finished with handwriting. For example, a missal printed in Cologne in 1512 was afterwards illuminated; in fact, printed matter that was subsequently coloured by hand was a widespread phenomenon. This practice stems from late medieval manuscript production, in which the scribe and the rubricator usually worked separately, with writing and illustrating thus being different activities.[80] To a certain extent, this procedure is continued in the age of printing. In the case of the abovementioned missal, the illustrations were available as woodcut prints, but were subsequently coloured by hand and the text embellished with borders.[81] Although the missal was already characterised by features of quality (folio format, parchment pages, red and black printing ink), only the intervention of handwriting via the illuminations seems to have made the book a true object of prestige. The significance of the content must be visible via the materiality, and this obviously includes the colouring by hand, as this is what serves to convey a sense of uniqueness and thus exclusivity. The practice of embellishing by hand remains or becomes a distinguishing feature and a marker of prestige in the print era, quite independent of the underlying material, be it parchment or paper.[82]

On the other hand, however, we find manuscripts in which printed texts have been copied by hand and recompiled (e. g. prayer books, chronicles, etc.).[83] In contrast to conventional printed books, handwritten copying allows one to select template texts and compile them as one likes, which leads to an increased individualisation of the artefact.

But the transcription of printed text by hand goes beyond mere copying; through the process of writing by hand, the texts regain their variability and can therefore be

---

[79] Cf. the anthology Brockstieger/Hirt 2023, produced within the CRC 933 subproject B13 'The Order of Knowledge and Biographical Writing. Calculated Handwriting in Printed Books of the Early Modern Period (16th and 17th Century)'.
[80] Cf. Schweitzer-Martin 2023.
[81] Cf. Rautenberg 2003, 169–176.
[82] For more on the increase in value of handwritten writing (with the pen) in the age of printing, see Wernli 2021. For more on the use of parchment in printed missals, see Schweitzer-Martin 2022b.
[83] On this, cf. Heinzer 2003; Rautenberg 2003.

compiled, i. e. 'mixed', however one likes. The collecting of rare texts and the compiling of text fragments on a specific topic are both practices that were already common before the invention of printing and are also maintained in the printing age.[84] Writing by hand can break up and relativise what seems fixed and unchangeable in print "by returning what is printed to the fragile individuality of what is handwritten and thus to the status of being provisional and changeable."[85] Through this individualisation, the manuscript obtains an exclusive character and thus experiences an increase in value.

These examples show that handwriting performs important functions that typography cannot. While the former was used for text preservation and distribution before the invention of printing, this task has now been taken over by printing. Yet handwriting acquires a new function by taking on the role of something special in book production and becoming a distinguishing feature; "via a retrospective/conservative (or anachronistic) link to the medieval codex, handwritten writing is able to survive in the public sphere in the printing age."[86] While the material and the production method do not change, the attributions of meaning, evaluations, and practices of use shift.[87] The deliberately differentiated use of both production techniques testifies to the fact that the choice between old and new in terms of material, practice, and technique was perceived as an enrichment.[88]

A somewhat different perspective emerges from the history of the book in East Asia. In this cultural area, the predominance of woodblock printing (see also the considerations on block books above in Thesis 19) meant, on the one hand, that printing could faithfully reproduce manuscripts, making the dichotomy between the two media less strict,[89] and, on the other hand, that printing costs were much lower than with movable type, which led to diverse forms of self-publishing alongside more commercial ventures. A sign of a respectable house was "the perfume of books"[90], regardless of whether such works be manuscripts or prints. Although woodblock printing had been used in China since the late eighth century, printing did not gain the upper hand over manuscripts until the mid-sixteenth century, and even then, manuscript production did not wane.[91]

---

84 Cf. Thorley 2015, 493–494; cf. McDermott 2006, 78.
85 Heinzer 2003, 158. (Our translation, German text: "indem [es] das Gedruckte wieder in die fragile Individualität des Handschriftlichen und damit in den Status des Vorläufigen und Veränderbaren zurückversetzt".)
86 Rautenberg 2003, 186, our translation, German text: "über eine retrospektiv-konservative (oder anachronistische) Anknüpfung an den mittelalterlichen Kodex kann handschriftliches Schreiben im öffentlichen Raum im Druckzeitalter überleben".
87 Cf. Mentzel-Reuters 2010, 474.
88 Cf. Rautenberg 2003, 183.
89 For a discussion of these characteristics with regard to Japan, see Davis/Chance 2006, 112.
90 Brokaw 2005, 3.
91 Cf. McDermott 2006, 43–47. Copying a book by hand remained the preferred form of acquiring its content, cf. ibid., 76–77.

This has to do with the slow change of conventions in the handling and appreciation of textual material. In the treatise *Dushu fa* 讀書法 ('On Reading'), printed in the thirteenth century, the Neo-Confucian scholar Zhu Xi recommends intensive, repeated reading of the classics so as to fully grasp their inner meaning. This reading practice refers to the text in terms of bodily metaphors: "Go down layer by layer, past skin to flesh, past flesh to bones, past bones to marrow. If you read in desultory fashion you'll never attain this."[92] This seems to be a continuation of the reading practices characteristic of manuscript cultures (see Thesis 20 above). Yet Zhu Xi was criticised by his contemporaries precisely for what was seen as a change in reading practice. Similar concerns about misinterpretation also led Shen Defu, the author of one of the most famous Ming-era works of popular fiction, *Jing Ping Mei* 金瓶梅 ('The Plum in the Golden Vase', first published in 1610), not to print his novel at first and to circulate it in manuscript form instead. His fear was twofold. First, he was worried that people would think he was a profit-hungry publisher, as the ideal of the literati who unselfishly pursued knowledge and self-improvement was incompatible with the practices of commercial publishers. Second, Shen Defu was afraid that printing the novel—especially given its erotic content—would make it accessible to unsophisticated readers whose minds it might corrupt.[93]

Commercial publishers embraced these concerns and increasingly advertised the ease of reading and learning, and even the moral edification, of print by constructing an "apologetics of the vernacular" through prefaces and altered textual features.[94] Towards the end of this long process of ebb and flow between manuscript and print production, the value of texts copied by hand changed: they were valued less for their rarity than for the beauty of their calligraphic style. During the same period, literati found ways to continue the authentication practices of manuscript culture in print. This included, above all, the support of professional colleagues; their comments on the manuscript drafts of the text were sought out and subsequently included in a limited edition.[95] The printed works thus envisaged a complex audience composed of at least two strata: an 'inner circle' of the literati, who were oriented towards the manuscript culture, and an 'outer circle' of readers who emulated the literati's values.

A similar phenomenon occurred in Japan, but in the absence of a firmly defined group of literati, more socially diverse communities engaged in cultural activities such as the production of poetry following the model of the pre-existing elite practices of the local manuscript culture.[96] Within these communities, printing was used in the seventeenth century to disseminate poetic production and thus maintain social and financial links between geographically dispersed practitioners. Alongside this 'inner circle',

---

92 McLaren 2005, 155.
93 Cf. Son 2018, 18–19.
94 McLaren 2005, 153.
95 Cf. Son 2018, 6.
96 Cf. Ikegami 2005.

emerging commercial publishers printed encyclopaedias, manuals, and other kinds of instructional texts (*ōrai mono* 往来物) that expounded and disseminated knowledge and practices previously confined to oral teaching and elite chains of transmission.[97] In this process, formats, layouts, and materials particular to manuscript traditions were adapted and imitated. As a result, manuscript formats became more desirable, which led to their increased production.[98] For example, existing popular fiction (*otogi zōshi* 御伽草子) was printed in an elongated format (*yokobon* 横本) that mimicked the experience of reading in manuscript format.[99] Furthermore, the covers of the printed editions were often decorated with silver foil and hand-painted idyllic scenes, so that their external appearance was indistinguishable from that of actual manuscripts. Doing so allowed printed editions to fulfil the same function as their handwritten counterparts did: they came to be conspicuously displayed on special occasions such as weddings and at the new year. Another relevant example from Japan are the early modern oaths (*kishōmon* 起請文). These materially hybrid texts were originally temple talismans, stamped on one side and inscribed by hand on the other side in ink (and often even in blood). In the seventeenth century, the use of these oaths diversified when they were integrated into pledges of allegiance between women from prostitution districts and their clients.[100] This phenomenon was a continuation of an older layer of print culture in the form of temple and shrine seals that were used as a form of authentication and developed in parallel with the rise of commercial printing in urban centres.

In summary, while the recourse to traditional production techniques has comparable effects on the meaning and use of texts across cultures, these changes are not rooted in the technology itself. Rather, they are modulated by cultural and social contexts in a complex scriptorial environment where different forms of manuscript and print production exist side by side.

Thesis 23
Changes in actors in the course of material change coincides with shifts in power relations and social contexts.

Material change should not be understood in a linear way, but rather as something that develops over the course of dynamic processes of change conditioned by several factors. However, the practices of production and those of reception do not necessarily change synchronously. These processes of change can be exemplified by early book printing in Latin Europe. The early prints from Mainz, for instance, were bibles, psal-

---

97 Cf. Berry 2007.
98 Cf. Davis/Chance 2006.
99 Cf. Ishikawa 2020.
100 Cf. Leca 2022b.

ters, and letters of indulgence, all of which were written in Latin. These so-called incunabula, some of which had also been printed on parchment, successfully imitated the handwritten versions of these genres. However, they were not reproduced by a process of handwritten copying, but rather by the setting of movable type. Components such as the incipit were often added by hand or—as already mentioned in the preceding thesis—the text was rubricated by hand, with its ornamental design imitating that of manuscripts.[101]

Even though handwritten artefacts and printed ones bore a strong resemblance to one another, they differed significantly in who produced them. While up to this point in time, it was monastic scriptoria (and in individual cases, urban centres of production, such as that of Diebold Lauber) that reproduced texts on a larger scale, the actors in text production now changed. In the period of the incunabula or first printed works, only about twenty monastic presses are documented,[102] which appears to be quite a marginal phenomenon when compared to the more than two hundred places of printing we know of, some of which had several smaller print workshops.[103] This meant that the majority of production was being carried out by laymen, but their clientele did not change immediately and clients making print commissions also remained initially stable.

In the Jewish sphere, there were no institutionalised places of book production akin to monastic scriptoria.[104] By contrast, we find workshops run by the same scribes who were also responsible for the production of important ritual objects such as *tefillin* and *mezuzot*.[105] Others were scholars who copied books for themselves and others, but often hired themselves out as itinerant workers.[106] This changed with the advent of early prints. A single scribe was now replaced by several people, each of whom had a different function: the typesetter, the proofreader, a tradesman who maintained the printing press, and sometimes another financier.

---

101 Cf. Schmitz 2018.
102 Cf. Schmitz 2018, 11–41, 183–186; Duggan 2008; Eisermann 2013; Schmitz 1990.
103 Cf. Rautenberg 2000.
104 Cf. Beit-Arié 1993, 77–108.
105 *Tefillin* are leather straps and leather cases containing small pieces of parchment inscribed with Bible verses (Exod 13:8–10, 11–16; Deut 6:4–9, 11:13–21), which people wear by tying them to their arms and forehead at the time of the so-called *shacharit* (morning prayer) on weekdays (but not on Shabbat and holidays) (the term is related to the Hebrew word for 'prayer', *tefilla*). This custom developed from Deut 6:8. A *mezuza* (Hebrew for 'doorpost') is a small tube containing a piece of parchment on which are handwritten the first two sections of the *Shema Yisrael* (Deut 6:4–9, 11:13–21). Even today, a *mezuza* is placed on every doorpost in a Jewish home, with the exception of the bathroom and toilet, a custom going back to Deut 6:9.
106 It was rare for the main text in a manuscript to be written by more than one hand (*pecia* system); in editions of biblical texts, however, it was quite common for one hand to be responsible for the consonantal text and two or more other hands to be charged with adding in punctuation, accent marks, and masora. Nevertheless, R. Meir ben Baruch of Rothenburg (ca. 1215–1293) wrote in a responsum that a book written by several hands should be classified as less valuable (cf. Beit-Arié 1993, 78).

Many early prints show that the typesetters were not necessarily specialists in the sense of the aforementioned scribal 'artist', but rather were print artisans who often lacked the necessary education pertaining to the texts at hand and whose prints therefore had to be subsequently corrected by specific persons charged with this task.[107] For this reason, many of the incunabula, even if they come from Jewish printers, are noticeably faulty and do not meet the high philological standards evident in the manuscripts.[108] Many Jewish scriptural prints contain only the consonant text; vowels, accents, and other reading aids, not to mention commentaries, were simply omitted in the initial days of printing. Some printers were partly to blame here, simply because they did not know enough Hebrew to spot such discrepancies or deficiencies in the prints, but at the same time, it was not yet fully technically possible to incorporate this interpretive apparatus and these reading aids.

At the beginning of the sixteenth century, printing became a "business crossing confessional lines that was structured according to the political rules of the printing privileges that were granted and the economic rules of the profits to be made in printing".[109] In this process, the protagonists of the Reformation also played an important role.[110] In Italy, Christian entrepreneurs hired typesetters who were Jewish and/or converts from Judaism for their printing houses in order to appropriate the latter's knowledge of Hebrew. The Hebrew manuscript of biblical texts, which should be characterised as a 'Jewish' book since it was designed by Jews (only) for Jews, became the Christian printed 'Old Testament' for the humanistically educated scholars and Christian Hebraists. Additionally inserted texts, such as papal dedications, were intended to assign the book its distinct confessional status. Related to this, it has been shown that different reading and layout traditions as well as different bindings and ply formats are reflected in the prints and point to different social fields. The binding of the partial prints determined whether the so-called five *megillot*[111] were bound after the Pentateuch or amongst the historical texts (*ketuvim* or 'writings'). Here, different affordances and contexts of reception become quite clear: Jewish audiences wanted the megillot for liturgical reading on corresponding holidays in the context of the Torah; whereas Christian Hebraist practice, itself a scholarly context, classified them with the historical texts. Conversely, the Pratensis edition designed for Christian readers in 1517 (printed in 1521) underwent a Jewish 'remake' through the omission of the papal dedication and the integration of the so-called Masora.[112]

---

107 Cf. Grafton 2011, 23.
108 For the early Bible prints and commentaries, cf. for instance Ginsburg 1897; Zafren 1982.
109 Petzold 2019, 34, our translation, German text: "konfessionsübergreifendes Geschäft, das sich nach den politischen Regeln der erteilten Druckprivilegien und den ökonomischen Regeln der im Druck zu erlösenden Gewinne gestaltete".
110 Cf. Kaufmann 2019, 15–52.
111 Scrolls read in conjunction with festivals: namely, the books of Ruth, Song of Songs, Qohelet (Ecclesiastes), Lamentations, and Esther.
112 Cf. Petzold 2009, 54–73.

The printing of the Hebrew Bible and of the Jewish (Hebrew) Bible commentaries by Christian parties was driven by the Church's conviction of having sole interpretive authority over the 'Hebrew faith' *(fides de Hebraeis)*. In this faith, the Church valued the 'Hebrews' just as much as it bitterly persecuted the 'Jews' and their books, especially the Talmud. Thus the printing of Hebrew books served to Christianise the Hebrew Bible and also cemented the hegemony of the Christian study of Hebrew in academic biblical exegesis (up to the present day, in the case of the German academic tradition). The Jewish minority had to surrender its monopoly over the *veritas hebraica* to the Christian majority.

A similar process of change from handwriting to a rapidly spreading print culture (although diverging in the details from the preceding) took place in Japan from the 1590s to the 1620s. While it is true that the first mass printing dates back to the years from 764 to 770, when Empress Shōtoku's (718–770) colossal programme of printing one million *dhāraṇī-sūtras* was carried out,[113] the cultural technique of printing only found sporadic use, given the prevailing view that it was possible to improve one's karma by copying sutras and other Buddhist writings by hand. Printing was thus primarily reserved for the social elite at the imperial court in Miyako (present-day Kyoto) and for Buddhist clerics.

It was only through a transcultural process of exchange and appropriation, as well as social upheaval between 1590 and the 1620s, that a rapid development in the mass production and distribution of printed texts and illustrations occurred beyond the halls of the imperial court. On the one hand, the *shōgun* Tokugawa Ieyasu produced reprints of Chinese books (and used bronze types for this).[114] On the other hand, a printing press and printed Christian texts were brought to Japan by the Italian missionary Alessandro Valignano (1539–1606) in 1590. The technique of movable type first spread in missionary circles and amongst Japanese converts in the south of the country, but soon made its way to the capital of Miyako as well. The latest research also proves that the technology of movable type, in addition to the layout design that had been introduced from Europe, was adapted by the merchants and important supporters of culture who were living in the capital for the reproduction of Japanese literary classics and poetry in the 1610s.[115]

Thus, instead of the Buddhist clergy, the educated and wealthy class of townspeople living in Miyako emerged as actors in the production of printed writings. In the 1610s, they primarily printed classical and newer works of poetry, such as *Ise monogatari* 伊勢物語 ('The Tales of Ise') with movable type on high-quality coloured paper.[116] The editions of these books produced in the 1610s—in a European context, one would rather speak of 'notebooks' on account of their material nature—were limited, as they were aimed at a small circle of intellectuals in the capital.

---

113 Cf. Kornicki 2012. The author suspects that the figure of one million could just be a claim on the part of the empress.
114 Cf. Kornicki 1998, 130–131; Pitelka 2013.
115 Cf. Koakimoto 2021.
116 Cf. Kornicki 1998, 131–132.

It was not until the 1620s in Miyako—which remained the centre of the printing industry in Japan until the 1660s—that an increasingly commercially oriented production of printed books developed, and with it the large-scale reproduction of textual content focusing on popular historical hero stories, such as war epics. Central to this was the proliferation of illustrations, which changed with each of the numerous new editions. In order to come closer to the character of illuminated manuscripts and thus also to achieve greater sales, colours applied by untrained hands were added to the illustrations in the mid-1620s, called *tanrokubon* 丹緑本 ('red-green books') due to the limited colour palette.[117] These printed and bound books, in turn, served from the 1650s onward as models for extremely opulent handscrolls painted with rich gold leaf and costly pigments. These were commissioned not so much by the urban population as by wealthy feudal lords from across the Japanese island chain, who sought them out, among other reasons, as dowry gifts for their daughters.[118]

In particular, the colophons common in the early prints of medieval Europe are an interesting example of how certain practices of book design, whether in terms of colours or paratexts, changed only slowly, yet their impact and the influence of their creators were by contrast all the greater since printing managed to penetrate social fields that had previously been less frequently addressed or not addressed at all, including the crafts and other trades. Although a colophon in a manuscript today provides information on purchasing and production practices, its most important feature is its explicit reference to individual and private circumstances: information that usually remained private because a manuscript was often intended for private use and its sphere of influence was consequently limited.

Liturgical manuscripts are of course an exception here, but they did not contain colophons precisely because they left the private for the public sphere of the synagogue or church. The scribes of such works often inserted themselves into the text in a rather hidden way.[119] At the dawn of the printing era, the colophon in a printed book was not very different from that of a manuscript; but it had a completely different function, since it could inform an entire reading community—even in the early prints, we are talking already of several hundred persons[120]—with basic information, not only about the text and its author, but above all about the production process, its costs, or the number of books per edition. They also partially took on a function of approval. What was emphasised here, then, was trade and various craftsmanship skills, which also already makes clear what the ultimate goal of book production was: namely, the financial profits of the printing industry. This is shown, for example, in the early prints of the Hebrew Bible and Bible commentary texts, in which the printers

---

[117] Cf. Yoshida 1984.
[118] Cf. Trinh/Bauer/Trede 2021, 246–249.
[119] Cf. Beit-Arié 2015, 16–18. According to ibid., 17, the Worms Maḥzor is an exceptional case, as it was not made for personal use.
[120] On circulation levels: Eisermann 2017; Green/McIntyre 2016.

explain in detail within the colophon that printing was not only a philological enterprise, but above all a technical task, and a costly one at that.[121]

For the Jewish sphere, especially in Italy from 1469 onwards, it can be assumed that the early Hebrew prints were cheaper to produce than it was to copy a single manuscript. However, the question of who was meant to be reading from these first prints is not easy to answer. At the same time as Jewish recipients of the texts, Christian Hebraists were also increasingly demanding Hebrew books, so the prints would have been able to satisfy a growing market there. At the beginning of the fifteenth century, this double reception also led to a marked improvement in the philological quality of the prints, since Christian printing houses availed themselves of educated Jewish printers and proofreaders. In the case of the Hebrew Bibles, different denominational editions were printed from the same printing block, which were distinguished merely by different bindings.[122] This shows that printing was also shaped by financial considerations from the outset.

The incunabula as well as prints from the early modern period were sometimes traded over long distances, as can be seen from their bindings and ownership marks, among other things. With printing, a differentiated book trade developed with bookkeepers and, at the end of the fifteenth century, the emergence of fixed shops for books. In addition to their production, the sale and distribution of books had changed, too.[123] Such changes were also reflected in the development of title pages for Latin and vernacular incunabula. Although there had also been specially designed title pages, opening initials, and highlighted headings in manuscripts, the conventions for title pages became standardised at the end of the fifteenth century. These now contained more information about authors and titles, and later also about publishers, printers, and the printing date, or were decorated with woodcuts in a bid to attract the eye of potential readers.[124] This development was a process that can also be seen in Hebrew prints. The first Hebrew prints of Bibles and Bible commentaries before 1500 had no title page; by contrast, the cover page of the first Bomberg Bible from 1517 is elaborately designed.[125]

The change in the actors involved in the material transformation from manuscript to book also brought other changes in its wake. Not only do we find that production processes changed and other groups were the main protagonists in production than was previously the case; we also find the formation of new communities of readers and users. This also resulted in shifts in the use and interpretation of what was written.

---

[121] Cf. for example the colophon in the printed *Pentateuch with commentary by Rashi and the Targum* (Bologna 1482; cf. Tychsen 1780, esp. 83–84). Colophons of Christian and secular works also often refer to the supposed text quality, correction efforts, and production process. On scribal notes, cf. Wallenwein 2017.
[122] For a good overview, see Petzold 2019, 26–77.
[123] Foundational here is Duntze 2013. Even in antiquity, there had already been professional booksellers.
[124] Cf. Rautenberg 2008; Smith 2000.
[125] Figure: https://commons.wikimedia.org/wiki/File:Titelseite_der_ersten_Mikraot_Gedolot_-_Felix_Pratensis_-_Daniel_Bomberg_-_1517.pdf (accessed 16/5/2023).

The assignment of a book's materiality and its cultural context—something which had been clear until this point in time—breaks down in processes that sometimes spanned decades. Research into the history of the first prints, however, has not been limited to examining various changes, but has also offered the possibility of assessing the influence of these changes on the construction of both individual and communal identity.

If, for example, it was assumed that the printing of a Jewish book also changed the attitude towards the book's 'Jewishness', this was intended to mean that printing enabled a wider circulation of the book not only as a specific product but also as a 'bearer' of ethnic, religious, and cultural content. Such content then came into contact with the broader circulation and transformation of ideas and thus necessarily became involved in a highly relevant transcultural process. From a methodological point of view, it is important to bear in mind that these cultural relations are never unambiguous, but always require reciprocity. This is the case even when they collide with unilaterally expressed cultural rigidity, as in the case of censorship more generally, or in the case of the ecclesiastical censorship of Jewish books, to be more specific here. In any case, what we have here is a transcultural process that strongly impacts how each party involved defines its own identity.

It is important to make another methodological remark at this point. The change in the nature of the Hebrew book in its transition from being produced by hand to being printed typographically does not only lie in the nature of the material or the technical means that made this development possible. This change also concerns the altered conditions of use that resulted from the spread of printing, and especially the fact that Jewish printing in Renaissance Italy never constituted a distinct cultural and technological sphere. Jewish printed works became very popular mainly through the activities of Christian printing houses. These set up shop in Venice and, thanks to their good contacts with the Christian authorities, obtained permission to print Jewish books, even if such tomes might be considered by the same ecclesiastical bodies as containing 'compromising' material.[126] The example of a Hebrew Bible print with a rich ornamental border (cf. Fig. 7) is particularly revealing.[127]

---

126 This is exemplified by the Jewish prints of Daniel Bomberg. He hired converted Jews and still printed Jewish books without necessarily subjecting himself to self-censorship. From this point of view, it becomes clear that the Jewish press in Venice developed within a cultural sphere that was dependent on the surrounding Christian world, and indeed it owed much of its happiness and success to this connection. By contrast, the Jewish press run by (non-converted) Jewish printers often had to adhere to forms of preventive self-censorship in order not to get into trouble with the Christian authorities, who often suppressed Jews socially and fiscally in ways inspired by the Inquisition (cf. Roth 1972, 45). However, the case of the Jewish press also offers quite revealing examples of cross-cultural transmissions. This is the case with the first Hebrew prints of the Bible, printed by Joshua Solomon Soncino, but decorated with plates that had already been used for prints by Greek and Latin authors.
127 An iconographically similar border was used in 1488 by Soncino for the *editio princeps* of the Bible (*Torah, Nevi'im, Ketuvim* [Pentateuch, Prophets, Writings]), printed by Abraham ben Ḥayyim for Joshua Solomon Soncino. This border, however, had first been used by the Italian printer Francesco Del Tuppo in his 1485 edition of Aesop's Fables. Cf. Roth 1972, 45.

Fig. 7: Frontispiece of a printed Hebrew Bible (*Torah, Nevi'im, Ketuvim* ['Pentateuch, Prophets, Writings']), Naples ca. 1492, printed by Joshua Solomon Soncino, parchment, GW 4199. Oxford, Bodleian Library Holk. c. 1. Photo: © Bodleian Libraries, University of Oxford (CC BY-NC 4.0).

The exchange, loan, or sale of typographical material—typefaces, frames, plates, and illustrations—was not uncommon, especially at the beginning of the printing age when the technical and economic capacities for producing typographical material were still relatively limited. It is interesting to note, however, that there was a willingness on the part of Jews to compromise with the surrounding Christian environment in order to satisfy the ambitions of producing Jewish prints of a certain typographical quality and aesthetic.

The text of the Soncino Bible (Fig. 7) is framed by an ornamental border. The small naked figures depicted here are striking and may be erotica based on ancient models; nonetheless, such depictions are forbidden according to Jewish law. These borders were used without any explicit warning to Jewish readers because the decorations were clearly 'non-Jewish'. This shows the contrast or tension between the text and its aesthetic form. On the other hand, this border also shows the technical and cultural dependence of early Jewish prints on the complex world of non-Jewish printing houses or those subject to Christian authorities. The fact that a Jewish printer used these border decorations can probably also be explained by the fact that they were very elaborately designed and therefore expensive, so that it could be economically more advantageous to reuse such decorative elements that had already been crafted for other purposes. It is important to note, however, that these borders, which profoundly violated the biblical prohibition against making a human image, were readily accepted not only by the printer but also by the readers themselves, who apparently did not complain and even bought these new Bibles. This suggests that the limited agency of Jewish actors led to a cultural and transcultural flexibility that arose perhaps primarily due to technical concerns. Apart from a certain tolerance of the customs of the Renaissance world, it can be assumed that printing as a technical innovation led Jewish printers and readers to accept aesthetically what they might not have accepted under other circumstances.

The example of the Soncino Bible illustrates the complexity of the material change that went hand in hand with a pragmatism on the part of those actors involved in the context of Jewish and Christian prints in Europe. Depending on the perspective, the processes can be described as both standardisation and pluralisation.

The transition to print of all kinds also enables processes of standardisation and the pluralisation of audiences, meanings, and uses of texts to take place simultaneously in early modern Japan, although these processes can have a lengthy and circuitous development. Almost a century after the development of commercial printing, the Kyoto illustrator Nishikawa Sukenobu turned what had become a standard format for organising knowledge into a vehicle for his covert political agenda.[128] At first glance, his 1743 work *Jokyō Ogura shikishi* 助教小倉色紙 ('Poem Cards for the Instruction of Women') looks like a standard textbook for the female audience named in the

---

128 Cf. Preston 2013. On the development of commercial printing in early modern Japan, see Kornicki 1998, 169–179.

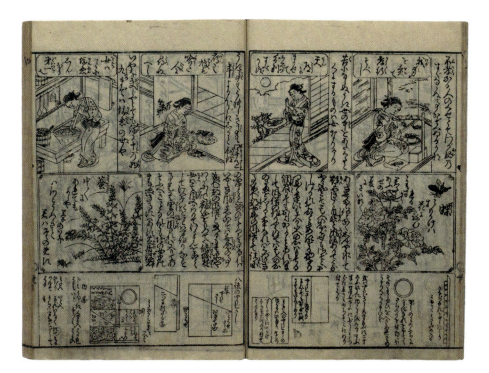

Fig. 8: Nishikawa Sukenobu, *Jokyō Ogura shikishi* 助教小倉色紙 ('Poem Cards for the Instruction of Women'), pp. 10v–11r, 1743, woodcut, ink on *washi*, 24.3 × 17.8 cm. © Atomi University Library, Tokyo, Japan, https://adeac.jp/adeac-arch/viewer/001-mp002619-200010/001-1001920501/ (accessed 27/01/2022).

title (cf. Fig. 8). Its complex layout testifies to the "accumulative tendency" of Japanese culture, as is also evident in the increasing density of information in textbooks over time.[129] On a single page, Sukenobu accommodates five separate cartouches with varying numbers of cross-references around the main theme of proper behaviour in society. Visual elements are also cleverly integrated into a moral dialectic: one of the women in the upper register is a housewife whose servant ties her sash from behind, while the other is a courtesan who ties her own sash. However, a close reading of the text reveals the use of political metaphors. For example, the combination of butterfly and peony imagery with the word *kimi* 君, which can mean both "courtesan/prostitute" and "ruler/emperor", in the cartouche in the centre of the right-hand page, almost certainly suggests a pro-imperial message.[130] These would only have been deciphered by a certain community of those supporting the restoration of de facto imperial

---

[129] Cf. Goree 2020, 114.
[130] The combination of butterfly and peony was a symbol for the proponents of the restoration of the Ming dynasty after its defeat and transition to the Qing dynasty; see Chiem 2020, 86.

rule over the military regime—a community which otherwise communicated predominantly via handwritten formats.

Often, letterpress printing is seen as a means of standardising and unifying access to textual material. However, the materiality of print was part of a complex media environment in which it negotiated its relationship to handwritten texts as well as the oft-competing interests of publishers, authors, financiers, authorities, and readers. As can be seen from the case studies presented here, printed texts—as components of textual ecosystems—contained textual and paratextual features that allowed for multiple simultaneous uses. The pluralisation of audiences, uses, and meanings thus depended on the standardisation made possible by print, which to a large extent determined how texts were used. Often they opened texts to new social fields and in this way also shifted power relations beyond the texts and their production.

Bibliography

Abbreviations and Sigla

GW   *Gesamtkatalog der Wiegendrucke,* 2nd ed., vols. 1–7 ed. by the Kommission für den Gesamtkatalog der Wiegendrucke, Stuttgart 1968, vol. 8ff., published by the Staatsbibliothek zu Berlin, Stuttgart 1978ff. (online version: http://www.gesamtkatalogderwiegendrucke.de/).

Sources

Shiba Kōkan, *Shiba Kōkan zenshū,* vol. 2, ed. by Asakura Haruhiko, Tokyo 1993.
Johannes Trithemius, *De Laude Scriptorum. Zum Lobe der Schreiber,* intr., ed. and transl. by Klaus Arnold (Mainfränkische Hefte 60), Würzburg 1973.

Research Literature

Augustyn, Wolfgang (2003), "Zur Gleichzeitigkeit von Handschrift und Buchdruck in Deutschland – Versuch einer Skizze aus kunsthistorischer Sicht", in: Gerd Dicke and Klaus Grubmüller (eds.), *Die Gleichzeitigkeit von Handschrift und Buchdruck* (Wolfenbütteler Mittelalter-Studien 16), Wiesbaden, 5–47.
Beckmann Petey, Alice (2021), "Verlage und Druckereien leiden unter Papiermangel", in: *Handelsblatt,* 4/9/2021, https://www.handelsblatt.com/27580396.html (accessed 7/3/2023).
Beit-Arié, Malachi (1993), *The Making of the Medieval Hebrew Book: Studies in Palaeography and Codicology,* Jerusalem.
Beit-Arié, Malachi (2015), "Commissioned and Owner-Produced Manuscripts in the Sephardi Zone and Italy in the Thirteenth–Fifteenth Centuries", in: Javier del Barco (ed.), *The Late Medieval Hebrew Book in the Western Mediterranean; Hebrew Manuscripts and Incunabula in Context,* Leiden/Boston, 13–27.

Berry, Mary Elizabeth (2007), *Japan in Print: Information and Nation in the Early Modern Period*, Berkeley, CA.
Berti, Irene/Haß, Christian D./Krüger, Kristina/Ott, Michael R. (2015), "Lesen und Entziffern", in: Thomas Meier, Michael R. Ott, and Rebecca Sauer (eds.), *Materiale Textkulturen. Konzepte – Materialien – Praktiken* (Materiale Textkulturen 1), Berlin/Munich/Boston, 639–650, https://doi.org/10.1515/9783110371291.639.
Blair, Ann (2020), "Managing Information", in: James Raven (ed.), *The Oxford Illustrated History of the Book,* Oxford, 169–194.
Bolle, Katharina (2020), *Materialität und Präsenz spätantiker Inschriften. Eine Studie zum Wandel der Inschriftenkultur in den italienischen Provinzen* (Materiale Textkulturen 25), Berlin/Boston, https://doi.org/10.1515/9783110633566.
Bolle, Katharina/Höh, Marc von der/Jaspert, Nikolas (eds.) (2019), *Inschriftenkulturen im kommunalen Italien. Traditionen, Brüche, Neuanfänge* (Materiale Textkulturen 21), Berlin/Boston, https://doi.org/10.1515/9783110642261.
Brandis, Tilo (1997), "Die Handschrift zwischen Mittelalter und Früher Neuzeit. Versuch einer Typologie", in: *Gutenberg-Jahrbuch* 72, 27–57.
Braudel, Fernand (1977), "Geschichte und Sozialwissenschaften. Die longue durée", in: Marc Bloch, Fernand Braudel, and Lucien Febvre (eds.), *Schrift und Materie der Geschichte. Vorschläge zu einer systematischen Aneignung historischer Prozesse* (edition suhrkamp 814), Frankfurt (Main), 47–85.
Brendecke, Arndt (2005), "Durchschossene Exemplare. Über eine Schnittstelle zwischen Handschrift und Druck", in: *Archiv für Geschichte des Buchwesens* 59, 50–64.
Brockstieger, Sylvia (2018), *Sprachpatriotismus und Wettstreit der Künste. Johann Fischart im Kontext der Offizin Bernhard Jobin* (Frühe Neuzeit 227), Berlin/Boston.
Brockstieger, Sylvia/Hirt, Rebecca (eds.) (2023), *Handschrift im Druck. Annotieren, Korrigieren, Weiterschreiben* (Materiale Textkulturen 39), Berlin/Boston, https://doi.org/10.1515/9783111191560.
Brockstieger, Sylvia/Schweitzer-Martin, Paul (eds.) (2023), *Between Manuscript and Print. Transcultural Perspectives, ca. 1400–1800* (Materiale Textkulturen 40), Berlin/Boston, https://doi.org/10.1515/9783111242699.
Brokaw, Cynthia J. (2005), "On the History of the Book in China", in: Cynthia J. Brokaw and Kai-Wing Chow (eds.), *Printing and Book Culture in Late Imperial China*, Berkeley, CA, 3–54.
Burnyeat, Myles F. (1997), "Postscript on Silent Reading", in: *The Classical Quarterly* 47 (1), 74–76.
Cavallo, Guglielmo (2016), "Codex, I. Kulturgeschichte", in: *Der Neue Pauly. Enzyklopädie der Antike*, vol. 3, Darmstadt, 50–53.
Chartier, Roger (1987), *The Cultural Uses of Print in Early Modern France,* Princeton.
Chiem, Kristen (2020), *Hua Yuan (1682–1756) and the Making of the Artist in Early Modern China,* Leiden.
Davis, Julie/Chance, Linda (2006), "Manuscript and Print: Issues of Format and Medium in Japanese Premodern Books", in: *Manuscript Studies* 1 (1), 90–114.
De Monticelli, Roberta (1990), *Le Confessioni di Agostino. Introduzione, traduzione, note e commenti,* Milan.
Dicke, Gerd/Grubmüller, Klaus (eds.) (2003), *Die Gleichzeitigkeit von Handschrift und Buchdruck* (Wolfenbütteler Mittelalter-Studien 16), Wiesbaden.
Dover, Paul M. (2021), *The Information Revolution in Early Modern Europe* (New Approaches to European History), Cambridge.
Duggan, Mary Kay (2008), "Bringing Reformed Liturgy to Print at the New Monastery at Marienthal", in: *Church History and Religious Culture* 88 (3), 415–436.

Duntze, Oliver (2013), "Verlagsbuchhandel und verbreitender Buchhandel von der Erfindung des Buchdrucks bis 1700", in: Ursula Rautenberg (ed.), *Buchwissenschaft in Deutschland. Ein Handbuch,* vol. 1, Berlin, 203–256.

Dussel, Konrad (2004), *Deutsche Tagespresse im 19. und 20. Jahrhundert* (Einführungen. Kommunikationswissenschaft 1), Münster.

Eisermann, Falk (2013), "A Golden Age? Monastic Printing Houses in the Fifteenth Century", in: Benito Rial Costas (ed.), *Print Culture and Peripheries in Early Modern Europe: A Contribution to the History of Printing and the Book Trade in Small European and Spanish Cities,* Leiden, 37–67.

Eisermann, Falk (2017), "Fifty Thousand Veronicas. Print Runs of Broadsheets in the Fifteenth and Early Sixteenth Centuries", in: Andrew Pettegree (ed.), *Broadsheets. Single-Sheet Publishing in the First Age of Print* (Library of the Written Word 60 / The Handpress World 45), Leiden/Boston, 76–113.

Elias, Norbert (1939), *Über den Prozeß der Zivilisation,* Basle.

Embach, Michael (2000), "Skriptographie versus Typographie: Johannes Trithemius' Schrift 'De laude scriptorum'", in: *Gutenberg-Jahrbuch* 75, 132–144.

Feuerstein-Herz, Petra (2017), "Weiße Seiten. Durchschossene Bücher in alten Bibliotheken", in: *Zeitschrift für Ideengeschichte* 11 (4), 101–114.

Flachmann, Holger (2003), "Handschrift und Buchdruck bei Martin Luther", in: Gerd Dicke and Klaus Grubmüller (eds.), *Die Gleichzeitigkeit von Handschrift und Buchdruck* (Wolfenbütteler Mittelalter-Studien 16), Wiesbaden, 121–140.

Focken, Friedrich-Emanuel/Ott, Michael R. (eds.) (2016), *Metatexte. Erzählungen von schrifttragenden Artefakten in der alttestamentlichen und mittelalterlichen Literatur* (Materiale Textkulturen 15), Berlin/Boston, https://doi.org/10.1515/9783110417944.

Fox, Richard/Panagiotopoulos, Diamantis/Tsouparopoulou, Christina (2015), "Affordanz", in: Thomas Meier, Michael R. Ott, and Rebecca Sauer (eds.), *Materiale Textkulturen. Konzepte – Materialien – Praktiken* (Materiale Textkulturen 1), Berlin/Munich/Boston, 63–70, https://doi.org/10.1515/9783110371291.63.

Garncarz, Joseph (2016), *Medienwandel,* Constance.

Gavrilov, Alexander K. (1997), "Techniques of Reading in Classical Antiquity", in: *The Classical Quarterly* 47, 56–73.

Gertz, Jan Christian/Schultz, Sandra/Šimek, Jakub/Wallenwein, Kirsten (2015), "Abschreiben und Kopieren", in: Thomas Meier, Michael R. Ott, and Rebecca Sauer (eds.), *Materiale Textkulturen. Konzepte – Materialien – Praktiken* (Materiale Textkulturen 1), Berlin/Munich/Boston, 585–596, https://doi.org/10.1515/9783110371291.585.

Ginsburg, Christian D. (1897), *Introduction to the Massoretico-Critical Edition of the Hebrew Bible,* London, 779–976.

Goree, Robert (2020), *Printing Landmarks: Popular Geography and 'Meisho Zue' in Late Tokugawa Japan,* Cambridge, MA.

Grafton, Anthony (2011), *The Culture of Correction in Renaissance Europe* (The Panizzi Lectures 2009), London.

Green, Jonathan/McIntyre, Frank (2016), "Lost Incunable Editions: Closing in on an Estimate", in: Flavia Bruni and Andrew Pettegree (eds.), *Lost Books. Reconstructing the Print World of Pre-Industrial Europe* (Library of the Written Word 46 / The Handpress World 34), Leiden, 55–72.

Günther, Johann (2007), *Digital Natives & Digital Immigrants,* Innsbruck/Vienna/Bolzano.

Heinzer, Felix (2003), "Handschrift und Druck im Œuvre der Grafen Wilhelm Werner und Froben Christoph von Zimmern", in: Gerd Dicke and Klaus Grubmüller (eds.), *Die Gleichzeitigkeit von Handschrift und Buchdruck* (Wolfenbütteler Mittelalter-Studien 16), Wiesbaden, 141–166.

Heller, Marvin J. (2004), *The Sixteenth Century Hebrew Book. An Abridged Thesaurus,* vol. 1, Leiden/Boston.

Heller, Steven (2011), *Remarkable Graphic Design Selected by Designers, Illustrators, and Critics,* Beverly.
Herweg, Mathias (2010), "Wider die Schwarze Kunst? Johannes Trithemius' unzeitgemäße Eloge auf die Handschriftenkultur", in: *Daphnis* 39, 391–477.
Hillner, Matthias (2009), *Virtual Typography* (Basics Typography 1), London.
Ikegami Eiko (2005), *Bonds of Civility: Aesthetic Networks and the Political Origins of Japanese Culture,* New York.
Illich, Ivan (1993), *In the Vineyard of the Text: A Commentary to Hugh's "Didascalicon",* Chicago.
Ishikawa Tōru (2020), "Nara ehon emaki no kenkyū to shūshū 11 – yokogata nara ehon to otogi bunkobon", in: *Nihon kosho tsūshin* 1093, 30–32.
Jackson, Terrence (2016), *Networks of Knowledge: Western Science and the Tokugawa Information Revolution,* Honolulu.
Johns, Adrian (2002), "The Book of Nature and the Nature of the Book", in: David Finkelstein and Alistair McCleery (eds.), *The Book History Reader,* London, 59–76.
Kanai Toranosuke (1989), *Saikaku kō: Sakuhin, Shoshi,* Yagi Shoten.
Kaufmann, Thomas (2019), *Die Mitte der Reformation. Eine Studie zu Buchdruck und Publizistik im deutschen Sprachgebiet, zu ihren Akteuren und deren Strategien, Inszenierungs- und Ausdrucksformen* (Beiträge zur historischen Theologie 187), Tübingen.
Koakimoto Dan (2021), "Sagabon to sono zenshi no issōbō", in: *Hōsei Daigaku gakubu kiyō* 82, 21–36.
Komatsu Shigemi (1972), *Kohitsu,* Kodansha.
Kornicki, Peter (1998), *The Book in Japan: A Cultural History from the Beginnings to the Nineteenth Century,* Leiden.
Kornicki, Peter (2012), "The Hyakumanto Darani and the Origins of Printing in Eighth-Century Japan", in: *International Journal of Asian Studies* 9 (1), 43–70.
Kornicki, Peter (2019), "Japan's Hand-Written Culture: Confessions of a Print Addict", in: *Japan Forum* 31 (2), 272–284.
Kuhn, Thomas S. (1976), *Die Struktur wissenschaftlicher Revolutionen,* Frankfurt (Main).
Leca, Radu (2022a), "Dynamic Scribal Culture in Late Seventeenth-Century Japan: Ihara Saikaku's Engagement with Handscrolls", in: *Japan Review* 37, 77–100.
Leca, Radu (2022b), "Vengeful Promises: The Agency of Love Oaths as Materially Hybrid Texts in Late Seventeenth-Century Japan", in: *East Asian Publishing and Society* 12 (1), 46–72.
Leipziger, Jonas (2021), *Lesepraktiken im antiken Judentum. Rezeptionsakte, Materialität und Schriftgebrauch* 1800 (Materiale Textkulturen 34), Berlin/Boston, https://doi.org/10.1515/9783110732764.
Liss, Hanna (2024), "Early Hebrew Printing and the Quality of Reading: A Praxeological Study", in: Katrin Kogman-Appel and Ilona Steimann (eds.), *Premodern Jewish Books, their Makers and Readers in an Era of Media Change,* Turnhout, 251–274.
Luhmann, Niklas (1990), *Die Wissenschaft der Gesellschaft,* Frankfurt (Main).
Lukacs, Gabor (2008), *Kaitai Shinsho: The Single Most Famous Japanese Book of Medicine & Geka Sōden. An Early Very Important Manuscript on Surgery,* Utrecht.
Malkmus, Sarah (2020), "Hochschule Fulda: Keine Zeugnisse – weil etwas Wichtiges fehlt", in: *Fuldaer Zeitung,* 26/6/2020, https://www.fuldaerzeitung.de/fulda/hochschule-fulda-zeugnisse-papier-lieferengpass-coronavirus-antje-mohr-90005365.html (accessed 7/3/2023).
Marcon, Federico (2020), "The 'Book' as Fieldwork: 'Textual Institutions' and Nature Knowledge in Early Modern Japan", in: *BJHS Themes* 5, 131–148.
Marks, Richard B. (1980), "A Cologne Benedictine Scriptorium ca. 1490 and Trithemius' 'De Laude Scriptorum'", in: *Mittellateinisches Jahrbuch* 15, 162–171.
McDermott, Joseph (2006), *A Social History of the Chinese Book,* Hong Kong.

McLaren, Anne E. (2005), "Constructing New Reading Publics in Late Ming China", in: Cynthia J. Brokaw and Kai-Wing Chow (eds.), *Printing and Book Culture in Late Imperial China,* Berkeley, CA, 152–183.

McLuhan, Marshall (1962), *The Gutenberg Galaxy,* London.

Mentzel-Reuters, Arno (2010), "Das Nebeneinander von Handschrift und Buchdruck", in: Ursula Rautenberg (ed.), *Buchwissenschaft in Deutschland. Ein Handbuch,* New York, 411–442.

Meyer-Schlenkrich, Carla (2018), *Wann beginnt die Papierzeit? Zur Wissensgeschichte eines hoch- und spätmittelalterlichen Beschreibstoffs,* Heidelberg (machine-written habilitation, forthcoming 2024 as Materiale Textkulturen 45).

Meyer-Schlenkrich, Carla/Schweitzer-Martin, Paul (2023), "The Risk to Print History in the Late 15th Century. Johann Koelhoff's Chronicle Project in 1499", in: Sylvia Brockstieger and Paul Schweitzer-Martin (eds.), *Between Manuscript and Print. Transcultural Perspectives, ca. 1400–1800* (Materiale Textkulturen 40), Berlin/Boston, 9–41, https://doi.org/10.1515/9783111242699-002.

Meyer, Carla/Schneidmüller, Bernd (2015), "Zwischen Pergament und Papier", in: Thomas Meier, Michael R. Ott, and Rebecca Sauer (eds.), *Materiale Textkulturen. Konzepte – Materialien – Praktiken* (Materiale Textkulturen 1), Berlin/Munich/Boston, 349–354, https://doi.org/10.1515/9783110371291.349.

Needham, Paul (2015), "Book Production on Paper and Vellum in the Fourteenth and Fifteenth Centuries", in: Carla Meyer, Sandra Schultz, and Bernd Schneidmüller (eds.), *Papier im mittelalterlichen Europa. Herstellung und Gebrauch* (Materiale Texkulturen 7), Berlin/Boston, 247–274, https://doi.org/10.1515/9783110371413.247.

Ogburn, William F. (1965), *Kultur und sozialer Wandel. Ausgewählte Schriften,* Neuwied.

Peltzer, Jörg (2020), "The Roll in England and France in the Late Middle Ages. Introductory Remarks", in: Stefan G. Holz, Jörg Peltzer, and Maree Shirota (eds.), *The Roll in England and France in the Late Middle Ages. Form and Content* (Materiale Textkulturen 28), Berlin/Boston, 1–20, https://doi.org/10.1515/9783110645125-001.

Peritz, Moritz (1894), *Ein hebräischer Brief Elijah Levita's an Sebastian Münster nach der von letzterem im Jahre 1531 besorgten Ausgabe aufs Neue herausgegeben und mit einer deutschen Übersetzung und Anmerkungen versehen,* Breslaw.

Petzold, Kay Joe (2019), *Masora und Exegese. Untersuchungen zur Masora und Bibeltextüberlieferung im Kommentar des R. Schlomo ben Yitzchaq (Raschi)* (Materiale Textkulturen 24), Berlin/Boston, https://doi.org/10.1515/9783110627121.

Pitelka, Morgan (2013), "The Tokugawa Storehouse: Ieyasu's Encounters with Things", in: Paula Findlen (ed.), *Early Modern Things: Objects and their Histories, 1500–1800,* London/New York, 297–315.

Prebor, Gila (2007), "From Jerusalem to Venice: The Life of Domenico Yerushalmi, His Writings and His Work as a Censor", in: *Peʿamim: Studies in Oriental Jewry* 111/112, 215–242.

Preston, Jenny (2013), "Allegories of Love", in: *Japan Review* 26 (Special Issue Shunga), 117–135.

Proust, Jacques (2002), *Europe through the Prism of Japan,* Notre Dame, IN.

Rautenberg, Ursula (2000), "Von Mainz in die Welt. Buchdruck und Buchhandel in der Inkunabelzeit", in: Die Stadt Mainz (ed.), *Gutenberg. Aventur und Kunst. Vom Geheimunternehmen zur ersten Medienrevolution,* Mainz, 236–247.

Rautenberg, Ursula (2003), "Medienkonkurrenz und Medienmischung – Zur Gleichzeitigkeit von Handschrift und Druckschrift im ersten Viertel des 16. Jahrhunderts in Köln", in: Gerd Dicke and Klaus Grubmüller (eds.), *Die Gleichzeitigkeit von Handschrift und Buchdruck* (Wolfenbütteler Mittelalter-Studien 16), Wiesbaden, 167–202.

Rautenberg, Ursula (2008), "Die Entstehung und Entwicklung des Buchtitelblatts in der Inkunabelzeit in Deutschland, den Niederlanden und Venedig. Quantitative und qualitative Studien", in: *Archiv für Geschichte des Buchwesens* 62, 1–105.

Raz-Krakotzkin, Amnon (2007), *The Censor, the Editor, and the Text. The Catholic Church and the Shaping of the Jewish Canon in the Sixteenth Century,* Philadelphia.

Reas, Casey/Fry, Ben (2014), *Processing. A Programming Handbook for Visual Designers and Artists,* Cambridge, MA.

Reiner, Elchanan (1997), "The Ashkenazi Élite at the Beginning of the Modern Era: Manuscript versus Printed Book", in: Gershon David Hundert (ed.), *Jews in Early Modern Poland* (Polin. Studies in Polish Jewery 10), London/Portland, 85–98.

Reudenbach, Bruno (2015), "Der Codex als Verkörperung Christi. Mediengeschichtliche, theologische und ikonographische Aspekte einer Leitidee früher Evangelienbücher", in: Joachim Friedrich Quack and Daniela Christina Luft (eds.), *Erscheinungsformen und Handhabungen Heiliger Schriften* (Materiale Textkulturen 5), Berlin/Munich/Boston, 229–244, https://doi.org/10.1515/9783110371277.229.

Roth, Cecil (1972), *Studies in Books and Booklore,* Farnborough (UK).

Sarri, Antonia (2017), *Material Aspects of Letter Writing in the Graeco-Roman World. 500 BC – AD 300,* (Materiale Textkulturen 12), Berlin/Boston, https://doi.org/10.1515/9783110426953.

Sasaki Takahiro (2023), "Manuscript Features of Early Japanese Movable Type Books. On the Intersection of Eastern and Western Typesetting Techniques", in: Sylvia Brockstieger and Paul Schweitzer-Martin (eds.), *Between Manuscript and Print. Transcultural Perspectives, ca. 1400–1800* (Materiale Textkulturen 40), Berlin/Boston, 187–207, https://doi.org/10.1515/9783111242699-008.

Schade, Richard E. (1984), "Kunst, Literatur und die Straßburger Uhr", in: Kunstmuseum Basel (ed.), *Spätrenaissance am Oberrhein. Tobias Stimmer 1539–1584* (Ausstellung im Kunstmuseum Basel, 23. September bis 9. Dezember 1984), Basle, 112–117.

Schmidt-Biggemann, Wilhelm (1983), *Topica Universalis. Eine Modellgeschichte humanistischer und barocker Wissenschaft,* Hamburg.

Schmitz, Wolfgang (1990), "Klösterliche Buchkultur auf neuen Wegen? Die Entstehungsbedingungen von Klosterdruckereien im ersten Jahrhundert nach Gutenberg", in: Engelbert Plassmann and Paul Kaegbein (eds.), *Buch und Bibliothekswissenschaft im Informationszeitalter,* Munich, 345–362.

Schmitz, Wolfgang (2018), *Grundriss der Inkunabelkunde. Das gedruckte Buch im Zeitalter des Medienwechsels* (Bibliothek des Buchwesens 27), Stuttgart.

Schneider, Irmela (2000), "Anthropologische Kränkungen – Zum Zusammenhang von Medialität und Körperlichkeit in den Mediendiskursen", in: Barbara Becker and Irmela Schneider (eds.), *Was vom Körper übrig bleibt: Körperlichkeit – Identität – Medien,* Frankfurt (Main), 13–39.

Schneider, Ulrich Johannes (ed.) (2006), *Seine Welt wissen. Enzyklopädien in der Frühen Neuzeit,* Darmstadt.

Schneidmüller, Bernd/Schweitzer-Martin, Paul (2020), "Massenkommunikation als Motor einer neuen Zeit", in: *Ruperto Carola Forschungsmagazin* 16, 137–143.

Schweitzer-Martin, Paul (2022a), *Kooperation und Innovation im Speyerer Buchdruck des ausgehenden Mittelalters* (Materiale Textkulturen 37), Berlin/Boston, https://doi.org/10.1515/9783110796599.

Schweitzer-Martin, Paul (2022b), "Material und Format liturgischer Inkunabeldrucke. Eine Fallstudie zur Offizin Johannes Sensenschmidt", in: Philipp Hegel and Michael Krewet (eds.), *Wissen und Buchgestalt* (Episteme in Bewegung. Beiträge zur einer transdisziplinären Wissensgeschichte 26), Wiesbaden, 301–321.

Schweitzer-Martin, Paul (2023), "Handschriftliche Elemente im Inkunabeldruck", in: Sylvia Brockstieger and Rebecca Hirt (eds.), *Handschrift im Druck (ca. 1500–1800). Annotieren, Korrigieren, Weiterschreiben* (Materiale Textkulturen 39), Berlin/Boston, 23–42, https://doi.org/10.1515/9783111191560-002.

Screech, Timon (2002), *The Lens within the Heart,* Honolulu.
Seifert, Arno (1976): *Cognitio historica. Die Geschichte als Namensgeberin der frühneuzeitlichen Empirie* (Historische Forschungen 11), Berlin.
Sina, Kai/Spoerhase, Carlos (eds.) (2017), *Nachlassbewusstsein. Literatur, Archiv, Philologie* (Marbacher Schriften, NF 13), Göttingen.
Small, David (1999), *Rethinking the Book* (PhD dissertation, Massachusetts Institute of Technology), https://acg.media.mit.edu/projects/thesis/DSThesis.pdf (accessed 31/1/2024).
Smith, Margaret M. (2000), *The Title-Page. Its Early Development, 1460–1510,* London/New Castle.
Son Suyoung (2018), *Writing for Print: Publishing and the Making of Textual Authority in Late Imperial China,* Cambridge, MA.
Stammen, Theo/Weber, Wolfgang E. J. (eds.) (2004), *Wissenssicherung, Wissensordnung und Wissensverarbeitung. Das europäische Modell der Enzyklopädien,* Berlin.
Stock, Brian (2009), *Augustine the Reader. Meditation, Self-Knowledge, and the Ethics of Interpretation,* Cambridge.
Svenbro, Jesper (1988), *Phrasikleia: Anthropologie de la lecture en Grèce Ancienne,* Paris.
Thomanek, Judith (2017), *Zeugnisse christlicher Zensur des frühen hebräischen Buchdrucks im Greifswalder Gustav Dalman-Institut,* Leipzig.
Thorley, David (2015), "Inscription, Print, and Miscellaneity: Reading John Donne's Poems in a Princeton Copy of Deaths Duell", in: *The Princeton University Library Chronicle* 76 (3), 476–494.
Trinh, Khanh/Bauer, Estelle/Trede, Melanie (eds.) (2021), *Liebe, Kriege, Festlichkeiten. Facetten der narrativen Kunst aus Japan,* Zürich.
Tychsen, Oluf Gerhard (1780), "O. G. Tychsen's kritische Beschreibung des Bononischen Pentateuch's vom J. 1482 / Kritische Beschreibung des Bononischen Pentateuchs'", in: *Repertorium für Biblische und Morgenländische Litteratur* 6, 65–103.
Wagner, Bettina (2012), "Idealtyp und Individuum. Blockbücher im Medienwandel des 15. Jahrhunderts", in: Bettina Wagner (ed.), *Vom ABC bis zur Apokalypse. Leben, Glauben und Sterben in spätmittelalterlichen Blockbüchern,* Lucerne, 11–26.
Wagner, Bettina (2017), "Die Erfassung von Wasserzeichen aus Handschriften, Blockbüchern und Inkunabeln in der Bayrischen Staatsbibliothek München. Mit neuen Erkenntnissen zur Datierung und Lokalisierung der Blockbücher von Hans Sporer", in: Erwin Frauenknecht, Gerald Maier, and Peter Rückert (eds.), *Das Wasserzeicheninformationssystem (WZIS). Bilanz und Perspektiven* (Sonderveröffentlichungen des Landesarchivs Baden-Württemberg), Stuttgart, 65–78.
Wallenwein, Kisten (2017), *Corpus subscriptionum. Verzeichnis der Beglaubigungen von spätantiken und frühmittelalterlichen Textabschriften (saec. IV–VIII)* (Quellen und Untersuchungen zur lateinischen Philologie des Mittelalters 19), Stuttgart.
Werle, Dirk (2007), *Copia librorum. Problemgeschichte imaginierter Bibliotheken 1580–1630* (Frühe Neuzeit 119), Tübingen.
Wernli, Martina (2021), *Federn lesen. Eine Literaturgeschichte des Gänsekiels von den Anfängen bis ins 19. Jahrhundert,* Göttingen.
Widmann, Hans (1973), *Vom Nutzen und Nachteil der Erfindung des Buchdrucks – aus der Sicht der Zeitgenossen des Erfinders,* Mainz.
Yoshida Kogoro (1984), *Tanrokubon: Rare Books of Seventeenth-Century Japan,* Tokyo/New York/San Francisco.
Zafren, Herbert C. (1982), "Bible Editions, Bible Study, and the Early History of Hebrew Printing", in: *Eretz-Israel: Archaeological, Historical and Geographical Studies* 16, 240–251.

Chapter 5
Sacralisation

Tobias Frese, Wolf Zöller, Stefan Ardeleanu, Nikolaus Dietrich, Dennis Disselhoff, Annette Hornbacher, Lisa Horstmann, Jiří Jákl, Tino Licht, Hanna Liss, Giuditta Mirizio, Anett Rózsa, Anna Sitz, Mandy Telle, Sebastian Watta, Franziska Wenig

Chapter 5
Sacralisation

Tobias Frese, Wolf Zöller, Stefan Ardeleanu, Nikolaus Dietrich, Dennis Disselhoff, Annette Hornbacher, Lisa Horstmann, Jiří Jákl, Tino Licht, Hanna Liss, Giuditta Mirizio, Anett Rózsa, Anna Sitz, Mandy Telle, Sebastian Watta, Franziska Wenig

Within the Abrahamic religious tradition, it is obvious that writing is something important, indeed fundamental: the written word is the medium through which the eternal Word of God and his revealed truth is believed to be communicated. The obviousness of this statement is called into question, however, as soon as we investigate the significance of inscribed artefacts in sacred contexts from a cross-religious, cross-epochal, and cross-cultural perspective.[1]

Apart from the simple observation that writing is of no significance whatsoever in some religions, we must concede that its status cannot even be unambiguously determined in distinct writing cultures, much less in the so-called 'religions of the book'. For the latter, but also with respect to many other cultures and religions—we can generally assert first of all that writing has hierographic potential (Thesis 24). However, the way in which this potential was used and activated differs greatly, depending on a variety of ideological and cultural factors. In Balinese rituals, for example, an inherently powerful effect is ascribed to individual written characters and their pictographic arrangement,[2] while in rituals of sacralisation in classical antiquity, the connection between what is written and what is spoken played a major role, with the use of writing in such instances being often possible, but not always necessary. In the Christian Middle Ages, by contrast, we find an almost ambivalent appraisal of the sanctity of writing. On the one hand, the Bible itself could be regarded as offering a sceptical view (seen, for instance, in the juxtaposition of the "letter [that] kills" with the "Spirit [that] gives life" [2 Cor 3:6]), while on the other hand, this very same book was regarded as 'Holy Scripture' and cultically venerated in its manifold material forms.

The sacred in itself eludes the analytical methods of both the natural sciences and the humanities. In material culture, however, we can identify attributions of a sacred quality to objects, places, or people, as is demonstrated for example in the creation and hierarchical structuring, or internal differentiation, of sacred spaces. These complex processes of 'sacralisation'[3] can be described as processes of discursive construc-

---
[1] This cannot be done with the same intensity for all world religions. In what follows, we focus on Graeco-Roman antiquity, Christianity, and Judaism, as well as on East Asian religious cultures.
[2] In this case, writing not only indicates *sacrality,* but also *sacralises* the object.
[3] When we refer to sacralisation through writing, we mean (ritual) acts by means of which objects, spaces, and persons can be both sacralised and also desacralised, either through (active) writing or

tion which often involve diverse media and where the sacred quality is recurrently and repeatedly ascribed or perceived by the people involved, thus becoming accessible to academic research.[4] Looking across cultures and different time periods, we encounter a mind-boggling diversity of concepts of the sacred that are implemented in this way and are also very dynamic in character.

If we inquire into the concrete role of writing in the production of sacred spaces and artefacts, we find that this role is highly flexible and takes on an extremely diverse array of forms. Thus, inscriptions often served to mark and protect the boundary[5] between the profane and the sacred; at the same time, however, writing could also make these boundaries permeable, generate its own intermediate spaces, and moderate existentially significant transitions (Thesis 25). Since sacral status is always in jeopardy, writings were also regularly deployed to authenticate, legitimise, and stabilise sacrality over the long term (Thesis 26). Finally, inscriptions were used to define and establish sacred spaces, but they were also positioned so that they profited 'parasitically' from the sacredness of a space, as it were (Thesis 27).

As diverse and in part contradictory as these functions of writing in sacred contexts may be, what they all have in common is a fundamentally dynamic quality and performative character. By participating in processes of sacralisation, inscribed artefacts were always more than mere external signs of transcendent messages. On the contrary, they had their own "communicative agency"[6] and effect, and they were always integrated into complex 'writing rituals'.[7] However, these ritual acts of writing took place not only in the context of religions with a strong, emphatic concept of sacred scriptures, but also in religions whose use of scripture was optional in character, and even (or especially) in a 'religion of the book', whose theologians polemicised against magical writing practices.

---

through the reception of writing. Cf. the etymological references to the terms 'sacralisation' ("Sakralisierung") or 'de- and resacralisation' ("De- und Resakralisierung") in Herbers 2013, esp. 12–13.
4 Cf. Gemeinhardt/Heyden 2012, 421–422. On church construction: Watta 2018, 21–24; Jäggi 2011.
5 Cf. the emphasis on the boundary or demarcation in Eliade 1958, 1, who posits "that the sacred and the religious life are the opposite of the profane and the secular life"; cf. Herbers 2013, 12: "Derived from this is *sancire*, 'to demarcate something as sacred', understood as a juridical act. What is demarcated is the *sanctum*; if one demarcates a person, that person is a *persona sancta* or *sanctus/sancta*" (our translation, German text: "Abgeleitet davon ist *sancire*, etwas als heilig abgrenzen, verstanden als ein juristischer Akt. Das Abgegrenzte ist das *sanctum*, grenzt man eine Person ab, ist diese eine *persona sancta* oder *sanctus, sancta*.").
6 Tilley 2002, 25. In general: Wieser 2008.
7 Cf. Frese/Keil 2015.

Thesis 24
Writing has hierographic potential.

Inscribing an artefact can sometimes lend it a sacred status. We refer to this possibility of direct sacralisation through inscribing as the hierographic potential of writing (from Gr. ἱερός ['sacred'] and γράφω ['to write/draw'], and thus in the sense of 'inscribing sacrality'). By the 'sacred status' of an artefact, we understand here any efficacy attributed to it which we can ascribe to the realm of the sacred, provided we also keep its ambivalent nature in mind.[8] Traditionally in some scholarly disciplines, such as Egyptology or papyrology, the concept of the magical has been used to describe such 'sacred efficacy' of artefacts and associated practices, with this efficacy understood to involve supernatural powers. This term is also used in the following, in contexts where it is established as a *terminus technicus;* yet we remain nonetheless aware of the problematic nature of this category, by means of which certain phenomena considered particularly irrational have been artificially separated from the continuum of cultural practices.[9] We speak of hierographic writing, then, when the inscribing of an artefact can be understood as an inscribing of sacred status that coincides with a qualitative change of this artefact in terms of its efficacy.

This qualitative change can either be 'merely' indicated by writing or, in a stronger sense, only come about in the first place through such writing. As we shall illustrate below via a number of significant objects and practices, this hierographic potential of writing is explored in different epochs, cultures, and religions to different degrees and in different ways. In comparing the concrete forms that the hierographic potential of writing can assume, the following questions in particular arise: what is the relationship of hierographic writing to orality and the spoken word, which is often central to forms of performative ritual action? What role does the meaning of the text play with regard to the hierographic quality of writing in relation to the materiality of what is written? To what extent is the act of writing itself significant? Does the audience play a role as a potential recipient group of what is written or of the act of writing? And finally: what is the relation of what is written to the concrete efficacy of the artefact?

The concept of hierographic writing can be used to describe some contemporary practices of the Balinese script,[10] which we will discuss here at the outset in order to counteract any impression of a linear historical development. Special visual arrangements of mystical characters *(aksara modré)* are applied to or carved into objects or onto the bodies of initiates in visible and 'invisible' form (by means of paint, liquid wax, or sanctified water for example). What we have here is a process of transforma-

---

8 An example of this is Agamben's analysis of the *homo sacer* and the latter's ambivalent status between being cursed and being consecrated to God. Cf. Agamben 2017.
9 On the reception and discourse history of the term: Otto 2011.
10 Cf. Hornbacher/Neumann/Willer 2015.

tion of the respective object or person, the goals of which can vary greatly. Amulets or metals with *aksara modré* can protect those bearing them or the buildings in whose foundation they are embedded from harmful influences, while mystical characters applied by a priest to the human body serve to spiritually purify or transfigure an initiate, e. g., from the state of an ignorant child to that of a discerning adult in the context of ritual tooth filing *(metatah)*. Depending on the arrangement of the characters and the objective of the specialist, such pictograms can promote physical and spiritual life, but also destroy it.[11] Yet written pictograms are also commonly used in public ritual contexts on Bali, and this far more frequently than hitherto observed. Thus, in the context of elaborate death and cremation rituals *(ngaben)*, various effigies are crafted (e. g., *kajang, puspa)* that manifest the physical, ethereal, or divine body of a deceased person by adorning material writing supports (white cotton cloth, leaves, sandalwood) with arrangements of characters.

The Indo-Malay world can boast of a longstanding tradition of ritual text practices that are more oriented around the spoken word and at the same time reminiscent of Agamben's *homo sacer,* the cursed outlaw who through a broken oath belongs entirely to the god by whom he swore. Ancient Malay stone inscriptions from the late seventh century CE refer to a similar concept and use writing as a powerful manifestation of the eternally valid royal word, for example on oath tablets. In such cases, water would be poured over a stone inscription on which a king's retainers swore an oath, which included their accursedness should they break it. The water thus 'imbued' with potential curses would be collected through a spout at the bottom of the stone tablet and drunk by the participants of the ritual. One such stone tablet, still extant today, was erected by Talang Tuwo in 683 CE on the occasion of a major campaign by Sumatran troops against the island of Java. The royal word, 'imbibed' by the soldiers in this same manner together with its concomitant provisions, was intended to ensure military discipline.[12] What is remarkable, by contrast, about the above-mentioned writing practices from contemporary Bali, is that the efficacy in the premodern example lies not in the representation of an authoritative word or oath, but decidedly in the written arrangement of characters. These characters are effective less through being read, heard, or understood as individual characters or a whole text (i. e., through the semantic reception of what is written), but rather through the characters' being visualised, which can also be ephemeral in nature. Thus, certain inscribed effigies unfold their agency in the process of being burnt.[13] Writing here is less a representation of authoritative speech than a semantically overdetermined manifestation of cosmological or spiritual speculations, which in many cases are no longer phonetically 'legible'.[14]

---

11 Hooykaas 1980, 75–79; Fox/Hornbacher 2016.
12 Casparis 1956.
13 Hornbacher 2019.
14 Hornbacher 2016, 98.

The semantically unambiguous understanding (and observance) of eternal oaths written down on the ancient Javanese stone tablets is contrasted here with writing as a visual and material manifestation of a cosmological reality that need not be understood in order to be efficacious. Such efficacy is often described by practitioners as an emanation of energy that involves spatial proximity and a particular way of dealing with what is written. The hierographic quality of writing therefore differs significantly from case to case. In the ancient Javanese example, writing works as the materialisation and internalisation of an oath, whereas in contemporary Balinese rituals, it works as the manifestation of creative energies which refer to the process of cosmogonic emanation and form a deeper, hidden layer *(niskala)* of visible/material reality *(sekala)*.

This absolute equation of the hierographic with the individual written character is not necessarily found in the very writing system in which one would most readily expect it: namely, in the ancient Egyptian writing system of the hieroglyphics (from Gr. ἱερός ['sacred'] and γλυφή ['carving, carved work']). The Egyptians themselves already imputed a sacred character to their writing, calling their script *zẖ₃.w-n-mdw.w-nṯr*, the "script of divine words". According to some sources, the hieroglyphs were created by Ptah, the primordial creator god.[15] But it was also the speaking of words that played an important role during the creation of the world.[16] Even in Graeco-Egyptian magical practices—such as those which have come down to us in large numbers on inscribed magical gems, lead tablets, and papyri, of both private and public nature—the efficacy of the artefacts does not seem to have been based solely on the hierographic quality of what is written on them. The sacralisation of the artefacts (in the sense of charging them with magical power) usually also took place with the help of spoken words in the form of a recitation for instance, in addition to other ritual acts.[17] The perpetuation of the power was then ensured by writing down the spoken formulas. Thus, this act of writing definitely has a hierographic quality, as it can permanently change the status of the mobile or immobile[18] artefact and endow it with supernatural powers.[19] However, this ritual act of writing is no independent work, but rather carried out in conjunction with a speech act.

The same is true, for example, in the case of the so-called *defixiones* documented in Greek and Latin since the late sixth century BCE. These are written lead tablets by which one could secure 'legal protection' as a means of punishment or as a protective measure from the gods by 'fixing' a potential enemy, not least by writing down his name (Lat. *defigo*, 'to make fast, to fix'; Gr. καταδέω, 'to bind, tie down'). Even though this 'effective' act of writing the name proves the hierographic quality of the writing

---

[15] This is also known from other cultures; see for example Schulz 2020, 41–42 on the invention of the runes in Old Norse mythology.
[16] A. Assmann/J. Assmann 2003
[17] Cubelic/Lougovaya/Quack 2015; Meyer-Dietrich 2010.
[18] Theis 2015.
[19] On the transfer of power to the artefact: Speyer 1992.

here, the *defixiones* nevertheless remained integrated into a specific ritual act (one of harm) that had a performative and oral character.[20]

Biblical tradition also recognises the hierographic quality of writing in connection with ritual acts: the so-called 'Ordeal of Jealousy' (Num 5:11–31), known in rabbinic literature as the *inyan soṭa*, is a ritual that a man can have performed if he suspects his wife has not been faithful. In the ritual, the woman must drink a solution of holy water which has been mixed with dust from the floor of the tabernacle and to which is added a formula invoking a curse on her in the case of guilt. This curse is written onto a scroll, with the writing being washed off by the priest into the water that is to be drunk. If she is innocent, the woman should remain physically unharmed.[21] The special significance of what is written is shown in the description of a medieval magical fragment from the genizah in Cairo. This text mentions that running water and dust from the synagogue are physical components of the ritual, but additionally prescribes more precisely that what is to be written out are (secret) divine names that are to be given to the woman to drink.[22]

Magical gems are another example of hierographic writing on account of the divine names, individual wishes, and magical signs and words *(charaktēres* and *voces magicae)* often inscribed on them.[23] For such gems, a consecration rite (Gr. τελετή) has come down to us[24] in which the actors temporarily received the power of the deity in question and transferred this power to the artefact.[25] The *charaktēres* consisted of script-like magical signs that were meant to convey magical qualities, even if people did not necessarily understand them.[26] Here, the meaning of the text was not a priority; rather, the signs reinforced the artefacts' function as a means of communicating with supernatural beings. Once the consecration had taken place, the presence of the writing and the knowledge that it was present was alone sufficient for the characters to be effective.[27] A public audience was not always necessary for the reception process, which in turn means that it was not necessary for the writing to be visible and

---

[20] Faraone 1991; Frankfurter 2019; Graf 2011; Kropp 2011. Graf 2005, 247: "Prayers, curses, and oaths are spoken rites that are closely interrelated. All three are performative utterances in which the action described in words and the action itself coincide." (Our translation, German text: "Gebet, Fluch und Eid sind gesprochene Riten, die eng miteinander verwandt sind. Alle drei sind performative Äußerungen, in denen die in Worte beschriebene Handlung und die Handlung selber zusammenfallen.")
[21] Cf. for example Liss 2007.
[22] Veltri 2002.
[23] On magical gems in general: *The Campbell Bonner Magical Gems Database* (CBD), online at http://classics.mfab.hu/talismans/ (accessed 16/12/2022). Cf. also Dasen/Nagy 2019; Endreffy/Nagy/Spier 2019.
[24] Such statements can be made on the basis of magical papyri that functioned as manuals for such consecration rituals while being physically separated from the artefacts in question.
[25] Eltram 1939.
[26] Gordon 2014; Dzwiza 2019.
[27] Quack 2014; Keil et al. 2018.

legible. Finally, these artefacts were often partially or completely hidden and concealed, and thus potentially served as instances of what might be called "restricted scriptural presence".[28]

From the same time period and cultural area, we know of another classic case in which writing has a hierographic quality in the literal sense of inscribing sacrality: namely, consecration inscriptions such as can be found on votive offerings in ancient Greek sanctuaries, for example. While *defixiones* and magical gems required performative rituals and speech acts in order to activate the hierographic quality of what was written on them, Greek votive inscriptions were less likely to be read as written traces of something spoken, as is made clear by the typical form in which such inscriptions are found. This kind of inscription, usually a more or less abbreviated form of the statement "X has consecrated [it] to the deity Y", can be found on all manner of consecrated objects within such sanctuaries, from humble clay vessels to colossal statues. In most cases, the reference to what was respectively consecrated remains implicit in the consecration formula, with the inscribed artefact itself usually taking the place of the accusative-case direct object in the phrase. The interweaving of material writing support and text can hardly be more concrete: as a spoken text without the writing support, the sentence would be grammatically incomplete and meaningless. The ritualistic understanding of consecrative inscriptions as being the written trace of spoken consecration formulae, something obvious in the case of *defixiones* and magical gems, thus becomes considerably less plausible here. Only in their material connection to the respective votive offerings do the dedicatory inscriptions retain their meaning.

While such short dedicatory inscriptions thus do not function as autonomous texts, the votive offerings by contrast can still function quite well without any consecratory wording. Unlike Christian relics, whose sacred status depends on a perceived reliable identification,[29] dedicatory inscriptions do not fulfil any urgent need for authentication. Even more numerous than the dedicatory inscriptions that have come down to us are votive offerings without dedicatory inscriptions in ancient Greek sanctuaries. This applies, for instance, to dedicated weapons, a particularly important type of votive gift in the archaic and early classical periods for which thousands of examples have survived in the sanctuary of Zeus at Olympia. These include bronze helmets, greaves, breastplates, shields, lances, and swords, all of which found their way into the sanctuary as dedications of booty (or, more rarely, as dedications of one's own weaponry) in gratitude for victories in battle. Only a fraction of these precious offerings is also inscribed,[30] one such artefact being a Corinthian helmet from around 500 BCE (Fig. 1). This helmet owes its fame to the fact that it was consecrated by none other than Miltiades, the Athenian commander who was victorious at the Battle of

---

28 Hornbacher/Frese/Willer 2015, 87–100; Willer 2015. Foundational here: Frese/Keil/Krüger 2014.
29 Ferro 2021.
30 According to H. Frielinghaus, only 5–6 % of the helmets and greaves dedicated at Olympia bear inscriptions.

Fig. 1: Helmet votive dedication from Olympia with dedicatory inscription along the lower edge: Μιλτιάδες ἀνέ[θ]εκεν [ː τ]ōι Δί ('Miltiades dedicated [it] to Zeus'), ca. 500 BCE. Olympia, Archaeological Museum, inv. no. B 2600. Photo: Oren Rozen (via Wikipedia, CC BY-SA 3.0)

Marathon against the Persian army in 490 BCE.[31] Beginning on the left cheek-guard, the simple inscription—Μιλτιάδες ἀνέ[θ]εκεν [ː τ]ōι Δί. (IG I³,2 1472, "Miltiades dedicated [it] to Zeus")—stretches from there across to the back of the neck screen.

Continuing along the undulation of the helmet's lower seam, the etched inscription submits to the morphology of the object, instead of taking pride of place via a more frontal positioning (which could end up demoting the helmet to the status of a mere writing support). Now, this inscription was undoubtedly legible, but we must bear some other factors in mind. First, this kind of dedication of weaponry or armour usually stood for but a short period of time within the sanctuary fixed to wooden posts

---

31 Olympia, Archaeological Museum, inv. no. B 2600. See Frielinghaus 2011, 383, cat. no. D 478 (with bibliography) and 548, no. 40 (on the inscription), table 114.3. See also Dietrich 2022. That the Miltiades mentioned in the inscription is actually identical with the historical figure cannot be proven beyond a doubt, yet does not seem implausible.

before being taken down.³² Second, deciphering the inscription also requires close-up observation of the artefact, which would entail a special attention that surely would have only very rarely been accorded to a single helmet amidst so many others. The inscription does not so much proclaim its content as a communicative act to the outside world as much as it etches it into the object (both literally and figuratively). The relationship between the consecrator and the receiving deity, based on the principle of *do ut des* and maintained through the practice of votive offerings, is additionally affirmed in the case of this helmet by the inscription of the names of Miltiades and Zeus, thus becoming part of the helmet's materiality. However, since such consecrative inscriptions could just as well be absent, the object does not necessarily require the written text to possess a hierographic quality in order to attain sacral efficacy as a votive offering.³³

The positions taken in Christianity on the hierographic quality of writing are much more ambivalent. As in other monotheistic 'religions of the book', the written word initially plays a central role in the Christian faith: after all, the Bible is not only understood as a documentary account of divine deeds, but is also regarded as being the Word of God itself. In the liturgy, 'Holy Scripture' guarantees the presence of the divine Logos and is not only used as a book, but is also revered and venerated: in entrances into churches and in processions, it is solemnly carried by the clergy and literally staged on the altar. The celebrants treat the book of the Gospels with great reverence; priests and deacons still kiss it during the Roman Catholic liturgy.³⁴ Even if the solemn reading from the Gospels and the epistles is certainly the most important act of reception (in the Liturgy of the Word), the book-object itself is obviously attributed great power and efficacy in liturgical acts: for example, during the consecration of a bishop, it is customary to hold the Gospel book or codex over the head and neck of the ordinand.³⁵

However, such sacralising acts of scripture are not limited to the handling of the Bible or the Gospel book in Christian liturgy. We find attestations of them elsewhere, with the so-called 'abecedary' of a church consecration serving as an impressive example.³⁶ In this consecration ritual, the bishop writes out—in rows and in their entirety—the Latin and Greek alphabets on the ground with his staff. Each letter is

---

32 On the length of time during which such dedications of weaponry remained standing at Olympia, see Frielinghaus 2011, 170–183.
33 This distinguishes such dedicatory inscriptions on votive weapons from the practice of inscribing graphemes on weapons, known from the Balinese cultural area. Here, the hierographic effectiveness of the inscription applies to such weapons, which—unlike weapon votive offerings—were still intended for practical use in battle and, which such dedication intended to increase the weapons' fighting power. See Hooykaas 1980.
34 Hermans 1984, 186–187; Ganz 2017, 93.
35 The process is described by Rupert of Deutz (d. 1129/1130), *Vita Herberti*, 45–46. On the consecration of the bishop himself, see also Engels 1987. In detail and with further examples: Schreiner 2011, 284–307; also Kehnel/Panagiotopoulos 2015, 3–5.
36 See Forneck 1999, 201–202; Schmitt 2004, 475–478 and Schreiner 2006.

written in scattered ashes or even traced out invisibly directly on the bare stone, with the rows of the letters forming an X-shaped cross. The bishop here is neither presenting a sacred text nor conveying a Christian message. Rather, this sequence of letters is only visible for a short time (if at all) and is not intended to be read in the literal sense of the word. What counts is the act of writing, with which a profane space is transformed into a consecrated and sacred one. Now, on the one hand, we can assume that this rite has its roots in older pagan customs,[37] but on the other hand, a specific Christian re-interpretation and legitimation of this writing ritual can be expected (God as the alpha and omega, following Rev 1:8; 21:6; 22:13).[38] In the ancient sense, the abecedary was believed to have an apotropaic, i. e. defensive or protective, power that could guard the church against demonic influences.[39]

In Jewish understanding, it is not so much the holy book of the 'Bible' *in toto* as much as the handwritten Torah scroll with the Pentateuch text that can be identified as the decisive artefact (Fig. 2). The starting point of this 'artefact theology', however, was likely not (only) the hierographic power of what was written (especially the names of God), but also the need to protect the cultic handling of the Torah scroll (bowing before the Torah; kissing the Torah mantle;[40] using the Torah scroll to ward off demons[41]) from the accusation of idolatry in terms of religious law and theology. This need emerged because the Torah scroll is a man-made artefact, and the anti-image polemics found in Isaiah (Isa 40–46) were often applied by Jews to Christians' handling of the cross and the Bible. Therefore, medieval Jewish theologians in Western Europe—especially the mystic circle around R. Yehuda ben Shmuel of Regensburg, called 'the Pious' (*he-ḥasîd;* d. 1217)—developed a kind of 'Torah artefact theology', in which the Torah scroll as bearer of the divine names vouches for God's presence and power. In R. Yehuda's theology, the upper (divine) and lower worlds (Torah) are conceived of as belonging together in a quasi-substantive way. Bowing before the Torah does not simply function as a substitute for the contemplation of the Eternal One which can no longer be accomplished; rather, such an act is itself that very contemplation of the Eternal One. In this way, the Torah guarantees the immediate presence and tangible experience of the divine presence.[42] Just like the prophetic vision, the Torah scroll before which the pious prostrate themselves becomes a (real) symbol of

---

37 Stapper 1937, 143–144.
38 God and Christ themselves are symbolically designated by John in his book of Revelation with the Greek letters alpha (Α) and omega (Ω) (Rev 1:8; 21:6; 22:13) as an expression of the beginning and the end of all that is created and has come into being, which coincides in God. Cf. Schreiner 2000, 64–65. The Word is the beginning of everything: cf. John 1:1 ("ἐν ἀρχῇ ἦν ὁ λόγος, καὶ ὁ λόγος ἦν πρὸς τὸν θεόν, καὶ θεός ἦν ὁ λόγος"; "In the beginning was the Word, and the Word was with God, and the Word was God").
39 Schreiner 2006, 184. Cf. Dornseiff 1925, 69–81 and Glück 1987, 219–220.
40 Liss 2014, 209–211.
41 Cf. Liss 2015, 169–172.
42 Liss 2001, 281–291.

Fig. 2: Mantled Torah scrolls with Torah shield *(tas)*, Torah pointer *(yad)*, and Torah crown *(keter)*, or two Torah crowns *(rimonim)* in the Torah shrine *(aron ha-qodesh)*. Heidelberg, synagogue. Photo: Hanna Liss.

the divine presence and thus enables an immediate realisation of (and participation in) the divine world. The Torah becomes *pars pro toto* the vehicle of the divine. In the Torah, the Creator himself — his essence, his wisdom, but also his power — is revealed to and made tangible for human beings.

If these writing practices are strong evidence for an emphatic understanding of writing and scripture, the objection has to be raised in the same breath that positions that were explicitly sceptical of writing and possibly inspired by (Neo-)Platonism have also played a major role in Christianity. Thus, we find influential theologians from Augustine to Thomas Aquinas always speaking out against the permissibility and meaningfulness of the practice of scriptural magic, which was particularly popular and prevalent in lay piety.[43] If we think again of the aforementioned cultic veneration accorded to 'Holy Scripture' in the liturgy, we might be further astonished by writing practices that testify to a remarkably irreverent treatment of this book-object. Thus,

---

[43] See Schreiner 1990 for more detail. The practice of curing illnesses of the head (physical or mental) through contact with the Bible, a practice apparently already known in late Christian antiquity, was tolerated by Augustine. Cf. Schreiner 2002, 82.

the same liturgical book venerated within the Christian liturgy could be destroyed only a short time later, regarded as an obsolete and irrelevant manuscript and economically recycled as scratch paper or flyleaves (maculature).[44] Was no supra-temporal permanence accorded to the hierographic quality of the writing, to its sacral power and presence?

Surely, we must understand the ambivalent values and practices of the Christian Middle Ages in the context of a genuinely ambivalent understanding of scripture, such as was prefigured in patristic literature, but also previously in the New Testament itself.[45] In Paul's Second Letter to the Corinthians, for example, we learn that the living God inscribed himself "not with ink [...] on tablets of stone but on tablets of human hearts" (2 Cor 3:3) and that "the letter kills, but the Spirit gives life" (τὸ γὰρ γράμμα ἀποκτείνει, τὸ δὲ πνεῦμα ζωοποιεῖ, 2 Cor 3:6). In this sense, according to Paul, true believers are not 'servants of the letter' but 'servants of the Spirit'. Without a doubt, this Pauline polemic helped in part to shape the theological understanding of scripture in the Christian Middle Ages. From this perspective, it was hardly possible to understand writing in the substantial sense as something sacred or effective: the hierographic potential of writing always had to play out in the ritual connection with the spoken word and liturgical action. Against this background, however, it is remarkable that popular and paraliturgical practices of sacralisation through writing, written characters, and books—extending even to mantic and magical usages[46]—have long remained a part of Christian piety despite the vast criticism and objections against them from the quill and pen of theologians.

Thesis 25
Writing opens up possibilities for the separation of profane and sacred space, thus creating spaces of liminality.

Already in the ancient Mediterranean world, writing served to separate profane from sacred space: stone inscriptions were sometimes used to mark the boundaries of ancient Greek sanctuaries and ensure that these boundaries were not crossed accidentally or carelessly. This task was primarily assigned to the precinct walls or *horos* (boundary) stones and their Greek inscriptions. Basically, horos stones could mark all kinds of boundaries and borders in the Greek world: inter-state borders, asylum

---

[44] Senzel 2018. Such waste paper—i. e., paper and parchment that has already been written on—can be used as flyleaves to reinforce the bindings of new prints and manuscripts. In the process, no value is attached to the writing itself, whereas the material finds use and importance. Kühne-Wespi/Oschema/Quack 2019, 15–16.
[45] On this also: Frese 2014; Reudenbach 2021.
[46] Further examples in Schreiner 2000.

areas, administrative and settlement borders (i. e., those of specific demes), the borders of public areas and buildings, and those of private property.⁴⁷ In the Athenian Agora, a carved stone from the fifth century BCE declares: "I am the boundary of the Agora" (hόρος εἰμὶ τε̃ς ἀγορᾶς).⁴⁸ This and other similar stones served to ensure that anyone entering the agora abided by its rules; for example, murderers were not allowed to enter this space. This concern for the control of boundaries was again of particular urgency in the case of sanctuaries. On a fifth-century-BCE stone from the island of Aigina, we can read: "Boundary stone of the sanctuary of Athena" (hόρος τεμένος Ἀθεναίας).⁴⁹ At first glance, this text read as a simple declarative statement: the stone identified itself as a horos, thus establishing a boundary and designating the area beyond it as a sacred space belonging to Athena (which also thus constituted a distinct legal sphere). Beyond this literal reading, however, such an inscription also had to be understood by the recipient as an appeal: as an invitation to stop and check one's own right to enter.⁵⁰ Accordingly, in the Greek worldview, only those who were free of any 'defilement' (Gr. μίασμα) were allowed to enter the sanctuary.⁵¹ Such ritual defilement could arise from 'unclean' events, some of which were beyond human control, such as a birth or a death in the household. A person thus 'defiled' who entered the sanctuary risked nothing less than the entire community being punished.

In an inscription at a sanctuary in Priene (Asia Minor), the concern for purity was formulated as follows: "One should enter the sanctuary pure in white garments" (εἰσίναι εἰς τὸ ἱερὸν ἁγνὸν ἐν ἐσθῆτι λευκῆι; second century BCE).⁵² Here, the appeal to the potential visitor of the sanctuary was not merely implicit, but rather expressed with utter clarity. The boundary between the profane and the sacred was transformed into an area where one should not only pause to reflect on one's ritual purity, but also where one could do something concrete about this pure state (or lack thereof), such as purifying oneself with sanctified water or washing one's hands in the blood of a sacrificed animal. In this sense, the inscribed stone did not simply mark a 'hard' boundary line, but rather opened up a space for reflection and action: namely, a liminal space of transition.

The reference to the concept of 'liminality',⁵³ a subject of intense discussion within the field of cultural studies, is obvious here. Very much in the vein of the basic

---

47 Seifert 2006.
48 IG I³,2 1087; Lagner 2017, 69. For other 'speaking objects': Edelmann-Singer/Ehrich 2021.
49 IG IV²,2 792; Seifert 2006, 30–33.
50 Ober 1995, 93.
51 Carbon/Peels-Matthey 2018. The following, however, must be borne in mind here: "A convincing unifying account of Greek pollution remains elusive [... it] is an immensely flexible metaphor that could be applied in many different spheres" (Parker 2018, 27).
52 Blümel/Merkenbach 2014, 402.
53 'Liminality' is an anthropological concept originally developed in the context of the study of rites of passage. See van Gennep 1909 [2005]; Turner 1964. For the adoption of the concept in more recent art and cultural studies, see Kern 2013; Krüger 2018; Foletti/Doležalová 2020.

anthropological inquiry as to how existentially significant transitions were moderated in societies by means of rituals, we can pose an analogous question here: what significance was accorded to inscriptions at 'critical' transitions, i. e., at gates, thresholds, and entrance areas? And in our context: what specific tasks did writing take on at sanctuary thresholds? As anthropological research has repeatedly emphasised, transitions that effected a change in status were perceived in pre-modern societies as something that fundamentally threatened the existing order. For this reason, 'containing' the potential threat posed by liminal spaces through rituals, ceremonies, and images always seems to have been especially important.[54] In this sense, we can assume that the use of writing (inscriptions, shields, sacred books, pictorial text, metaphysical texts in narratives) at or within a liminal space not only served to define more clearly the respective 'in-between space' and to fill the latter with content, but also contributed to stabilising a potentially dangerous location in a symbolic way. For example, rites of initiation into ancient mystery cults included various practices that involved secret objects and aimed at the ritual transmission of secret, unwritten knowledge. However, the specific rules required for many different rituals could be chiselled in stone at the entrance to the sanctuary.[55]

Writing's potential power to reinforce boundaries and generate liminal space is particularly evident in the early Christian period (fourth–sixth centuries CE), during which ritual defilement was considered to be less problematic than individual sinfulness.[56] Various inscriptions from the late antique Near East that were placed in church vestibules or at their entrances addressed the need for visitors to make a self-examination before entering the sanctuary, with such persons being admonished to reflect before entering on whether they had prepared themselves and were worthy to encounter God and his saints in the church space.[57] There was always the danger of damaging the sacred character of the church space and incurring punishment for this, should physical (but especially spiritual) purity be lacking.[58]

---

54 On images at the threshold and receptive performativity in entryways, cf. Bawden 2014; Kern 2004.
55 Harris 2015; I. Petrovic/A. Petrovic 2018.
56 Cf. van Opstall 2018.
57 For example, in a damaged mosaic inscription in the Church of the Martyrs (al-Khadir) in Madaba, Jordan (second half of the sixth century/early seventh century): "Let whoever enters here carry a pure palm branch (?) with him, preserving the memory of the most holy martyrs, and praising God as is fitting"; on the inscription: Di Segni 2006, 586; Denis Feissel has suggested the reading "a pure heart", see Feissel/Gatier 2008, 754–755 (no. 571). On the building: Watta 2018, 246–247 no. 61 with figs. 74, 166; Piccirillo 1997, 129–131 with figs. 142–157.
58 Clement of Alexandria, for example, identified both forms of purity as an essential prerequisite for contact with God and the saints around 200 CE in his treatise *The Pedagogue*, and not only for the clergy but for the congregation as well: "[…] the man and woman each must come to the church dressed becomingly, with an unaffected walk, respecting silence, possessing 'charity unfeigned' [cf. Rom 12:9], pure of body and pure in heart, prepared to offer worship to God" (English transl. by Simon P. Wood, C. P.: Clement of Alexandria, *Christ the Educator*, 259; cf. *Clementis Alexandrini Paedagogus* III 11, 79, 3–4).

Unlike in ancient Greece, Christians had a holy book from which they could quote, and biblical texts written on church doors called on those viewing them not only to self-reflect but also to repent inwardly before entering the sacred space.[59] Ps 117:20 (LXX) was a particularly popular choice: "This is the gate of the Lord; righteous ones shall enter in it" (αὕτη ἡ πύλη τοῦ κυρίου, δίκαιοι εἰσελεύσονται ἐν αὐτῇ)—in its original context a reference to the holy temple in Jerusalem and, even in Christian belief, a prototype of the heavenly Zion.[60] Through this written reference, the threshold to the church building was ennobled as the "gate of the Lord" (πύλη τοῦ κυρίου) and in this way accentuated as a special place between the profane and the sacred, the earthly and the heavenly kingdom, the present and the future.[61] It is interesting to note that this 'gate' apparently also inspired everyday visitors time and time again to adorn the threshold with inscriptions of their own. Engraved graffiti (prayer texts, crosses, etc.) can often be found at entrances to sacred areas—for example, at a Greek temple near Aphrodisias that was converted into a church (Asia Minor, around 500 CE) (Fig. 3). Here we find both official and unofficial instances of writing or signs in the form of crosses (both professionally engraved ones and graffiti), a reference to the resurrection of Christ, and petitions for divine assistance.[62] The overlapping texts form a palimpsest on marble that points to the supra-temporal significance of entering a church; this collection of graffiti suggests that various actions took place in this liminal space: pausing, looking, reflecting, as well as ritual activity.[63]

However, the significance of this boundary of the sacred building was not only supposed to be apparent to those entering therein. In individual cases, inlaid floor mosaic inscriptions in the area of the main and side entrances to late antique churches and chapels (which speak about the construction or beseech salvation, eternal rest, etc.), or extended areas of mosaic work decorated with figures, were oriented towards the west or outwards. They were thus obviously directed at visitors who were leaving the church buildings and thus sought to preserve the salience of the messages represented by them at the moment when people would be going out through these portals.[64] This is also the case in the use of the aforementioned verse from the Psalms:

---

[59] Even though the ancient Greeks also had a category of texts (not always in written form) which they called 'sacred accounts' (ἱεροὶ λόγοι): Henrichs 2003.
[60] Leatherbury 2020, 258–267; Breytenbach 2012, 389–394; Watta 2018, 84–85, 92. English translation of LXX text: NETS, 606.
[61] Frese/Krüger 2019.
[62] Reynolds/Roueché/Bodard 2007, 1.21 and 1.22.
[63] Yasin 2009, 143; Sitz 2019, 151.
[64] For example, in the church of the apostles at Anemurium in Turkey: intercessory inscription (Leatherbury 2020, 120–121 fig. 3.26); in the northern church at Herodion in Israel: intercessory and psalmic inscription (Leatherbury 2020, 265–268 fig. 6.16); in the basilica of Dometios (Basilica A) at Nicopolis in Greece: building and psalmic inscription (Leatherbury 2020, 80 n. 220, 141–142, 265); in the Basilica of Anastasia at Arkasas in Greece: building inscription (Leatherbury 2020, 64–66, 267–268). For Jordan, see Watta 2018: cat. 47.1., 48, 52, 63 (inscriptions); cat. 43, 47.1., 47.2., 48, 52, 64 (elements of figural scenery).

Fig. 3: Marble doorpost with graffiti, ca. 500 CE and later, Aphrodisias (near present-day Geyre, Turkey), entrance to the sanctuary of Aphrodite, converted into a church. Photo: Anna Sitz.

if church visitors left the so-called Acropolis Church of Ma'in, Jordan (719/720 CE) through the western entrance, they would see inside directly in front of the threshold a west-facing *tabula ansata* with the building inscription. This text was connected with the quotation from Ps 117:20 (LXX) mentioned above, but here also supplemented by another quotation, this time from Ps 86:2 (LXX): "The Lord loves the gates of Sion more than all the dwellings of Jacob." The entrance area of the church is thus also directly associated with God here and subordinated to his power. The connection of the church portal with the 'gates of Sion' relates the Christian sacred building even more clearly to the 'City of God', the Heavenly Jerusalem.[65] In various Middle Eastern church buildings, inscriptions with this psalm verse also served as a kind of apotropaic protection at the entrances through their assignment to God's power, meaning

---

[65] On the church: Watta 2018, 248–250 no. 63 with fig. 76, 169–170; Piccirillo 1997, 200–201 with fig. 304–312. Note on the inscription SEG 35, 1579; Gatier 1986, 186–187 no. 158. On the psalm inscriptions in general: Leatherbury 2020, 249–270; Watta 2018, 84–86; Vriezen 1998. English translation of LXX text adapted from NETS, 590.

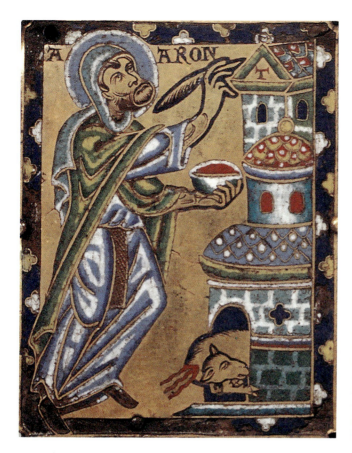

Fig. 4: Crucifix, detail: Aaron draws the letter T on the gable of a house with the blood of the lamb, twelfth century, champlevé enamel. London, Victoria and Albert Museum, inv. no. 7234. Reproduction from Schreiner 2000, 73.

that the positioning in this liminal area was apparently much more decisive than the orientation towards either the inside or the outside.[66]

In medieval Christendom, however, sacralising effects were attributed not only to crosses and certain sentences of the Bible, but also to the alphabet as a whole[67] and even to individual letters.[68] In the context of liminality, great importance was attached in particular to the Greek letter tau (τ) or the Latin letter T. In this case, it was first of all the figurative resemblance of the letter to the cross that made it a symbol for salvation. Furthermore, medieval Christian theologians were convinced that the Israelites had already marked the "two doorposts and [...] the lintel" (Exod 12:7) with this sign on the Feast of Passover in order to be spared from the final Egyptian plague (Fig. 4). The

---

66 Vriezen 1998, 249 n. 5 with examples. Likewise, apotropaic elements in the floor mosaics of imperial villa complexes are not always oriented towards the visitor entering from the outside; Swift 2009, 43 with n. 77.
67 Cf. note 36 above.
68 The Greek letter pairs of chi and rho, as well as that of alpha and omega, can be mentioned as prominent examples. Cf. Debiais 2017.

Hebrew Bible does not report anything about writing on the doorposts in this context; instead, this interpretation of the apotropaic effect of writing possibly harks back to the prophetic description in Ezek 9:4–6, where a divine messenger is sent to place a 'mark' *(tāw;* also the name of the last letter of the Hebrew alphabet [ת] and the equivalent to Greek tau and Latin T) on the foreheads of the God-fearing men of Jerusalem so as to protect them from death.[69]

Christian exegesis was extremely consequential for the interpretation of the letter T as a sign marking a boundary and protecting a space. This did not necessarily have to be an architecturally delimited ecclesiastical space, but could also refer to the spiritual 'space' within an individual believer. In the case of book art, it was in turn the "sacred writing space"[70] of a codex that could be structured by initials.

A prominent example here is a sacramentary[71] of the East Frankish King Henry II, dating from the early eleventh century and probably produced in Regensburg (Fig. 5). In this liturgical manuscript, a magnificent panel adorned with an initial is presented on fol. 16r, where we find the beginning of the Roman Canon: *Te igitur, clementissime pater* ("[We] therefore [humbly pray and beseech] you, most gracious Father [...]"). The first letter of the text is highlighted in the manuscript by a large initial letter T. The letter's interior is marked by interweaving decoration and entwined with golden tendrils, enabling the initial to attract the reader's attention and captivate his gaze. The T certainly had a strong effect both as a symbol and as a signal in the context of the celebration of the Mass. Thus, the reader (i. e., the celebrant) was clearly made

---

69 The word תָו in the Hebrew *urtext* is ambiguous and can mean the letter (ת/*tāw*) as such, or else another common meaning, namely 'sign'. The Septuagint text here reads simply τὸ σημεῖον ('the sign', Ezek 9:4–6). In the Vulgate, both readings are represented (*signa thau,* Ezek 9:4; *thau,* Ezek 9:6). The interpretation of this sign mentioned by Ezekiel as the letter tau can be found—despite the differences mentioned—in the patristic theology of both the East and the West. Cf. Suntrup 1980, 290–294; Schreiner 2000, 69–77. See also Liss 2008, esp. 30–32. As a sign of admonition, though without apotropaic effect (and thus also with an anti-magical implication), the Book of Deuteronomy calls for people of Israel to write the confession of the unity of God *(Shema Yisrael)* on their doorposts. To this day, the placing of a *mezuzah* (a small tube into which have been placed the scriptural verses Deut 6:4–9 and 11:13–21, written on parchment) on every internal and external doorpost of a house (except for the bathroom and toilet) is obligatory. By this, a Jewish home becomes neither a sacred nor a specially protected space, but rather a space distinguished from the external environment, which through the mezuzah symbolises the duty to live a law-abiding life and which never releases the Jewish person inside it from this duty. This relation of the creation of distinct spaces by means of writing is encountered everywhere in Jewish tradition, although we must stress that it is the writing that constitutes the spaces, and not that the spaces attribute meaning to what is written. Cf. also Liss 2014.

70 On this concept of "sacred writing spaces" (our translation, German text: "sakrale Schrifträume"): Frese/Krüger 2019.

71 A sacramentary contains the prayers and blessing formulae that a priest had to recite during the Mass. The most important part, the Canon of the Mass, begins with a direct address of the priest to God: "We therefore humbly pray and beseech you, most merciful Father, through Jesus Christ your Son our Lord [...]" *(Te igitur, clementissime pater, per Iesum Christum Filium tuum Dominum nostrum, supplices rogamus ac petimus [...]).*

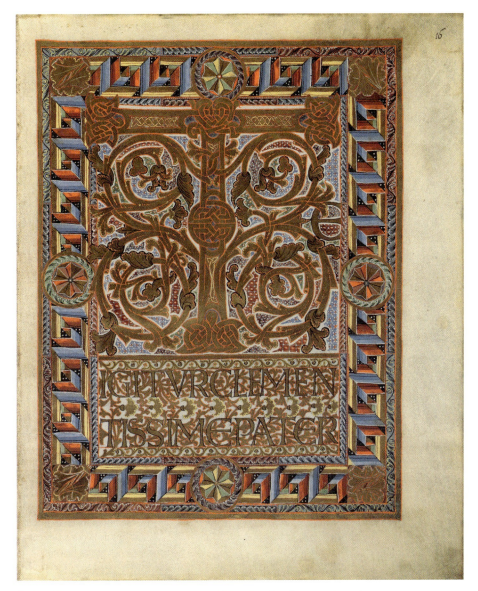

Fig. 5: *Te Igitur* page from the Sacramentary of Henry II, after 1002 CE, Bavarian State Library Munich, Clm 4456, fol. 16r.

aware that the Liturgy of the Word with its readings had been concluded and that the celebration of the Liturgy of the Eucharist was about to begin. The T thus marked an important caesura not only within the text, but also within the event of the Mass itself. In this way, the scriptural space of the manuscript corresponded to the liturgical space of the sacrificial prayer, into which the celebrant—as we read in an early medieval

Order of the Mass—was to enter "alone" and "silently".[72] In this sense, the golden tendrils that spread across the nearly illegible majuscule letters in the lower area acted on the one hand like a metal grille, warning against unauthorised entry.[73] On the other hand, the celebrant also had a divine sign of protection before his eyes at this point, which illustrated to him the certainty of sacramental salvation during the transition into the Canon of the Mass.

Liminally significant inscriptions can also be found in spiritual narratives from the European Middle Ages. Here, narrative spaces with profane connotations are separated from sacred spaces via inscriptions appearing in the narrative.[74] Spaces not already explicitly designated as sacred—such as a church room, a monk's cell, a hermitage, and so on—can be sacralised within the narrative by means of inscriptions that are immanent in the text. Instances of writing with explicitly spiritual/religious content (Bible texts, credal formulae, liturgical phrases), letters (tau, alpha, and omega) and signs (the cross) also mark out sacred spaces in texts. Just as in the real-world contexts described in the foregoing, these sacred characters placed above portals and doors in texts must be perceived, deciphered and read before one enters the space on the other side within the story. Moreover, since they indicate a threshold between two disparate spaces (profane vs. sacred), they often play an important role in the narrative.

The Latin version of *Wisdom's Watch upon the Hours (Horologium Sapientiae,* fourteenth century)[75] by Heinrich Seuse (a.k.a. Henry Suso, a medieval mystic from southern Germany) recounts for example a spatial allegory that marks off a sacralised space from a secular one via such a text-immanent inscription. To the protagonist of this mystical account, a "disciple" on a quest for the "wisdom of all the ancients",[76] there appears in a vision "a golden sphere, amazingly vast in extent and beautifully adorned with gems, in which there lived countless masters and students of all the arts and sciences".[77] This allegorical space—a school—is divided into two 'hemispheres': in the one, the liberal arts are taught, while in the other, the focus is on the teaching of theological truth. Three kinds of students and scholars learn and teach in the school of theology.[78] An inscription above the entrance, giving information about the afore-

---

[72] "The bishop alone rises and silently enters into the Canon" *(Surgit solus pontifex et tacito intrat canonem). Ordo secundum Romanos (Ordo V),* in: Andrieu 1948, 209–227 (our translation).
[73] Frese 2019, 49–51. Cf. the elaborate physical barriers that separated the sanctuary—the holiest area of a Byzantine church—from the nave where the congregation was gathered; on this, see Pallis 2017.
[74] Cf. Lieb 2015, 18–19.
[75] Heinrich Seuse, *Horologium Sapientiae,* 519–521 and 525–526; English transl. by Edmund Colledge: Henry Suso, *Wisdom's Watch upon the Hours.*
[76] Heinrich Seuse, *Horologium Sapientiae,* 519: *sapientia omnium antiquorum.* English transl. by Edmund Colledge: Henry Suso, *Wisdom's Watch upon the Hours,* 234.
[77] Heinrich Seuse, *Horologium Sapientiae,* 520: *sphaeram auream, mira amplitudine diffusam et pulchritudine gemmarum perornatam, ubi cunctarum artium et scientiarum magistri et scholares innumeri degebant.* English transl. by Edmund Colledge: Henry Suso, *Wisdom's Watch upon the Hours,* 234.
[78] Heinrich Seuse, *Horologium Sapientiae,* 521: *tres studentium ordines atque doctorum.*

mentioned, marks off as profane space the School of Liberal Arts by identifying the space behind it as sacred: "This is the school of theological truth, in which Eternal Wisdom is teacher, truth subject matter, and eternal felicity end."[79] The space that opens up behind the entrance is only receptively distinguished as being sacred when the inscription above the threshold is perceived: "When he [sc. the disciple] read this, he hastened to enter the academy, longing with all his heart to be one of its pupils, for he hoped through it to attain his desired end."[80] The writing is linked to the formulation of a religious haven that has everlasting bliss as its goal (cf. also Augustine, *On the Blessed Life*) and thus literally guides the recipient to enter the new space in a transgressive way, while at the same time enabling him to assume the role of disciple and pupil. This disciple, who passes through a liminal phase as he internalises the received inscription and its writing, becomes affiliated with the institution of the 'School of Theology' through his entry (in the broadest sense of the term) into the sacralised space and thus evidently also comes to be numbered amongst its pupils and teachers.

The allegorical narrative of the 'spherical' school is, as it were, integrated into the *Horologium Sapientiae* as a good example of the theme of the 'spiritual meaning of scripture'. Before a kind of voice *(quasi vox)* conclusively interprets the allegorical meaning of what is seen—"The three divisions that you [i. e., the disciple] have seen are three ways of studying and teaching Sacred Scripture"—the narrative inscription is first descriptive in function while at the same time explanatory as to the subsequent allegorical reading of the vision.[81] Here, the inscription serves as a prelude to the decoding of what has been seen and marks the disciple's new status as being part of the School of Theology.[82]

In summary, we can say that writing in ancient, late antique, and medieval spaces often had the task of commenting on, reinforcing, or even determining the division between profane and sacred areas. It is significant here that in all the examples mentioned, it is only through the use of writing that the local boundaries were transformed into a liminal threshold space—a reflexively significant, critical in-between space. The inscriptions and characters set at boundary points were used to prevent impure or unworthy persons, but also demonic powers, from entering, and in this way were

---

[79] Heinrich Seuse, *Horologium Sapientiae*, 520: *Haec est schola theologicae veritatis, ubi magistra aeterna sapientia, doctrina veritas, finis aeterna felicitas.* English transl. by Edmund Colledge: Henry Suso, *Wisdom's Watch upon the Hours*, 235.

[80] Heinrich Seuse, *Horologium Sapientiae*, 520: *Quibus perlectis festinanter accurit, et scholas intravit, cupiens totis visceribus huius scholae discipulus esse, per quam sperabat se ad finem desideratum pervenire.* English transl. by Edmund Colledge: Henry Suso, *Wisdom's Watch upon the Hours*, 235.

[81] Heinrich Seuse, *Horologium Sapientiae*, 525: *Tres ordines, quos vidisti, tres modi sunt studendi atque docendi sacram scripturam.* English transl. by Edmund Colledge: Henry Suso, *Wisdom's Watch upon the Hours*, 240. On this, cf. Disselhoff 2022, 71.

[82] Heinrich Seuse, *Horologium Sapientiae*, 526: *Igitur discipulus, aliis omissis, cupiebat cum his mansionem habere.* On this, cf. Disselhoff 2022, 74.

deployed to protect the sacred sphere. Furthermore, such written characters could also serve to moderate the liminal phase of crossing said boundary, ensuring the protection of those entering (and exiting) and encouraging self-reflection. Apart from the narrative texts analysed towards the end, we can assume that (materially real) inscriptions and characters did not fulfil these functions alone, but rather in interaction with special actions, prayers, and rituals. In the Christian context, writing at the border of sacred spaces also had a strong prophetic character:[83] writing at entrances, whether implicitly or explicitly, made the promise of individual salvation and heavenly bliss clear to whoever should enter.

> **Thesis 26**
> The status of sacrality is always endangered. The demonstrative use of writing serves to authenticate, legitimise, and stabilise sacrality.

Whether sacrality is endangered or potentially able to be lost or revoked is bound up with the question of the existence of religiously neutral spheres. Especially in polytheistic religions, we find ideas of the omnipresence of the sacred, which would suggest a negative answer. However, Roman antiquity—like other ancient cultures—knows of an opposition of sacred and profane and develops an understanding of divine right *(ius divinum)*, a distinction between (not fully) private and public sacrality, and a notion of divine property. In these contexts, we find terms used for transferring something from the holy *(sacrum)* to the non-holy *(profanum)* or vice versa: profanation *(profanatio)* and consecration *(consecratio)*, or in slightly older English, 'unhallowing' and 'hallowing'. In addition to representational and local categories, there is also the category of the personal (e. g., the word *profani* in reference to the uninitiated).[84] The Latin Church Fathers understand what is pagan (as well as what is heretical) to be non-holy and replace the traditional term *sacer* with *sanctus*. Something similar happens in Greek. Analogously, every religious transformation ends up using forms of erasure, profanation, renaming, and rededication to express the overcoming of old cults and religions. The extent to which sacrality is lost or absorbed here must be judged on a case-by-case basis and is certainly a matter of opinion. In any case, though, there are numerous examples of the continuity of old sanctuaries that sometimes have a multi-layered history of changes in cult, but in which remnants of 'original' sacrality are visibly carried over. What sacralises a place or object is a question of religious specifications. Nature-related notions of sacrality recognise a presence of the

---

83 On prophecy as an important "threshold coordinate" (our translation, German text: "Koordinate der Schwelle"), cf. Bawden 2014, 28–29.
84 De Souza 2010.

sacred in whatever is high up or elevated (a tree or mountain), separated (a spring), or planted (a grove). Institutionalised religions and their practices make use of distinctively enclosed areas with assembly rooms or sacred buildings as cult centres. As discussed in Thesis 25, writing serves to mark, delimit, and stabilise such spaces; epigraphic research operates with its own type of consecration inscription along with a characteristic protocol. In order to understand the function of writing, we could step back from the technical aspect of the term 'inscription' and speak instead of 'consecratory superscription'. Examples of such consecratory superscriptions can be found wherever writing and written characters form part and parcel of established cultural techniques.[85]

In what follows, we limit ourselves to the phenomena of consecratory superscription and the sacral function of writing, respectively. These can be best understood in contexts that are well-documented with regard to praxeology, such as Christian sacred spaces and the liturgical rites connected to these, for example. In many sacred spaces, writing is a defining element. Whether it be in the apse within the sanctuary, on windows, in wall paintings, frescoes and mosaics no matter the location, on the altar itself, on the reredos or on objects around and on the altar (such as on liturgical vessels and implements), in the form of valuable codices or on and in reliquaries: writing serves to document the sacred quality of a place. The fact that this quality is endangered can be traced back to various aspects. This status can be forgotten or even revoked; the space itself and the artefacts representing this status can be destroyed. The (e)valuation of the place can change or be rejected through competition and rivalry that can lead to a reinterpretation of status. For this reason, there is a need to authenticate, legitimise, and stabilise sacred status. The latter can be traced back to the place itself, the saints venerated there, and the rites dedicated to them, but also to the high material value of the artefacts in question, which can serve to illustrate sacred glory and divine splendour. We can also observe here reciprocity between places and artefacts with regard to sacrality: objects can become elevated in status on account of where they are placed or kept, or they can imbue a formerly neutral or profane place with sacrality by their very presence (cf. Thesis 27).

That sacrality can indeed be lost through forgetting is shown by the ubiquitous efforts to combat such oblivion. There is an awareness that the annual cycle of feast days is a stabilising force for memory. As Archbishop Peter Chrysologus (d. ca. 450) of Ravenna put it: "It is for a purpose that the birthdays of the martyrs are celebrated every year with joy: that that which happened in the past should remain in the memory of devout men of every century."[86] Alongside the temporal dimension of *memoria*,

---

[85] Campanelli 2016, 161–162.
[86] Petrus Chrysologus Sermo 129, 2: *Idcirco ergo natales martyrum annua laetitia celebrantur, ut quod semel actum est, per omne aeuum in memoria maneat deuotorum* (see *Sancti Petri Chrysologi Collectio sermonum*, 793–794; English translation by George E. Ganss, S. J.: Saint Peter Chrysologus, *Selected Sermons*, 214).

we find a spatial one: the place associated with those who are venerated becomes the place of worship. On the oldest dated Christian authentics (inscribed labels attached to relics), it is not the relics themselves that are referred to, but rather their 'commemoration'. Thus, the former did not initially read 'the relics of Saint *N.*' (*reliquiae Sancti*) but rather 'commemoration of Saint *N.*' (*memoria Sancti*), as in the case of an authentic made from slates of mica for relics of Saint Julian, datable to 543 CE and discovered during excavations at Henchir Akrib in Algeria.[87] That such a remembrance or commemoration was not fixed in place and immobile is easy to see and prove: just as the bodies and other physical remnants of saints moved, so too did the location of their cult: in the case of Augustine from Hippo via Sardinia to Pavia; in the case of Benedict from Montecassino to Fleury; in the case of Isidore from Seville to León.[88]

If sacrality can be lost and transferred, then it can also be revoked or removed. In 962, Bishop Rather (d. 974) robbed the Veronese faithful of their saint, Metro, and justified this in a penitential sermon to them, giving as reason for his actions the lack of veneration in literary form towards their holy patron.[89] From the research carried out by Jutta Fliege, we know that Metro's body was brought to Gernrode, where a new place of his veneration subsequently arose.[90] If a place is revalued or increases in value in this way (e. g., by housing relics), a new sacred place can be established even where there once was desolation. The three churches founded by Pope Paschalis I (d. 824) in Rome—Santa Prassede, Santa Cecilia in Trastevere, and Santa Maria in Domnica—are examples of this (Fig. 6).[91] Whereas the veneration of the relics of many Roman saints initially took place outside the city walls near the cemeteries in chapels, oratories, basilicas, and in the catacombs themselves, Paschalis judged some saints to be so worthy of veneration that he transferred their mortal remains into the urban space proper.[92] Among other things, the tituli of the apse mosaics bear witness to this: in Santa Prassede, the titulus informs us that it was the pope who brought the bones of many saints to that place,[93] while the one in Santa Cecilia shows that it was only through Paschalis's involvement that it was possible to transform the house of Saint Cecilia, which lay in ruins, into a splendidly radiant house of God into which the bones of the saints could be transferred from the catacombs of Praetextatus. Once in ruins as well, Santa Maria in Domnica was transformed under this pope's leadership into a place worthy of the veneration of the Virgin. All three buildings stand as evidence that Paschalis was also interested in demonstrating *intra muros* that his

---

87 Edition information in Licht/Wallenwein 2021, XXXIII–XXXIV.
88 On the establishment of several places of worship for Augustine during the sixth, and again in the nineteenth/twentieth centuries, see Ardeleanu 2019 and Ardeleanu 2020.
89 Berschin 1999, 53–58.
90 Fliege 1990.
91 Thunø 2015, 1–3.
92 Goodson 2010, 198–199; Poeschke 2009, 190–205.
93 Goodson 2010, 228.

Fig. 6: Apsis mosaic, between 817–824 CE, Rome, S. Maria in Domnica. Reproduction from Poeschke 2009, 193; photo by Abbrescia Santinelli, Rome.

supra-temporal understanding of sanctity went further than had been cultivated up to that point.[94] In order to authenticate and legitimise the correctness of his actions, he established a connection between the martyrdoms and the relics, securing their identity by means of cult objects and inscriptions.

As the following example shows, such decisions were not without far-reaching consequences. In less prominent cases, where there was no single obvious place of veneration, but rather competing local traditions, a decision on the right place or object of veneration had to be made based on documentary evidence. At the beginning of the twelfth century, Abbot Guibert of Nogent (d. 1124) discusses such a case in his remarkable text on relics, *On the Saints and their Tokens (De sanctis et eorum pigneribus)*. According to Guibert, Saint Firminus, the first bishop and martyr of Amiens, had been moved to a new tomb by one of his successors, but no authentic was found next to the supposed body of the saint. Accordingly, a lead tablet was inscribed and placed with the body in the new reliquary casket. At the same time, the abbot of Saint-Denis had reburied at his own monastery a body, in the nostrils of which was found an authentic identifying the body as "Firminus, martyr of Amiens". Guibert of Nogent recommended that careful consideration be made, concluding that the case might need to be decided in favour of Saint-Denis, since there one could rely on something written that had not been reproduced later on. As Guibert himself

---

94 Goodson 2010, 1–4, 197, 255–256.

Fig. 7: Early medieval authentication of unknown relics: *Hic sunt reliquias* [sic] *nescimus quales* ('Herein are relics, we know not which ones'), ca. 800 CE, height 2.2 cm, length 5.5 cm. Sens, Trésor de la cathédrale (CEREP-Musées), J 36.

pondered rhetorically: "What is a greater sacrilege than to venerate as holy something that is not?"[95]

What is unexpected about Guibert's remarks is not only the fact that in the case of the founding bishop of Amiens, the abbot recommends against deciding in favour of the saint's own cathedral, but also the basis on which Guibert grounds his decision. It is not an appeal to a tradition or a reference to some miraculous event that is decisive, but rather the rational faculty *(ratio)* which literally chairs the dispute and does so by making use of writing. For Guibert, written evidence is a factual aid in decision making on the question of the authenticity of the saint's body. Let us consider here the tension between the supposedly marginal documents—the labels superscribed on relics were barely the size of a modern-day doorbell label—and their inherent documentary value. Given this, the loss of an authentic could have dire consequences. Authentics are amongst the few witnesses of older literacy of which we often have duplicates preserved together with the original: the older original and/or copies verify the tradition of the saint, while more recent copies serve to update legibility and stabilise sacrality. Incidentally, Guibert's attitude that unjustified veneration should be considered as sacrilege was by no means a special or idiosyncratic position. The words *Hic sunt reliquias* [sic] *nescimus quales* ("Herein are relics, we know not which ones") are written on an authentic made around or soon after 800 CE and preserved in the holdings of the cathedral of Sens (Fig. 7).[96] Here too, we see that one wished to avoid committing the sacrilege of recording false saints' names.

---

95 Guibert of Nogent, *De sanctis et eorum pigneribus*, 103–104; English translation: Head 2000, 418.
96 Wallenwein 2021, 259; further examples in ibid., 269, n. 26.

Fig. 8: So-called Prudentia shrine, ca. 1230–1240, gilt silver plate, embossed, stamped, engraved, nielloed, gilt copper, filigree, precious stones, and so-called 'Alsen gem'. Oak wood centre. Height 69.5 cm, width 41.5 cm, length 102.5 cm. Beckum, Catholic parish church of St Stephen. Photo: Stephan Kube, Greven.

Similar potential for conflict arises from the history of the so-called Prudentia Shrine (made ca. 1230–1240) in the Provost Church in Beckum, Germany (Fig. 8). An inscription on one of the outer gilded mouldings of the artefact lists the names of saints Stephen, Sebastian, and Fabian, although the three are absent from the pictorial programme. Stephen can be proven as being the patron saint of the town of Beckum since 785, while Sebastian is first mentioned as such via the inscription on this shrine. Fabian's feast day coincided with that of Sebastian on 20 January, which is probably why he was also included in the inscription.[97] Whether there were actually relics of the three inside the shrine, and whether they were also provided with corresponding authentics, is to be expected on account of the inscription. However, neither in Beckum itself nor in the diocese of Münster, which today is responsible for the administration of many sources hailing from the town, have any medieval or early modern inventory registers with corresponding references been preserved.[98] From the Middle Ages until 1814, the shrine was carried through the streets of Beckum to surrounding chapels in a large, seven-hour procession on the feast of Saint Vitus (15 June) and later

---

[97] Gesing 2007, 26.
[98] Many thanks to Prof. Dr. Thomas Flammer for the reference.

on that of Saint John the Baptist (24 June).⁹⁹ The inscription referring to the saints suggested—at least to those who knew how to read—that relics of the saints who were mentioned were in fact contained within the artefact, thus certifying the latter's sacred quality.

The fact that sacrality was endangered by the loss of relics or their authentics is also shown in a letter from the parish dean Hagemann to the mayor Marcus, dated 16 May 1836. The cleric alludes to the absence of particles of the saint's relics and to the concomitant loss of status brought about by the ban on processions that was in effect at the time as a result of secularisation: "Since it is now ecclesiastically forbidden to carry around such objects during processions, the casket no longer has any value for the church here [...]".¹⁰⁰ In 1881, relics of Saint Prudentia were therefore transferred to the shrine, which the former chaplain of Beckum, Johann Bernhard Brinkmann, had received from Pope Pius IX during a visit to Rome in 1878. A certificate confirming the authenticity of the relic fragment is held in the parish archives in Beckum¹⁰¹ and demonstrates that relics had to be authenticated via inscriptions. Ever since, the shrine has been known as the Prudentia Shrine.¹⁰²

It thus becomes apparent that sacrality in the Christian contexts discussed here is not encountered in the essentialist sense as a 'fixed', perpetual, or even pre-figured state/status, but was apparently already regarded as insecure and fragile in late antiquity and the Middle Ages and therefore had to be commemorated, updated, and revitalised. Threats such as the forgetting, revoking, or transferring of saints and sanctity were taken into account and prevented, in particular through the use of inscribed artefacts, which in turn assumed the functions of authentication and of the guaranteeing of sacrality.

---

99 Gesing 2007, 83.
100 Gesing 2007, 86, and Kreisarchiv Warendorf, Stadt Beckum B 333 (our translation, German text: "Da nun das Herumtragen solcher Gegenstände bei den Prozessionen kirchlich verboten ist, so hat der Kasten für die hiesige Kirche keinen Werth mehr [...]"). In the chronicle of Beckum, Chaplain A. Pollack also records on 14 October 1875 the absence of relics in the shrine and that in light of secularisation, "[...] it was in danger of being put under the hammer or sent to the museum in Berlin as an antique. Afterwards it has still happily escaped such profanation or destruction. [...] May it soon be returned to its old purpose as a reliquary and find a more suitable place" (Gesing 2007, 87, our translation, German text: "[... es] in Gefahr stand, unter den Hammer gebracht zu werden oder ins Museum zu Berlin als Antiquität zu wandern. Danach ist er noch glücklich solcher Profanation oder Destruction entgangen. [...] Möchte er recht bald wieder seinem alten Zwecke als Reliquienschrein zurückgegeben werden, und einen passenderen Platz finden").
101 Gesing 2007, 28 and n. 12.
102 Gesing 2007, 9.

Thesis 27
Sacred places (temples, churches, altars) attract writing: inscribed artefacts partake there of the sacred, while simultaneously contributing to sacralisation themselves.

The study of sacred places boasts of a long tradition in the disciplines of classical and medieval studies. However, in the treatment of individual manifestations of the sacred—or of the respective hagiographic, epigraphic, and archaeological sources—the sacred usually appears as being firmly defined and absolute. Sanctuaries, churches, or temples hardly seemed to require explanation as far as of their 'sacrality' is concerned. Yet for a long time, the question as to which elements contributed decisively to the sacralisation of spaces (be they of an urban, funerary, religious, or private nature) hardly lay at the heart of research on antiquity or the Middle Ages. It is only recently, under the influence of constructivist theoretical approaches and an increased interest in cult practices, that special attention has been given to the production of sacrality and to processes of sacralisation in various spatial contexts.[103] Likewise, the sanctity of cities and even of entire landscapes, along with the sacrality of objects or of concepts such as 'dominion' are increasingly being put up for discussion,[104] especially from a diachronic and interdisciplinary perspective.[105] Nevertheless, the role of inscribed artefacts in these analytical contexts—i.e. the part they play in the creation, demarcation, and legitimation of sacrality—has so far only been considered via isolated case studies and without the necessary systematisation.[106]

In ancient studies, inscriptions from sacred contexts are increasingly perceived as important 'actants' in the sacralisation of spaces. The role of consecrative inscriptions and normative epigraphic regulations in ancient Greek sanctuaries and in early Christian churches has already been discussed above (cf. the remarks on 'hierographic quality' in Thesis 24 and on 'liminality' in Thesis 25). Such texts guaranteed and documented the correct worship of the gods and thus the correct performance of the cult. But within the sanctuaries, there is also an immense number of official, public documents on stone. These include contracts between cities, letters from kings and emperors, as well as manumissions of slaves dating from the archaic to the late

---

103 Hamm/Herbers/Stein-Kecks 2007; Beck/Berndt 2013; Herbers/Düchting 2015; Bihrer/Fritz 2019. On sacrality in urban space: Ferrari 2015; Lafond/Michel 2016. On the relationship between space and liturgy: Bauer 2010.
104 On power/dominion: Erkens 2002; Herbers/Nehring/Steiner 2019; as well as Chapter 6 'Political Rule and Administration'. On landscape: Walaker Nordeide/Brink 2013; Belaj et al. 2018. On objects: Beck/Herbers/Nehring 2017.
105 Hamm/Herbers/Stein-Kecks 2007; Ferrari 2015; Bergmeier/Palmberger/Sanzo 2016; Belaj et al. 2018.
106 Egypt: Luft 2014, esp. 33–34. From the Archaic to imperial era: Dihle 2003 (on the ancient vocabulary of sanctity); Parker 2012; Borgeaud/Fabiano 2013; Roels 2018. Late antiquity: Yasin 2009; van Opstall 2018; Watta 2018, 73–99.

Fig. 9: Marble column with inscriptions from the second/third century CE, Klaros (near present-day Ahmetbeyli, Turkey), oracular temple of Apollo. Photo: Anna Sitz.

antique periods (sixth century BCE to fourth century CE).[107] Entire cities sought out the sanctuary of Apollo at Delphi in central Greece so as to consult the oracle, issue civic documents, and consecrate victory monuments after wars fought against both Greek and non-Greek opponents. In imperial-era Klaros (near present-day Ahmetbeyli in the Menderes district of İzmir Province, Turkey), delegations from various cities immortalised records of their visit on the pillars and steps of the temple, furnishing the latter with an unusual 'inscribed skin' (Fig. 9).[108] Initially, it may seem that these 'profane' documents hardly contributed to the sacrality of the sanctuaries discussed here, but rather benefited from this sacrality, acquiring an inviolable or sacred status by being entrusted to the gods. In reality, however, these written testimonies linked rulers, cities, and gods in a web of relationships, in which the political success of the mortal actors confirmed and thereby reinforced the sacral aura of the deity.

Late antique churches and burial spaces also serve as promising fields of inquiry for our questions.[109] Recent contextual analyses show that inscriptions not only played a major role in the creation of sacred spaces, but also qualified, structured, hierarchised,

---

[107] Roels 2018; Drauschke 2019.
[108] Ferrary 2014.
[109] Churches: Jäggi 2007; Bergmeier 2017; Watta 2018. Tombs: Duval 1982; Ardeleanu 2018. Not all periods of antiquity saw tombs as part of sacred spaces. In Greek sanctuaries, for example, burial was prohibited within the *temenos*.

and protected the latter to a considerable extent through their own communicative character. In the excellently preserved churches of Jordan dating to the fifth–eighth centuries CE, veritable 'inscribed carpets' with psalm quotations, intercessory inscriptions, and building inscriptions directed the gaze (and thus also the movement) of visitors towards the sanctuary and other central cultic zones (e. g., the baptistery) (Fig. 10).[110] The area in front of the sanctuary, which was closed off and accessible only to clergy, served as the terminus for the range of movement of lay visitors and was the closest they could get to the liturgical happenings at the altar. It thus constituted a special 'place of attention', with the floor covered with particularly elaborate mosaic fields replete with large-format inscriptions and detailed figurative representations.[111] Various quotations from Holy Scripture were probably recited or sung as part of the liturgy or the commemoration of the dead, thus significantly contributing to the sacred effect of the space.[112]

Monumental inscriptions on church façades, on the other hand, could announce the sacrality of the place as soon as one entered (cf. the explanations in Thesis 25).[113] When these texts were spoken aloud (partly in the first person), they made it possible to experience sacred places in a personal way. The accumulation of endowments near the altar, observed in the mosaic inscriptions from donors in *Histria et Venetia,* demonstrates that the holiest place in the church offered the donors the maximum potential for acquiring prestige (Fig. 11).[114] Inevitably, however, the concentration of such inscriptions also entailed a further ennobling of the holiest zones in purely visual terms, irrespective of the question of the public's literacy. In addition to the character of this area as a zone of special attention and increased prestige, the accumulation of donor images and inscriptions in front of the sanctuary barriers of the late antique churches located in present-day Jordan points to another motive of the patrons of those buildings. In the media of image and inscription, which were understood as veritable entities of representation, such persons sought to draw near to the altar and

---

110 Cf. Watta 2018, 74–99, who emphasises the "multiple use of designations of the conceptual field of the 'sacred'" in the inscriptions (our translation, German text: "vielfache Nutzung von Bezeichnungen des Begriffsfeldes 'heilig'"). The gaze-directing framing of the inscriptions by *tabulae ansatae*, contraposed pairs of animals, or circles must also be considered: Leatherbury 2020, 97–124; cf. Chapter 2 'Layout, Design, Text-Image'.
111 Watta 2018, 52, 71, 93, 106.
112 Papalexandrou 2007; Yasin 2009, 143, 226–228; Cubelic/Lougovaya/Quack 2015; Leatherbury 2020, 14–18; of ca. 800 biblical quotations in late antique inscriptions, 163 are attested from funerary contexts. There, they could function apotropaically and in relation to the funerary cult, but also purely as captions and 'permanent prayers' in the context of resurrection: Felle 2006, 406–408; cf. inscriptions that explicitly call for chanting/prayer, e. g. CIL VIII, 20 903: *omnis sacra canens manus porrigere gaudet / sacramento Dei* [...] (Ardeleanu 2018, 482–487).
113 Papalexandrou 2007; Leatherbury 2020, 168–169; on portal inscriptions cf. Dickmann/Keil/Witschel 2015, 126–127.
114 Yasin 2009, 123–129; Bolle/Westphalen/Witschel 2015, 494–498; cf. the database 'Mosaikinschriften auf den Fußböden von Kirchenräumen in der spätantiken Provinz Venetia et Histria' (https://mosaikinschriften.materiale-textkulturen.de/).

Fig. 10: Baptismal complex with mosaic carpets, 530 CE. Room adjoined to the pilgrimage church at the shrine of the Prophet Moses on Mount Nebo (Jordan). Reproduction from Piccirillo 1998, 273, fig. 12 (Courtesy of the Studium Biblicum Franciscanum, Jerusalem).

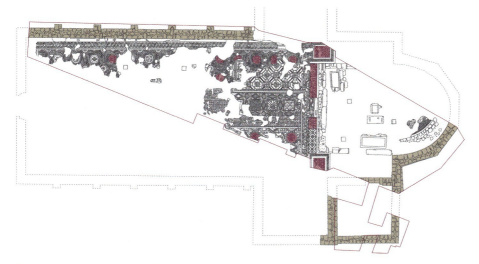

Fig. 11: Donor inscriptions (fifth/sixth century CE) in front of the altar area. Trieste, church on the Via Madonna del Mare. Photo from: https://mosaikinschriften.materiale-textkulturen.de/plaene.php (SFB 933, redrawing by Christoph Forster).

the saving Eucharistic liturgy performed there through a permanent commemorative presence within the medium.[115]

Since the fourth century CE, one widespread strategy for transferring ideas of sanctity to the church building as a whole, but also to the area of the sanctuary in particular, has been the creation of parallels with Old Testament sanctuaries and above all with the temple in Jerusalem. There are many corresponding references that can be found not only in sermons, but also in architecture and furnishings, in pictures and inscriptions.[116] For example, the mosaic field in front of the altar of the chapel of the Theotokos within the memorial church dedicated to Moses on Mount Nebo in Jordan, completed in the early seventh century, shows a combination of an inscription bearing Ps 50:21 (LXX) ("Then they will offer calves on your altar") and a depiction of the Jerusalem Temple with the Holy of Holies and the altar of burnt offering, flanked by two bulls (Fig. 12). For the viewers, central components of Old Testament temple sacrality were transferred via the ritual to the present-day Christian cult building and its liturgy, with Old Testament and Christian themes of offerings and sacrifices standing in parallel with one another.[117]

The above example shows that inscriptions can never be considered in isolation. In the sacralisation process, symbols such as crosses or nimbi/haloes, luxury mate-

---

[115] Watta 2018, 93, 105–106, 143–144; on the accumulation of donor representations at focal points of the liturgy, cf. also Bauer 2013, 185–233.
[116] Branham 2012; Ousterhout 2010; McVey 2010.
[117] SEG 8, 321; Piccirillo 1997, 133–151; Branham 2012; Watta 2018, 86–88. On the chapel of the Theotokos: Watta 2018, 216–217 no. 46.8. English translation of LXX text: NETS, 572.

Fig. 12: Mosaic floor with a quotation from Ps 50:21 (LXX) and figurative depictions, early seventh century CE, sanctuary of the Chapel of the Theotokos at the shrine of the Prophet Moses on Mount Nebo (Jordan). Reproduction from Piccirillo 1998, 301, fig. 74 (Courtesy of the Studium Biblicum Franciscanum, Jerusalem).

rials, targeted lighting, architectural decoration, wall paintings, barriers, etc. took on central roles.[118] The creation of sacred spaces can also be traced in late antique buildings that had a funerary function. Such burial spaces must first be understood as social spaces that were regularly visited for the commemoration of the dead. In North Africa, numerous such buildings increasingly took on the features of churches in the course of the fourth century (naves, barriers, apses, altars, baptisteries), with inscriptions supporting this sacralisation process. The commemoration of deceased parishioners was 'codified' in the church floor by commemorative as well as funerary inscriptions at neuralgic points of liturgical rites.[119] The donors emphasised the parts of the church they had 'sacralised' (*sancta altaria fulgent*: 'the holy altars shine'; *limina sancta*: 'the holy thresholds'; *clausula iustitiae*: 'the threshold of justice') and hoped for a special reward in the age to come through the targeted positioning of their funerary inscriptions at liturgically relevant locations and the collective reci-

---

[118] Jäggi 2007; Bergmeier 2017.
[119] The decisive factor here was the position and reading direction: Duval 1982; Yasin 2009, 56–100; Ardeleanu 2018.

Fig. 13: So-called Basilica of Alexander (right) with martyrs' burial ground (left) from the fourth to the sixth century CE, Tipasa (Algeria). Red: inscriptions *in situ* with reading direction. Light green: reconstructed liturgical sequence. Reproduction from Ardeleanu 2018, fig. 3.

tation of the former in the course of worship, respectively (Fig. 13).[120] The sacrality of such buildings was also greatly augmented through the deposition of martyrs' relics, which were often only brought into the buildings over a period of time. Inscriptions above or at the 'graves' announced in striking fashion the presence of the saint.[121] Individuals could partake permanently of this sacrality by having themselves buried as close as possible to the 'graves of the saints' *(ad sanctos)*.[122]

With later centuries in mind, it is equally possible to discuss the extent to which inscriptions in ecclesiastical or sacred spaces contributed to charging such space or even imbuing it with sanctity in the first place. Instead of providing a broad overview, we refer here to a pertinent case study in which the questions raised so far were not only dramatically acute, but also ritually staged. What is meant—and what is up for discussion—is the sanctity of places that seemingly needed no further attribution of sacrality, at least according to common Christian conceptions: namely, the *loca sancta* of the Bible in Palestine connected with the life and Passion of Jesus.

A unique epigraphic witness from twelfth-century Jerusalem demonstrates that the problem outlined here is not merely the product of modern academic discourse,

---

120 CIL VIII, 20 903; 20 906; 20 914. In detail on the inscription quotations mentioned above: Ardeleanu 2018, 478–492.
121 Duval 1982; Bergmeier 2017.
122 Some of the epitaphs explicitly referred to the physical proximity to the saints' tombs: AE 1973, 650 (from Tipasa): *co[r]pus sanc[tae] martyris [Sa]ls(a)e Clim[ene(?)?] adiun[cta] est sep[ultura(?)]*.

but was already being critically reflected upon by contemporaries of that time. To wit, we are talking about the inscription commemorating the dedication of the new, Crusader-era building of the Church of the Holy Sepulchre in 1149; this inscription unfortunately no longer survives in material form, but its wording has survived in copy. The patrons or authors (who can be identified as the protagonists of the liturgical dedication of the cathedral and hence equated with the Latin patriarch and cathedral chapter of Jerusalem) used the inscription to express their conviction, also attested elsewhere (e. g., in charters and other documents), that the centre of their religious life, the place of Christ's crucifixion and resurrection, was sanctified by his blood alone and would not acquire any additional sacral potency through their own intervention. In their view, the place of worship erected over the sites of the Passion and resurrection of Jesus Christ had merely been formally and newly consecrated. The decisive beginning of the inscription reads as follows:

> This holy place has been sanctified by the blood of Christ / Through our consecration we add nothing to this holiness / But the house built around and over the holy place / Has been consecrated [literally, 'sanctified'; translator's note] on 15 July [...].[123]

The statements made here contrast, of course, with the rites of consecration that were carried out with great performative power. In the context of efforts to legitimise the still relatively new Latin rule over the holy sites of the Promised Land, these rites were accorded the highest political and theological significance and served to create a sense of identity and belonging in the ecclesiastical and cultural life of the Latin diocese and kingdom of Jerusalem.[124] From this point in time onwards, the feast of the 'dedication of the church of the Holy Sepulchre' *(dedicatio ecclesiae sancti Sepulchri)* was to be celebrated annually, and even overlapped with the so-called liberation of Jerusalem by the Crusaders, which was commemorated on the very same day and which, in 1149, dated back exactly fifty years. In this context, it was no coincidence that the inscription itself referred to the very biblical passages on which the Roman rite of the dedication of the church *(dedicatio ecclesiae)* was based and which were incorporated in several places into the newly composed festal liturgy.[125]

Reflecting on one's own actions and existence in the face of what was held to be the very source of salvation nurtured an almost paradoxical relationship between

---

123 Our translation, Latin text: *Est locus iste sacer sacratus sanguine Christi / Per nostrum sacrare sacro nichil addimus isti / Sed domus huic sacro circum superedificata / Est quinta decima Quintilis luce sacrata* [...]. Reconstruction of the text according to medieval and early modern pilgrim reports in Linder 2009, 31–32. Cf. also *Peregrinationes tres*, 123 and 156; and Franciscus Quaresimus, *Historica, theologica et moralis terræ sanctæ elucidatio*, 483.
124 On the liturgy in Crusader-era Jerusalem in general, see most recently Shagrir/Gaposchkin 2019. On the rite of the Canons of the Holy Sepulchre, see Dondi 2004 as well as the overview in Zöller 2018, 93–107.
125 Linder 2009, 35–37.

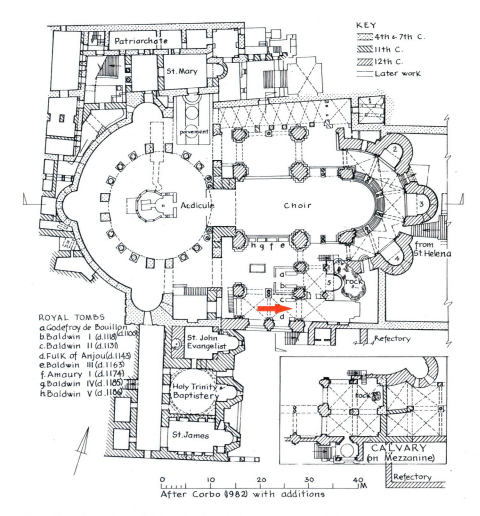

Fig. 14: Floor plan with possible location (arrow) of the Crusader-era dedicatory inscription, twelfth century, Jerusalem, Church of the Holy Sepulchre. Reproduction from Pringle 2007, 39.

two poles, i. e. the explicit conception of the unalterable sacrality of the Holy Sepulchre on the one hand, and, on the other, the epigraphic proclamation and inscribing of this sanctity into the material substance of the church, which was peppered with references to the corresponding actions and pious formulae used in these rites. Right next to the stairway to the Crusader-era Calvary Chapel, the supposed site of Jesus' crucifixion located above the rock of Golgotha (i. e., in the immediate vicinity of the main portal of the cathedral, only a few steps away from the entrance to the church's interior), the inscription monumentalises in an architecturally prominent position the credo of the seemingly inviolable sacrality of the site, which, supposedly, lay beyond the reach of mortals (Fig. 14). At the same time, however, the text commemorates the earthly events surrounding the rededication of the church, the act of sacralisation as well as the clerical dignitaries involved in or responsible for the latter.

The necessarily selective choice of the examples in the foregoing illustrates that sacred places, or places considered as such, attracted to themselves with particular intensity acts of writing or invited people to inscribe and superscribe buildings and objects in a variety of ways. At the same time, we find that complex webs of interaction unfolded in such spatial configurations between the ascribed, constructed sanctity of the place and the inscribed artefacts that were found and/or created there and which participated in or benefited from processes of sacralisation to various extents and degrees. Inscriptions at sacred sites not only proclaimed the outstanding specific character of the space in question, which set it apart from profane spheres; they also motivated and supported the performance of central cultic and religious practices. From a topological and praxeological perspective, these inscriptions assumed important functions in the creation, maintenance, and safeguarding of sacrality. In outstanding cases, they even bear witness to the reflection on and critical engagement with contemporary concepts of sacrality.

Bibliography

Abbreviations and Sigla

AE *L'Année Épigraphique*, Paris 1888–.
CIL VIII *Corpus Inscriptionum Latinarum*, vol. VIII: *Inscriptiones Africae Latinae*, 7 partes, coll. Gustav Wilmanns, ed. by Theodor Mommsen, Berlin 1881.
IG I³,2 *Inscriptiones Graecae*, vol. I, ed. 3: *Inscriptiones Atticae Euclidis anno anteriores*, fasc. 2: *Dedicationes, catalogi, termini, tituli sepulcrales, varia, tituli Attici extra Atticam reperti, addenda*, ed. by David Lewis and Lilian Jeffery in cooperation with Eberhard Erxleben, Berlin 1994.
IG IV²,2 *Inscriptiones Graecae*, vol. IV, ed. 2: *Inscriptiones Argolidis*, fasc. 2: *Inscriptiones Aeginae insulae. Schedis usus quas condidit Hans R. Goette*, ed. by Klaus Hallof, Berlin 2007.
NETS *A New English Translation of the Septuagint and the Other Greek Translations Traditionally Included under That Title*, ed. by Albert Pietersma and Benjamin Wright, 2nd revised ed., Oxford/New York 2007.
SEG 8 *Supplementum Epigraphicum Graecum*, vol. VIII, ed. by J. J. E. Hondius, Amsterdam 1937.
SEG 35 *Supplementum Epigraphicum Graecum*, vol. XXXV, ed. by H. W. Pleket and R. S. Stroud, Amsterdam 1988.

Sources

Clementis Alexandrini Paedagogus, ed. by Miroslav Marcovich in cooperation with Jacobus C. M. van Winden (Supplements to Vigiliae christianae 61), Leiden/Boston 2002.
Clement of Alexandria, *Christ the Educator,* transl. by Simon P. Wood, C. P. (Fathers of the Church 23), New York 1954.
Franciscus Quaresimus, *Historica, theologica et moralis terræ sanctæ elucidatio,* vol. II, Antwerpen: Balthasar Moretus 1639.
Guibert of Nogent, *De sanctis et eorum pigneribus,* in: Guibert of Nogent, *Quo ordine sermo fieri debeat. De bucella iudae data et de veritate dominici corporis. De sanctis et eorum pigneribus,* ed. by Robert B. C. Huygens (Corpus Christianorum. Continuatio Mediaevalis 127), Turnhout 1993.
Heinrich Seuse, *Horologium Sapientiae,* ed. by Pius Künzle using the preliminary work of Dominikus Planzer O. P. (Spicilegium Friburgense 23), Fribourg (CH) 1977.
Henry Suso, *Wisdom's Watch upon the Hours* (The Fathers of the Church. Medieval Continuation 4), transl. by Edmund Colledge, Washington, D. C., 1994.
Peregrinationes tres: Saewulf, John of Würzburg, Theodericus, with a Study of the Voyages of Saewulf by John H. Pryor, ed. by Robert B. C. Huygens (Corpus Christianorum. Continuatio mediaevalis 139), Turnhout 1994.
Sancti Petri Chrysologi Collectio sermonum, vol. 3, ed. by Alexander Olivar (Corpus Christianorum. Series Latina 24B), Turnhout 1982.
Saint Peter Chrysologus, *Selected Sermons* [and Saint Valerian, *Homilies*], transl. by George E. Ganss, S. J. (Fathers of the Church 17), Washington, D. C., 1953.
Rupert of Deutz, *Vita Herberti. Kritische Edition mit Kommentar und Untersuchung,* ed. by Peter Dinter (Veröffentlichungen des Historischen Vereins für den Niederrhein 13), Bonn 1976.

Research Literature

Agamben, Giorgio (2017), "I. *Homo Sacer:* Sovereign Power and Bare Life", in: Giorgio Agamben, *The Omnibus Homo Sacer,* transl. by Daniel Heller-Roazen, Stanford, CA, 5–159.
Andrieu, Michel (1948), *Les ordines romani du haut moyen age,* vol. 2 (Spicilegium Sacrum Lovaniense 24), Paris.
Ardeleanu, Stefan (2018), "Directing the Faithful, Structuring the Sacred Space: Funerary Epigraphy in its Archaeological Context in Late-Antique Tipasa", in: *Journal of Roman Archaeology* 31, 475–501.
Ardeleanu, Stefan (2019), "Zum funerärepigraphischen Habit des spätantiken Hippo Regius. Gräber, Kirchen mit Bestattungen und Grabinschriften in ihrem urbanen und sozialen Kontext", in: *Römische Mitteilungen* 125, 401–448.
Ardeleanu, Stefan (2020), "Hippo Regius – Bûna – Bône. Ein Erinnerungsort im Spiegel der kolonialzeitlichen Augustinusrezeption", in: *Römische Quartalschrift* 115, 29–56.
Assmann, Aleida/Assmann, Jan (2003), "Hieroglyphen: altägyptische Ursprünge abendländischer Grammatologie", in: Aleida Assmann and Jan Assmann (eds.), *Hieroglyphen. Stationen einer anderen abendländischen Grammatologie,* Munich 2003, 9–25.
Bauer, Dieter R. (ed.) (2013), *Heilige – Liturgie – Raum* (Beiträge zur Hagiographie 8), Stuttgart.
Bauer, Franz Alto (2013), *Eine Stadt und ihr Patron. Thessaloniki und der Heilige Demetrios,* Regensburg.
Bawden, Tina (2014), *Die Schwelle im Mittelalter: Bildmotiv und Bildort,* Cologne/Weimar/Vienna.

Beck, Andrea/Berndt, Andreas (eds.) (2013), *Sakralität und Sakralisierung. Perspektiven des Heiligen* (Beiträge zur Hagiographie 13), Stuttgart.

Beck, Andrea/Herbers, Klaus/Nehring, Andreas (eds.) (2017), *Heilige und geheiligte Dinge: Formen und Funktionen* (Beiträge zur Hagiographie 20), Stuttgart.

Belaj, Juraj/Belaj, Marijana/Krznar, Siniša/Sekelj Ivančan, Tatjana/Tkalčec, Tatjana (eds.) (2016), *Sacralization of Landscape and Sacred Places. Proceedings of the 3rd International Scientific Conference of Mediaeval Archaeology of the Institute of Archaeology. Zagreb, 2nd and 3rd June 2016*, Zagreb.

Bergmeier, Armin (2017), *Visionserwartungen. Visualisierung und Präsenzerfahrung des Göttlichen in der Spätantike*, Wiesbaden.

Bergmeier, Armin/Palmberger, Katharina/Sanzo, Joseph Emanuel (eds.) (2016), *Erzeugung und Zerstörung von Sakralität zwischen Antike und Mittelalter*, Heidelberg.

Berschin, Walter (1999), *Biographie und Epochenstil im Lateinischen Mittelalter*, vol. IV/1 (Quellen und Untersuchungen zur Lateinischen Philologie des Mittelalters 12,1), Stuttgart.

Bihrer, Andreas/Fritz, Fiona (eds.) (2019), *Heiligkeiten: Konstruktionen, Funktionen und Transfer von Heiligkeitskonzepten im europäischen Früh- und Hochmittelalter* (Beiträge zur Hagiographie 21), Stuttgart.

Blümel, Wolfgang/Merkelbach, Reinhold (2014), *Die Inschriften von Priene* (Inschriften griechischer Städte aus Kleinasien 69), Bonn.

Bolle, Katharina/Westphalen, Stefan/Witschel, Christian (2015), "Mosaizieren", in: Thomas Meier, Michael R. Ott, and Rebecca Sauer (eds.), *Materiale Textkulturen. Konzepte – Materialien – Praktiken* (Materiale Textkulturen 1), Berlin/Munich/Boston, 485–501, https://doi.org/10.1515/9783110371291.485.

Borgeaud, Philippe/Fabiano, Doralice (eds.) (2013), *Perception et construction du divin dans l'antiquité*, Genf.

Branham, Joan R. (2012), "Mapping Sacrifice on Bodies and Spaces in Late-Antique Judaism and Early Christianity", in: Bonna D. Wescoat and Robert G. Ousterhout (eds.), *Architecture of the Sacred. Space, Ritual and Experience from Classical Greece to Byzantium*, New York, 201–230.

Breytenbach, Cilliers (2012), "Psalms LXX and the Christian Definition of Space: Examples Based on Inscriptions from Central Asia Minor", in: Johann Cook and Hermann-Josef Stipp (eds.), *Text-Critical and Hermeneutical Studies in the Septuagint*, Leiden, 381–394.

Campanelli, Sara (2016), "Family Cult Foundations in the Hellenistic Age", in: Markus Hilgert (ed.), *Understanding Material Text Cultures* (Materiale Textkulturen 9), Berlin/Boston, 131–202, https://doi.org/10.1515/9783110417845-005.

Carbon, Jan Mathieu/Peels-Matthey, Saskia (eds.) (2018), *Purity and Purification in the Ancient Greek World. Texts, Rituals, and Norms*, Paris.

Casparis, Johannes G. de (1956), *Selected Inscriptions from the 7th to the 9th Centuries A. D.*, Bandung.

Cubelic, Danijel/Lougovaya, Julia/Quack, Joachim Friedrich (2015), "Rezitieren, Vorlesen und Singen", in: Thomas Meier, Michael R. Ott, and Rebecca Sauer (eds.), *Materiale Textkulturen. Konzepte – Materialien – Praktiken* (Materiale Textkulturen 1), Berlin/Munich/Boston, 651–663, https://doi.org/10.1515/9783110371291.651.

Dasen, Véronique/Nagy, Árpád M. (2019), "Gems", in: David Frankfurter (ed.), *Guide to the Study of Ancient Magic* (Religions in the Graeco-Roman World 189), Leiden, 406–445.

De Souza, Manuel (2010), "Repousser les profanes. Les progrès du militantisme religieux d'apres les sources latines de Virgile à Augustin", in: Èric Rebillard and Claire Sotinel (eds.), *Les frontières du profane dans l'Antiquité tardive* (Collection de l'École Française de Rome 428), Rome, 55–71.

Debiais, Vincent (2017), "Writing on Medieval Doors: The Surveyor Angel on the Moissac Capital (ca. 1100)", in: Irene Berti, Katharina Bolle, Fanny Opdenhoff, and Fabian Stroth (eds.),

Writing Matters: Presenting and Perceiving Monumental Inscriptions in Antiquity and the Middle Ages (Materiale Textkulturen 14), Berlin/Boston, 285–308, https://doi.org/10.1515/9783110534597-012.

Di Segni, Leah (2006), "Varia Arabica. Greek Inscriptions from Jordan (Pls. 53–56)", in: Michele Piccirillo (ed.), "Ricerca storico-archeologica in Giordania XXVI – 2006", in: *Studium Biblicum Franciscanum. Liber Annuus* 56, 578–592, https://doi.org/10.1484/J.LA.2.303660.

Dickmann, Jens-Arne/Keil, Wilfried E./Witschel, Christian (2015), "Topologie", in: Thomas Meier, Michael R. Ott, and Rebecca Sauer (eds.), *Materiale Textkulturen. Konzepte – Materialien – Praktiken* (Materiale Textkulturen 1), Berlin/Munich/Boston, 2015, 113–128, https://doi.org/10.1515/9783110371291.113.

Dietrich, Nikolaus (2022), "Inscribed Classical Victory Offerings at Olympia in the *longue durée*. Past as Present", in: Nikolaus Dietrich and Johannes Fouquet (eds.), *Image, Text, Stone. Intermedial Perspectives on Graeco-Roman Sculpture* (Materiale Textkulturen 36), Berlin/Boston, 321–359, https://doi.org/10.1515/9783110775761-012.

Dihle, Albrecht (2003), "Das Vokabular der Heiligkeit", in: József Herman and Hannah Rosén (eds.), *Petroniana: Gedenkschrift für Hubert Petersmann,* Heidelberg, 215–233.

Disselhoff, Dennis (2022), "Inschriftenallegorese. Zur Funktion inschriftentragender Sakralobjekte in geistlichen Texten des Mittelalters", in: Laura Velte and Ludger Lieb (eds.), *Literatur und Epigraphik. Phänomene der Inschriftlichkeit in Mittelalter und Früher Neuzeit* (Philologische Studien und Quellen 285), Berlin, 53–78.

Dondi, Cristina F. (2004), *The Liturgy of the Canons Regular of the Holy Sepulchre of Jerusalem: A Study and a Catalogue of the Manuscript Sources* (Bibliotheca Victorina 16), Turnhout.

Dornseiff, Franz (1925), *Das Alphabet in Mystik und Magie,* 2nd ed., Leipzig.

Drauschke, Marie-Kathrin (2019), *Die Aufstellung zwischenstaatlicher Vereinbarungen in griechischen Heiligtümern,* Hamburg.

Duval, Yvette (1982), *'Loca sanctorum Africae'. Le culte des martyrs en Afrique du 6e au 7e s. ap. J.-C.,* Rome.

Dzwiza, Kirsten (2019), "Magical Signs: An Extraordinary Phenomenon or Just Business as Usual?", in: Kata Endreffy, Arpád M. Nagy, and Jeffrey Spier (eds.) (2019), *Magical Gems in their Contexts: Proceedings of the International Workshop held in the Museum of Fine Arts, Budapest, 16–18 February 2012,* Rome, 59–83.

Edelmann-Singer, Babett/Ehrich, Susanne (eds.) (2021), *Sprechende Objekte. Materielle Kultur und Stadt zwischen Antike und Früher Neuzeit,* Regensburg.

Eitrem, Samson (1939), "Die magischen Gemmen und ihre Weihe", in: *Symbolae Osloenses* 19 (1939), 57–85.

Eliade, Mircea (1958), *Patterns in Comparative Religion,* transl. by Rosemary Sheed, New York.

Endreffy, Kata/Nagy, Arpád M./Spier, Jeffrey (eds.) (2019), *Magical Gems in their Contexts: Proceedings of the International Workshop held in the Museum of Fine Arts, Budapest, 16–18 February 2012,* Rome.

Engels, Odilo (1987), "Der Pontifikatsantritt und seine Zeichen", in: *Segni e riti nella chiesa altomedievale occidentale* (Settimane di studio del Centro italiano di studi sull'alto Medioevo XXXIII), vol. 2, Spoleto, 707–766.

Erkens, Franz-Reiner (ed.) (2002), *Die Sakralität von Herrschaft. Herrschaftslegitimierung im Wechsel der Zeiten und Räume,* Berlin.

Faraone, Christopher A. (1991), "The Agonistic Context of Early Greek Binding Spells", in: Christopher A. Faraone and Dirk Obbink (eds.), *Magika Hierà. Ancient Greek Magic and Religion,* Oxford, 3–32.

Feissel, Denis/Gatier, Pierre-Louis (2008), "Syrie, Phénicie, Palestine, Arabie", in: "Bulletin épigraphique", in: *Revue des Études Grecques* 121.2, 745–756.

Felle, Antonio (2006), *Biblia epigraphica. La Sacra Scrittura nella documentazione epigraphica dell'Orbis Christianus antiquus (III–VIII secolo),* Bari.

Ferrari, Michele (ed.) (2015), *Saints and the City. Beiträge zum Verständnis urbaner Sakralität in christlichen Gemeinschaften (5.–17. Jh.),* Erlangen.

Ferrary, Jean-Louis (2014), *Les mémoriaux de délégations du sanctuaire oraculaire de Claros, d'après la documentation conservée dans le Fonds Louis Robert,* Paris.

Ferro, Eva (2021), "Zum Verhältnis von Reliquien und Beschriftung im frühen Mittelalter. Eine Durchsicht der Quellen", in: Tino Licht and Kirsten Wallenwein (eds.), *Reliquienauthentiken. Kulturdenkmäler des Frühmittelalters,* Regensburg, 59–76.

Fliege, Jutta (1990), "Der heilige Metro und Gernrode im Harz", in: Friedhilde Krause (ed.), *Von der Wirkung des Buches. Festgabe für Horst Kunze zum 80. Geburtstag,* Berlin, 122–132.

Foletti, Ivan/Doležalová, Klára (2020), *The Notion of Liminality and the Medieval Sacred Space* (Convivium Supplementum 3), Turnhout.

Forneck, Torsten-Christian (1999), *Die Feier der Dedicatio ecclesiae im Römischen Ritus. Die Feier der Dedikation einer Kirche nach dem deutschen Pontifikale und dem Meßbuch vor dem Hintergrund ihrer Geschichte und im Vergleich zum Ordo dedicationis ecclesiae und zu einigen ausgewählten landessprachlichen Dedikationsordines* (Theologische Studien), Aachen.

Fox, Richard/Hornbacher, Annette (eds.) (2016), *The Materiality and Efficacy of Balinese Letters. Situating Scriptural Practices* (Brill's Southeast Asian Library 6), Leiden/Boston.

Frankfurter, David (2019), "The Magic of Writing in Mediterranean Antiquity", in: David Frankfurter (ed.), *Guide to the Study of Ancient Magic* (Religions in the Graeco-Roman World 189), Leiden, 626–658.

Frese, Tobias (2014), "'Denn der Buchstabe tötet' – Reflexionen zur Schriftpräsenz aus mediävistischer Perspektive", in: Tobias Frese, Wilfried E. Keil, and Kristina Krüger (eds.), *Verborgen, unsichtbar, unlesbar – zur Problematik restringierter Schriftpräsenz* (Materiale Textkulturen 2), Berlin/Boston, 1–16, https://doi.org/10.1515/9783110353587.1.

Frese, Tobias (2019), "'Kommt und seht den Ort' – sakrale Schrifträume im Sakramentar Heinrichs II.", in: Tobias Frese, Wilfried E. Keil, and Kristina Krüger (eds.), *Sacred Scripture / Sacred Space. The Interlacing of Real Places and Conceptual Spaces in Medieval Art and Architecture* (Materiale Textkulturen 23), Berlin/Boston, 37–62, https://doi.org/10.1515/9783110629156-003.

Frese, Tobias/Keil, Wilfried E. (2015), "Schriftakte/Bildakte", in: Thomas Meier, Michael R. Ott, and Rebecca Sauer (eds.), *Materiale Textkulturen. Konzepte – Materialien – Praktiken* (Materiale Textkulturen 1), Berlin/Munich/Boston, 633–638, https://doi.org/10.1515/9783110371291.633.

Frese, Tobias/Keil, Wilfried E./Krüger, Kristina (eds.) (2014), *Verborgen, unsichtbar, unlesbar – zur Problematik restringierter Schriftpräsenz* (Materiale Textkulturen 2), Berlin/Boston, https://doi.org/10.1515/9783110353587.

Frese, Tobias/Krüger, Kristina (2019), "Sacred Scripture / Sacred Space. The Interlacing of Real Places and Conceptual Spaces in Medieval Art and Architecture. An Introduction", in: Tobias Frese, Wilfried E. Keil, and Kristina Krüger (eds.), *Sacred Scripture / Sacred Space. The Interlacing of Real Places and Conceptual Spaces in Medieval Art and Architecture* (Materiale Textkulturen 23), Berlin/Boston, 1–10, https://doi.org/10.1515/9783110629156-001.

Frielinghaus, Heide (2011), *Die Helme von Olympia. Ein Beitrag zu Waffenweihungen in griechischen Heiligtümern* (Olympische Forschungen 33), Berlin.

Ganz, David (2017), "Touching Books, Touching Art. Tactile Dimensions of Sacred Books in the Medieval West", in: *Postscripts. The Journal of Sacred Texts, Cultural Histories, and Contemporary Contexts* 8 (1–2), 81–113.

Gatier, Pierre-Louis (1986), *Inscriptions de la Jordanie,* vol. 2: *Région centrale: Amman, Hesban, Madaba, Main, Dhiban* (Inscriptions grecques et latines de la Syrie 21,2 / Bibliothèque archéologique et historique 114), Paris.

Gemeinhardt, Peter/Heyden, Katharina (2012), "Heilige, Heiliges und Heiligkeit in spätantiken Religionskulturen", in: Peter Gemeinhardt and Katharina Heyden (eds.), *Heilige, Heiliges und Heiligkeit in spätantiken Religionskulturen* (Religionsgeschichtliche Versuche und Vorarbeiten 61), Berlin/Boston, 417–438.

Gennep, Arnold van (1909 [2005]), *Les rites de passage,* Paris.

Gesing, Martin (2007), *Der Schrein der heiligen Prudentia in der Propsteikirche zu Beckum,* Beckum.

Glück, Helmut (1987), *Schrift und Schriftlichkeit. Eine sprach- und kulturwissenschaftliche Studie,* Stuttgart.

Goodson, Caroline J. (2010), *The Rome of Pope Paschal I. Papal Power, Urban Renovation, Church Rebuilding and Relic Translation, 817–824,* Cambridge.

Gordon, Richard G. (2014), "'Charaktêres' between Antiquity and Renaissance: Transmission and Re-Invention", in: Véronique Dasen and Jean-Michel Spieser (eds.), *Les savoirs magiques et leur transmission de l'Antiquité à la Renaissance,* Florence, 253–300.

Graf, Fritz (2005), *Fluch und Verwünschung* (Thesaurus Cultus et Rituum Antiquorum 3), Los Angeles.

Graf, Fritz (2011), "Magie et écriture: Quelques réflexions", in: Magali de Haro Sanchez (ed.), *Écrire la magie dans l'antiquité. Actes du colloque international,* Liège, 227–238.

Hamm, Berndt/Herbers, Klaus/Stein-Kecks, Heidrun (eds.) (2007), *Sakralität zwischen Antike und Neuzeit* (Beiträge zur Hagiographie 6), Stuttgart.

Harris, Edward (2015), "Toward a Typology of Greek Regulations about Religious Matters: A Legal Approach", in: *Kernos* 28, 53–83.

Head, Thomas (2000), *Medieval Hagiography: An Anthology,* New York.

Henrichs, Albert (2003), "'Hieroi Logoi' and 'Hierai Bibloi': The (Un)Written Margins of the Sacred in Ancient Greece", in: *Harvard Studies in Classical Philology* 101, 207–266.

Herbers, Klaus (2013), "Sakralität: Einleitende Bemerkungen", in: Andrea Beck and Andreas Berndt (eds.), *Sakralität und Sakralisierung. Perspektiven des Heiligen* (Beiträge zur Hagiographie 13), Stuttgart, 11–14.

Herbers, Klaus/Düchting, Larissa (eds.) (2015), *Sakralität und Devianz: Konstruktionen, Normen, Praxis* (Beiträge zur Hagiographie 16), Stuttgart.

Herbers, Klaus/Nehring, Andreas/Steiner, Karin (eds.) (2019), *Sakralität und Macht* (Beiträge zur Hagiographie 22), Stuttgart.

Hermans, Jo (1984), *Die Feier der Eucharistie. Erklärung und spirituelle Erschließung,* Regensburg 1984.

Hooykaas, Christiaan (1980), *Drawings of Balinese Sorcery,* Leiden.

Hornbacher, Annette (2016), "The Body of Letters: Balinese Aksara as an Intersection between Script, Power and Knowledge", in: Richard Fox and Annette Hornbacher (eds.), *The Materiality and Efficacy of Balinese Letters. Situating Scriptural Practices* (Brill's Southeast Asian Library 6), Leiden/Boston, 90–99.

Hornbacher, Annette (2019), "Schriftverbrennung als kosmologische Realisierung. Eine balinesische Perspektive auf die Handlungsmacht von Schrift", in: Carina Kühne-Wespi, Klaus Oschema, and Joachim Friedrich Quack (eds.), *Zerstörung von Geschriebenem. Historische und transkulturelle Perspektiven* (Materiale Textkulturen 22), Berlin/Boston, 315–338, https://doi.org/10.1515/9783110629040-011.

Hornbacher, Annette/Frese, Tobias/Willer, Laura (2015), "Präsenz", in: Thomas Meier, Michael R. Ott, and Rebecca Sauer (eds.), *Materiale Textkulturen. Konzepte – Materialien – Praktiken* (Materiale Textkulturen 1), Berlin/Munich/Boston, 87–100, https://doi.org/10.1515/9783110371291.87.

Hornbacher, Annette/Neumann, Sabine/Willer, Laura (2015), "Schriftzeichen", in: Thomas Meier, Michael R. Ott, and Rebecca Sauer (eds.), *Materiale Textkulturen. Konzepte – Materialien – Praktiken* (Materiale Textkulturen 1), Berlin/Munich/Boston, 169–182, https://doi.org/10.1515/9783110371291.169.

Jäggi, Carola (2007), "Die Kirche als heiliger Raum: Zur Geschichte eines Paradoxons", in: Berndt Hamm, Klaus Herbers, and Heidrun Stein-Kecks (eds.), *Sakralität zwischen Antike und Neuzeit* (Beiträge zur Hagiographie 6), Stuttgart, 75–89.

Jäggi, Carola (2011), "'Heilige Räume'. Architektur und Sakralität – Geschichte einer Zuschreibung", in: Angelika Nollert, Matthias Volkenandt, and Rut-Maria Gollan (eds.), *Kirchenbauten in der Gegenwart. Architektur zwischen Sakralität und sozialer Wirklichkeit,* Regensburg, 23–30.

Kehnel, Annette/Panagiotopoulos, Diamantis (2015), "Textträger – Schriftträger: Ein Kurzportrait (statt Einleitung)", in: Annette Kehnel and Diamantis Panagiotopoulos (eds.), *Schriftträger – Textträger. Zur materialen Präsenz des Geschriebenen in frühen Gesellschaften* (Materiale Textkulturen 6), Berlin/Munich/Boston, 1–13, https://doi.org/10.1515/9783110371345.1.

Keil, Wilfried E./Kiyanrad, Sarah/Theis, Christoffer/Willer, Laura (eds.) (2018), *Zeichentragende Artefakte im sakralen Raum. Zwischen Präsenz und UnSichtbarkeit* (Materiale Textkulturen 20), Berlin/Boston, https://doi.org/10.1515/9783110619928.

Kern, Margit (2004), "Performativität im Bereich von Tür und Tor. Eine Ikonologie der Bewegung", in: Margit Kern, Thomas Kirchner, and Hubertus Kohle (eds.), *Geschichte und Ästhetik. Festschrift für Werner Busch zum 60. Geburtstag,* Munich/Berlin, 32–48.

Kern, Margit (2013), "Liminalität", in: Jörn Schafaff, Nina Schallenberg, and Tobias Vogt (eds.), *Kunst – Begriffe der Gegenwart. Von Allegorie bis Zip* (Kunstwissenschaftliche Bibliothek 50), Cologne, 147–151.

Kropp, Amina (2011), "Schriftlichkeit in der Schadenzauberpraxis am Beispiel der vulgärlateinischen *defixionum tabellae*", in: Anne Kolb (ed.), *Literacy in Ancient Everyday Life,* Berlin, 261–286.

Krüger, Klaus (2018), *Bildpräsenz – Heilspräsenz. Ästhetik der Liminalität,* Göttingen.

Kühne-Wespi, Carina/Oschema, Klaus/Quack, Joachim Friedrich (2019), "Zerstörung von Geschriebenem. Für eine Phänomenologie des Beschädigens und Vernichtens", in: Carina Kühne-Wespi, Klaus Oschema, and Joachim Friedrich Quack (eds.), *Zerstörung von Geschriebenem. Historische und transkulturelle Perspektiven* (Materiale Textkulturen 22), Berlin/Boston, 1–40, https://doi.org/10.1515/9783110629040-001.

Lafond, Yves/Michel, Vincent (eds.) (2016), *Espaces sacrés dans la Méditerranée antique,* Rennes.

Lagner, Martin (2017), "Urbane Qualitäten hochklassischer Zeit. Treffpunkte als städtische Angebote an die Bürger Athens", in: Alexandra W. Busch, Jochen Griesbach, and Johannes Lipps (eds.), *Urbanitas – urbane Qualitäten. Die antike Stadt als kulturelle Selbstverwirklichung,* Mainz, 69–89.

Leatherbury, Sean V. (2020), *Inscribing Faith in Late Antiquity. Between Reading and Seeing,* New York.

Licht, Tino/Wallenwein, Kirsten (2021), "Frühe Authentiken. Eine Einführung", in: Tino Licht and Kirsten Wallenwein (eds.), *Reliquienauthentiken. Kulturdenkmäler des Frühmittelalters,* Regensburg, IX–XXXVI.

Lieb, Ludger (2015), "Spuren materialer Textkulturen. Neun Thesen zur höfischen Textualität im Spiegel textimmanenter Inschriften", in: Beate Kellner, Ludger Lieb, and Stephan Müller (eds.), *Höfische Textualität. Festschrift für Peter Strohschneider* (Germanisch-romanische Monatsschrift, Beiheft 69), Heidelberg, 1–20.

Linder, Amnon (2009), "'Like Purest Gold Resplendent': The Fiftieth Anniversary of the Liberation of Jerusalem", in: *Crusades* 8, 31–51.

Liss, Hanna (2001), "Die Offenbarung Gottes in der mittelalterlichen Bibel- und Gebetsauslegung", in: *Mitteilungen für Anthropologie und Religionsgeschichte* 13, 1998 (erschien 2001), 271–292.

Liss, Hanna (2007), "Das Problem des eifernden Mannes: Das 'Eifer'-Ordal in der biblischen Überlieferung und in der jüdischen Tradition", in: Sylke Lubs, Louis Jonker, Andreas Ruwe, and Uwe Weise (eds.), *Behutsames Lesen. Alttestamentliche Exegese im interdisziplinären Methodendiskurs. Christof Hardmeier zum 65. Geburtstag* (Arbeiten zur Bibel und ihrer Geschichte 28), Leipzig, 197–215.

Liss, Hanna (2008), "Das destruktive Potential des Heiligen und seine 'Bändigung' durch die Tora", in: Katharina von Bremen (ed.), *Wie gefährlich ist der Heilige Geist? Ordnung – Geist – Anarchie* (Tagungsprotokolle – Institut für Kirche und Gesellschaft), Schwerte, 27–40.

Liss, Hanna (2014), "Vom *Sefer Tora* zum *sefer*: Die Bedeutung von Büchern im 'Buch der Frommen' des R. Yehuda ben Shemu'el he-Chasid", in: Joachim Friedrich Quack and Daniela Christina Luft (eds.), *Erscheinungsformen und Handhabungen Heiliger Schriften* (Materiale Textkulturen 5), Berlin/Munich/Boston, 207–227, https://doi.org/10.1515/9783110371277.207.

Liss, Hanna (2015), "The Torah Scroll and its Function as a Ritual Object in Jewish Culture", in: Hendrik Schulze (ed.), *Musical Text as Ritual Object,* Turnhout, 165–174.

Luft, Daniela C. (2014), "Einleitung: Heilige Schriften und ihre Heiligkeit in Umgang und materieller Präsenz. Zu Zielen und Ergebnissen des Workshops", in: Joachim Friedrich Quack and Daniela Christina Luft (eds.), *Erscheinungsformen und Handhabungen Heiliger Schriften* (Materiale Textkulturen 5), Berlin/Munich/Boston, 3–38, https://doi.org/10.1515/9783110371277.3.

McVey, Kathleen E. (2010), "Spirit Embodied. The Emergence of Symbolic Interpretations of Early Christian and Byzantine Architecture", in: Slobodan Ćurčić and Evangelia Hadjitryphonos (eds.), *Architecture as Icon. Perception and Representation of Architecture in Byzantine Art,* New Haven/London, 39–71.

Meyer-Dietrich, Erika (2010), "Recitation, Speech Acts, and Declamation", in: Willeke Wendrich (ed.), *UCLA Encyclopedia of Egyptology,* Los Angeles.

Ober, Josiah (1995), "Greek Horoi: Artifactual Texts and the Contingency of Meaning", in: David Small (ed.), *Methods in the Mediterranean: Historical and Archaeological Views on Texts and Archaeology,* Leiden, 91–123.

Opstall, Emilie van (ed.) (2018), *Sacred Thresholds. The Door to the Sanctuary in Late* Antiquity, Leiden.

Otto, Bernd-Christian (2011), *Magie: Rezeptions- und diskursgeschichtliche Analysen. Von der Antike bis zur Neuzeit,* Berlin.

Ousterhout, Robert G. (2010), "New Temples and New Solomons. The Rhetoric of Byzantine Architecture", in: Paul Magdalino and Robert Nelson (eds.), *The Old Testament in Byzantium. Selected Papers from a Symposium Held Dec. 2006, Dumbarton Oaks* (Dumbarton Oaks Byzantine Symposia and Colloquia 2), Washington, D. C., 223–253.

Pallis, Georgios (2017), "Messages from a Sacred Space: The Function of the Byzantine Sanctuary Barrier Inscription (9th–14th Centuries)", in: Irene Berti, Katharina Bolle, Fanny Opdenhoff, and Fabian Stroth (eds.), *Writing Matters. Presenting and Perceiving Monumental Inscriptions in Antiquity and the Middle Ages* (Materiale Textkulturen 14), Berlin/Boston, 145–158, https://doi.org/10.1515/9783110534597-007.

Papalexandrou, Amy (2007), "Echoes of Orality in the Monumental Inscriptions of Byzantium", in: Liz James (ed.), *Art and Text in Byzantine Culture,* Cambridge, 161–187.

Parker, Robert (2012), "Epigraphy and Greek Religion", in: John Davies (ed.), *Epigraphy and the Historical Sciences,* Oxford, 17–30.

Parker, Robert (2018), "Miasma: Old and New Problems", in: Jan-Mathieu Carbon and Saskia Peels-Matthey (eds.), *Purity and Purification in the Ancient Greek World. Texts, Rituals, and Norms,* Liège, 23–33.

Petrovic, Ivana/Petrovic, Andrej (2018), "Purity of Body and Soul in the Cult of Athena Lindia: On the Eastern Background of Greek Abstentions", in: Jan-Mathieu Carbon and Saskia Peels-Matthey (eds.), *Purity and Purification in the Ancient Greek World. Texts, Rituals, and Norms,* Liège, 225–260.

Piccirillo, Michele (1997), *The Mosaics of Jordan* (American Center of Oriental Research Publications 1), 2nd ed., Amman.

Piccirillo, Michele (1998), "The Mosaics", in: Michele Piccirillo and Eugenio Alliata (eds.), *Mount Nebo. New Archaeological Excavations 1967–1997* (Studium Biblicum Franciscanum/Collectio maior 27), Jerusalem, 265–371.

Poeschke, Joachim (2009), *Mosaiken in Italien, 300–1300,* Munich.

Pringle, Denys (2007), *The Churches of the Crusader Kingdom of Jerusalem. A Corpus,* vol. 3: *The City of Jerusalem (Appendix),* Cambridge.

Quack, Joachim Friedrich (2014), "Die Drohung des Unlesbaren und die Macht des Ungelesenen. Zwei Fallbeispiele aus dem Alten Ägypten", in: Tobias Frese, Wilfried E. Keil und Kristina Krüger (eds.), *Verborgen, unsichtbar, unlesbar – zur Problematik restringierter Schriftpräsenz* (Materiale Textkulturen 2), Berlin/Boston, 33–41, https://doi.org/10.1515/9783110353587.33.

Reudenbach, Bruno (2021), "Enigmatic Calligraphy: Lettering as Visualized Hermeneutic of Sacred Scripture", in: Jörg B. Quenzer (ed.), *Exploring Written Artefacts. Objects, Methods, and Concepts,* Vol 2. (Studies in Manuscript Cultures 25), Berlin/Boston, 773–794.

Reynolds, Joyce/Roueché, Charlotte/Bodard, Gabriel (eds.) (2007), *Inscriptions of Aphrodisias,* Online Corpus: http://insaph.kcl.ac.uk/iaph2007/index.html (accessed 28/2/2023).

Roels, Evelien (2018), "The Queen of Inscriptions Contextualized. The Presence of Civic Inscriptions in the Pronaos of Ancient Temples in Hellenistic and Roman Asia Minor (4th cent. BCE–2nd cent. CE)", in: Emilie van Opstall (ed.), *Sacred Thresholds. The Door to the Sanctuary in Late Antiquity* (Religions in the Graeco-Roman World 185), Leiden, 221–253.

Schmitt, Hanno (2004), *"Mache dieses Haus zu einem Haus der Gnade und des Heiles". Der Kirchweihritus in Geschichte und Gegenwart als Spiegel des jeweiligen Kirchen- und Liturgieverständnisses im 2. Jahrtausend* (Paderborner theologische Studien 4), Paderborn.

Schreiner, Klaus (1990), "Volkstümliche Bibelmagie und volkssprachige Bibellektüre", in: Peter Dinzelbacher and Dieter R. Bauer (eds.), *Volksreligion im hohen und späten Mittelalter,* Paderborn, 329–373.

Schreiner, Klaus (2000), "Buchstabensymbolik, Bibelorakel, Schriftmagie. Religiöse Bedeutung und lebensweltliche Funktion heiliger Schriften im Mittelalter und der Frühen Neuzeit", in: Horst Wenzel, Wilfried Seipel, and Gotthart Wunberg (eds.), *Die Verschriftlichung der Welt. Bild, Text und Zahl in der Kultur des Mittelalters und der Frühen Neuzeit* (Schriften des Kunsthistorischen Museums 5), Vienna, 59–103.

Schreiner, Klaus (2002), "Heilige Buchstaben, Texte und Bücher, die schützen, heilen und helfen. Formen und Funktionen mittelalterlicher Schriftmagie", in: Erika Greber, Konrad Ehrlich, and Jan-Dirk Müller (eds.), *Materialität und Medialität von Schrift,* Bielefeld, 73–89.

Schreiner, Klaus (2006), "Abecedarium. Die Symbolik des Alphabets in der Liturgie der mittelalterlichen und frühneuzeitlichen Kirchweihe", in: Ralf Stammberger (ed.), *"Das Haus Gottes, das seid ihr selbst". Mittelalterliches und barockes Kirchenverständnis im Spiegel der Kirchweihe* (Wissenschaftliche Fachtagung im Erbacher Hof, Akademie des Bistums Mainz, 23.–26.01.2002), Berlin, 143–188.

Schreiner, Klaus (2011), "Das Buch im Nacken. Bücher und Buchstaben als Zeichenhafte Kommunikationsmedien in rituellen Handlungen der mittelalterlichen Kirche", in: Klaus Schreiner, *Rituale, Zeichen, Bilder. Formen und Funktionen symbolischer Kommunikation im Mittelalter,* ed. by Ulrich Meier, Gabriela Signori, and Gerd Schwerhoff, Cologne/Weimar/Vienna, 283–322.

Schulz, Katja (2020), "Inscriptions in Old Norse Literature", in: Ricarda Wagner, Christine Neufeld, and Ludger Lieb (eds.), *Writing Beyond Pen and Parchment. Inscribed Objects in Medieval*

European Literature (Materiale Textkulturen 30), Berlin/Boston, 41–62, https://doi.org/10.1515/9783110645446-003.

Seifert, Aletta (2006), *Der Sakrale Schutz von Grenzen im Antiken Griechenland – Formen und Ikonographie* (Diss. Julius-Maximilians-Universität Würzburg).

Senzel, Dennis (2018), "Makulatur", in: Susanne Scholz and Ulrike Vedder (eds.), *Handbuch Literatur und Materielle Kultur* (Handbücher zur kulturwissenschaftlichen Philologie 6), Berlin, 422–424.

Shagrir, Iris/Gaposchkin, Cecilia (eds.) (2019), *Liturgy and Devotion in the Crusader States,* Abingdon.

Sitz, Anna M. (2019), "Hiding in Plain Sight: Epigraphic Reuse in the Temple-Church at Aphrodisias", in: *Journal of Late Antiquity* 12 (1), 136–168.

Speyer, Wolfgang (1992), "Das Buch als magisch-religiöser Kraftträger im griechischen und römischen Altertum", in: Peter Ganz (ed.), *Das Buch als magisches und als Repräsentationsobjekt. Vorträge gehalten anläßlich des 26. Wolfenbütteler Symposions vom 11.–15. September 1989 in der Herzog-August-Bibliothek,* Wiesbaden, 59–86.

Stapper, Richard (1937), "Kirchweihe und griechisches Alphabet im Korveyer Codex Wibaldi", in: *Westfälische Zeitschrift* 93, 143–150.

Suntrup, Rudolf (1980), "Te igitur-Initialen und Kanonbilder in mittelalterlichen Sakramentarhandschriften", in: Christel Meier and Uwe Ruberg (eds.), *Text und Bild: Aspekte des Zusammenwirkens zweier Künste im Mittelalter und früher Neuzeit,* Wiesbaden, 278–382.

Swift, Ellen (2009), *Style and Function in Roman Decoration. Living with Objects and Interiors,* Aldershot.

Theis, Christoffer (2015), "Mobile und immobile Schriftträger", in: Thomas Meier, Michael R. Ott, and Rebecca Sauer (eds.), *Materiale Textkulturen. Konzepte – Materialien – Praktiken* (Materiale Textkulturen 1), Berlin/Munich/Boston, 611–618, https://doi.org/10.1515/9783110371291.611.

Thunø, Erik (2015), *The Apse Mosaic in Early Medieval Rome. Time, Network, and Repetition,* Cambridge.

Tilley, Christopher (2002), "Metaphor, Materiality and Interpretation", in: Victor Buchli (ed.), *The Material Culture Reader,* London, 23–56.

Turner, Victor (1964), "Betwixt and Between: The Liminal Period in Rites de Passage", in: Melford E. Spiro (ed.), *Symposium on New Approaches to the Study of Religion. Proceedings of the 1964 Annual Spring Meeting of the American Ethnological Association,* Seattle, 4–20.

Veltri, Giuseppe (2002), "Das Ordal der ehebruchsverdächtigen Frau im jüdischen Mittelalter", in: Giuseppe Veltri, *Gegenwart der Tradition. Studien zur jüdischen Literatur und Kulturgeschichte,* Leiden/Boston/Cologne, 172–191.

Vriezen, Karel J. (1998), *Inscriptions in Mosaic Pavements in Byzantine Palaestina/Arabia Quoting Texts from the Old Testament,* in: Leonard V. Rutgers, Pieter W. Van der Horst, and Henriette W. Hevelaar (eds.), *The Use of Sacred Books in the Ancient World,* Leuven, 247–261.

Walaker Nordeide, Saebjorg/Brink, Stefan (eds.) (2013), *Sacred Sites and Holy Places: Exploring the Sacralization of Landscape through Time and Space,* Turnhout.

Wallenwein, Kirsten (2021), "Die Reliquienauthentiken von Baume-les-Messieurs", in: Tino Licht and Kirsten Wallenwein (eds.), *Reliquienauthentiken. Kulturdenkmäler des Frühmittelalters,* Regensburg, 255–273.

Watta, Sebastian (2018), *Sakrale Zonen im frühen Kirchenbau des Nahen Ostens. Zum Kommunikationspotenzial von Bodenmosaiken für die Schaffung heiliger Räume* (Spätantike – frühes Christentum – Byzanz. Reihe B: Studien und Perspektiven 45), Wiesbaden.

Wenzel, Horst (2000), "Die Schrift und das Heilige", in: Horst Wenzel, Wilfried Seipel, and Gotthart Wunberg (eds.), *Die Verschriftlichung der Welt. Text und Zahl in der Kultur des Mittelalters und der Frühen Neuzeit* (Schriften des Kunsthistorischen Museums 5), Vienna, 15–58.

Wieser, Matthias (2008), "Technik/Artefakte. Mattering Matter", in: Stephan Moebius and Andreas Reckwitz (eds.), *Poststrukturalistische Sozialwissenschaften,* Frankfurt (Main), 419–432.

Willer, Laura (2015), *'Beschreib es und trag es versteckt'. Sogenannt magische Papyrusamulette aus dem römischen Ägypten in der Praxis – Ihre Herstellung und Handhabung*, http://www.ub.uni-heidelberg.de/archiv/33755.

Yasin, Ann Marie (2009), *Saints and Church Spaces in the Late Antique Mediterranean. Architecture, Cult, and Community,* Cambridge.

Zöller, Wolf (2018), *Regularkanoniker im Heiligen Land. Studien zur Kirchen-, Ordens- und Frömmigkeitsgeschichte der Kreuzfahrerstaaten* (Vita regularis. Abhandlungen 73), Berlin.

Chapter 6
Political Rule and Administration

Abigail S. Armstrong, Rodney Ast, Enno Giele, Julia Lougovaya,
Hannah Mieger, Jörg Peltzer, Joachim Friedrich Quack,
Chun Fung Tong, Sarina Tschachtli, Banban Wang

Chapter 6
Political Rule and Administration

Abigail S. Armstrong, Rodney Ast, Enno Giele, Julia Lougovaya, Hannah Mieger, Jörg Peltzer, Joachim Friedrich Quack, Chun Fung Tong, Sarina Tschachtli, Banban Wang*

To convey a message across a larger expanse of time and space than was possible via oral communication and thus to fix a fleeting thought or utterance of speech as materialised, external memory: these two functions are usually posited to be at the very origin of writing as a cultural technique.[1] Writing is believed to have begun either as messages to a supernatural, sacred power—which could also be construed as a pathway to worldly authority—or out of a need for managing an ever more complex economy involving the revenue from and redistribution of state (or temple) resources.[2]

Perhaps not incidentally, both these functions also form the very foundation of most political rule and administration. Political rule is inextricable from what we shall pragmatically term 'states', that is, composites of hierarchical social action and structure that exceed the confines of small groups whose members know each other personally (such as families or village populations). Such rule depends on messages being disseminated among all group members, and needs to legitimise itself and make this legitimation persuasive and permanent.[3] Administration, too, needs messages to be circulated and sent to specific group members so as to coordinate their actions across space and time.[4] But even more so, it needs written records, which enumerate and list possessions and people, and archives or other forms of information repositories.[5]

---

[1] For a critical discussion of these assumptions, see the comments in Chapter 1, Thesis 1.
[2] Postgate/Wang/Wilkinson 1995. See also Martin 1988 (or its English translation: Cochrane 1994), who combines the competing theories mentioned above, but in a rather abstract way.
[3] The qualification of the size and type of political rule seems necessary, as there were and still are certainly polities and societies or "communities that have no overarching structure of leadership and authority, no sovereign, no chief, no king, no permanent council to direct or coordinate their affairs" and have thus been called "acephalous (that is headless […]) societies" (Goody 1986, 88). It is an open question whether, or to what extent, polities like these were dependent upon writing for upholding their leaderless collective action and how large they could become before succumbing to the kind of despotic rulership that previous generations of scholars have postulated as being inevitable.
[4] While for the collective action model—that is, for his 'acephalous societies'—Goody makes a point of assuring us that "[a]t this level literacy [and by extension: writing] played no part in the polity", he is equally certain that "[t]he segregation of administrative activities in a specific organization, the bureaucracy, […] is critically dependent […] on the capacity for writing to communicate at a distance, to store information in files, and to tend to depersonalise interaction" (Goody 1986, 89–90).
[5] Nissen/Damerow/Englund 2004.

---

* In alphabetical order.

These theoretical considerations highlight two spheres—namely, 'rulership'/'expression of authority' and 'administration'/'information management'—in which writing as a state practice has developed and thrived since its incipient days. Of course, administration and information management are not limited to state practices, but are also at the core of economic enterprises such as business management. But here, for pragmatic reasons, we will focus predominantly on state actors. In any case, the two abovementioned spheres define the most basic functions of writing. Hence we shall term texts that display, establish, and legitimatise political rule as 'rulership writing' (or 'Herrschaftsschrifttum'), while texts that solicit, provide, collect, summarise, archive, and retrieve relevant information (and thereby enable or support political rule) we shall call 'administrative writing' ('Verwaltungsschrifttum'). More often than not, the basic binary characterisations of writings—'public vs. restricted access', claims for 'truth vs. correctness', 'long-lasting vs. ephemeral or cyclical'—do conform rather neatly to the 'rulership vs. administrative writing' divide, although it bears stressing that these two categories are but hermeneutical devices rather than self-contained genres. There are certainly many transitions and overlaps between them.

Claiming political authority or justifying political rule of any kind requires *persuading* those who are ruled—as well as perhaps the ruling elite itself, other rulers, or the gods—of the legitimacy of that rule. Rather than simply *forcing* the ruled under the yoke by violent means, the legitimation of political rule entails a specific communicative situation with the following conditions.

The arguments for legitimation displayed in rulership writing usually constitute a unidirectional message by a sender (the rulers or their advocates) to a recipient (the ruled). While any claim to rulership can be challenged, it is not made with the intent that this should happen. Rulership writing is envisioned for the most part as a monologue, not a dialogue. Nevertheless, the message will need to be made public and accessible to as many recipients as possible. Like any argument, it has to make a truth claim. It cannot be based on doubt or a choice between equally valid alternatives. Even in a democracy, the suasion consists of the argument that certain political candidates (or incumbent politicians, for that matter) are best equipped to deal with a political situation and thus worthy of the political powers invested in them. Like any form of persuasion, rulership writings may operate on rational, irrational, or emotional levels, or even on all of these at once. Therefore, the medium may at times be more important than the actual message, the effect more valued than clarity. In this respect, the staging of a message becomes a crucial factor in strengthening its persuasive effect.

Finally, the argument usually contains, at least implicitly, the idea that the claimed rule is either permanently valid everywhere the message is conveyed or that it is at least valid for a specified period and in a well-defined territory. In other words, the claim may be indefinite (life- or dynasty-long and boundless; that is, worldwide or even cosmological) or limited and bounded, tied to certain conditions being met (for example, the mandate of Heaven, the graces of the gods).

None of this *has to* be formulated in written form. Charisma, which is so effective in suasion, is often better manifested in live performance, such as in speeches.[6] But with the publicity and permanence of the message also being important factors, writing is often used as a powerful tool for achieving both. Thus, the writing materials of choice will tend to support the persuasion through their size, beauty, impressiveness, durability, visibility, placement, and so on.

Information management, on the other hand, relies a good deal on interaction and dialogue, on confidentiality rather than publicity, clarity instead of an appeal to emotions, accuracy rather than 'truth' claims, and actuality rather than permanence. Information can be obtained by observation, but without the cooperation of some of the ruled (or at least those who may be called 'functionaries') submitting written reports, a state cannot be governed. Although bureaucratic language is infamous for being obscure and ambiguous (which at times may be on purpose), rulers or their proxies do rely at a very general level on unambiguous reports so as to be well informed. They also need to clearly communicate downwards if they want the ruled to enact their wishes. While many orders need to be made public for the same reason, rulers or administrators always need to keep their informational edge over the ruled. If they cannot, they at least need to appear to know more and to retain the power to control access to sources of information, impose processes for gathering intelligence, or to decide which facts matter. It is clearly advantageous to rulers if the information they have is not only clear, but also accurate and comprehensive. It does not have to be 'true' in a moral or justifying sense, but making decisions on the basis of wrong information is not conducive to government. For the same reason, information for the ruler needs to be up to date. Information gathering does not aim at acquiring knowledge once and for all, but rather at regularly keeping such knowledge up to date and maintaining the steady flow of incoming messages. The goal is to build up an information repository that can be conveniently tapped at any time by those wielding power.

Again, not all administratively relevant information *has to* be committed to writing. For security reasons, some messages may only be relayed orally. But if and where writing is used to store and convey information as the basis for successful and efficient administration, it can make good use of the memory-keeping function of writing, resulting in the establishment of archives, access to which must be controlled.[7]

As in the case of authoritative rulership writing, the materials and practices chosen for administrative writing are expected to serve the specific purposes of information management, which are different from the purposes of claims to authority. The writing materials used in administration must be designed for fast production,

---

6 This does, of course, refer to personal charisma in the Weberian sense of charismatic rule ('charismatische Herrschaft'); see Weber 2009 [1922], 221; see also his claim that even other types of rule based to a large extent on bureaucracy cannot, in fact, completely forego personal charisma on the part of leaders (ibid., 218).

7 See Chapter 3 'Memory and Archive'.

handling, and conveyance; they are usually available in adequate number, conveniently portable, and easy to produce, at least by the functionaries and those who are meant to use them (but not necessarily by anyone else). These writings also need to be archivable, which entails that they be easy to organise, store, retrieve, discard, and replace. Even though some information may be unchanging and permanent, as a rule of thumb good day-to-day administration relies on a lot of information that is more or less ephemeral, and which (literally) does not need to be 'hewn in stone'. Information gathering in this context is usually a cyclical and repetitive affair. Unlike claims of authority generated by rulers, an administration may face the problem of too little or too much information, since its information is not entirely self-generated, but rather relies on opportune and external sources of information.

These communicative situations make certain types of materiality seem more adequate than others.[8] However, once these material conventions are established, they become a code with which its users can play. Therefore, we sometimes see administrative writing staged as rulership writing, and when this happens, it is often accompanied by a shift in materiality. This is the case, for instance, when administrative lists are published in order to demonstrate a ruler's magnanimity and may then be transferred from an ephemeral material such as wood, bamboo, papyrus, or paper to something more durable such as stone or metal. Likewise, size, layout, colour, embellishment, etc. are all parameters that in most cases will be employed differently in public claims of authority, be they blatant or subtle (in the case of rulership writing) as opposed to the hurried or meticulous yet efficient, matter-of-fact day-to-day information gathering and bookkeeping (as in administrative writing).

In some areas, the distinction between rulership and administrative writing is less clear. Legal texts, for instance—those pertaining to legislation and legal codification, and their promulgation and jurisdiction—tend to be of a dual or ambiguous nature. Jurisdiction exists to regulate and decide legal situations case by case so as to guarantee the smooth functioning of society, much like administration does; yet in the premodern era, juridical court decisions (not to mention the very act of legislating) were the prerogative of political powers and definitely also served to enhance their political authority. By their very nature, legal codes, such as royal or imperial edicts and decrees, must display authority. At the same time, they also serve the very practical ends of organising and directing the behaviour of the masses. Accordingly, they must be at once 'awe-inspiring' and understandable and clear. What is more, such legal texts pose a practical problem for any administration: they are constantly accruing and their sheer volume over time becomes a challenge for archiving and retrieval while also potentially leading to political 'embarrassment' when previous laws, oaths, treaties, or alliances become obsolete and must be concealed or surreptitiously deleted.

---

[8] In addition to the communicative situation, the materiality of administrative and rulership writings also affects the actual territorial expanse that is to be governed or administered. On this point, see Innis 2007 [1950], 26–27, who distinguishes between the suitability of different media.

Moreover, in many non-typographical societies, there was an element that could blur the distinction made here between 'rulership writing' and 'administrative writing': namely, the oftentimes transcendent or cosmological justification of rule. Because of this, administrative writings—even more palpably than in modern times—came to represent political rule by their mere existence, and the presence of them reminded their users of the power relations of which they were part. Hence, anything that represented the rulers' words, such as their name or depiction, was often embellished by means of precious materials, specific layouts, unusual or large sizes, as well as the use of colour, terminology and special protocols during the production and reception processes—even if the content of the writing served purely administrative purposes. Therefore, while this chapter will frequently refer to 'rulership' and 'administrative writing' as two basic categories, in order to better situate and classify concrete historical examples, this classification is less useful in other instances, for which other contextualisations must serve and support the hermeneutical purpose.

One such context is provided by the structure of the following narrative. This context is governed by the diachronic framework evidently provided by the process of producing inscribed artefacts and the different circumstances of that production. Within this framework, eight theses—often purposefully simplistic—are provided, which in turn are fine-tuned or contrasted with counter-examples.

The first section (Thesis 28) deals with the cultural contexts that make the objects and actions we analyse possible in the first place. These are language and writing systems, without which no official writing culture can be established. In particular, this includes issues such as multilingualism and translation. The second section (Thesis 29) analyses the spatial and performative context: namely, the importance of the location, setting, and staging of rulership and administrative writings, which includes public display and restricted access. The third section (Thesis 30) discusses the physical properties (the shape or form) and the dimensions of the inscribed artefacts, in addition to aspects of the production and standardisation of writing supports before any writing is applied to them. In short, we speak here about the choice of writing materials. Following the production process further, the subsequent three sections elaborate how writing supports received their writing, as well as possible illustrations and/or proof of authenticity, and how all of these elements were consciously deployed to achieve certain goals. In the fourth section (Thesis 31), we focus first on the layout of the writing on the support. The focus of the fifth section (Thesis 32) is the type of script, that is, the execution of the writing itself as cursive, standard, elaborate etc. The sixth section (Thesis 33) briefly turns to the use of imagery in rulership and administrative writings. The seventh section (Thesis 34) concludes the discussion of the production process by exploring means of authentication, with particular focus on seals and tally-notches. Finally, the eighth section (Thesis 35) will look at common types of reaction to and interaction with the finished inscribed artefacts on the part of the recipients of rulership and administrative writings.

> **Thesis 28**
> Rulers and administrators of multilingual realms consciously chose which languages and writing systems were materialised in writing. Inscribing a text in multiple languages on a monument almost always served primarily to visualise authority.

At the very outset of the discussion on material text cultures in the context of rulership and administration stands the observation that writing is not a precondition for ruling. Putting a language down in writing, a process one might term the 'materialisation' of language, is a choice. This choice becomes even more pertinent if the rule in question extended over people speaking different languages, or if the rulers and/or their administration attempted to address people outside their realms who might speak other languages (such as merchants). In multilingual polities, which can be observed from very early on in history and which were probably the norm rather than the exception, the question of which language(s) became materialised and which one(s) did not is of some significance for understanding the respective political and administrative culture.

To illustrate the potential of such an enquiry, we shall briefly touch upon the materialisation of language(s) in a small number of multilingual polities ranging from ancient Egypt to medieval England. We first provide a general outline of how rulers addressed the issue of multilingualism in their respective realms and whether there was a ranking amongst the languages, before tackling the question of the extent to which multilingualism was reflected in the writings of local administrators. Finally, we shall speak briefly about a specific phenomenon of rulership writing, namely the use of several languages on publicly displayed monuments.

Languages Materialised in Manuscripts: Choosing between Ideology and Pragmatism

One example of an empire that united several originally independent political and linguistic groups under its rule and fixed the language (and writing) of the dominant political group for the top level of administration is the Roman Empire, which used Latin in the west and Greek in the east. But basic administrative needs required that one also takes the divergent languages of local peoples into consideration. A remarkable case is the Old Persian Empire, which did not make Persian the administrative language, but rather Aramaic, as observed in documents from the far west (Egypt) to the far east (Bactria).[9] This language and script was not specific to a politically domi-

---

[9] For Egypt, see Porten/Yardeni 1986–1999; for Bactria, see Naveh/Shaked 2012. Overall, see Tavernier 2017.

nant group, but was comparatively easy to learn and had already played a role in the administration of the Neo-Assyrian and Neo-Babylonian empires before the Persian conquest.

Compared to the Roman or Persian Empire, the Kingdom of England in the eleventh century was a small realm. And yet, on the eve of the Norman Conquest in 1066, it was home to a number of languages: Old English, Norse, various Celtic languages, and even Norman French were spoken in the British Isles. Yet this multilingualism appears only partially in the documents issued by the Anglo-Saxon kings; these were written in Latin and Old English and thus materialised only those languages associated with royal authority.[10]

The use of a vernacular in official charters was exceptional in the English context and set Old English clearly apart from other contemporary spoken languages, almost marking it as the 'official' vernacular of the realm. This contrast can be seen in the activity of the Norman conquerors who were used to a different practice: their spoken language, French, was not materialised in the charters they drafted, but rather they were all written in Latin, the *lingua franca* of such documents in Europe at the time.

Upon his conquest of England, however, the new King William (r. 1066–1087) did not immediately introduce this Latin-based practice. At first, he continued to issue charters in Old English, employing personnel who had already served under the Anglo-Saxon King Edward the Confessor (r. 1042–1066). Remarkably, Old English was practically the only language used in royal writs and charters during the first years of William's rule — only one writ in Latin has survived from before 1070.[11] The continuing use of Old English was first and foremost a political statement and not so much the result of practical considerations (for instance, existing administrative routines or comprehensibility of decisions on the part of the English populace). Even though William was eager to make forgotten the short-lived rule of his opponent at Hastings, Harold (r. 1066), he was keen to connect his own kingship with that of Harold's predecessor Edward and position himself as the latter's legitimate successor. The use of Old English may well have served to suggest a certain level of continuity between the reigns of Edward and William. Furthermore, it may also have been considered a signal to the Anglo-Saxons, especially members of the surviving elite, of William's willingness to work together with them. However, when William ended his policy of cooperation with such native elites in 1070 and actively sought to replace them with Normans, the practice of writing royal documents exclusively in Old English came to an end.[12]

Yet Old English did not disappear altogether. A notable, if infrequent, feature of William's documents issued after 1070 were bilingual writs, in which (save in one case)

---

10 Keynes 2013, 135–137.
11 *Regesta regum Anglo-Normannorum*, 48. The writ (no. 35) was very probably issued before 1070. Another one dating from before 1069 is a Latin translation of an Old English writ, no. 32. On post-conquest vernacular documents in general, see Pelteret 1990.
12 *Regesta regum Anglo-Normannorum*, 50.

the Latin text came first, followed by the Old English.[13] In this particular case, the order of the languages made clear who were the conquerors and who were the conquered.

While Latin thus became the only materialised language of the ruling elite, it was not the only language associated with the new rulers, with the vernacular French spoken by the conquerors being at least as indicative and effective a marker of social difference. In contrast to the situation in the Anglo-Saxon kingdom and the Norman duchy, where the spoken language of the ruling elite was shared by the ruled, in post-conquest England the vernacular of the invaders was almost exclusively theirs, a language not shared with their subordinates. This also shows that the materialisation of a language as such — through its written form — did not automatically create an exclusive association between that language and the ruler(s). The written (materialised) word was not necessarily more important than the spoken word. Moreover, the recognition of the vernacular was not limited to French. Documents issued by the royal chancery explicitly addressed not only French speakers, but also English, Danish, Gaelic, Welsh, and Cornish speakers. The conquerors recognised the multilinguistic reality of their kingdom and their focus on a particular language (and in the rare instances of charters in Latin and Old English, on two) was not directed at denying the existence of other languages or even at suppressing them.[14]

Thus the choice of which language would actually be materialised depended on various factors. It is important to note that there were no universally applicable rules that determined the choice of the language(s). It cannot even be taken for granted that the language spoken by the ruler was the one to be materialised. Nor did the concern that the writing was to be understood by all recipients always dictate the choice. Which language rulers used for their writings was by and large an ideological choice in the widest possible sense of the word, which could be imposed by custom, concrete political aims or other reasons.

Likewise, it cannot be taken for granted that the writings of local governmental agents reflected the potentially multilinguistic background of the people with whom they were dealing. While there seems to be a certain correlation between the degree of literacy in society and the use of multilingual documents by local administrators (that is, the greater the literacy, the higher the likelihood of multilingual documents), there is no automatism based on this correlation. The extent to which local administrative documents were drafted multilingually remained a choice, which could be determined by pragmatic reasons as much as by ideological ones. Whether there existed a difference between administrative and rulership writing as concerns multilingualism must thus be studied in each individual case.

The conditions of lower-level administration often made it advantageous not to use multilingual texts, but rather only the locally used language and script (and, if

---

[13] *Regesta regum Anglo-Normannorum*, 50–52.
[14] Sharpe 2011.

necessary, translations from other tongues into the local language). The necessity of translating some forms of administrative writing can be documented by Demotic Egyptian letters from Achaemenid Egypt[15] which either indicate explicitly that they have been translated from Aramaic or can be recognised as such from their unidiomatic use of Demotic Egyptian. There is also a Demotic Egyptian letter written in hieratic script from Roman-period Egypt which indicates that it has been translated from the Greek.[16]

In the Graeco-Roman world, administrative texts at the local level tended to be written in the language of the local administration, which was the same as that of at least one large part of the population; but again, as in medieval England, it may not have been the language of the central authority. Thus, decrees, letters, or other orders from high-ranking government representatives issued in Latin would routinely be translated into Greek in the eastern part of the Empire. An illustrative example is furnished by an ostracon bearing a prefectural letter found at Mons Claudianus, the site of Roman imperial quarries in the Eastern Desert of Egypt, which were under the control and protection of the army.[17] The text on the ostracon is a Greek translation of the Latin original in which the prefect of Egypt ordered that his judgement on the case regarding two soldiers accused of abandoning their comrades in an attack by local barbarians be publicised in the military forts around the quarries. The involvement of the prefect of Egypt (who served as governor over the entire province) as opposed to a lower functionary was due to the severity of the offence. The governor spoke Latin, but he had his order circulate in Greek translation, since that was the language of the majority of the soldiers stationed there as well as of the local administration.

In some administrative documents, both Greek and Latin were used, but the texts written in each of them usually differed in content and function. For example, a text in one language could be a summary of the original in the other, such as we find with the birth certificate of a daughter born to the Roman soldier Longinus by his concubine in Philadelphia in the Fayum on 26 December 131 CE. The wax tablet in question first provides a Latin text mentioning among other things the military affiliation of Longinus, the names of his daughter and concubine, and the place and date of the girl's birth. This is followed by a summary in Greek, which encompasses a simple acknowledgement of birth and refers to details in the text above it—that is, to the Latin document.[18]

The different functions of the two languages are most conspicuous in Roman and late antique legal proceedings from Egypt. In these, the highly formalised header of the document would be in Latin, the description of the case in Greek, and the judge's ruling in Latin, which would sometimes itself be followed by a translation of the verdict in Greek. Evidently, the parties to such lawsuits were Greek-speaking, while the

---

[15] That is, Egypt under Persian rule (526–404/401 BCE); see Quack 2021.
[16] Quack 2020.
[17] For an edition of the letter (O.Claud. inv. 7218), see Bülow-Jacobsen 2013.
[18] Viereck/Zucker 1926, no. 1690. For the image, cf. the *Berliner Papyrusdatenbank* online at https://berlpap.smb.museum/04001/ (accessed 28/9/2021).

Fig. 1: Letter from the Governor Qurra ibn Šarīk, 709 CE. P. Heid. inv. Arab. 12 recto. © Institut für Papyrologie, Universität Heidelberg.

legal ruling was pronounced in Latin and then made accessible to the Greek-speaking audience. For the same reason, the notarial authentication[19] of Greek documents was often made in Latin.

An illustrative example of a multilingual document from medieval Egypt is a letter from the Arabic Governor Qurra ibn Šarīk dated to 709 CE (Fig. 1), which addresses the settlement of Aphrodito in Upper Egypt and demands that a local tax be paid. Presumably so as to make the document more understandable at the local level, the Arabic text in the first seven lines was translated below into Greek. Additionally, instead of

---

19 See Thesis 31 below.

the Islamic Hijri calendar date mentioned in the upper part, the lower Greek text uses the corresponding date according to the local pre-Islamic Alexandrian calendar.[20]

In antiquity, the combination of texts of equivalent content in more than one language is rare in administrative documents. A notable exception is an edict aiming to curb abuse of the postal or transport system (*vehiculatio* or *cursus publicus*), issued by the governor of Galatia, Sextus Sotidius Strabo Libuscidianus after ca. 14 CE and inscribed on stone in Latin and Greek. Since the edict regulates in minute detail what travellers are entitled to and what the local population is obliged to provide them with, it functions as local administrative writing and aims to address not only the governing elite, but also the widest strata of the population. Both the choice of the inscriptional form for the document, which was also widely circulated on portable media, and the inclusion of the original Latin can be explained by the efforts at enforcing the regulations (hence the monumental form and positioning of the Latin text before the Greek) and by the necessity of expanding the text's audience. Since abuse was perpetrated mostly by travelling soldiers, many of whom were Latin speakers even in this eastern province, the promulgation of the Latin version helped to ensure that no one could plead ignorance of the governor's decree.[21]

The cases from Egypt and Rome show attempts at accommodating in what is written the reality of a multilingual audience to whom documents were addressed, yet they hardly reflect the entirety of languages spoken in these places. This points to the significance of the spoken word in executing administrative measures on the ground.

This can clearly be seen in post-conquest England in the late eleventh and early twelfth centuries. As far as we can trace the documents of local agents in this period, they do not differ from those issued by the king in terms of language; they were written in Latin.[22] Nevertheless, the bulk of the practical administrative work on the ground was conducted orally, and if royal agents were unable to communicate with locals, they had to make use of interpreters. This shows firstly that local administration did not depend on the written word; governance by the spoken word continued to play an important role especially in multilinguistic polities. Secondly, the documents issued by the king and those by his agents or indeed other lords provided a very coherent picture in terms of their language. Indeed, this coherence may have been their major aim: to convey first and foremost the authority of rulers. This also means that the deployment of language did not reflect or communicate a dichotomy between the ruler on the one side and his agents on the other: when it came to communicating lordly authority, they used the same materialised language. In this respect, rulership and administrative writings were one, and as a consequence, the practical necessities of multilingual communication were left to the sphere of orality.

---

20 SB I 5638; cf. Richter 2010.
21 Mitchell 1976.
22 The practice of latinising English words in writing points to the practical limits of multilingualism.

Multilingual and Multiscriptal Monuments and Manuscripts: Claims to Imperial Rule

Multilingualism was also well suited to bolstering the positive image of a ruler, be it as part of the display of military successes or the proclamation of prominent administrative measures. Although numerous examples inscribed in just one language exist,[23] the presence of several languages and scripts is not infrequent in this genre of texts.

In Ancient Egypt, rare occasions make it possible to compare royal inscriptions on quite different media. For the struggle of King Kamose (ca. 1550 BCE) against the Hyksos, who were of Asiatic descent and had occupied part of Egypt, there exist versions of the royal deeds written in hieroglyphs on stone stelae as well as in cursive 'hieratic' writing on a wooden board. The differences are limited to orthographic matters without any real difference on the linguistic level.

Multilingual decrees from Ptolemaic Egypt, including the one preserved on the famous Rosetta Stone, recorded the decisions of priestly synods that had an administrative impact, such as regulations on the celebration of feasts or the creation of new priestly groups. That such decisions were not only preserved, but also engraved monumentally on stone or metal—as was already prescribed at the end of the original text—shows that they also fulfilled the function of rulership writings. The languages and scripts used include not only Greek and Demotic Egyptian as the then-contemporary languages, but also hieroglyphs, which created a link to the millennia-old indigenous tradition of the country. This symbolically highly-loaded hieroglyphic version of the text comes first on the Rosetta Stone on the upper part of the stele, whereas Greek was placed at the bottom, even though it was the language of the ruling class at the time.

Examples of purely monumental rulership texts that do not contain practical decisions hail from the Achaemenid Empire. The large inscription of Darius I (r. 522–486 BCE) at Bisitun (Behistun)—a long record of the deeds of the king, especially his fight against different rebels and 'lying kings'—was made in cuneiform script in Old Persian as the language of the political elite; in Elamite, the local administrative language; and in Babylonian, the language of neighbouring Mesopotamia (Fig. 2). Fragments of a version on a stele found in Babylon only give the Babylonian version; a papyrus found at Elephantine in Egypt presents a translation into Aramaic. The Canal Stele documenting the creation of a waterway between the Nile and the Red Sea gives an Old Persian and a hieroglyphic Egyptian version. A statue of Darius I, discovered in Susa but probably originally conceived for erection in Heliopolis in Egypt, also preserves hieroglyphic Egyptian, cuneiform Old Persian, Elamite, and Babylonian inscriptions. The inscriptions stress that the statue should serve as a witness to the Persian conquest of Egypt; that is probably the reason why the different cuneiform

---

23 As in the case of the first Chinese empire, see Kern 2000.

Fig. 2: Bisitun rock inscription in Old Persian, Elamite, and Babylonian, all in cuneiform script. Public Domain, via Wikimedia Commons: https://commons.wikimedia.org/wiki/File:Behistun_inscription_reliefs.jpg (accessed 28/9/2021).

versions are utilised in three different languages, more than would be needed for those actually interacting with it in its original context.[24] Note that monuments such as the Rosetta Stone or the Bisitun Inscription may be termed both 'multilingual' as well as 'multiscriptal', since over the course of millennia, both languages (such as Egyptian) as well as writing systems (such as cuneiform) changed so much that the concepts of a unitary 'language' and 'writing system' become blurred.

The multilingualism of the Bisitun inscription[25] finds later parallels in monumentally published accounts of royal achievements in the Hellenistic and Roman periods in the Mediterranean and other regions. The choice of languages can serve the pragmatic purpose of broadcasting the message to a wider population, but it can also be symbolic, since a language may carry a claim to political and cultural associations. Furthermore, although there is usually little difference in content among versions in different languages, a translation may display concerted efforts to accommodate the

---

[24] Schmitt 2009, 36–96. On the Canal Stele, see Mahlich 2020.
[25] Part of the inscription reads: "I am Darius the king, [...] the King of Kings, [...] the king of Persia [...] These are the countries that listen to me [...]: Persia, Elam, Babylonia, Assyria, Arabia, Egypt, the Sealand, Sardis, Ionia, Media, Urartu, Cappadocia, Parthia, Drangiana, Aria, Choresmia, Bactria, Sogdiana, Gandhara, Scythia, Sattagydia, Arachosia, and Maka, in total twenty-three countries. [...]" (translation by Van De Mieroop 2016, 328). Instead of 'countries that listen to me' the Babylonian version reads 'countries that obey me' while the Elamite text states 'countries that call themselves mine' (our translation from German provided by Borger/Hinz 1983–1985, 424).

concepts of the original message to its translated version and to the cultural expectations of the local audience.

Such intentions are apparent in the edicts of the Emperor Ashoka of the Mauryan Empire (mid-third-century BCE) in India, which comprised historical accounts along with a collection of the moral and religious precepts the emperor strove to implement. The edicts, composed in Prakrit, were promulgated and inscribed in various Indic scripts, as well as in Greek and Aramaic translations. The Greek version shows considerable effort to align the original to the Hellenistic cultural background of the Greek colonists in Alexandria in Arachosia (modern Kandahar).[26]

The most famous accounts of Roman imperial achievements, the *Res gestae divi Augusti* ('Deeds of the Divine Augustus'),[27] originally composed in Latin ca. 14 CE, survive in three inscriptional publications from the distant province of Galatia, where they were inscribed either in both Latin and Greek, or in only one of the languages, with the choice apparently depending on the composition of the local population. Remarkably, the Greek version employs at least four Greek words to render different shades of meaning of the Latin word *imperium*, attesting to the particular effort put into translating concepts of special significance.[28]

The tradition of multilingual records of deeds was continued by the rulers of kingdoms at the borders of the Roman Empire. Thus, the *Res gestae divi Saporis* ('Deeds of the Divine Shapur', before 272 CE)—a trilingual inscription set up during the reign of the Sasanian King Shapur I northwest of Persepolis, in today's Fars Province of Iran—comprised versions of the text in Middle Persian, Parthian, and Greek.[29] The translation of the text, which extolled the king's victories against the Romans, into Greek may have been both pragmatic (by addressing a wider audience) as well as symbolic (by linking into the tradition of Roman *res gestae* literature).

If the materialised languages used different sign systems, it was particularly easy to distinguish the languages even from afar. While the contexts in which such monuments can be found greatly varied, a common message links them all, sometimes more prominently than on other occasions: namely, the ruler's claim to imperial rule (in this context meaning the rule over several distinct polities). Yet multilingualism was only one aspect of monumental writing. It is therefore necessary to turn our attention to the topology of writing and to look closer at how and where rulership writings could be staged and displayed.

---

26 I. Estremo Oriente, nos. 290–292.
27 Cf. Chapter 2, p. 99.
28 For a recently updated edition, see *Res gestae divi Augusti* (ed. by John Scheid). See also Cooley 2012 and the next section.
29 Huyse 1999.

Thesis 29
Geographical or geopolitical space may contribute to the prestige and authority of a rulership text by associating the agent behind the text with the authority of the place.

The efficiency of the inscribed message, its authority and its audience, could be affected by non-textual parameters, among which the textual topology is of particular significance. Topology might endow a rulership text with power, regardless of whether or not the authority behind the message is explicitly named in the text, since the inscribed text may exploit the authority of the location of the monument or object on which it is inscribed. In the case of administrative texts, authority could be affected by such factors as access to and use of the texts or circumstances surrounding their deposition. Moreover, a change of setting could lead to a change in function, from that of administrative to rulership writing.

Location: Geographical or geopolitical space—whether at the 'centre of the world' (for example, Delphi in Greece) or at the heart of the empire in Rome—contributed to the prestige and authority of the inscribed message. The text of the abovementioned *Res gestae divi Augusti* details how the emperor placed "the whole world" under the sovereignty of the Roman people. Promulgated probably in papyrus copies across the Roman Empire and inscribed on various monuments in its provinces, the text opens with a declaration that the account is a copy of the text engraved on bronze pillars in Rome.[30] This very statement endows the message displayed in a remote province with the authority of the original's location in the centre of the empire, while making manifest the subordination of the place where the inscription stands to the power of Rome.

In non-typographical societies, the spreading of information entailed access to and control over an assembly of people. Whereas in the modern age information comes to people—be it in the form of a newspaper or television or any other kind of mass media—in non-typographical societies, people had to go to the source of the information, whether it was in the form of an oral announcement or a publicly displayed text. A place frequented by people, such as one of particular religious or civic significance, would be a fitting location not only for the most efficient spreading of the message, and would also enhance the prestige of any text displayed or proclaimed there. Since the publication of a text in such a location would be restricted to a governing body, the displayed message encompassed the authority of that body and functioned thereby as rulership writing, no matter whether the ruler was an emperor or a body of citizens. Thus, the ten taxiarchs, high-ranking military leaders in classical Athens, posted conscription lists inscribed on whitened boards in the Agora, presum-

---

[30] *Res gestae divi Augusti* 1.

ably the most frequented place in the city, as a manifestation of their authority over the conscription process for upcoming military expeditions.[31]

It is probably due to public accessibility and the function of the location where a message is displayed that there is a tendency across various cultures to display rulership texts in places of religious significance. The combination of affording public attention with the placement of the message under the protection of the divine comes into play. For example, the display of many archaic and classical Greek interstate treaties on bronze tablets affixed to the walls of the sanctuary of Zeus in Olympia or the practice of inscribing laws on the walls of the major temple of a polis emphasise the interplay of rulership and religion.[32]

The importance of the location in which administrative texts are deposited is well illustrated by the frequent storage of civic documents in Greek sanctuaries. The purpose of this is usually the preservation of the documents and possibly also the limitation or at least the regulation of access to them, which aims to prevent tampering with the documents and thus to ensure their validity. The official administrative records of the city of Athens were kept in the Metroon, which was not only a sanctuary of the Mother of the Gods but also the state archive.[33] Also, citations of administrative texts, be they in public inscriptions or in copies from law texts, frequently referred to the archival deposition of the base texts, buttressing the notion that the texts were valid and authentic.[34]

Setting: The interplay of a monumentally inscribed text and its setting is well illustrated several centuries later by the charters of Emperor Henry V (r. 1099–1125), which he had inscribed on the façade of the cathedral of Speyer in August 1111 on the occasion of the burial of his father, Emperor Henry IV (r. 1056–1106).[35] Speyer cathedral, which had been the spiritual centre and the burial place of Henry V's forebears, the Salian emperors, was the embodiment in stone of the Salians' self-perception as the vicars of Christ on earth. Yet, the charters Henry V had engraved on the façade of the cathedral did not confer further privileges on the church, but rather granted liberties to the citizens of Speyer.

Henry's choice of the façade was not simply rooted in the fact that the cathedral was the most prominent building in Speyer; the choice in and of itself was also a statement. First, by appropriating the cathedral's façade, Henry V made clear who was in charge; he ruled not only over the state, but over the church as well. Second, he used the cathedral to manifest a change of policy towards the church, because the liberties

---

31 Cf. Andrewes 1981; Lougovaya 2013.
32 Hölkeskamp 1992; Christ 2001. For an updated list of published inscribed bronze tablets from Olympia, see Siewert 2018.
33 Wycherley 1957, 150–160; Sickinger 1999, esp. 114–138.
34 For Chinese legal texts, see Loewe 1965.
35 Most recently discussed by Scholz 2011a–c.

Henry granted the citizens limited the rights of the bishop. While there is no doubt that Speyer retained some importance for Henry as an imperial bishopric and as the family's burial place, it is also clear that the bishop and his cathedral were no longer cornerstones of Henry's kingship which they had been under his forebears. Henry instead turned to other sources, especially to the citizens of the flourishing towns, which were to reshape the political, social and economic landscape for centuries to come. To put all this on the cathedral's wall in golden letters was as drastic a message as could be imagined.

While the meaning and authority of inscribed texts might be informed by their setting, the process is reciprocal, because inscriptions can mark and thus create meaningful context. This can be seen in inscriptions associated with sanctuaries, which display texts announcing the special status of their grounds.[36] For example, four stelae inscribed with copies of a royal decree granting the right of asylum and inviolability to the sanctuaries of Isis and Penephros in Theadelphia in the Fayum were set up in order to mark literally the territory covered by such rights.[37] Personal conduct or the performance of rituals within the sanctuary could also be regulated by means of inscriptions, which range from the frequently attested requirements of purity on the part of those entering the sanctuary[38] to the mysterious prohibition on boiling falcon heads in the newly excavated Falcon Shrine in the town of Berenike.[39] These inscriptions literally proclaim rulership over the spaces they delineate by displaying the rules that apply within them.

Staging: The promulgation of commands necessarily implies the usage of portable media or oral communication. In societies that did not make use of writing or refrained from using it in certain types of communications, such as that described in the Homeric epics, a set of codified rituals could accompany the delivery of a rulership message, for example, the use of a scepter by a herald charged with delivering the message. With the advance of writing, a royal letter becomes one of the most common ways of exercising power. The staging of such transmission of power may sometimes endow the message with more power than the issuer himself or the content of the message could have effected, as is illustrated both in Herodotus and in medieval German romances, to give only two examples.

In the story of the fall of Oroetes, a satrap of Lydia appointed by Cyrus the Great, the protagonist outlives both Cyrus and his successor, Cambyses, indulging in his growing power for the sake of which he does not shun turning against the Persian nobles who dared to cross him. When Darius becomes king, he is wary of the power

---

36 See also Chapter 5, Thesis 25.
37 Two copies of the former (I.Fay. II 112 and II 113, dated 19/2/93) and three of the latter (I.Fay. II 116–118, dated 22/10/57) survive.
38 Cf. for example, Petrovic/Petrovic 2018.
39 Oller Guzmán et al. 2022.

and atrocities of Oroetes, yet wishes to avoid direct confrontation with the satrap, whose guard comprises a thousand spearmen. Bagaeus, a Persian noble, comes up with a plan: he goes to Sardis, the seat of Oroetes, with many letters bearing Darius's seal. There, he hands them one after the other to the royal scribes to read out, all while watching their reaction. Seeing that they have great respect for the rolls and what is written on them, he proceeds to give the scribes a letter demanding that the guards abandon Oroetes. As the command is read out, the guards lay down their spears. When Bagaeus hands over the final letter, in which King Darius charges the Persians to kill Oroetes, the spearmen immediately do so. The message of the king, through the cunning staging of its delivery, achieves what the king, in person, might not have been able to achieve.[40]

Letters were also a common way of communication between authorities later on in the Middle Ages. The thirteenth-century chivalric romance *Willehalm von Orlens* by Rudolf von Ems describes letters exchanged between King Witekin of Denmark and King Amilot of Norway and shows that not only writing itself, but also its staging, could function as a demonstration of power. The visual-haptic presence of King Witekin's letter is narrated in detail, with the letter being richly decorated with a golden seal.[41] Even though political letters in this specific cultural context were usually sealed—in contrast to private communication by letters—this particular material of the seal needs to be highlighted, since the seal itself not only serves as a mechanism of authentication and a protection, but the fact that it is made of gold also demonstrates Witekin's wealth and power.[42] It is effective even before the letter is read. Furthermore, in presenting the letter, the messenger executes a performative function. He stages King Witekin's rulership and foresight, all the more so by handing out two more letters that are sealed in the same way. Witekin does not wait for Amilot's answer; instead, he presents documents of both King Girat of Estonia and King Gutschart of Livonia, who in turn guarantee their support of the Danish king against his Norwegian counterpart. The material presence of these two letters overshadows their content, which is only briefly summarised.[43] Ultimately, the materiality of the letters and their successive presentations, especially with the use of the same golden seal for all three letters, are shown to be more important than the content of the message they contain.

Finally, it bears mentioning that it is not only the delivery of the rulers' commands that may be staged. By contrast, for the effect of memorials or petitions to the ruler, it can be even more critical how their submission is staged because the status of their sender or the circumstances of regular delivery do not always imbue such missives with the kind of importance or urgency that the sender may regard as essential or desirable. In these cases, a certain amount of theatrics are in order. In the early Chinese empires,

---

40 Herodotus, *Historiae* 3.127. Cf. Briant 2002, 344–345.
41 Rudolf von Ems, *Willehalm von Orlens*, line 10 549.
42 For more on seals, see the section on authentication below.
43 Rudolf von Ems, *Willehalm von Orlens*, lines 10 652–10 653.

for instance, memorials by high-ranking officials were usually handed in and read out aloud to the emperor and the assembled ministers in the large audience hall to which only the privileged had access. The only chance for the common folk to have their petitions heard by the emperor, however, was to try and elbow their way to a particular streetside palace gate in order to hand in their petitions to a palace official. Sometimes, though, if a high-ranking official wanted to draw particular attention to his memorial, he would also choose this self-deprecating way of handing in a petition instead and creating the scandal necessary for garnering for himself the desired attention.[44]

Thesis 30
A change in the materiality of a particular text often signals a shift in the function of the document.

This section looks at the production, physical properties, size or dimension, and form or shape of inscribed artefacts, all while seeking to address the following questions: what motivated rulers, administrators, or other producers of inscribed artefacts operating within a state to choose specific types of writing support? Why were particular types of stelae or other monumental or non-monumental artefacts chosen for official purposes? How did their choice influence the reception of the inscribed artefact in the communicative process?

Material Properties and Conditions: The physical (and chemical) properties of any writing material are experienced as hardness, colour, mass, density, structure, and durability in terms of the raw materials used, which could include naturally occurring stone, clay, bone, wood, bark, bamboo, hide, etc., or processed materials such as metal, textiles (esp. silk), papyrus, parchment, or paper. Moreover, factors such as abundance and accessibility can also affect how the material is perceived.

Mass, hardness, abundance, or accessibility, in addition to production conditions, set limits for the size afforded by a specific writing material. A rare substance such as gold cannot be made into monumental stelae (although it can be used to gild such stelae). The dimensions of cloth depend on the size of the loom used in weaving; those of traditionally produced paper, on the dimensions of the screen used.

Size as well as shape and weight also determine the potential mobility of an inscribed artefact. The size of some naturally shaped materials—for example, bovine shoulder blades, elephant tusks, turtle shells, or palm leaves—does of course limit the size of the inscribed artefact produced from them. But even the internal biological or physical structure of a raw material may influence the possible sizes and shapes of the artefact to be made from it. The vertical growth and fibrous structure of fast-growing

---
[44] Giele 2006, 109–111.

bamboo, for example—possibly the first writing material in China—may have affected the design of narrow, oblong writing slips as well as their vertical orientation, and thus predisposed the writing of Chinese script to the vertical direction, a situation that survived nearly into the present as the predominant direction of writing for the language.[45]

There is also the economic side to writing materials. An artefact's production cost and its prestige are determined not only by the rarity or abundance of its basic material substance, but also by the skill and labour required to transform it into a suitable writing surface and then to inscribe a message on it. That inscriptions on bronze, for example, required engravers or casters who possessed specialised skills and tools was a major reason for the limited supply and exceptional prestige of inscribed bronze vessels. Equally important is the fact that bronze could only be produced with access to tin. It is therefore no coincidence that, in many societies, a list of names inscribed in bronze or gold is perceived as being more significant than one made on inexpensive materials (for example, papyrus or ceramic sherds), even when both inscribed artefacts carry an identical text.

Ascribed Values: Beyond the physical properties, natural occurrence, and economic value, material substances usually have culturally or individually ascribed values. Types of stone such as granite, marble or limestone are examples of substances of choice for monumental inscriptions, which are then rather immobile. Marble in particular is a medium that was found by the Greeks and Romans to be very suitable for carving inscriptions because of its relative malleability, durability, and availability in many places (though not in Egypt, where marble was rare). It is also regarded by many as being beautiful, and certain varieties deemed exceptionally valuable (esp. Parian marble or, in the Roman imperial period, marble from Proconessus) could be chosen to enhance the prestige invested in the inscribed message.[46]

Gold's prestige as a 'royal' material par excellence in the west (but less so in China, where jade was highly valued instead) can be attributed not only to its rarity, but especially to its near absolute resistance to chemical changes. In practice, characters engraved in or applied to stone could be gilded or formed with metal: gold foil could be affixed to small tiles *(tesserae)* and used in the formation of words in mosaics, and in monumental texts bronze lettering often imitates gold. In short, these materials and colours were (and are) typically more highly regarded than other options such as limestone (stationary) and ceramic sherds (portable).

Other examples of materials and colours associated with a ruler's authority are purple, green, and—to a lesser extent—vermilion, again due to the rarity of the substance (Tyrian purple or the mineral cinnabar, respectively) or to the conspicuousness or similarity of the colour itself to (precious) blood. Transmitted sources record that the decrees of the Han emperors were to be sealed with purple clay and packed in

---

45 See also Chapter 2, Thesis 7.
46 On the ideological aspects of the use of marble, cf. Maischberger 1997; Paton/Schneider 1999.

green bags.⁴⁷ In the Byzantine Empire as well as in medieval Europe, purple parchment inscribed with gold or silver letters was sometimes used for biblical codices or charters, such as the purple marriage charter of Otto II (r. 973–983) for his wife Theophanu.⁴⁸ However, while purple is decidedly a dye for imperial clothes in the Roman and Byzantine tradition, it seems not as common a colour or substance for writing. Neither was vermilion cinnabar, or in general bright red, necessarily exclusively associated with political rulership in Rome or Byzantium. The most prominent example of this connection being made are the 'vermilion endorsements' added by the emperor himself in Qing Chinese documents.⁴⁹ In Egypt as well as medieval Europe, on the other hand, red ink simply served to highlight ('rubricate') lettering, without connoting any association of text or inscription to royal authority.⁵⁰

Shape and Size: Shapes and sizes, too, tend to be influenced by cultural values, even when other forms and dimensions than the ones encountered would be possible to produce. The connection between form and textual content could sometimes be so close that a mere glance at the form sufficed to recognise the authority conveyed by an artefact. Consider the Qin-Han (221 BCE–220 CE) edicts: despite being written on everyday (and less permanent) materials such as wood or bamboo, the size of their writing supports was larger than that used for other types of administrative writing.⁵¹ Transmitted sources also indicate that during the Han period, legal codes were to be written on bamboo or wooden strips approximately 55.5 cm long, which was much longer than what was used for day-to-day administrative documents.⁵² When the Han emperor sent a diplomatic note to his counterpart, the khan of the Huns or Xiongnu, the khan used wooden strips for writing that were two centimetres longer than those of the Chinese emperor, thus clearly making a political statement expressed not in words per se, but rather in the material conveying such words.⁵³

This was also the case with the military diplomata issued across the Roman Empire to non-citizen veterans. These usually take the form of diptych-like bronze rectangular tablets, hinged together and sealed with wax. On both of the inner sides is inscribed the

---

47 Green was another colour closely associated with the Han emperor, as it symbolised the notion of birth. Such a symbolic meaning continued in the early medieval period, where it was reported that the imperial decrees of Western Jin (266–316 CE) emperors were written on green paper; see Tomiya 2010, 22–28.
48 Niedersächsisches Staatsarchiv, Wolfenbüttel, 6 Urk. II.
49 Wilkinson 2012, 280.
50 For red ink being used in ancient Egypt, see Posener 1951.
51 Additionally, appellations such as 'Your/His Majesty' or the clause 'The imperial decision says: approved' were usually highlighted to stress rulers' authority: cf. Giele 2006, 100–101; Tomiya 2010, 31–38; Staack 2018, 275, n. 101.
52 Tomiya 2010, 44–45.
53 Sima Qian et al., *Shiji* 110, 2899; for an English translation, see Sima Qian et al., *The Grand Scribe's Records*, vol. IX, 274.

extract (twice, usually in different hands) of the *ad personam* imperial decree granting Roman citizenship to the veteran and legal status to his wife; on one of the outer sides is inscribed once again the extract; the other outer side has the names of the witnesses with a seal. This unique arrangement of the texts on the mass-produced artefact evokes both the administrative authenticity and the authority given to the artefacts.[54]

There are also many culturally specific names and terms for the different formats of writing materials, too many in fact to recount here. However, what seems to act almost globally as a unifying force is the principle of affordance. Viewed from the side of the recipient or handler, the dimensions of writing materials have certainly also been shaped by the size and functionality of the human body. When the Sumerians picked up a lump of clay from the ground to form a writing tablet, they made sure that it fit snugly into their hands, which determined both the tablet's size and shape. Furthermore, it cannot be a coincidence that in many cultures, the dimensions and shapes of sheet-like writing supports (such as is used in state administration and other types of everyday writing) are similar to the distance formed by two hands casually extended outwards, that is, about shoulder-width or a bit shorter (20–40 cm) for some purposes. Another factor is that the length of a line of written text that the human eye is usually able to capture at close reading distance during one saccade (that is, in a single glance or period of fixation) is shorter than twenty centimetres.[55] These biological conditions of the human species may have determined the usual length of a line of writing.[56] Thus, it is not surprising to find standard writing materials of similar dimensions around the world, especially in the area of day-to-day administrative writing, while enlarging these dimensions—a phenomenon also seemingly encountered across the world—could betray a ruler's intention to impress.

Writing Material in the Context of Political Rule and Administration: Rulership writing seeks to display, establish, and legitimise political rule, and is often publicly displayed to this end. It also needs to be long-lasting, at least until the next ruler produces writings to support his or her own claim to power. All this would imply that writing materials for rulership writing should be not only durable and capable of monumentality (so as to be publicly visible), but also perhaps impressive, awe-inspiring, and beautiful, so that the message might be supported by the appeal of the medium and become all the more persuasive.

This is why rulership writing is frequently found inscribed on prestigious surfaces—often immobile and monumental (such as a cliff, rock or wall)—but also on small, mobile precious artefacts. By contrast, administrative writing, which occured

---

54 For a short introduction to this type of document, see Speidel 2015, 338, and Eck 2003; see also the discussion in Thesis 31 below.
55 Naturally, this biological fact also applies differently to different writing systems (alphabetical or logographical) and different writing directions (vertical or horizontal); see Behr/Führer 2005, 32–33.
56 See also Chapter 2 'Layout, Design, Text-Image'.

ubiquitously and in much larger volumes than rulership writing, could not have been too expensive and should have been easy to handle and standardise with respect to size and shape. After all, in a large polity, many government personnel—not all of whom were highly trained—had to handle such documents. The materials for administrative writing in general, therefore, has to be flexible, portable, easy to transport, and suitable for a variety of applications, including effective archiving. Though stone-like durability is certainly not required, since administrative information in general tends to be ephemeral, such materials cannot be too fragile or volatile so as to withstand the conditions of transportation and archiving.

Finally, writing materials may also be chosen with a view to preventing fabrication and forgery. In non-typographical societies, exceptional functionality, high production costs, and premium-quality materials—seen, for example, in gold coins bearing the portrait of a potentate—defined or increased the efficacy of inscribed artefacts bearing rulership writing, since the message partook of the aura of its material and had the potential to evoke awe in those beholding it. On the other hand, everyday inscribed artefacts made of humble and/or inexpensive materials but which participated in political or economic administrative processes—such as ceramic jars onto which an inscription specifying their contents and volume had been applied—represent administrative writings, not only because of their mundane function, but also on account of their materiality.

If there is a shift in the materiality whereby the inscribed artefact acquired enhanced exclusivity, this suggests that regardless of the textual content, authority was intended to be displayed. If the materials became more ordinary, this testifies to a more prosaic, pragmatic administrative function.[57] One such example of a shift in function through material change and monumentalisation are the inscribed building accounts from the Acropolis in Athens, which were carved on a marble stele in 408/407 BCE.[58] To inscribe the Athenian building accounts in stone for public display, in addition to writing them down with ink and stowing them away in the relative seclusion of an archive, was an expression of authority, a sign of the grandeur of the building enterprise and a symbol of political accountability.

It is noteworthy that monumentalisation did not always enhance the authority of the ruler alone. In many cultures (though far from all), the political authority invested by a potentate in any document which granted rights or privileges also encouraged the ruled to make copies of the document by using even more prestigious materials, glorifying both themselves and the ruler. Examples include Eastern Han stelae inscribed with the text of official letters pertinent to the regulations instituted by the central government or agreements made between a local government and a private individual or

---

[57] See also Chapter 3, Thesis 17.
[58] IG I³,1 476, dated 408/407 BCE; text and translation: https://www.atticinscriptions.com/inscription/IGI3/476 (accessed 27/9/2021); image: https://commons.wikimedia.org/wiki/File:EPMA_6667-IG_I(3) 476-Erechtheion_accounts-1.JPG (accessed 27/9/2021).

a community.⁵⁹ One should additionally note that users of this type of administrative 'letter monuments' also usually endeavoured to recreate the layout and other material traits of the original letters despite the change in material. This is exemplified by two stelae datable to 153 and 159 CE respectively from Shandong and Henan provinces.⁶⁰

The dynamics between the two factors of 'function' and 'materiality' sometimes make it difficult to determine if an inscribed artefact conveys authority because of the specific material(s) used to produce it, or if the authority of a ruler as the ultimate or ostensible origin of a written message encourages a writer to choose a prestigious material for the task. At any rate, the authority (or lack of authority) of what is written on such artefacts is embodied in their materiality. Therefore, setting materiality and its concomitant practices (which may also translate into production or transaction costs) as a decisive criterion helps us to discern more clearly the spectrum between the poles of rulership writing and administrative writing. This would be difficult to do if the criteria were only textual content or intent, as these aspects are not readily quantifiable, whereas material and transactional costs are.

A good example for the applicability of the materiality criterion is the genre of travel permits or visas, in which we observe an astonishing range of practices and documents, even within a single culture. In China under the Western Han (206 BCE–9 CE), long-distance travel was strictly limited and commoners were required to apply for permits for their journeys through checkpoints along the way. Usually, applicants had to submit information such as personal characteristics, criminal records, type of vehicle used, belongings, travel companions, and so on to the authorities, who would verify the submitted data and, if approved, issue the requisite permits or visas. Such travel documents were written on wooden or bamboo writing supports not particularly large in size and inscribed in non-decorative clerical script. Thus they were by no means extraordinary with regard to their material characteristics.

By observing the materiality and associated practices of these travel documents more closely, however, we can make out quantifiable grades. A first parameter that is readily quantifiable (and visible) is any change in size. Moreover, even a run-of-the-mill small travel permit could increase in material- and transaction-based prestige if it acquired a seal from an issuing authority; this prestige would be even greater in the case of a multi-piece tally. Furthermore, in case the authority's parts of the tallies were to be transported to the checkpoint in special bags or containers, or delivered by special courier, the sovereign's authority and/or the urgency of the affair would again have been heightened to a certain degree. Finally, the realm of rulership writing is once again encountered with a set of travel and tax-exempt trade permits or tallies, such as

---

59 One specimen dated to 153 CE documents an imperial edict approving the creation of an additional junior official exclusively serving in the Temple of Confucius in Qufu, Shandong, as well as the subsequent correspondence between the central and provincial governments with regard to the selection of a suitable candidate for this new position; see Hou 2014.
60 For images, see *Kandai sekkoku shūsei*, nos. 70 and 80; cf. also Chapter 2, Thesis 11.

Fig. 3: Two of five travel permits by Qi, Lord of E, cast in bronze in the shape of bamboo segments with gold-inlay writing, dated to 323 BCE, Hubei Province, China. Photo from the catalogue of the bronzes kept at the Museum of Anhui Province. © Anhui Museum.

those for merchants issued by Qi, the sovereign of the regional state of E, dated to the year 323 BCE, which form a set of five oversized pieces, cast in bronze in the shape of bamboo tube segments and inlayed with ornate golden characters (Fig. 3).[61]

---

[61] For discussions of commoners' requirements for passport applications in the Western Han period, see Sou 2018, 229–230, and Takatori 2020. For the bronze permits from the regional state of E, see Falkenhausen 2005.

Having discussed the various materials, their affordances, and how they can be shaped to serve as rulership and administrative writings, we now narrow our focus to look at layout, script, the use of iconography, and means of authentication.

> **Thesis 31**
> Layout can considerably alter the significance of texts and allows for a distinction between rulership writing and administrative writing. From the layout, one can gauge the degree of sophistication and standardisation of an administration.

Once a writing support has been selected and created, writing as well as (potentially) images can be inscribed on or applied to it. The choice of layout is important as it defines the relationship between different parts of the writing or writing and images.[62] As with the writing itself and potential images, the neatness and complexity of the layout is an indicator of how much care has been invested in the drafting process. At the outset, the properties of the material provide a framework for the layout: the size of a sheepskin or the shape and condition of a rock, for instance. Within that framework, regularity, neatness, and complexity can be used not only to estimate the degree of sophistication and standardisation of an administration, but also to identify different production steps and consequently a certain procedural hierarchy within an administration. Drafts are by nature less carefully executed than final versions.[63]

Layout can serve to direct the reader's attention and to clarify content. For example, tax lists, financial accounts, and similar texts tend towards a tabulated layout; items are written out at the start, while the corresponding numbers or amounts are positioned (with some space before them) in a margin or at the bottom in order to facilitate the final calculations. Depending on the context of an inscribed artefact, the layout can differ even when the texts themselves deal with similar or identical matters. When, for example, we look at land registers from Graeco-Roman Egypt, differences between manuscript and monumental writing are obvious. Manuscript versions of land registers contain brief entries, which are summarised to a minimum and employ a well-tabulated layout. By contrast, a hieroglyphic monumental inscription in the temple of Edfu listing all land owned by the temple makes use of very elaborate signs, but the numerical indications are difficult to spot due to the *scriptio continua*.[64] In this case, the two kinds of inscribed artefacts differ in almost all aspects of their materiality, signalling a clear distinction of administrative from rulership writing.

---

62 On this thesis, see also Chapter 2 'Layout, Design, Text-Image'.
63 Holz 2022.
64 Quack 2015.

If the similarities between inscribed artefacts are much greater, differences in layout can indicate differences in meaning or significance. This is demonstrated by examples from the chancery of the counts palatine of the Rhine. The counts palatine, who were among the top-ranked princes in the Holy Roman Empire, began keeping written records of their seignorial privileges, prerogatives, and rights, as well as of their outgoing charters from the fourteenth century onwards. The earliest register of outgoing charters was begun in 1355,[65] with the earliest cartulary (that is, a register of incoming charters) being commissioned in 1356.[66] The almost contemporaneous register and cartulary dealt with the same content (charters), and yet their materiality makes it very evident that they are very different documents. The layout of the register is a very basic listing of copies of outgoing documents on pages from top to bottom within more or less regular margins. The manuscript is written in a cursive script, but lacks any table of contents, illuminations, or rubrics. The register thus conveys the impression of a very pragmatic, business-like document, written at speed for potential internal use only.[67] By contrast, the layout of the first cartulary shows carefully aligned copies of charters in a double column. The script is a Gothic book hand, and while illuminations are also lacking here, each entry is headed by a rubric. A table of contents is also present, facilitating orientation. In comparison with the register, the book hand and neatly arranged double column layout of the cartulary convey a much higher level of execution. Moreover, the script and layout echo the style of contemporary liturgical manuscripts, particularly those of the Bible. While it would be a step too far to attribute any liturgical character to the cartulary, the design clearly sets it apart from the register, which shows all the marks of everyday chancery work.

Thus, in relation to both administrative and rulership writing, layout provides several layers of interpretation. As a general rule of thumb, there is a correlation between the standardisation of the layout and the cleanliness of its execution on the one hand, and the professionalisation of the administration on the other hand. The validity of this observation can also be extended to working processes within an administration. The cleaner the copy, the more it approaches the final version. But there is more to layout than clean lines and an experienced hand: irrespective of the professionalisation of the writing process, the choice of the layout for texts of similar content could alter their significance quite considerably, leading to a clear distinction between texts of a more purely administrative nature and those pertaining to rulership writing. The means to communicate between the lines and in the margins, however, must be analysed on a case-by-case basis.

These observations suggest a strong relationship between layout and script at all stages: in the writing, reading, and understanding of the inscribed artefact. Therefore, we should now turn to the writing itself.

---

65 Landesarchiv Baden-Württemberg, Generallandesarchiv Karlsruhe, 67/804.
66 Landesarchiv Baden-Württemberg, Generallandesarchiv Karlsruhe, 67/799.
67 Cf. Spiegel 1996, vol. 1, 108–114.

> **Thesis 32**
> Simplified cursive handwriting, shorthands, or abbreviations are characteristic of basic forms of administrative writing. Rulership writing tends to use scripts that can convey care, durability, and faithfulness, which often leads to 'monumental' applications of script.

When processing administrative acts, speed in noting them down is of the essence. Therefore, the pressure towards faster, more economical, and more fluid forms of writing results in the development of abbreviated or simplified character shapes optimised for flowing lines. Such a running and/or simplified script is usually called 'cursive'.

Given these considerations, the form of a script appears at first to provide a relatively straightforward means of distinguishing between administrative and rulership writing. Indeed, there are many cases where such a distinction can easily be drawn, an extreme example of which is provided by Egyptian script. The immediately pictorial system of hieroglyphs remained in use as a compulsory medium for monumental inscriptions for more than three millennia, but alongside this script developed a form of cursive writing, leading eventually to the so-called hieratic script. Once this had become standardised, there was a phase of relative stability concerning long-term archiving of texts of a literary or religious nature. However, with the exception of a few specific time periods and applications, hieratic was not used in monumental display. This administrative and everyday script was more open to change and development than the complicated system of hieroglyphs, and in the early first millennium BCE, there was an innovative drive for the development of an even quicker, more cursive form: namely, the so-called Demotic script. This script is characterised not only by the significantly simpler character forms, but also (and especially) by the frequent use of abbreviations for words pertaining to administration, such as terms for grain, farm animals, or types of money. There is always a balancing act between the trend towards (time-saving) shorthand and the desire for (justiciable) clarity. The optimisation value achieved depended to a large extent on what was written and who was addressed by it. Terse notes that only the writer had to be able to read (and which were often only of ephemeral relevance) constitute the lowest requirement of refinement. Letters that were read by the sender and recipient, but not necessarily by more people, could also place lower demands on objective clarity, especially if the people in question were familiar with the individual writing habits of each other due to previous contact. Documents intended for permanent archiving such as religious and literary texts, which in the future could also be potentially read by people without prior familiarity with the writer's hand, required a higher degree of clarity.

But we would be greatly mistaken to generalise this and to say categorically that cursive script is reserved for administrative writing, whereas non-cursive script indicates rulership writing. Especially in the worlds of Chinese and Arabic writing, particularly cursive or 'fluid' calligraphy has attained high prestige as a skill and art form, thus becoming both monumentalised (transferred onto stone stelae as calligraphic models) and being used to represent rulership.

The case of Chinese or Arab cursive calligraphy epitomising high cultural and social standards and thus even being used by rulers themselves again suggests a clear dichotomy between representational rulership writing and more mundane administrative writing, which also valued cursive script but in which calligraphy as an art form played less of a role. However, the matter is even more complicated. Across times and ruling cultures, cursive scripts could be used in a very 'fluid' way across the divide between administrative and rulership writing. The Romans, for example, had firm ideas about which type of script was adequate for which function and on what type of writing support. For instance, inscribed imperial decrees and laws on tablets and/or marbles were usually in well-carved, square 'monumental' script, while administrative texts written in the private sphere — for instance, everyday contracts issued by a competent authority — were usually executed in cursive script.[68]

For administrative writing in the Roman empire, the balancing act between time-saving records and recognisable unambiguity can also be found in the usage of Latin cursive scripts. The rapid sophistication of the administrative system in the Roman Empire called for quick communication media in written form, which in turn required scripts marked by both speed and clarity. At the edge of the Empire, scribes in Londinium and Vindolanda used a cursive script (Old Roman Cursive) to write military documents, letters, and accounts. Words that appear very frequently, including monetary denominations and the names of military ranks, were abbreviated or expressed with symbols used throughout the Empire.[69] Scribes could write more efficiently and with little concern for misunderstanding by using cursive script and employing symbols and shorthand in administrative documents, since the writing system in question was considerably standardised and widely understood across the geographic area under Roman rule.

Interestingly, the dichotomy between cursive and monumental scripts frequently became blurred as their perceived functionality or the neatness of their execution varied considerably. An imperial decree from 368 CE ordered that the local chanceries not imitate the type of letters used in the imperial chancery,[70] revealing that there were

---

[68] It must be noted, though, that the function of the inscribed artefact also played a role. In principle, an edict could be transcribed in cursive or in monumental script, depending on the function of the written copy. For the distinction between cursive hands and 'epigraphic hand', namely block hands with more epigraphic elements, see Mugridge 2010.
[69] For the palaeographic features of the Vindolanda tablets, see the introduction by Alan K. Bowman and John D. Thomas in *The Vindolanda Writing Tablets*, 47–63; for Old Roman Cursive and its development in general, see Tjäder 1979 and recently Mullen/Bowman 2021.
[70] CTh 9.19.3.

different levels of hierarchy within cursive scripts at the time. On rare occasions, we can observe cursive script in inscriptions, such as in late antique imperial decrees that probably reproduced the writing of their text exactly as it appeared on the manuscript master copies.[71] On most notarised copies of Roman military diplomata, the script was square-shaped and well-carved—though not as neat as on the Lyon Tablet—in order to imbue the copies symbolically with the power of the issuing authority, namely the emperors.[72] Even many private inscriptions, such as epitaphs and private votive artefacts, are inscribed in squared letters, though less neatly than in imperial inscriptions. Broadly speaking, the material choices, locations, and intended functions of what was written all influenced scripts, which we can situate on a spectrum ranging between the two poles of cursive scripts and non-cursive, monumental ones.

The futility to consider cursive script as being a marker purely of administrative writing in contrast to rulership writing across various writing cultures is neatly exemplified by fourteenth-century charters from the governments in England and the Holy Roman Empire. These do not make use of a script distinct from other documents of the same administrations, but rather seem to be instances of rulership writing clothed in the 'business-as-usual' garb of administrative writing. It is true that the writing of these royal or imperial charters demonstrates a particularly careful and neat execution and thus could distinguish itself from charters issued by other less carefully working chanceries.[73] Nonetheless, the writing of royal charters was not itself distinguished in terms of a completely different style, as was the case for instance between the Gothic book hand and cursive script. While the charters of Emperor Louis IV (r. 1314–1347) followed the general tendency towards a more cursive script,[74] the English royal charters portrayed the general characteristics of all documents issued by the chancery.[75] In the latter case, the 'royal hand', if at all, may have been a distinguishing factor common to all documents issued by the royal chancery, but such a claim would have to be tested against detailed studies of writings issued by secular and ecclesiastical lords.[76]

While it can be argued that non-cursive, monumental scripts—with the exception of the special cases of artful calligraphy in East Asia and the Arabic-writing world—were more closely tied to rulership writings than to administrative writings,

---

[71] For an exemplary case, a stele inscribed with an imperial decree, see Feissel 2000. The decree was later compiled into *Codex Theodosianus* (CTh 1.16.8).
[72] See Eck 2003.
[73] Cf. the difference in quality between the writing of the charters of the counts palatine and those of the rulers of the Holy Roman Empire, Spiegel 1996, vol. 1, 22.
[74] Bansa 1968, 107–227; cf. Wrede 1980, 19.
[75] Danbury 2018, 270.
[76] Oftentimes, there are also methodological difficulties: the attempt to prove the existence of a certain script style that is particular to a centre of power is hampered in many disciplines (including papyrology and Early China Studies) by the fact that the vast majority of manuscript sources hail from peripheral regions and comparatively low-ranking personnel, so that originals written at the political centre by the elite simply do not survive.

an exclusive connection cannot generally be claimed here, even for Europe. Depending on the individual writing cultures, cursive scripts could also be used to represent the ruler and his or her authority.

Thesis 33
Images can reinforce the message of rulership writing, visualise the ideological framework of societal order, and address larger, less literate audiences, but they are not always an integral part of rulership writing.

The subject of the relationship between text and image is too large to be dealt with here adequately.[77] The evidence is manifold, ranging from doodles scribbled down by (bored) scribes in administrative documents to elaborate images in rulership writings, and even on seals and money.

As a medium highly controlled by the state, and moreover one produced in large quantities, coins have great potential to convey rulership messages to a large audience across the area of their use through written legends or images, which includes original designs but also countermarks.[78] While in the Sinosphere, coins normally bore their denominations and beginning in medieval times, also the era name in writing,[79] coins west of the Pamir Mountains served as 'monuments in miniature' and thus were covered with images of deities, civic symbols, rulers, or religious calligraphy together with legends, all selected by the issuing authorities to address audiences ranging from the rulers (as a kind of panegyric) to the end-users of coins (as a kind of premodern propaganda).[80]

The vast volume of coin production and the wide distribution of currency brought the symbols on them to areas speaking different languages far away from ruling centres. The Aramaic-speaking Jesus knew the emperor's portrait and inscription on the denarius when facing the Pharisees,[81] and Emperor Julian (r. 361–363 CE) became angry when people in Antioch mocked his beard and the pagan symbols on his coinage.[82] The coins of early Greek city states had very sparse legends, if at all, but were immediately recognisable and also explicitly addressed by the image they showed (oftentimes a 'heraldic' animal, such as an owl, a turtle, or horse)—a clear sign of identity

---
[77] See also the section 'Writing and Image' in Chapter 2, pp. 77–78.
[78] See Fig. 5 below for an example of countermarks on the coinage of Emperor Nero.
[79] For old Chinese coins, see Thierry 2017.
[80] Elkins 2019 offers a great overview on imagery on Roman coinage; he was the first to coin the term 'monuments in miniature' (Elkins 2015).
[81] Cf. *The Oxford Annotated Bible with Apocrypha*, Matt 22:15–22.
[82] Cf. Emperor Julian, *Misopogon* ('Beard-Hater') 355d.

creation. After Alexander the Great (r. 336–323 BCE) had conquered the Achaemenid Empire, coinage in that area began to show local potentates from very diverse cultural and linguistic backgrounds, imitating Alexander's own coins with his image (posture and paraphernalia)—a clear sign of identity imitation and political aspirations. The imagery of early Roman round coins, on the other hand, due to the Republican nature of their state, did not depict a potentate, but rather other symbols of Rome, such as a quadriga and a god or goddess—also a clear expression of political identity, when compared to the cases above.[83] These historical facts alone show that imagery on coins irrespective of any written language was consciously chosen and carried a message, which in these cases would also have been intelligible to the vast majority of illiterate people as well as the semi-literate with a limited, functional literacy allowing them to recognise and differentiate between set phrases or words on inscribed artefacts such as coins. In everyday use, however, multiple factors played a role in the efficacy of the political communication attempted via images on coinage.[84]

It is interesting to note that one of the earliest (non-monumental) expressions of a ruler's authority and glory consists more of image than of text. This is the famous Nar-Meher Palette, which displays an elaborate iconography celebrating the victorious pharaoh, with only a minimal amount of hieroglyphs scattered in between, which even at first glance seem to be merely part of the illustration. Incidentally, these have been recognised as some of the earliest phonetic writing in the world, dating to before 3000 BCE. In Egyptian royal decrees, one can see that the oldest monumentalised implementations remain purely textual (and also very faithfully imitate the complex layout of such documents on papyrus), but from the second millennium BCE onwards, we increasingly find an image added on top of the stele; mostly showing the king before one or several deities.[85]

On other instances of rulership writing, images offer the opportunity to visualise more abstract concepts of rulership and societal organisation. For example, above the text of the laws, the stele bearing the Code of Hammurabi depicts the ruler standing before the sun god, who was also the guardian of justice.[86] While this image reinforces the message inscribed on the stele, it first and foremost conveys the message that the ruler is the one to make and to enforce laws by divine providence.

---

83 A brief overview of all these cases with superior reproductions is found in Eagleton/Williams 1997, 30–43.
84 Noreña 2011 and Woytek 2018 discuss the agencies of imagery communication from the perspectives of issuers and users, respectively. Moreover, Picard 2010 and Callataÿ 2016 have described how Romans in the second century BCE paid their mercenaries in the Eastern Mediterranean mostly in various coinage bearing Hellenistic civic images in the widely recognised Attic weight standard, only introducing Roman symbols in the first century BCE as mercenaries in the Hellenistic period began to prefer coinage with higher silver content. On the interaction of users with coins, see Thesis 35 below.
85 Quack 2012.
86 Van De Mieroop 2016, 121.

Fig. 4: Louis IV's charter for Otto I and Barnim III of Pomerania-Stettin in 1338. Greifswald, Landesarchiv, Repositur 2, no. 73. © Landesarchiv Greifswald.

If we turn again to the fourteenth-century charters of the Holy Roman Emperor, Louis IV, we also occasionally find illuminations in these. A well-studied case is the charter issued in 1338 to the Pomeranian dukes Otto I (r. 1295–1344) and Barnim III (r. 1320/1344–1368), by which Louis enfeoffed them and granted them the rank of imperial prince (Fig. 4). The initial 'L' of the charter is transformed into an image representing the scene of the investiture: the emperor is seated on his throne, while Otto and Barnim kneel in front of him and hold the lance with the banner representing their new status granted by the emperor.

Just as in the case of the Code of Hammurabi, the image not only reinforces the text of the charter, but also conveys the much more general message that it is the emperor who grants the dignity of an imperial prince; the princes' authority derives from that of the emperor, who is at the helm of the Empire's social and political order. On another level, the image also communicates that from now on, Otto and Barnim were part of the elite group of imperial princes. The drawing therefore communicated — in addition to its primary message of a hierarchical relationship between the emperor and the imperial princes — a message of affiliation.[87]

Yet, if we look more closely at Louis' charters, we find that the majority of them contain no illuminations. The same can be said for the charters of his successor, Emperor Charles IV (r. 1346/7–1378). This was by no means exceptional; the contempo-

---

[87] Peltzer 2019, 22–23, with further references.

raneous English royal chancery under Edward III (r. 1327–1377) presents a similar situation. The practice of illuminating the initial of a royal charter was well known, but as in the Holy Roman Empire, this was not deployed as a regular means of royal propaganda in the English realm.[88] This points to a very important fact: even if rulers and their administrations knew about the power of images and disposed of the means to employ them on their inscribed artefacts, they could opt against using images on a regular and systematic basis. The explanation for this is a healthy reminder that the propagation of the royal image was not necessarily a priority for royal government. In England, as in the Holy Roman Empire, the recipients paid for the charters, and this payment also extended to the execution of any drawings or images to be included.[89] The decision, therefore, whether to illuminate an initial lay with the recipient and not with the royal chancery. In other words, the administrative routine behind the production of the charters outweighed the possibilities of trumpeting the royal cause. As a consequence, the parchment and letters of a charter did not serve as a platform for a systematically developed and displayed royal iconography. In connection—literally—with charters, this was left to the seal, the charter's principle means of authentication.

Thesis 34
Rulership or administrative texts, particularly those written on portable media, often required some means of material authentication in order to prove the validity of the artefact.

Once an inscribed artefact had been produced, it would often undergo a final step by which the artefact was validated so as to prove the legitimacy of its contents. Such verification processes were ubiquitous across societies, serving political, legal, and economic functions and ranging from notes or initials to signatures and seals; these all could be quite small, plain, and straightforward, or else large, ostentatious, and elaborate to emphasise a ruler's power. The focus of this section is on two examples commonly used in the context of administrative and rulership writing and which are particularly interesting from a material perspective: the seal and the tally.

Validation via seals has a long history stretching back to the ancient world. As such, different disciplines utilise the term 'seal' differently, referring either to the object making an impression (such as stamp seals) or to the imprint created using such a device (the seal impression or sealing).[90] Stamp seals are already attested in the

---

[88] Peltzer 2019, 37, with further references.
[89] Peltzer 2019, 38, with further references; Danbury 2018; for the charters of Louis IV, see Bansa 1968, 274–280; Wrede 1980, 13.
[90] For a more detailed discussion of the development and use of seals, see Giele/Oschema/Panagiotopoulos 2015.

Chalcolithic Near East (fifth and fourth millennia BCE),[91] remaining common in Egypt as well as in India long thereafter and still in use to the present day in the Sinosphere. Mesopotamia by contrast largely used cylinder seals.[92]

Whereas for this earlier period, seals were the object that made the impression, in medieval Europe, the seal was understood to be the end product, the impression made into or onto a malleable material by a seal matrix or die. The medieval European seal would be appended to a written document by a cord of parchment or thread, or else affixed to the body of the charter itself *(en placard),* combining both text and image, which represented the ruler and his claims to rulership. In order to receive the imagery and text impressed upon them, seals had to be made of a reasonably soft material. Most medieval seals were made of beeswax,[93] but could also be made of more precious or durable materials, such as lead and gold.[94] The use of these two metals, however, was rare and often reserved for the most solemn or important documents, a famous example of which being the Golden Bull of Charles IV from 1356, which regulated the election of the Holy Roman Emperor. Like the writing of the charter, its sealing was also paid by the recipient.[95] Therefore, the choice of a material more durable or prestigious compared to wax would be used to display such prestige. Of the seven copies of the Golden Bull of 1356, only one was sealed with wax,[96] with the remaining copies being sealed with gold to demonstrate the high status of the recipients, namely, the imperial electors. Nevertheless, for the majority of medieval charters, a wax seal appears to have been sufficient for the needs of most.

The government of early Chinese empires also utilised seals to authenticate administrative writings. Inscribed artefacts unearthed from the northwestern frontier regions reveal that administrative manuscripts were always sealed close by their senders, even when their contents were supposed to be displayed publicly. This indicates that the practice of applying a seal or seals was not only meant to safeguard a message but also to authenticate it with an official's authority.[97]

Another means of material authentication, particularly of administrative artefacts, may not necessarily involve any text. In early Chinese empires, wooden tallies would be carved with notches to denote the number of items exchanged in a transaction (including, but not limited to, transactions between the government and non-officials).[98] The tally would then be split into two or three parts as necessary and distrib-

---

[91] Keel-Leu 1991.
[92] Collon 1987; Keel-Leu/Teissier 2004.
[93] The malleability of beeswax is evident in its use as a coating for wooden boards to provide a reusable writing surface: Clanchy 2013, 120.
[94] For sealing materials in medieval Europe, see Stieldorf 2004, 60.
[95] See the earlier discussion of recipients paying for the writing of charters at the end of Thesis 33, p. 286.
[96] Staatsarchiv Nürnberg, Reichsstadt Nürnberg Urkunden 938.
[97] Tomiya 2010, 80.
[98] For wood as a writing material, see Berkes et al. 2015.

uted to the involved parties.[99] At the audit, these transaction tallies would be used to check the amount recorded in official accounts, and in the case of any discrepancies, other parties might be asked to submit their tallies to authenticate the number.[100] A similar practice occurred in medieval England, where wooden tally sticks with notches representing cash sums were used as receipts to indicate how much sheriffs had paid at the royal exchequer, with the stick split lengthwise to provide both the sheriff and the exchequer with an identical copy of the tally as proof of payment.[101] These examples convey how materiality (notches) delimited, augmented, or possibly even contradicted the interpretation of the text of an inscribed artefact (tally).

Thesis 35
Administrative writing included some of the most interactive forms of inscribed artefacts, whereas rulership communication was usually intended to be unidirectional.

While the previous sections mainly illustrate the factors of materialisation of administrative and rulership writing based on their respective material contexts, this section focuses on what happened *after* these writings were committed to stone, wood, paper, or parchment. While rulers intended to impose their wills unidirectionally on the subjects through instances of rulership writing, different audiences could still react to and interact with the inscribed artefacts.

The following discusses the material reaction to and interaction with inscribed artefacts of the state. By 'reaction', we mean the copying and reproduction of texts on the one hand or replies to communication on different artefacts (which may be made of the same or different material[s]) on the other hand, as well as metatextual reflections about those artefacts. By 'interaction', we understand the editing, addition, emendation, erasure of, as well as reply to, text on the same artefact. Although literacy is an important aspect of these issues, it is too large a topic to be comprehensively dealt with here.

Interactive Administrative Artefacts: Administrative communication flows in multiple directions or even cyclically, and is almost conversational in nature, as information is relayed between and within governments and the governed. The artefacts produced within this system of information gathering and retrieval are often more interactive

---

99 For the use of notches and the production of wooden tallies during the Qin and Han periods, see Momiyama 2015; Ma 2017.
100 Lai/Tong 2016.
101 Stone 1975.

in nature, a result of being the work and product of many people and sources. On the one hand, in order to rule effectively, rulers needed to be informed both about the situation on the ground and about how their will was being implemented; on the other hand, subjects could also petition or appeal to rulers in order to benefit from their authority. Either way, the communication between parties involved in administrative procedures often left material traces in the writing they produced, from which we can determine how their texts were received as well as how responses to these texts were generated.

Many administrative records exhibit this exchange or dialogue of information gathering on the artefacts themselves. Specific types of documents could be created, much like a fill-in form, whereby one individual would complete the framework of information that the document was to contain, while another person, who had retrieved the requisite information, would then complete the document by filling in the blanks. In medieval England, these fill-in style forms were used to draft manorial and other financial accounts as part of the audit process, whereby a lord's officials would be held accountable for all income and expenditures associated with their respective office. Often, clerks would draw up the bulk of the account but leave key information, such as specific figures or totals, blank.[102] The auditor could then complete these gaps as he checked and approved the sums, without affecting the layout or legibility of the records that would be archived for future reference.[103] Conversely, if an account had been written in full on submission to the audit, the auditors could substantially edit the document, deleting erroneous figures or excising claims for expenditures that had not been authorised by the lord. In both types of accounting documents—the fill-in form style and fully completed one—medieval manorial records demonstrate and display the administrative conversation of the audit, whereby an official proffered his version of events and the lord (through his auditor) responded, approving or rejecting the official's claims.

Interaction undertaken for approval or rejection could also take the form of simple notes, as the more powerful party could exert its authority with just a few words on the same artefact. In one particular Roman administrative procedure, a high official responded to a petition on the same papyrus originally submitted to him. On a veteran's petition in Greek to the prefect of Egypt dated between 222 and 255 CE,[104] there is a subscription approving the petition, also in Greek, at the bottom of the papyrus sheet in a hand different from that of the main text, as well as the remark *recognovi* ("I certify") in Latin.[105] Such *subscriptiones* can even remain when the text had been copied onto other materials. On a stele inscribed with administrative serial correspon-

---

102 Harvey 1976, 42.
103 For the storing and archiving of inscribed artefacts, see Chapter 3, 'Memory and Archive'.
104 Sänger 2011, no. 10. A link to an image of this papyrus is available online at *Papyri.info*, see: https://papyri.info/ddbdp/p.vet.aelii;;10 (accessed 30/9/2021).
105 Discussed in Haensch 1994 and Thomas 2003.

dence from late antique Didyma,[106] we also find the remark *edantur* ("they should be published") in Latin, decorated with ivy-leaves.

Reacting to and Interacting with Rulership Artefacts: In contrast to administrative records, rulership artefacts (that is, inscribed artefacts fulfilling the function of rulership writing, including commemorative stelae, coins, certain kinds of manuscript communications emanating from the government, etc.) were intended to be unidirectional: that is, part of a top-down process, with the message of the rulers imposed upon their subjects through the written word. Despite this intention—and because it was often widely promulgated and displayed in public—rulership writing would easily provoke interactions and reactions both from its contemporaries as well as from later generations. Of course, much of this remained relegated to the realm of uttered comments or gestures that have left no permanent trace; but some reactions were manifested materially. Written artefacts could be enhanced or monumentalised, or damaged or altered in a way that we can still observe today.

One of the possible strategies of reacting to rulership writing was through monumentalisation. While monumental inscribed artefacts displaying political rule could have been destroyed along with the demise of the political authorities that created them, many of these have ended up outlasting the rule and rulers that commissioned them. A number of factors can account for this phenomenon. For instance, later rulers might leverage the rulership writing of earlier rulers to bolster their own legitimacy. Likewise, such inscribed monuments can become symbols for the collective memories of different social groups.[107] Although these groups were simply supposed to receive such rulership writing, their subsequent use of monumentality served as a technique allowing them to exceed the inscribed artefacts' designated function of expressing political authority. Through that technique they also honoured and commemorated themselves locally. Given that many inscribed monuments were created by local communities rather than a central government, such multifunctionality was intended from the monuments' inception.

The abovementioned Chinese stele from 153 CE with an edict granting privileges to the descendants of Master Kong (Confucius) is a good example of such multifunctionality.[108] This stele was carefully preserved by the Kong lineage in Qufu long after the collapse of the Eastern Han authorities. This move was likely motivated by the fact that the monumentalised imperial edict and the magistrate's instruction became proof of the sagacity of their ancestor, Confucius, and the prominence and privilege of his lineage. This stele, therefore, was made as much for the ruler as for its users. Aside from the more universal framework of imperial largesse to which the stele also refers, the memories and identities that it helped to evoke or construe were more localised,

---

106 For further details, see below p. 291.
107 Assmann 1988, 90–91. Cf. Allgaier et al. 2019.
108 See above p. 276.

specified, and layered. Presumably, artefacts bearing an identical rulership text can even evoke different local memories in cases in which they have been created by different social groups. In this respect, the monumentalisation of a rulership text gave its users a certain amount of leeway so as to leverage the monument's authority. This sets what is written here apart from the immediate political agenda that the text's original authors might have had in mind.

The Eastern Han phenomenon just mentioned mirrors the situation in the Roman Empire, especially during its later phase. Many late Roman documentary inscriptions faithfully reproduced features that were originally found on other materials (presumably bearing the original text) in order to retain the message's credibility. This sometimes led to the inconsistent use of scripts or the emergence of multilingual texts. Under the reign of Justinian I (r. 527–565 CE), a tripartite dossier of correspondence related to the exemption from civic tribute was inscribed on a tall stele in Didyma. From the text on the stele, three consecutive acts can be reconstructed reflecting a specific administrative process: an imperial edict; a hearing before the praetorian prefect of the East on the next day; and a declaration of the provincial governor of Caria, to which Didyma belonged. Of special interest here is the hearing, of which the stele text offers an extract. It reproduces not only what the prefect said in Greek, but also interpolates this with the Latin text of the edict itself, which must have been originally written on papyrus.[109] In reaction to the reception of these texts, the local decision makers chose to reproduce the full dossier on stone rather than only the imperial edict. This reinforces the notion of administrative procedure as a source of authority.

In contrast to the direct and immediate interactions between government personnel in official accounts and correspondences (that is, administrative writing), interaction with rulership writing was often indirect and sometimes even took place in a context different from that of the original writing. Often a reaction to artefacts bearing rulership writing or images reflects a personal response of a viewer or recipient and addresses the public or other viewers, not necessarily the ruler or government as the sender of the message. The original message of rulership writing could be appended, distorted, or ridiculed in order to demonstrate the response of a later ruler or the ruled. As a result of these actions, the materiality of the original rulership writing might be altered or destroyed. Much like the modern defacing of political posters or slogans that abound nowadays during popular elections, graffiti and targeted acts of damage—as well as non-targeted instances of vandalism—were usual forms of such destructive interactions in pre-modern times as well.[110]

Alternatively, destruction could also happen by command. In the premodern world, memory sanctions (often referred to anachronistically as *damnatio memoriae*)

---

109 For an edition of this source, see Feissel 2004, 304–306. For a discussion of the extract, see Manservigi/Mezzetti 2016, 210–234.
110 A practice long in the focus of the CRC 933; see for instance Mauntel et al. 2015 and Kühne-Wespi/Oschema/Quack 2019.

Fig. 5: Bronze *as* of Nero, with the obverse portrait being countermarked with *SPQR* on the neck. © American Numismatic Society, 1953.171.1308.

at the local and empire-wide level purportedly aimed at the total erasure of an individual's material existence in writing and imagery, most commonly of an emperor considered wicked or harmful to the world. However, for a variety of reasons this erasure was never implemented completely across an empire. The practice existed in the early Roman Empire and continued into early Christianity, when the names of pagan deities and anti-Christian emperors were sometimes erased.[111] But the local communities usually carried out memory sanctions against such disgraced emperors in a way that might have preserved the authority of the written monuments. In late antique Aphrodisias, a predominantly Christian city, for instance, the locals erased only the *cognomen* of the disgraced anti-Christian Emperor Julian, and later inscribed the name of the new Emperor Theodosius onto the erased surface, but Julian's titles and even his first two names remained intact.[112]

The continuation of legal authority combined with dissociation from the original context of rulership through defacing can also be seen in imperial Roman bronze coinage, the value of which depended not only on its metallic content, but to a large degree on the financial and political credentials of the issuing authority. After an emperor was condemned, coins issued under his authority often received countermarks showing the recognition of new authorities. Following the reign of Nero, the Roman Senate frequently applied countermarks with the legend *SPQR* (an abbreviation of the phrase *Senatus populusque Romanus,* 'the Senate and People of Rome') on the neck of Nero's portrait on the obverse of his bronze coins (Fig. 5); the new Emperors Galba and Vespasian also used countermarks with their own names on Nero's face. The interaction

---

[111] For memory sanctions and the role of locals, see Omissi 2016 (Roman), Schwedler 2021 (early Christianity).
[112] IAph2007 8.405.

of original coin design and later countermarks therefore imbues such coins with new political authority while recognising the economic value of an existing artefact bearing rulership imagery and carrying out economic functions.[113]

Moreover, there were also certain forms of rulership artefacts that expected or elicited a response on the same artefact. Appended texts or addenda were one of the common ways of materialising responses to rulership writing. In China in 210 BCE, the Second Emperor of Qin (r. 210–207 BCE) added his own edict next to the inscriptions that his father, the First Emperor, had left ubiquitously on stelae, measures and weights. This additional edict foregrounded the First Emperor's achievements and was complementary to existing rulership writing.[114] By highlighting his relationship with his revered predecessor, the young and inexperienced Second Emperor in turn enhanced his own authority.

Metatextual Interaction: Another way of interacting with rulership writing was through various genres of metatext, such as critique, commentary, and fiction. Often, such responses differed diametrically from the original messages of specific instances of rulership writing, or could have little to do with the forms and contents of the actual inscribed artefacts they mentioned. The metatextual interaction with rulership writing, therefore, reveals how both contemporaries and later people appropriated the ruler's authority for their own agendas.

In premodern China, the panegyrical stele inscriptions of the First Emperor of Qin (r. 247–221 BCE as king over a rapidly increasing realm, and r. 221–210 BCE as emperor without peer) almost became a laughing stock for later generations. Soon after the Qin regime's demise, the Western Han thinker Jia Shan (fl. 175 BCE) contrasted the narratives in the inscriptions from the Kuaji and Langye mountains with the brevity of the Qin Empire, suggesting that the Qin emperor was ignorant about his own faults and overestimated his own virtue.[115] As time progressed, however, the negative reception of these stelae waned.[116] One of the most intriguing accounts concerning the First Emperor's stelae comes from the Tang statesman Du You (735–812 CE). In his encyclopaedic institutional history *Tongdian* Du portrays the materiality of the First Emperor's stele and other related artefacts on Mount Tai. In addition to the stele, Du writes, the Qin emperor's utterance to heaven was inscribed on a multistrip artefact made of gold and was put in a stone container, sealed with clay mixed with gold powder and bearing a jade label.[117] The description of this setting, however, was probably

---

113 On the defacing of Nero's portraits after his death, see Calomino 2016, 67–79. On countermarks for economic reasons, see Howgego 1986.
114 That the Second Emperor's edict never appears independently on weights or measures suggests that its intention was to accompany the writing of the First Emperor; see Sanft 2014, 60.
115 Ban Gu et al., *Hanshu* 51, 2332.
116 Lu Qinli, *Xian Qin Han Wei Jin Nanbeichao shi*, 921; Zhan Ying, *Wenxin diaolong yizheng*, 803.
117 Du You, *Tongdian* 54, 1508.

anachronistic and differed from the actual inscribed artefacts of the First Emperor.[118] In fact, Du You's description of the Qin emperor's golden scroll echoes the jade scroll used by the Tang emperors in their *feng* sacrifices.[119] By construing the materiality and text of the Qin-era rulership writing, Du traced the origin of a contemporaneous practice to the beginning of the imperial Chinese period. This fictional monument thus usurped the authority of the actual stele of the Qin emperor, turning it into evidence for the authority of the later Tang ruler.

Interactions with rulership writing can also be found in literature. To give only one example among many: in the seventeenth-century German drama *Ibrahim Sultan* by Daniel Casper von Lohenstein (1635–1683), the protagonist, a violent sultan, receives a letter of reprimand from his council. Before even reading the letter, the Sultan Ibrahim is angered that the letter had not been immediately burnt by his henchmen; the provocation here seems to be occasioned not by the letter's content, but by its mere presence. In reaching the addressee via the text-bearing artefact, the opposing party has managed to penetrate the inner circle of power. The sultan then refuses to read the letter and rips it apart, demanding that its shreds be sent back to the senders (along with the dismembered body of an ally). By destroying the letter, Ibrahim not only answers the missive, but also tries to annihilate its message retroactively. The scene epitomises how meaning is generated not only through what is written, but also in the transmission of this text—how it is delivered and received—and in the material interactions with the writing. Not least, it shows how rulers rely on the symbolic (and political) power of these interactions.

---

118 The stele inscription which Du You cites in his *Tongdian* does not match that which appears in other transmitted sources such as the *Shiji* by Sima Qian et al. A Northern Song (960–1279) witness, Liu Qi, who saw the First Emperor's stele on Mount Tai in 1108, makes no mention of the stone container in Du's account. Liu also reveals that the emperor's stele was only ca. 1.5 metres in height, and unlike stelae made by later rulers, the stone was "an irregular, roughly finished boulder"; its four sides, all of which were inscribed, were of unequal width. Liu's account conforms to extant rubbings of the stele inscription. This contrasts sharply with the lavish setting that Du You narrated in *Tongdian*; see Harrist 2008, 223.
119 Du You, *Tongdian* 54, 1514–1522. To date, no actual inscribed artefacts that the emperors used in the *feng* sacrifices to Heaven have been discovered. For an image of the 'jade' (in fact marble) multi-strip artefact used by Emperor Xuanzong of Tang (r. 713–756) in a *shan* sacrifice to Earth—which was as important as the *feng* sacrifice—dated to 725 CE, see the *National Cultural Heritage Database:* https://nchdb.boch.gov.tw/assets/overview/antiquity/20140421000006 (accessed 28/9/2021).

Bibliography

Abbreviations and Sigla

CTh *Theodosiani libri XVI cum constitutionibus Sirmondianis et leges Novellae ad Theodosianum pertinentes,* ed. by Theodor Mommsen and Paul M. Meyer, Berlin 1904.

IAph2007 *Inscriptions of Aphrodisias,* ed. by Joyce Reynolds, Charlotte Roueché and Gabriel Bodard, https://insaph.kcl.ac.uk/insaph/iaph2007/index.html (accessed 30/9/2021).

IG I³,1 *Inscriptiones Graecae,* vol. I, ed. 3: *Inscriptiones Atticae Euclidis anno anteriores,* fasc. 1: *Decreta et tabulae magistratuum,* ed. by David Lewis, Berlin 1981.

I.Estremo Oriente *Iscrizioni dello estremo oriente greco: un repertorio* (Inschriften griechischer Städte aus Kleinasien 64), ed. by Filippo Canali De Rossi, Bonn 2004.

I.Fay. *Recueil des inscriptions grecques du Fayoum,* I–III, ed. by Étienne Bernand, Leiden 1975–1981.

SB I *Sammelbuch Griechischer Urkunden aus Ägypten,* vol. 1, ed. by Friedrich Preisigke, Straßburg 1915.

Sources

Archival Sources
American Numismatic Society, 1953.171.1308
Greifswald, Landesarchiv, Repositur 2, no. 73.
Institut für Papyrologie, Universität Heidelberg, P. Heid. inv. Arab. 12
Landesarchiv Baden-Württemberg, Generallandesarchiv Karlsruhe, 67/799; 67/804.
Niedersächsisches Staatsarchiv, Wolfenbüttel, 6 Urk. II.
Staatsarchiv Nürnberg, Reichsstadt Nürnberg Urkunden 938.

Published Sources
Ban Gu 班固 et al., *Hanshu* 漢書 (The Writings of the Han), Beijing: Zhonghua shuju, 1962.
Berliner Papyrusdatenbank, online resource at: https://berlpap.smb.museum (accessed 31/1/2022).
Bible: *The Oxford Annotated Bible with Apocrypha,* ed. by Michael D. Coogan, Marc Z. Bretter, Carol A. Newsroom, and Pheme Perkins, Oxford 2010.
Du You 杜佑, *Tongdian* 通典 (Comprehensive Institutions), Beijing: Zhonghua shuju, 1988.
Herodotus, *Historiae,* ed. by Nigel G. Wilson, Oxford 2015.
Julian (Emperor), *Misopogon,* in: L'Empereur Julien, *Œuvres complètes,* Tome II: *Discours de Julien Empereur,* 2ᵉ Partie: *Les Césars, Sur Hélios-Roi, Le Misopogon,* ed. and transl. by Christian Lacombrade (Les Belles Lettres), Paris 1964, 141–199.
Kandai sekkoku shūsei. Zuhan shakubun hen 漢代石刻集成 — 図版・釈文篇 (Collection of Stele Inscriptions during the Han Period. Plates and Transcriptions), ed. by Nagata Hidemasa 永田英正, Kyoto 1994.
Lohenstein, Daniel Casper von, *Ibrahim Sultan. Sophonisbe,* ed. by Lothar Mundt (Sämtliche Werke, Dramen 3), Berlin 2012.
Lu Qinli 逯欽立, *Xian Qin Han Wei Jin Nanbeichao shi* 先秦漢魏晉南北朝詩 (Poems of Pre-Imperial, Early Imperial and Early Medieval China), 3 vols., Beijing 1983.

National Cultural Heritage Database Management System, Bureau of Cultural Heritage, Ministry of Culture, Taiwan, https://nchdb.boch.gov.tw/ (accessed 28/9/2021).
Papyri.info, online ressource at: https://papyri.info (accessed 31/1/2022).
Regesta regum Anglo-Normannorum. The Acta of William I (1066–1087), ed. by David Bates, Oxford 1998.
Res gestae divi Augusti: Hauts faits du divin Auguste, ed. by John Scheid (Collection des universités de France. Série latine 386), Paris 2007.
Rudolf von Ems, *Willehalm von Orlens,* intr. and transl. by Gisela Vollmann-Profe (Regensburger Studien zur Literatur und Kultur des Mittelalters 3), Berlin 2017.
Sima Qian 司馬遷 et al., *Shiji* 史記 (Records of the Scribe), Beijing: Zhonghua shuju, 1959.
Sima Qian 司馬遷 et al., *The Grand Scribe's Records,* Vol. IX: *The Memoirs of Han China, Part II*, ed. by William H. Nienhauser, transl. by J. Michael Farmer, Enno Giele, Christiane Haupt, Li He, Elisabeth Hsu, William H. Nienhauser, Jr., Marc Nürnberger, and Ying Qin, Bloomington 2011.
The Vindolanda Writing Tablets, vol. 2, ed. by Alan K. Bowman and John D. Thomas (tabulae Vindolandenses II), London 1994. Also available online in *Roman Inscriptions of Britain* at: https://romaninscriptionsofbritain.org/tabvindol/vol-II/introduction (accessed 22/5/2021).
Zhan Ying 詹鍈, *Wenxin diaolong yizheng* 文心雕龍義證 (Corroboration of the Meaning of the Wenxin diaolong), 3 vols., Shanghai 1989.

Research Literature

Allgaier, Benjamin/Bolle, Katharina/Jaspert, Nikolas/Knauber, Konrad/Lieb, Ludger/Roels, Evelien/Sauer, Rebecca/Schneidereit, Nele/Wallenwein, Kirsten (2019), "Gedächtnis – Materialität – Schrift. Ein erinnerungskulturelles Modell zur Analyse schrifttragender Artefakte", in: *Saeculum* 69 (II), 181–244.
Andrewes, Antony (1981), "The Hoplite *katalogos*", in: Gordon S. Shrimpton and David J. McCargar (eds.), *Classical Contributions: Studies in Honor of Malcolm Francis McGregor,* Locust Valley, NY, 1–3.
Assmann, Jan (1988), "Stein und Zeit: Das 'monumentale' Gedächtnis der altägyptischen Kultur", in: Jan Assmann and Tonio Hölscher (eds.), *Kultur und Gedächtnis,* Frankfurt (Main), 87–114.
Bansa, Helmut (1968), *Studien zur Kanzlei Kaiser Ludwigs des Bayern vom Tag der Wahl bis zur Rückkehr aus Italien (1314–1329)* (Münchener Historische Studien, Abteilung Geschichtliche Hilfswissenschaften 5), Kallmünz.
Behr, Wolfgang/Führer, Bernhard (2005), "Einführende Notizen zum Lesen in China mit besonderer Berücksichtigung der Frühzeit", in: Bernhard Führer (ed.), *Aspekte des Lesens in China in Vergangenheit und Gegenwart. Referate der Jahrestagung 2001 der Deutschen Vereinigung für Chinastudien (DVCS),* Bochum.
Berkes, Lajos/Giele, Enno/Ott, Michael R./Quack, Joachim Friedrich (2015), "Holz", in: Thomas Meier, Michael R. Ott, and Rebecca Sauer (eds.), *Materiale Textkulturen. Konzepte – Materialien – Praktiken* (Materiale Textkulturen 1), Berlin/Munich/Boston, 383–396, https://doi.org/10.1515/9783110371291.383.
Borger, Rykle/Hinz, Walther (1982–1985), "Die Behistun-Inschrift Darius' des Großen", in: Otto Kaiser (ed.), *Texte aus der Umwelt des Alten Testaments,* vol. 1: *Rechts- und Wirtschaftsurkunden. Historisch-chronologische Texte,* Gütersloh, 419–450.
Briant, Pierre (2002), *From Cyrus to Alexander. A History of the Persian Empire,* Winona Lake, IN.

Bülow-Jacobsen, Adam (2013), "Translation of a Letter of the *Praefectus Aegypti* (O. Claud. inv. 7218)", in: Rodney Ast, Hélène Cuvigny, Todd M. Hickey, and Julia Lougovaya (eds.), *Papyrological Texts in Honor of Roger S. Bagnall* (American Studies in Papyrology 53), Durham, NC, 47–51.

Callataÿ, François de (2016), "The Coinages Struck for the Romans in Hellenistic Greece: A Quantified Overview (mid 2nd – mid 1st c. BCE)", in: Florian Haymann, Wilhelm Hollstein, and Martin Jehne (eds.), *Neue Forschungen zur Münzprägung der Römischen Republik*, Bonn, 315–338.

Calomino, Dario (2016), *Defacing the Past: Damnation and Desecration in Imperial Rome*, London.

Christ, Matthew R. (2001), "Conscription of Hoplites in Classical Athens", in: *The Classical Quarterly* 51 (2), 398–422.

Clanchy, Michael T. (2013), *From Memory to Written Record: England 1066–1307*, 3rd ed., Chichester.

Cochrane, Lydia G. (1994), *The History and Power of Writing*, Chicago.

Collon, Dominique (1987), *First Impressions. Cylinder Seals in the Ancient Near East*, London.

Cooley, Alison (2012), "From Document to Monument. Inscribing Roman Official Documents in the Greek East", in: John Davies and John Wilkes (eds.), *Epigraphy and the Historical Sciences*, Oxford, 159–182.

Danbury, Elisabeth (2018), "The Study of Illuminated Charters, Past, Present and Future: Some Thoughts from England", in: Gabriele Bartz and Markus Gneiss (eds.), *Illuminierte Urkunden. Beiträge aus Diplomatik, Kunstgeschichte und Digital Humanities. Illuminated Charters. Essays from Diplomatic, Art History and Digital Humanities* (Archiv für Diplomatik, Schriftgeschichte, Siegel- und Wappenkunde 16), Cologne/Weimar/Vienna, 259–280.

Eagleton, Catherine/Williams, Jonathan (1997), *Money. A History*, London, 2nd ed., 2006.

Eck, Werner (2003), "Der Kaiser als Herr des Heeres. Militärdiplome und die kaiserliche Reichsregierung", in: J. J. Wilkes (ed.), *Documenting the Roman Army: Essays in Honour of Margaret Roxan*, Oxford, 55–87.

Elkins, Nathan T. (2015), *Monuments in Miniature: Architecture on Roman Coinage*, New York.

Elkins, Nathan T. (2019), "Money, Art, and Representation: A Look at the Roman World", in: Stefan Krmnicek (ed.), *A Cultural History of Money in Antiquity*, London, 105–121.

Falkenhausen, Lothar von (2005), "The E Jun Qi Metal Tallies", in: Martin Kern (ed.), *Text and Ritual in Early China*, Seattle/London, 79–123.

Feissel, Denis (2000), "Une constitution de l'empereur Julien entre texte épigraphique et codification (*CIL* III, 459 et *CTh* I, 16, 8)", in: Edmond Lévy (ed.), *La codification des lois dans l'Antiquité*, Paris, 315–337.

Feissel, Denis (2004), "Un rescrit de Justinien découvert à Didymes (1er avril 533)", in: *Chiron* 34, 285–365.

Giele, Enno (2006), *Imperial Decision-Making and Communication in Early China. A Study of Cai Yong's 'Duduan'*, Wiesbaden.

Giele, Enno/Oschema, Klaus/Panagiotopoulos, Diamantis (2015), "Siegeln, Stempeln und Prägen", in: Thomas Meier, Michael R. Ott, and Rebecca Sauer (eds.), *Materiale Textkulturen. Konzepte – Materialien – Praktiken* (Materiale Textkulturen 1), Berlin/Munich/Boston, 551–566, https://doi.org/10.1515/9783110371291.551.

Goody, Jack (1986), *The Logic of Writing and the Organization of Society*, Cambridge.

Haensch, Rudolf (1994), "Die Bearbeitungsweisen von Petitionen in der Provinz Aegyptus", in: *Zeitschrift für Papyrologie und Epigraphik* 100, 487–546.

Harrist, Robert E., Jr. (2008), *The Landscape of Words: Stone Inscriptions in Early and Medieval China*, Seattle.

Harvey, Paul D. A. (1976), *Manorial Records of Cuxham, Oxfordshire, circa 1200–1359*, London.

Hölkeskamp, Karl-Joachim (1992), "Written Law in Archaic Greece", in: *Proceedings of the Cambridge Philological Society* 38, 87–117.

Holz, Stefan G. (2022), *Rolle und Kodex. Die Schriftlichkeit der königlichen Finanzverwaltung Englands unter Eduard I. (1272–1307)* (Veröffentlichungen des Deutschen Historischen Instituts London 87), Berlin/Boston.

Hou Xudong 侯旭東 (2014), "Dong Han *Yi Ying bei* zengzhi zushi/cuishi shi suojian zhengwu chuli" 東漢《乙瑛碑》增置卒史事所見政務處理 (The Discharge of Governing Duties that Can Be Seen in the Affairs of Increasingly Established Lieutenant Scribes in the Eastern Han *Stele of Yi Ying*), in: *Zhongguo zhonggushi yanjiu: Zhongguo zhonggushi qingnian xuezhe lianyihui huikan* 中國中古史研究 — 中國中古史青年學者聯誼會會刊 (Historical Studies of the Chinese Middle Ages. Journal of the Association of Young Scholars of Chinese Medieval History) 4, Beijing, 43–69.

Howgego, Christopher (1986), *Greek Imperial Countermarks: Studies in the Provincial Coinage of the Roman Empire,* London.

Huyse, Philip (1999), *Die dreisprachige Inschrift Šābuhrs I. an der Ka'ba-i Žardušt (ŠKZ)* (Corpus Inscriptionum Iranicarum, Part III, Vol. I, Text I), London.

Innis, Harold A. (2007 [1950]), *Empire and Communications,* Lanham et al.

Keel-Leu, Hildi (1991), *Vorderasiatische Stempelsiegel. Die Sammlung des Biblischen Instituts der Universität Freiburg Schweiz,* Fribourg/Göttingen.

Keel-Leu, Hildi/Teissier, Beatrice (2004), *Die vorderasiatischen Rollsiegel der Sammlungen BIBEL + ORIENT der Universität Freiburg Schweiz,* Fribourg/Göttingen.

Kern, Martin (2000), *The Stele Inscriptions of Ch'in Shih-huang: Text and Ritual in Early Chinese Imperial Representation,* New Haven, CT.

Keynes, Simon (2013), "Church Councils, Royal Assemblies, and Anglo-Saxon Royal Diplomas", in: Gale R. Owen-Crocker and Brian W. Schneider (eds.), *Kingship, Legislation and Power in Anglo-Saxon England,* Rochester, NY, 17–182.

Kühne-Wespi, Carina/Oschema, Klaus/Quack, Joachim Friedrich (eds.) (2019), *Zerstörung von Geschriebenem. Historische und transkulturelle Perspektiven* (Materiale Textkulturen 22), Berlin/Boston, https://doi.org/10.1515/9783110629040.

Lai Ming Chiu 黎明釗/Tong Chun Fung 唐俊峰 (2016), "Liye Qinjian suojian Qindai xianguan, cao zuzhi de zhineng fenye yu xingzheng hudong" 里耶秦簡所見秦代縣官、曹組織的職能分野與行政互動 (The Division of Labour and Administrative Coordination between Guan and Cao Organisations in the Qin County Administration: Evidence from the Liye Manuscripts), in: *Jianbo* 簡帛 13, 131–158.

Loewe, Michael (1965), "The Wooden and Bamboo Strips Found at Mo-chü-tzu (Kansu)", in: *Journal of the Royal Asiatic Society* 1/2, 13–26.

Lougovaya, Julia (2013), "Inscriptions on the Attic Stage", in: Peter Liddel and Polly Low (eds.), *Inscriptions and Their Uses in Greek and Latin Literature,* Oxford, 255–270.

Ma Tsang Wing (2017), "Scribe, Assistant, and the Materiality of Administrative Documents in Qin–Early Han China: Excavated Evidence from Liye, Shuihudi, and Zhangjiashan", in: *T'oung Pao* 103 (4–5), 297–333.

Mahlich, Elena (2020), *Der Kanalbau unter Dareios I. Ein achämenidisches Bauprojekt in Ägypten,* Berlin.

Maischberger, Martin (1997), *Marmor in Rom. Anlieferung, Lager- und Werkplätze in der Kaiserzeit,* Wiesbaden.

Manservigi, Flavia/Mezzetti, Melania (2016), "The Didyma Inscription: Between Legislation and Palaeography", in: Markus Hilgert (ed.), *Understanding Material Text Cultures. A Multidisciplinary View* (Materiale Textkulturen 9) Berlin/Boston, 203–242, https://doi.org/10.1515/9783110417845-006.

Martin, Henri-Jean (1988), *Histoire et pouvoir de l'écrit,* Paris.

Mauntel, Christoph/Sauer, Rebecca/Theis, Christoffer/Trampedach, Kai (2015), "Beschädigen und Zerstören", in: Thomas Meier, Michael R. Ott, and Rebecca Sauer (eds.), *Materiale Textkulturen. Konzepte – Materialien – Praktiken* (Materiale Textkulturen 1), Berlin/Munich/Boston, 735–746, https://doi.org/10.1515/9783110371291.735.

Mitchell, Stephen (1976), "Requisitioned Transport in the Roman Empire: A New Inscription from Pisidia", in: *The Journal of Roman Studies* 66, 106–131.

Momiyama Akira 籾山明 (2015), *Shin Kan shutsudo moji shiryō no kenkyū: keitai, seido, shakai* 秦漢出土文字史料の研究 ― 形態・制度・社会 (Studies of Excavated Inscriptional Material from the Qin and Han Times: Form, System, Society), Tokyo.

Mugridge, Alan (2010), "Writing and Writers in Antiquity: two 'Spectra' in Greek Handwriting", in: *Proceedings of the 25th International Congress of Papyrology,* Ann Arbor, 573–580.

Mullen, Alex/Bowman, Alan (2021), *Manual of Roman Everyday Writing*, vol. 1: *Scripts and Texts,* Nottingham.

Naveh, Joseph/Shaked, Shaul (2012), *Aramaic Documents from Ancient Bactria,* London.

Nissen, Hans J./Damerow, Peter/Englund, Robert K. (2004), *Informationsverarbeitung vor 5000 Jahren. Frühe Schrift und Techniken der Wirtschaftsverwaltung im alten Vorderen Orient,* Hildesheim et al.

Noreña, Carlos F. (2011), "Coins and Communication", in: Michael Peachin (ed.), *The Oxford Handbook of Social Relations in the Roman World,* Oxford, 248–268.

Oller Guzmán, Joan/Abella, David Fernández/Pita, Vanesa Trevín/Kaper, Olaf E./Ast, Rodney/Sidebotham, Steven E. (2022), "A Falcon Shrine at the Port of Berenike (Red Sea Coast, Egypt)", in: *American Journal of Archaeology* 126, 567–591, https://doi.org/10.1086/720806.

Omissi, Adrastos (2016), "*Damnatio Memoriae* or *Creatio Memoriae?* Memory Sanctions as Creative Processes in the Fourth Century AD", in: *The Cambridge Classical Journal* 62, 170–199.

Paton, Sara/Schneider, Rolf Michael (1999), "Imperial Splendour in the Province: Imported Marble on Roman Crete", in: Angelos Chaniotis (ed.), *From Minoan Farmers to Roman Traders. Sidelights on the Economy of Crete,* Stuttgart, 279–304.

Pelteret, David A. E. (1990), *Catalogue of English Post-Conquest Vernacular Documents,* Woodbridge.

Peltzer, Jörg (2019), *Fürst werden. Rangerhöhungen im 14. Jahrhundert – Das römisch-deutsche Reich und England im Vergleich* (Historische Zeitschrift. Beihefte 75), Berlin/Boston.

Petrovic, Ivana/Petrovic, Andrej (2018), "Purity of Body and Soul in the Cult of Athena Lindia: On the Eastern Background of Greek Abstentions", in: Jan-Mathieu Carbon and Saskia Peels (eds.), *Purity and Purification in the Ancient Greek World: Texts, Rituals, and Norms,* Liège, 225–258.

Picard, Olivier (2010), "Rome et la Grèce à la basse période hellénistique: monnaies et impérialisme", in: *Journal des Savants* 2, 161–192.

Porten, Bezalel/Yardeni, Ada (1986–1999), *Textbook of Aramaic Documents from Ancient Egypt,* Jerusalem.

Posener, Georges (1951), "Sur l'emploi de l'encre rouge dans les manuscrits égyptiens", in: *Journal of Egyptian Archaeology* 37, 75–80.

Postgate, Nicholas/Wang Tao/Wilkinson, Toby (1995), "The Evidence for Early Writing: Utilitarian or Ceremonial?", in: *Antiquity* 69, 459–480.

Quack, Joachim Friedrich (2012), "Pharao und Hofstaat, Palast und Tempel: Entscheidungsfindung, Öffentlichkeit und Entscheidungsveröffentlichung im Alten Ägypten", in: Christina Kuhn (ed.), *Politische Kommunikation und öffentliche Meinung in der antiken Welt,* Stuttgart, 277–295.

Quack, Joachim Friedrich (2015), "Ägyptische Listen und ihre Expansion in Unterricht und Repräsentation", in: Susanne Deicher and Erik Maroko (eds.), *Die Liste. Ordnungen von Dingen und Menschen in Ägypten,* Berlin, 51–86.

Quack, Joachim Friedrich (2020), "Zwei demotische Briefe in hieratischer Schrift", in: Kim Ryholt (ed.), *Hieratic Texts from Tebtunis Including a Survey of Illustrated Papyri* (CNI Publications 45), Copenhagen, 141–149, pls. 28–31.

Quack, Joachim Friedrich (2021), "Under Persian Rule: Egypt", in: Bruno Jacobs and Robert Rollinger (eds.), *A Companion to the Achaemenid Persian Empire,* Hoboken, 553–566.

Richter, Tonio Sebastian (2010), "Language Choice in the Qurra Dossier", in: Arietta Papaconstantinou (ed.), *The Multilingual Experience in Egypt, from the Ptolemies to the Abbasids,* Farnham, 189–220.

Sanft, Charles (2014), *Communication and Cooperation in Early Imperial China. Publicizing the Qin Dynasty,* Albany, NY.

Sänger, Patrick (2011), *Veteranen unter den Severern und frühen Soldatenkaisern: Die Dokumentensammlungen der Veteranen Aelius Sarapammon und Aelius Syrion,* Stuttgart.

Schmitt, Rüdiger (2009), *Die altpersischen Inschriften der Achaimeniden. Editio minor mit deutscher Übersetzung,* Wiesbaden.

Scholz, Sebastian (2011a), "Die Urkundeninschriften in Speyer (1111), Mainz (1135) und Worms (1184) – Funktion und Bedeutung", in: Alexander Koch, Bernd Schneidmüller, and Stefan Weinfurter (eds.), *Die Salier. Macht im Wandel,* Munich, 163–165.

Scholz, Sebastian (2011b), "Die Urkundeninschriften Kaiser Heinrichs V. für Speyer aus dem Jahr 1111", in: Alexander Koch, Bernd Schneidmüller, and Stefan Weinfurter (eds.), *Die Salier. Macht im Wandel,* Munich, 167–173.

Scholz, Sebastian (2011c), "Die Urkunden Kaiser Heinrichs V. für die Bürger der Stadt Speyer, 7. und 14. August 1111", in: Alexander Koch, Bernd Schneidmüller, and Stefan Weinfurter (eds.), *Die Salier. Macht im Wandel,* Munich, 174–175.

Schwedler, Gerald (2021), *Vergessen, Verändern, Verschweigen: 'Damnatio memoriae' im frühen Mittelalter,* Göttingen.

Sharpe, Richard (2011), "Peoples and Languages in Eleventh- and Twelfth-Century Britain and Ireland: Reading the Charter Evidence", in: Dauvit Broun (ed.), *The Reality behind Charter Diplomatic in Anglo-Norman Britain,* Glasgow, 1–119.

Sickinger, James P. (1999), *Public Records and Archives in Classical Athens,* Chapel Hill, NC.

Siewert, Peter (2018), "Fragment einer hocharchaischen Bronzetafel aus Olympia mit Nennung der Eleer und des Mantis-Amtes (BrU 8)", in: *Tyche* 38, 177–182.

Sou, Daniel Sungbin (2018), "Crossing Borders. Control of Geographical Mobility in Early China", in: *T'oung Pao* 104, 217–250.

Speidel, Michael A. (2015), "The Roman Army", in: Christer Bruun and Jonathan Edmondson (eds.), *Oxford Handbook of Roman Epigraphy,* Oxford, 319–344.

Spiegel, Joachim (1996), *Urkundenwesen, Kanzlei, Rat und Regierungssystem des Pfalzgrafen bei Rhein und Herzogs von Bayern Ruprecht I. (1309–1390)* (Stiftung zur Förderung der pfälzischen Geschichtsforschung, Reihe B: Abhandlungen zur Geschichte der Pfalz 1), 2 vols., Neustadt (Weinstraße).

Staack, Thies (2018), "Single- and Multi-Piece Manuscripts in Early Imperial China: On the Background and Significance of a Terminological Distinction", in: *Early China* 41, 245–295.

Stieldorf, Andrea (2004), *Siegelkunde* (Hahnsche Historische Hilfswissenschaften 2), Hannover.

Stone, Willard E. (1975), "The Tally: An Ancient Accounting Instrument", in: *Abacus* 11.1, 49–57.

Takatori Yuji 鷹取祐司 (2020), "Kandai no minyō tsūkōshō to tsūkan meiseki. Kensui Kinkan ishi shutsudo tsūkan meiseki bunseki no tame no yobi sagyō" 漢代の民用通行証と通関名籍 ― 肩水金関遺址出土通関名籍分析のための予備作業 (Commoners Transit Visas and Travellers' Lists from the Han Period. Preparatory Work for the Analysis of Travellers' Lists from the Site of the Jin Checkpoint at Jianshui), in: *Ritsumeikan bungaku* 立命館文學 668, 325–343.

Tavernier, Jan (2017), "The Use of Language on the Various Levels of Administration in the Achaemenid Empire", in: Bruno Jacobs, Wouter F. M. Henkelman, and Matthew W. Stolper (eds.), *Die Verwaltung im Achämenidenreich – Imperiale Muster und Strukturen. Administration in the Achaemenid Empire – Tracing the Imperial Signature* (Classica et Orientalia 17), Wiesbaden, 337–412.

Thierry, François (2017), *Les monnaies de la Chine ancienne. Des origines à la fin de l'Empire,* Paris.

Thomas, J. David (2003), "The *subscriptiones* in *PSI* IX 1026 and *P. Oxy.* XLVII 3364", *Tyche* 18, 201–206.

Tjäder, Jan-Olof (1979), "Considerazioni e proposte sulla scrittura latina nell'età romana", in: Scuola Speciale per gli Archivisti e Bibliotecari (ed.), *Paleografia, diplomatica, et archivistica: studi in onore di Giulio Battelli,* vol. 1, Rome, 31–60.

Tomiya Itaru 冨谷至 (2010), *Monjo gyōsei no Kan teikoku: Mokkan, chikkan no jidai* 文書行政の漢帝国 — 木簡・竹簡の時代 (A Han Empire Managed through Manuscripts. The Period of Wooden and Bamboo Documents), Nagoya.

Van De Mieroop, Marc (2016), *A History of the Ancient Near East, ca. 3000–323 BC*, 3rd ed., Chichester/Malden/Oxford.

Viereck, Paul/Zucker, Friedrich (1926), *Ägyptische Urkunden aus den Staatlichen Museen zu Berlin. Griechische Urkunden,* vol. 7: *Papyri, Ostraka und Wachstafeln aus Philadelphia im Fayûm,* Berlin.

Weber, Max (2009 [1922]), *Wirtschaft und Gesellschaft. Herrschaft. Studienausgabe,* Tübingen.

Wilkinson, Endymion (2012), *Chinese History. A New Manual,* Cambridge, MA/London.

Woytek, Bernhard E. (2018), "The Depth of Knowledge and the Speed of Thought. The Imagery of Roman Republican Coins and the Contemporary Audience", in: Panagiotis P. Iossif, François de Callataÿ, and Richard Veymiers (eds.), *ΤΥΠΟΙ. Greek and Roman Coins Seen Through Their Images. 'Noble' Issuers, 'Humble' Users?,* Liège, 355–387.

Wrede, Christa (1980), *Leonhard von München, der Meister der Prunkurkunden Kaiser Ludwigs des Bayern* (Münchener Historische Studien, Abteilung Geschichtliche Hilfswissenschaften 17), Kallmünz.

Wycherley, Richard E. (1957), *The Athenian Agora,* vol. 3: *Literary and Epigraphical Testimonia,* Princeton, NJ.

Indexes

Indexes

Index I: Names (places, persons, figures) and works/artefacts

Individually mentioned artefacts can be found under the lemmata 'manuscripts', 'inscriptions', 'ostraca', and 'papyri'. Titles of works may be found under the respective author's name, while biblical passages can be found under 'Bible'.

Aesop
    – *Fables* 190
Agamben, Giorgio 46, 205f., 284
Aigina (Greek island) 215
Alexander of Macedonia (the Great) 284
Aphrodisias (Turkey) 217f., 292
Aphrodito (Kūm Išqāw, Egypt) 124f., 137, 262
Aragon 130, 136
Aristotle 45f., 95
Ashoka I (Indian ruler) 266
Assmann, Aleida 41, 75, 118f.
Assmann, Jan 75, 118, 141
Athena (goddess) 215
Athens *see also* inscriptions
    – Acropolis 72, 275
    – Agora 215
    – Metroon 268
Augustine 213, 226
    – *Confessions* (*Confessiones*) 165f.
    – *On the Blessed Life* (*De beata vita*) 223
Augustus (emperor)
    – *Res gestae* 99, 266f.

Bali 4, 32, 205f., 211
Barcelona 136
Barnim III (duke of Pomerania) 285f.
Beckum
    – Prudentia Shrine 229f.
Berthold von Henneberg (archbishop of Mainz) 177
Bible 88, 184f., 187–192, 203, 211f., 219f., 222, 237, 279
    – Hebrew Bible/Old Testament
        – Exod 12:7 219
        – Exod 13:8–10 and 11–16 185
        – Num 5:11–31 208
        – Deut 6:4–9 and 11:13–21 185, 220
        – Megillot 186
        – Psalms 233f.
        – Ps 50:21 (LXX) 235
        – Ps 86:2 (LXX) 218
        – Ps 117:20 (LXX) 217f.
        – Ezek 9:4–6 220f.
        – Dan 5 54
    – New Testament
        – Matt 1:18–19 80
        – Matt 22:15–22 283
        – John 1:1 212
        – John 8:1–11 54
        – John 19:19–20 55
        – 2 Cor 3:6 203, 214
Biernoff, Suzannah 46
Bomberg, Daniel (printer) 177, 189f.
Byzantium *see* Constantinople

Cairo
    – Genizah 208
Cato 128
Certeau, Michel de 34
Chambéry (castle) 134
Charles IV (Holy Roman emperor) 114, 285, 287
China 4, 99, 115, 182, 272, 275–277, 290, 293
Christ *see* Jesus Christ
Cicero 128
    – *On the Commonwealth* (*De re publica*) 140
Clement of Alexandria
    – *Pedagogue* 216
Codex Theodosianus 133, 282
Constantinople/Byzantium 127, 131, 273
    – Hippodrome 131
Darius I (Persian ruler) 264f., 269
Del Tuppo, Francesco (Italian printer) 190
Delphi 232, 267
Derrida, Jacques 34–40, 117
Dioskoros 124f.

Domenico Irosolimitana 178
Du You
— *Tongdian* 293f.

East Asia 163f., 169, 171
Edfu (Egypt)
— Temple 278
Edward the Confessor (English king) 259f.
Edward III (English king) 286
Egypt 130f., 137, 143, 207, 261–265, 278
Eliyyahu ben Asher (Elia Levita) 177
England 131, 258–263, 282, 286, 288f.
Eyck, Jan van
— *Portrait of a Man* (Fig. 6) 89f.

Fayum (Egypt) 261, 269
Felix Pratensis 177, 186
Firminus (Saint) 227
Fitz Neal *see* Richard fitz Nigel
Flachmann, Holger 180
Fliege, Jutta 226
Foucault, Michel 116
Frischlin, Nicodemus
— *Iulius Redivivus* 161

Galgenmeyer, Georg
— *Schreibkalender* (calendrical diary) 163
Genoa 91f.
Gernrode 226
Goody, Jack 253
Guibert of Nogent (abbot)
— *On the Saints and their Tokens* (*De sanctis et eorum pigneribus*) 227f.
Gumbrecht, Hans Ulrich 19, 43
Gutenberg, Johannes 161

Harold (English king) 259
Ḥayyim ben Bezalel of Friedberg
— *Vikkuaḥ Mayyim Ḥayyim* 176
Helena (Saint) 55
Heliodorus
— *Ethiopian Story* (*Aethiopica*) 50f.
Heliopolis 264
Henchir Akrib (Algeria) 226
Henry II (Eastern Frankish king) 220f.
Henry IV (Holy Roman emperor) 268
Henry V (Holy Roman emperor) 268f.
Herculaneum 54
Hermopolis 127, 131

Herodotus
— *Histories* 50, 269
Herzogenburg, Abbey 135
Hilgert, Markus 11, 51

Ihara Saikaku 163
— *The Great Mirror of Beauties* 174
Illich, Ivan 165
India 266, 287
Inscriptions, individual
— Athens, Epigraphical Museum, inscribed stele 71
— Beckum, Prudentia Shrine (Fig. 8) 229
— Bisitun (Behistun), rock inscription (Fig. 2) 265
— Cairo, Egyptian Museum, Nar-Meher Palette 284
— Changsha, wooden ledgers from Wuyi Square (Fig. 8b) 98
— Egypt, Rosetta Stone 264
— Henan (Chinese province), inscribed stelae 276
— Iran, *Res Gestae Divi Saporis* 266
— Istanbul, Hippodrome, Serpent Column 50
— Klaros, marble pillar (Fig. 9) 232
— London
    — British Museum, pediment stele (Fig. 3) 79
    — National Gallery, Jan van Eyck's *Portrait of a Man* (the so-called Timotheos) (Fig. 6) 90
    — Victoria and Albert Museum, crucifix (Fig. 4) 219
— New York, American Numismatic Society, bronze *as* of Nero 292
— Olympia, Archaeological Museum, helmet (dedication) (Fig. 1) 210
— Rome, inscription (*CIL VI* 9556) 101
— Shandong (Chinese province), inscribed stele 276
— Taiwan, wooden ledger from Juyan (Fig. 8a) 98
Isserles, Moshe ben Israel (ReMa) (Polish rabbi) 175
— *Torat ha-Ḥaṭṭat* 175
Italy 58, 127, 186, 189f.

Japan 4, 115, 162–164, 169–171, 183f., 187f., 192
Java 206f.
Jerusalem 217f., 220, 235–239
– Golgotha 239
– Holy Sepulchre 239
Jesus Christ 54f., 82, 91, 93, 212, 237–239, 283
John (evangelist) 54f., 212
John the Lydian
– *On the Magistracies of the Roman State* (*De magistratibus reipublicanae Romanae*) 131
Jordan 233–236
Judaean Desert 129
Julian (Roman emperor) 283, 292
Justinian (Roman emperor) 127, 291

Kallimachos
– Nike (Athens) 72
Klaros (Turkey) 232
Kohitsu tekagami (book on calligraphy) 164
Koishi Genshun 171
Kulmus, Johann Adam
– *Anatomical Tables* 169–171
Kuno of Falkenstein 84, 86

Latour, Bruno 9, 12
Lauber, Diebold 88, 185
Legend of the finding (*inventio*) of the cross 55
Libri Carolini 82
Lohenstein, Daniel Casper von
– *Ibrahim Sultan* 294
London (Londinium) 281
Louis IV (Holy Roman emperor) 282, 284f.
Lucian
– *How to Write History* (*Quomodo historia conscribenda sit*) 49
Luhmann, Niklas 40, 168
Luther, Martin 177

Madaba (Jordan) 216
Magnus Maximus 133
Maimonides (Jewish philosopher)
– *Mishneh Torah* 172 (Fig. 4)
– *Moreh ha-Nevukhim* 175
Mainz 184
Manuscripts *see also Ostraca, Papyri*
– Berlin, Staatsbibliothek, MS lat. fol. 286 (Aristotle, *Metaphysics*) 95 (Fig. 7)

– Dublin, Trinity College, MS 58 (Book of Kells) 93
– Florence, Biblioteca Medicea Laurenziana, Codex Florentinus 127
– Greifswald, Landesarchiv, Rep. 2 Ducalia, no. 73 284f.
– Heidelberg University Library
– Cod. Pal. Germ. 330 84, 87 (Fig. 5c)
– Cod. Pal. Germ. 389 85 (Fig. 5a)
– Hildesheim, Dom- und Diözesanmuseum, Guntbald Gospels 93
– Karlsruhe, Generallandesarchiv, 67/799 and 804 279
– Magdeburg, Landesarchiv Sachsen-Anhalt
– *Liber Privilegiorum Sancti Mauritii Magdeburgensis* 121 (Fig. 1a)
– Original document of Otto III 122 (Fig. 1b)
– Munich, Bayerische Staatsbibliothek, Clm 4456 (sacramentary of Henry II) 221f. (Fig. 5)
– Neuenstein, Hohenlohe-Zentralarchiv, GA 120, no. 5 139
– New York, Pierpont Morgan Library, MS G.54 (Fig. 5b) 84, 86
– Paris, Bibliothèque nationale de France, MS Nouv. Acq. Lat. 1203 (Godescalc Evangelistary) 80–83 (Fig. 4)
– Parma, Biblioteca Palatina, MS 1872 178f. (Fig. 6)
– Rome, Biblioteca Apostolica Vaticana, MS Vat. Lat. 5757 140
– St. Paul im Lavanttal, Stiftsbibliothek, Cod. 86b/1 (Reichenau exercise book) 138
– Wolfenbüttel, Niedersächsisches Staatsarchiv, 6 Urk. II (marriage certificate of Otto and Theophanu) 273
Māʿīn (Jordan)
– Acropolis Church 218
McLuhan, Marshall 42f., 159
Mesopotamia 115, 264, 287
Metro (Saint) 226
Miltiades (Athenian commander) 209f.
Miyako (Kyoto) 187
Mons Claudianus (Egypt) 261
Münster, Sebastian 177

Nanaion (temple)   130
Napoleon Bonaparte   123
Nar-Meher Palette   284
Nebo (mountain, Jordan)   234–236 (Figs. 10 and 12)
Nessana (Palestine)   130
Nishikawa Sukenobu (Japanese artist)
  – *Poem Cards for the Instruction of Women*   192f. (Fig. 8)
North Africa   236

Odano Naotake (Japanese painter)   170 (Fig. 3)
Olsen, Bjørnar   8
Oroetes (satrap of Lydia)   269
Ostraca, individual
  – O. BuNjem 8   101
  – O. Claud. II 308   101
  – O. Claud. Inv. 7218   261
  – O. Did. 406 (Qift, Archaeological storeroom Did. 131)   72f. (Fig. 2)
  – O. Krok. II   101
Otte (German poet)
  – *Eraclius*   48
Otto I (duke of Pomerania)   285

Palermo
  – Cappella Palatina   136
Papyri, individual
  – Copenhagen, Papyrus Carlsberg 2   99
  – Heidelberg, Papyrussammlung, P. Heid. Inv. Arabisch. 12   262f. (Fig. 1)
  – Leiden, Rijksmuseum van Oudheden, Papyrus Insinger   99f. (Fig. 9)
  – London, British Library, Papyrus 384   289
  – Petra Papyri   130
Paschalis I (pope)   226f.
Peter Chrysologus (archbishop of Ravenna)   225
Petrarca   114
Petrucci, Armando   58
Philippi
  – Church of St Paul   91
Pilate   55
Pisa
  – Cathedral   144
Pius IX (pope)   230
Plato
  – *Phaedrus*   35, 49
Pompeii   54

Porphyrios (bishop)   91
Priene (Asia Minor)   215
Prudentia Shrine, Beckum   229f.

Qimḥi, David (RaDaQ) (Provençal rabbi)   177f.

Rather (bishop of Verona)   226
Relic authentics *see also* Index II (*Artefacts*)
  – Sens, authentic of unknown relics   228 (Fig. 7)
Richard fitz Nigel (Fitz Neal)   77
Rome
  – Quirinal Hill, Dioscuri   141
  – Santa Maria in Domnica, apse mosaic   226f. (Fig. 6)
  – Temple of Saturn, *aerarium populi Romani*   127
Rudolf von Ems
  – *Willehalm von Orlens*   270
Rupert of Deutz
  – *Vita Herberti*   211

Saragossa   126
Schatzki, Theodore   12
Schneider, Irmela   168
Sedulius
  – *Carmen paschale*   126
Sem Tob de Carrión   47
Suso, Henry (Heinrich Seuse)
  – *Wisdom's Watch upon the Hours (Horologium Sapientiae)*   222f.
Shapur I (Sasanian king)   266
Shen Defu
  – *The Plum in the Golden Vase (Jing Ping Mei)*   183
Shiba Kōkan (Japanese painter)   171
Shōtoku (Japanese empress)   187
Small, David   166f. (Fig. 2)
Speyer
  – Cathedral   268f.
Stephan Matthias von der Neidenburg (bishop)   114

Talmud   166f., 175f., 187
Tegea (Greece)   78f.
Theodosius I (Roman emperor)   133, 292
Theodulf of Orléans
  – *Libri Carolini*   82
Thomas Aquinas   45f., 126, 213

Thomasin von Zerklaere
- *Der Welsche Gast* 84–88 (Fig. 5a-c)
Thucydides 50
Tipasa (Algeria)
- Church of Alexander 236f. (Fig. 13)
Tokugawa Ieyasu (Japanese shogun) 187
Torah *see also Bible* 186, 190–192 (Fig. 7), 212f. (Fig. 2)
Trieste
- Church in the Via Madonna del Mare 235 (Fig. 11)
Trimethius, John
- *De Laude Scriptorum* 173f., 176

Valignano, Alessandro (Italian missionary) 187
Vindolanda 281

Wagner, Peter 77
Wax tablet (Berlin, Papyrus 14008) 261
Weber, Max 255
William I (English king) 259f.

Yehuda ben Shmuel of Regensburg (German rabbi and Jewish theologian) 212f.

Zeus 209–211, 268
Zeus Labraundos 78f. (Fig. 3)
Zhang Chao (Chinese author) 163f.
Zhu Xi (Chinese philosopher)
- *Dushu fa* 183
Zumthor, Paul 42f.

Index II: Terms, Concepts, and Materials

accessibility (restricted) 16, 18, 115f., 119, 127–131, 133, 268, 271; *see also presence (restricted)*
actor-network theory (ANT) 9f., 12
administration/administrative writing 77, 97–99 (Figs. 8a–b), 253f., 258f.
affordance 15f., 18, 69f., 72f., 94, 134f., 142, 162, 165 173, 186, 274
agency/effectiveness of writing 12, 16f., 32f., 37, 39f., 44–48, 55, 69f., 96, 121, 132, 203–209, 211f., 214 *see also power*
aisthetic presence/permanence 38, 40, 43, 52–55, 74, 83
alphabet 141, 211f., 219
alphabetical script *see writing*
amulets *see artefacts*
archives
- family archives 121, 124, 128
- public archives 127–132
- seignorial archives 117, 124
archon, archivist 15, 117–120, 124f., 127–136, 139f.
artefact (term) 5, 15f.
artefact biography 54, 130f., 139, 144

artefacts, various *see also letters (i.e., epistles), manuscripts, papyri as well as Index I above*
- amulets 56f., 206
- Bible manuscripts 89, 94, 177f., 273, 279
- calendars/calendrical diaries 94, 162f., 181
- cartularies 279
- coins 97, 102, 114, 275, 283f., 290, 292
- defixiones 207f.
- Dirigierrollen (director's scrolls) 76
- (administrative) documents/certificates/deeds 89, 99, 101, 121–124, 128–136, 139, 259–263, 266, 268, 273, 279, 281f., 285–287
- dossier 116, 291
- gems 56, 102, 207–209, 229
- horos stones 214
- lead tablets 19, 42, 138, 207f., 227
- mezuza 185, 220
- military diplomata 273, 282
- notched wood/tallies 276, 287
- ostraca 68, 72f., 101, 261
- relic authentics 42, 126, 209, 226–230
- sacramentary 127, 220–222
- scarabs 56

- seals   47, 97, 134, 138, 184, 257, 270, 274, 276, 283, 286f.
- scrolls   20, 70, 89, 97, 130, 134, 140, 157, 164–167, 175, 188, 208, 269f., 294
    - English administrative scrolls (Pipe Rolls)   77, 93, 131
    - Torah scroll   212f.
- travel permits, travel documents   276f.

aura/auratic/auratic quality   53f., 115, 120, 139, 162, 232, 275
authenticity/authentication   34f., 120, 134, 139, 162, 183, 209, 228–230, 257, 262, 274, 286–288; *see also legitimation*
author(ship)   11, 31f., 126, 162
authorial intent   6, 11, 41f.
authority   53, 206, 253f., 256, 258–269, 272–276, 281f., 284–286, 287, 290–294
autograph   126, 162

Bible   203, 211f., 217, 219f., 222, 233, 237f.
Bible printing   184–192
blind ruling   94
bones *see materials*
book *see manuscript, scroll, destruction*
book printing (Jewish incunabula, Japanese horizontal scrolls)   4, 47, 94, 160–162, 175–194
border/boundary/demarcation *see space*
bronze *see materials*
bureaucracy *see administration*

calendar/calendrical diary *see artefacts*
calligraphy   48, 79, 164, 175, 281, 281–283
cartularies *see artefacts*
characters *see written characters*
citations/quotations   233, 236 (Fig. 12), 268
codex *see manuscript*
coins *see artefacts*
collection, archive and collecting/gathering   114–116, 133
colophons   92, 177–179, 188f.
colour of writing   82–84, 91, 187f., 272f.
communication
    - communicative function of writing   20, 31, 33f., 36f., 39f., 52–55, 232f., 253, 269f.
    - monologic/dialogic (interaction)   254, 290
    - oral as distinct from written   263, 269f.

consecrative inscriptions *see inscriptions*
content *see form*
context of writing   77–79, 82, 96, 116, 120, 123, 165
    - context of understanding   11
    - context of use   136–139, 143, 160, 171, 173, 175f., 186f.
    - (de-/re-)contextualisation   133, 144
    - sacred context   203f., 206, 220f.
conventionalisation   31, 76f., 97 *see also standardisation*
copies/transcriptions   83f., 97, 128, 137–139, 168, 171, 173–175, 181, 267, 275, 279, 282, 288 *see also writing practices*
corporeality/physicality of writing *see writing*
criticism/scepticism of writing   35, 203, 213
cults/worship *see space, rituals*
cultural transfer *see transcultural adaptation*
cultural turn   8

damnatio memoriae   125, 143, 291
defixiones see artefacts
destruction of writing   118, 141, 291
digital/digital age/digital turn   113, 120, 158–160, 166–168, 174
dipinti see artefacts
Dirigierrollen see artefacts
documents *see artefacts*
dossier *see artefacts*
durability/permanence of writing and writing supports   50, 52–55, 158, 174, 214, 254f., 268, 271f., 274f., 280, 287

effectiveness/efficacy of writing *see agency, power*
endurance of writing *see durability*
enigmatisation of writing   88–91 (Fig. 6)
ephemerality of writing *see durability*
epideixis   49
epistemology/epistemological conditions of writing   34, 36f., 40, 44–48, 52, 68, 159f.
epistolary network   57
Eucharist   221

figure poem (carmen figuratum)   76, 88f.
form (administrative document)   181, 288f.
form/form and content   35, 41, 46–48, 73, 76, 82, 88, 165–168, 171, 263, 271, 273f., 280, 293

format/formatting 17, 20, 70, 77, 88, 96, 101f., 134, 137, 139, 157, 162, 169–171, 175, 180–184, 186, 192–194, 274
formulae 209, 220, 227, 239
– consecrative formulae 209
– curse formulae 207f.

gates, doors *see inscriptions, space*
gems *see artefacts*
gift (reciprocal/offering/sacrifice) 209, 235
gloss/glossing *see writing practices*
gold *see materials*
graffiti *see inscriptions*

hermeneutics 6f., 10f., 40f. *see also meaning/ sense*
– limits of hermeneutics/criticism of hermeneutics 10, 19, 40–43
– extended hermeneutics 6, 10, 13, 31f., 41f.
hieroglyphics *see scripts/writing systems*
hierographic potential of writing 205–214; *see also agency, sacrality*
holy/holiness *see inscriptions, space, relics, sacralisation/sacrality*
horos stones *see artefacts*

iconoclastic discourses 38f., 79
images *see also pictoriality of writing*
– image and writing 38f., 47, 74f., 77f., 83–87 (Figs. 5a–c), 93–95 (Fig. 7), 99, 233, 283–286
information management 254–256, 267f., 288f.
initials (in manuscripts) 38, 76f., 84–87, 189, 220, 285
inscribed stelae *see inscriptions*
inscribed carpets 233
inscriptions 18f., 50–52 (in metatexts), 53, 56–58, 91f., 143f., 206, 214–224 (liminal function), 231–240, 264–266 (multilingual), 268f.; *see also artefacts, materials, relics, writing (i.e., process), writing (i.e., product)*
– on bodies 57
– on borders (horos stones) 214f.
– building inscriptions 18, 91f., 217f., 232–240

– burial/funerary inscriptions 101, 142f., 232f., 236f.
– in column fluting 72
– consecrative/dedicatory inscriptions 72, 75, 209–211, 224–230, 239
– *dipinti* 54
– documentary inscriptions 291
– on doorposts 219f.
– on external facades 233
– founder/donor inscriptions 233, 235
– graffiti 54f., 72, 217f.
– on the ground 218, 233–236
– helmet inscription 209f.
– inscriptions in narratives 48–58, 222–224
– inventory inscriptions 76
– *menetekel* 54
– monumental inscriptions 91f.
– mosaic inscriptions 91, 217
– on portals, gates, doors, thresholds 216–224
– on spolia 126, 144
– on shrines (reliquaries) 229f.
– at shrines/sacred places 70f., 231–235, 269
– on statues 68, 72, 264–265
– on stelae (inscribed stelae) 70–72 (Fig. 1)
– on temple walls 99
– tattooing/tattoos 57
– votive inscriptions 72, 209–211, 238
interaction with inscribed artefacts 288–294
interlinear glosses 87f. (Fig. 5c), 94f. (Fig. 7)
italics *see writing*

knowledge, knowledge texts, wisdom texts 53f., 94

language(s) *see also multilingualism*
– Aramaic 258
– Babylonian 264–265
– Celtic 259
– Czech 87f. (Fig. 5c)
– Demotic 99f., 261
– Elamite 264
– Greek 55, 89, 99, 138, 177, 207f., 211, 224, 258, 261–264, 266, 289
– Hebrew 55, 171–173, 186–189

– Latin   55, 76, 88, 89, 99, 101, 138, 177, 185, 189, 207f., 222, 224, 258–263, 289, 291
– lingua franca   259
– Old English   259f.
– (Old) French   89, 259f.
– Old Norse   259
– (Old/Middle) Persian   258, 264f. (Fig. 2), 266
– Parthian   266
– vernacular language   49, 141, 177, 183, 189, 259f.
– written language   31, 33f.
law/laws/legal texts   256, 268, 284
– legal/court proceedings   261f.
– legal texts/decrees   57, 70f. (Fig. 1), 97
layout   56, 67, 134, 162–168, 171–173, 184, 186f., 193, 278f. *see also material change*
– and (il)legibility   92f.
– and meaning   74–83
– and reception practices   92–96, 162f., 166f.
– and text type   96–102
– and writing supports   69–73, 101f.
– communicative function of   83–92
– conventions of, standardisation   77, 88, 92f., 96–98 (Figs. 8a–b), 99 – 102 (Fig. 9), 134f.
lead tablets *see artefacts*
legislation/legal text *see law*
legitimation/legitimisation   53, 212, 286–288 *see also authenticity*
– of rule through writing   97–99, 238, 253–256, 274f., 290
– of sacrality through writing   224–230
"The letter kills" *see criticism of writing*
letters (epistles)   57, 73 (Fig. 2) , 96f., 99–101 (Fig. 8a, 8b), 129, 135, 139, 181, 185, 214, 261, 269–271, 275f., 280, 294
letters (individual characters)   32, 47f., 56f., 68f. (meaningless sequence of), 72f. (Fig. 1), 76 (*masora figurata*), 82f., 88 (*versus intexti*) 89, 99, 101, 134, 141, 164, 203, 211f., 214, 219–222 (Fig. 4, Fig. 5), 269, 273, 282; *see also initials, writing*
– Alpha and Omega   212, 219, 222
– Chi-Rho   93
– Tau/T   219–222
– *Tāw*   220

library   53, 114f., 131, 159, 179
liminality, liminal function of writing   57f., 214–224 *see also rituals*
linguistic turn   8
lists   68, 76, 96, 101, 127f., 136, 138, 142, 256, 272, 278
literacy   34, 52, 228, 233, 260, 284
liturgy   211–214, 220–222, 233–235; *see also rituals*
locomobile/locostatic inscribed artifacts *see mobility*
logocentrism vs. phonocentrism   34–37, 45

magic   205 *see also agency, power*
– 'magical' power of the written word/magic of writing   32, 37, 44, 99, 207–209, 213f.
manuscript   67, 83–88, 97, 122, 133, 139, 177, 188f., 258, 264, 279, 287, 290; *see also artefacts as well as Index I for individual manuscripts*
– glossed manuscripts   77, 88, 94f. (Fig. 7), 97
– liturgical manuscripts   188, 213f., 220f., 279
manuscript culture and print culture   77, 158, 161–164 (esp. Japan), 166, 168, 175–178, 180–184
material change   157–160
– abundance of books/*copia librorum*   53, 159
material culture studies   7, 9–12
material turn   7–13
materials (text supports) *see also paper, papyrus, parchment*
– ash   212
– bamboo   70, 97f. (Figs. 8a–b), 256, 271–273, 276f. (Fig. 3)
– bones   56, 271
– bronze   97, 141, 187, 267f., 272–274, 277 (Fig. 3), 292 (Fig. 5)
– ceramic sherds   72f. (Fig. 2), 101, 272
– dust   54, 208
– gold   82, 84, 93, 141, 269–273, 275, 277 (Fig. 3), 293f.
– (golden glass) tesserae   91, 272
– ivory   135, 141f.
– lead   19, 42, 138, 207, 227, 287

– marble 16, 70, 92, 217f. (Fig. 3), 232 (Fig. 9), 272, 275, 281
– metal 56, 141, 206, 256, 264, 271f.
– rock crystal 141f.
– sand 54
– stone 15, 50–57, 67f., 89–92, 143, 206f., 214f., 231f., 256, 263–265, 271f., 274f., 281, 288, 291
– textiles 51, 56f., 271
– wax/wax tablets 53, 138, 205f., 261, 287
– wood 56, 97f. (Figs. 8a–b), 206, 256, 264, 271, 273, 276; see also notched wood
– writing materials 255f., 271f., 274f.
materiality (of writing) 17, 38, 47, 78, 256, 270, 293f.
– 'immaterial' writing 46–48
– material arrangement, artefact arrangement/collection (of written characters) 12f., 15f., 17f., 48, 57, 67–69, 76–78, 116–118, 123, 133, 135, 138, 203, 205f.
– value of materials 42, 141f., 225, 272f.
meaning/sense 6f., 10f.; see also hermeneutics
– auratic meaning 53
– cultural/historical significance 6–11, 16f.
– in competition with materiality, imagery, or presence 6f., 13, 38f., 213f.
– in interaction with layout/spatial arrangement 70f., 76f.
– meaning produced by the materiality and presence of writing 40–44, 56–58, 209
– meaningless text (nonsense inscriptions, lorem ipsum) 68f., 99
– semantics of what is written/textual meaning 31–33, 36, 205
– semanticisation 57
media theory 16, 35, 41f.
medium/media 16, 40, 42f., 82, 203, 254
memory/*memoria* 46, 50, 51–53, 57, 113f., 118–120, 123f., 141–143, 225, 253, 255, 290–292.
menetekel see artefacts
message/messenger 16, 31, 42f., 54, 142f., 204, 220, 253–255, 265–268, 269f., 275f., 283–287, 290–294

metal *see materials*
metatexts 10, 17, 19f., 32f., 42, 45, 48–52, 288, 293f.
military diplomata *see artefacts*
mobility/immobility of inscribed artefacts 56–58, 225, 271f., 275
monumentality of writing 67, 92, 268, 272, 274–275
monumentalisation 239, 281, 384, 289–291
mosaics 91, 217, 225–227, 233–236, 272
multilingualism 99, 257–267, 291
mysticism 212, 222f.

names of God/gods 208, 211, 212
names, written down
– in a harming ritual 208f.
– in consecrative inscriptions 211
non-typographic/al 4, 70f., 83, 113, 119, 126, 140, 267f., 275
notched wood *see artefacts*

oaths/curses 42, 99, 184, 206–208
orality 34, 184, 205, 208f., 253, 255, 263
– and writtenness/writing 34–38, 49f.
ostraka *see artefacts and materials (pottery sherds)*

palimpsest 58, 140, 217
paper 4, 20, 47f., 56, 69f., 122, 157, 160, 164, 169, 173f.
papyrus (text support), papyri 56, 70, 73, 135, 137
parchment 4, 15, 18, 20, 53, 56, 67, 93–95 (Fig. 7), 122, 136, 140f., 157, 174, 181, 185, 286–288
phonocentrism 34
pictogram 35, 206
pictoriality, iconic quality/impact of writing 20, 35, 38f., 41, 47, 74–76, 78–83, 142
place *see space, topology; see also Index I for specific places, countries, etc.*
poststructuralist 8f., 11, 41, 45
power/powerful effect/agency of writing 12, 16f., 32–34, 43–47, 52–55, 99, 115, 120, 132, 203f., 205–208, 211–214, 217f., 223f., 253
practices/praxeology 9–15, 37, 40–44, 48–51, 57, 117–120, 134–138, 142, 157f., 206f., 213, 225, 240, 276; see also writing practices

praxeologically oriented artefact analysis 5f., 11f., 15f.
praxeology, praxeological 9, 11–13, 15f., 18, 117, 123, 142, 160, 176f., 225, 240
prayers 99, 143, 185, 208, 217, 220f., 224, 233
presence of writing 11, 18f., 31f., 120, 139, 157, 208, 270, 294
– aisthetic (sensual) 34–40
– ephemeral 33
– of God in scripture 212f.
– of saints 225, 237
– permanent 33, 36, 235
– restricted 18, 33, 39, 57, 69, 93, 209, 257
prestige of a text 162, 164, 181, 233, 267f., 272, 276, 281
production/producers of writing 14–16, 51f., 69, 83–92 (Figs. 5a–c and 6), 120, 125–127, 257, 271
production process 52, 83, 188f., 257
public arena/sphere 57, 126–131, 158, 182, 188, 206–208, 231, 254–258, 268, 274f., 290f.; *see also topology*

quotations *see citations*

reading 10, 18, 38, 44, 82, 93, 165–168, 183f., 186; *see also reception*
– (il)legibility of writing 33f., 37f., 40, 92f.
– reading practices 18, 165f.
reception of writing 5–11, 18, 37f., 41, 44, 49f., 69f., 82–84, 92–96, 118, 120, 125–127, 142, 184, 186f., 190, 207, 209, 223; *see also reading*
– reactions to inscribed artefacts 288–294, 270
– reception according to groups of addressees 57, 88, 91, 99
– reception practice(s) 5f., 12, 17f., 92f., 134, 165–173
– reception situation 7–10, 19, 41, 54
– recognition without reading 101f.
– viewing 82, 93
– writing as a reception practice (Fig. 7) 93–96
recipients of writing 52, 69, 84, 91, 119f., 141f., 189, 205, 217, 286
referentiality, reference 38–41, 43f., 74, 228

registers 131f., 138, 229, 278f.
relics 125f., 209, 225–230, 237
– relic authentics *see artefacts*
religion *see sacralisation/sacrality*
– and rule 268
religions of the book 203f., 211
representation, representational function of writing 31, 75
restricted presence of writing *see presence*
rituals/cults 32, 205–209, 223, 268–270; *see also liturgy*
– abecedarium of the consecration of a church 211f.
– consecration 208–212
– consecration of a church 238
– cultic handling of Torah scroll 212f.
– rites of passage 215f.
– water poured over stone inscription/book scroll 208
rule, political 131f., 238, 253–255
runes *see scripts*

sacralisation/sacrality 203f.; *see also inscriptions, space*
– endangering of sacrality 224–230
– sacralisation of spaces 231–240
sanctuary 70, 209f., 215–218, 232–237 (Fig. 10–13)
scarabs *see artefacts*
scripts/writing systems 31, 34–36
– alphabet 34f., 97, 219f.
– (ancient) Egyptian script 99–101 (Fig. 9), 207, 261, 264f., 280
– Antiqua 76
– Balinese script 203, 205f.
– Bastarda 84, 87 (Fig. 5c)
– *capitalis rustica* 92f.
– Chancery script 89f. (Fig. 6), 281
– Chinese script 70, 97–99 (Fig. 8a-b), 169–171, 271–273
– Cuneiform 264f. (Fig. 2)
– Demotic script 99f. (Fig. 9), 129, 261–264, 280
– Greek alphabet 207–209, 211f., 214, 219f., 258, 261–264
– Hebrew alphabet 171–173, 177f., 220
– hieratic script 261, 264, 280

– hieroglyphics   34f., 128, 207–209, 264, 278, 280, 284
– italics   57, 76, 264, 280–283
– Latin alphabet   101, 211f., 219f., 258–263, 281
– majuscule script   56, 72, 89–92 (Fig. 6), 222, 281
– mathematical notation   35–37
– minuscule script   56, 84–86 (Figs. 5a–b), 92
– runes   56, 207
– shorthand   280–282
– syllabic writing/syllabary   34f.
scroll (amulet scroll/book scroll/*Dirigierrolle*/ Pipe Rolls/Torah scroll) *see artefacts*
seals *see artefacts*
semantics *see meaning/sense*
signatures   89f. (Fig. 6)
socialisation of inscribed artefacts/ writing   114–116, 119f., 134
space/spatiality *see also sacralisation, topology*
– burial spaces   236
– places of worship, sacred places   115f., 130, 226, 231–240
– sacred spaces, church spaces   217
– sacred vs. profane   204, 214–225, 240
– sacred written space   203f., 221, 225, 231–233, 240
– spatial allegory   222f.
spatial turn   17
speaking objects   32, 215
spells *see magic*
standardisation   88, 97, 102, 169, 192–194, 257, 274, 278f.; *see also layout (conventions of, standardisation), conventionalisation*
stone *see materials*
storage/institutions that store writing(s)/ knowledge storage   113–118, 121, 123
stigmata   57

tables, tabular structure   278
tallies *see artefacts*
tattooing/tattoos *see inscriptions*
temples   99, 115, 127f., 130f., 184, 217, 232–240
text anthropology   11, 83

text/textual content   6–10, 69, 273, 275; *see also meaning/sense, form*
text culture   4, 7, 11–20, 42, 69, 75, 83, 159, 168; *see also writing culture*
textiles *see materials*
theses, explanation of the approach and all theses in this volume   5, 21–25
tombs *see inscriptions as well as space (burial spaces)*
topology/writing within space   6, 11, 17–18, 57, 67, 123, 267–271; *see also space*
Torah   175–179, 186f., 189–192, 212f.; *see also Bible, scroll*
transcultural adaptation, cultural transfer of writing   169–171 (Fig. 3), 186–192 (Fig. 5)
– translation(s)   169–171 (Fig. 3), 177, 257, 259, 261–266
travel authorisations, travel permits *see artefacts*

validity
– of artefacts   286–288
– of documents   268
– of layout   68
– of writing   11, 53f., 114
value of materials *see materiality*
visibility/visualisation of writing *see writing (i.e., product)*
votive inscriptions *see inscriptions*

wood *see materials*
writing (act of)   33, 40, 50, 68, 93, 204, 207, 212, 240
writing (i.e, process/technique)   33, 40, 49–51, 54, 67, 74–76, 165f.6, 174, 181f., 253f.4, 259, 267, 269f., 274, 280–282; *see also writing (i.e., product), writing (act of)*
writing (i.e., practice)
– direction of writing   69–71, 75, 99, 272
– chiselling/inscribing of an artefact   51, 56, 68, 72, 89, 96, 205, 209–211, 216, 239, 272
– not writing   54
– writing implement/tool   75, 91, 165
– of individual letters (i.e., characters)   211f., 219f.
– writing subject   40, 47f.; *see also author(ship)*

writing (i.e., product)   14f., 32; *see also agency, durability, validity, inscriptions, communication, context, legitimation, power, materiality, mobility, monumentality, presence, space, reception, writing (i.e., process), scripts, topology, transcultural adaptation*
– and bodies   57, 75, 168, 206, 274
– and ornamentation   38, 68, 83, 93, 185, 190
– corporeality/physicality of writing   32f., 44–47, 75
– immaterial writing   47
– light writing   48
– operationality of writing   39–41
– referentiality (limits of)   34, 36–40
– representational function of writing (criticism of the)   34–40, 48
– self-reflection on writing   32f., 50f.; *see also metatexts*
– various types of writing/character systems/multiscripturalism (Fig. 6)   89–91, 264–266
– visibility/visualisation   38f., 57, 71, 82f., 91, 167, 207
writing culture   44, 55, 69f., 157, 203, 257, 282f.; *see also text culture*
writing practices   37, 49–51, 213f.
– glossing/commenting   77, 94, 162, 171–173, 175, 177–179, 186–189, 223
– copying (Figs. 5a–c)   83–88, 93, 133, 168, 171, 173–175, 181–189, 288
written characters   36, 37–40, 46f., 56, 67, 70, 74
– mystical/magical   203, 205–207
– sacred   213, 219, 221, 223
written word *see* reading, writing (i.e, process), writing (i.e., product)